Birth Control and American Modernity

How did birth control become legitimate in the United States? One kitchen table at a time, contends Trent MacNamara – as Americans reexamined old ideas about money, time, transcendence, nature, risk, and their relationship to family planning. By the time Margaret Sanger and other activists began campaigning for legal contraception in the 1910s, Americans had been effectively controlling fertility for a century, combining old techniques with explosive new attitudes. *Birth Control and American Modernity* charts those attitudes, capturing a movement that relied less on traditional public advocacy than dispersed action of the kind that nullified Prohibition. Acting in bedrooms and gossip corners where formal power was weak and moral feeling strong, Americans of both sexes gradually normalized birth control in private, then in public, as part of a wider prioritization of present material worlds over imagined eternal continuums. The moral edifice they constructed, like similar citizen movements around the world, remains tenuously intact.

Trent MacNamara is an assistant professor of history at Texas A&M University.

Birth Control and American Modernity

A History of Popular Ideas

TRENT MACNAMARA

Texas A&M University

CAMBRIDGE
UNIVERSITY PRESS

CAMBRIDGE
UNIVERSITY PRESS

University Printing House, Cambridge CB2 8BS, United Kingdom

One Liberty Plaza, 20th Floor, New York, NY 10006, USA

477 Williamstown Road, Port Melbourne, VIC 3207, Australia

314-321, 3rd Floor, Plot 3, Splendor Forum, Jasola District Centre, New Delhi - 110025, India

79 Anson Road, #06-04/06, Singapore 079906

Cambridge University Press is part of the University of Cambridge.

It furthers the University's mission by disseminating knowledge in the pursuit of
education, learning and research at the highest international levels of excellence.

www.cambridge.org
Information on this title: www.cambridge.org/9781108460538
DOI: 10.1017/9781108650465

First published 2018
Reprinted 2019
First paperback edition 2020

A catalogue record for this publication is available from the British Library

Library of Congress Cataloging in Publication data
NAMES: MacNamara, Trent, author.
TITLE: Birth control and American modernity : a history of popular ideas / Trent
MacNamara, Texas A & M University.
DESCRIPTION: Cambridge, United Kingdom ; New York, NY : Cambridge University
Press, 2018. | Includes bibliographical references and index.
IDENTIFIERS: LCCN 2018012846 | ISBN 9781316519585
SUBJECTS: LCSH: Birth control – United States – History.
CLASSIFICATION: LCC HQ766.5.U5 M24 2018 | DDC 363.9/60973–dc23
LC record available at https://lccn.loc.gov/2018012846

ISBN 978-1-316-51958-5 Hardback
ISBN 978-1-108-46053-8 Paperback

Contents

Figures

Tables

Acknowledgments

Special thanks to Matthew Connelly for sound advice at every turn, to Elizabeth Blackmar for searching questions, to William Leach for foundational discussions, and to Linda Gordon and Dennis Hodgson for insightful comments on the dissertation version of this project. Alan Brinkley, Rosalind Rosenberg, Sarah Phillips, Caroline Bledsoe, Emily Merchant, Katherine Lynch, Susan Pearson, Oliver Murphey, Simon Stevens, Stephen Wertheim, Ed Freedman, and Adam Bright commented on portions of this study, for which I am grateful. Parts of Chapter 2 appeared in "Why 'Race Suicide': Cultural Factors in U.S. Fertility Decline, 1903–1908," *Journal of Interdisciplinary History* 44:4 (2014); I appreciate the opportunity to use that material here. Family and friends encouraged me to pursue this project and helped me detach from it. Thanks to my parents and grandparents for instilling self-discipline and intellectual curiosity, to my friends for laughing at my cat joke, and to my children for enforcing occasional self-abandonment. Molly, Nate, and Josie, your appearance during this writing led wise people to wonder if I had truly mastered my subject. I am glad you do not have 4.04 additional siblings (as you would in 1800, according to the statistics) but each of you fill me with love and gratification. Never stop standing defiantly for what you know to be correct. Annmarie, I could not have done this without your strength, patience, and support. Thank you for being as you are and being here with me.

I

The Long History of Birth Control

If we have convictions, and cannot express them in words, then let us act them out, let us live them!

Margaret Sanger (1929)[1]

Man, like all other animals, has two main functions: to feed his own organism, and to reproduce his species. Ancestral habit leads him, when mature, to choose himself a mate ... If this profound impulse is really lacking to-day in any large part of our race, there must be some correspondingly profound and adequate reason for it.

Grant Allen (1894)[2]

**

INTRODUCTION

In 1800 the average American had seven offspring. "Every log cabin is swarming with half-naked children," wrote an English traveler on the Illinois frontier. "Boys of 18 build huts, marry, and raise hogs and children at about the same expence." Farms and streets teemed with children. The young republic's expanding population, thought Benjamin Franklin, Thomas Jefferson, and George Washington, guaranteed its security and expressed its citizens' health, wealth, and happiness.[3]

A century later Americans were having half as many children, on average. "There are regions of our land, and classes of our population, where the birth-rate has sunk below the death-rate," President Theodore Roosevelt warned Congress in 1906. The trend seemed to be spreading. "Willful sterility," Roosevelt chided, "is ... the one sin for which the penalty is national death, race death; a sin for which there is no atonement." The president's warnings went unheeded. By the mid-1930s the average American had just over two children, well below the period's rate of replacement.[4]

This steady decline in family size took place over a period when there were no major advances in contraceptive technology and very few outspoken advocates for reproductive rights. What changed, instead, were Americans' ideas about the place of childrearing in a good life. In order to understand that change, this book examines the ethical sensibilities of several thousand Americans (mostly white and middle class) who participated in America's first mass civic debates over fertility control. The central question is: how did birth control gain popularity and legitimacy in America?

Answering this question means investigating a topic, reproductive decision-making, that is at once universal, essential, and nearly invisible. Virtually all adults are forced to make decisions about their reproductive potential, and those decisions tend to feel important. But the reasons we make them can be hard to articulate to ourselves, much less to others.

Americans discussing birth control in the early twentieth century were no different. Reproductive questions' emotional charge and social volatility made them difficult to address. So did their complexity: for many Americans, the values relevant to reproductive action seemed so wide ranging, and the moral questions so abstract and deeply held, that it was difficult to capture the trend towards smaller families in any but the most sweeping terms. "The cause is multiplex," wrote a Baltimore editorialist in 1904, "lying partly in the material and partly in the spiritual and intellectual environment of our time."[5]

The struggle to explain the spread of family limitation has since passed to sociologists, demographers, and historians. Many theories have emerged. Traditionally, these have emphasized major social-historical shifts such as women's emancipation, urbanization, industrialization, mass education, and better access to contraceptive technology. Sometimes these shifts are lumped together as "modernization." "Almost anything that distinguishes traditional from modern societies has been considered relevant to the explanation of the fertility decline," as one demographer notes.[6]

Important as such factors have been in creating an environment favorable to smaller families, none of them – alone or in combination – has been shown to be necessary for fertility decline or sufficient to explain when and why people limit their families. Fertility has dropped precipitously among illiterate Bulgarian peasants, remained stubbornly high in industrial England, and risen mysteriously as contraceptive technology improved in mid-twentieth-century America. Often it has seemed that the brighter the lights aimed at fertility behavior, the darker the shadows. Some scholars have responded by declaring the causes of fertility decline to be irreducibly plural and local: too variable across place, time, and class for generalization. Yet the hunt for shared qualities continues, if only because it seems unlikely that hundreds of broadly simultaneous fertility transitions, across every corner of the world, would not share some common characteristics.[7]

That search continues, too, because low fertility has become a truly global phenomenon. Around half the world's people now live in countries where fertility is below replacement level, and that proportion is growing. It includes wealthy parts of Europe and North America where the trend was first perceived, but also countries from Brazil to Morocco, Korea to Colombia, and Thailand to Russia. Where birthrates remain above replacement they are generally trending downward, and within a century we are likely see a broad-based, voluntary end to human population growth, perhaps even a decline – events which seemed unfathomable fifty years ago. The benefits of these trends are obvious at the global level; locally, however, they threaten welfare states with bankruptcy and nations with the destabilizing politics of cultural extinction.[8]

Understanding fertility decline is above all a question of understanding subtle changes in the acting ideas of people with no special interest in birth control as a social cause. It is a question of half-articulate principles that span the borders between popular commonsense and abstract moral philosophy. In America, those ideas pertained above all to relationships of economy to morality, self to society, worldliness to transcendence, human to cosmic orders, and modernity to eternity.

A grand civic debate over these principles emerged in America in the wake of Roosevelt's denunciation, in 1903, of "race suicide" among "the average men and women who make up the nation." The U.S. birthrate's apparent trajectory towards zero, warned the young president, promised to extinguish the American experiment. "A new race ... will take your place," he thundered, "because you will have shown that you are not fit to cumber the ground."[9]

Roosevelt's words struck a nerve – not just for their discordant pessimism, but because Americans were unaccustomed to hearing heads of state address such earthy topics. In the subsequent controversy, which lasted many years and grew to include counterarguments by Margaret Sanger and other pro-birth control activists, millions of Americans asked themselves, "Under what circumstances is it acceptable to avoid childbearing?"

Open debate ultimately encouraged many Americans to come to terms with birth control's immense private popularity – accepting semisecret practices as facts of life and even public virtues. Along the way, however, countless Americans wondered if a virtuous and sustainable society could publicly condone birth control. Would people continue to have children if family limitation were publicly acceptable? Would the liberalization of reproduction fatally alienate American democracy from God and nature?

Most parties to the debate came from America's numerically and politically dominant culture – white, native-born, nonindigent – and concerned themselves with the reproductive future of their own kind. This frame of reference was obvious to them. Few evinced much thought or care for groups living beyond the civic pale: "new" immigrants, the destitute, and African-Americans, who together constituted around a quarter of the country's population. Perhaps those groups would multiply and inherit the land; or perhaps they too would vanish after adopting the small-family norm. Some middle-class whites worried about the former scenario; some black or immigrant Americans worried about the latter. But vastly more words were spilled on self-examination by the enfranchised majority. Debate centered on inward-looking questions of moral order in a virtuous and sustainable society. Much of the commentary was mystical, introspective, and uncertain.[10]

This debate over reproductive ethics has much to teach us about the roots of birth control's legitimation in America. Each chapter of this book accordingly focuses on several hundred Americans' views on fertility control, as recorded in a variety of media: newspapers, letters, field reports, and responses to a radio program. This approach – using bulk qualitative sources to uncover the views of ground-level actors – bridges the gap between the two dominant approaches to birth control history, historical demography and narrative history.

Demographers see fertility control's spread as a "revolution without generals" conducted by ordinary women and men responding to socioeconomic and other structural factors. But this sort of data alone, most demographers now believe, cannot provide a complete account of fertility motivation. We also need research into "cultural factors." "Fertility decline is now the stuff of history," as one demographer writes. Efforts to explain it rely "more on qualitative argument and less on the elaborate statistical modeling."[11]

[handwritten margin note: most of the debate centered this pop]

Qualitative argument is the stock in trade of narrative history, but historians of birth control have largely focused on a small corps of out-spoken activists – despite "the systematic divergence," in the words of three demographic historians, "between popular values and practices and those of the tiny minority in the intelligentsia who made birth control and sexuality their business to discuss, investigate, and legislate."[12]

Though that divergence was strong, the stories of dedicated advocates like Sanger – who in 1914 launched a feminist campaign to legalize, legitimize, and distribute birth control – remain essential to birth control history. Activists delivered contraceptive services to hundreds of thou-sands of the neediest cases, shifted the terms of public debate, and success-fully prompted community leaders to forthrightly acknowledge their private support for fertility control. Activist stories underscore the role of human agency in big-picture social reform, reminding us that change derives from living and breathing moral action, not ghostly trends and averages.

Still, just as historical demographers have been unable to write a grand formula for fertility decline, traditional historians have been unable to establish the importance of any particular individual or organization to birth control's de facto legitimation, a process which was largely complete by the time activists gave it voice. If there is more to the birth control story, it seems to lie somewhere between history and demography, in the applied ideas of millions of Americans who were able to justify birth control to themselves, their families, and communities.

Like the collapse of Prohibition, the rise of birth control is best understood as the product of a sprawling mass movement. If no leader or group was central to the movement, nor any single struc-tural trend, then local people acting in small, interconnected groups were collectively indispensable. In kitchens, foundries, bars, churches, and picnic grounds, Americans observed and enacted new reproduc-tive codes, judging and rejudging themselves and their peers. Often they were uncertain. "Having to live and rear a child or children in two or three rooms, and oftentimes in the rear of a store, is enough to break the spirit of the stoutest heart," wrote a Midwestern woman, Ruby Poley, in a characteristically ambivalent 1927 letter. "Our boys should be taught (and our girls too) that parenthood is not all hard-ship and that only in building for the future on a good foundation can happiness be found."[13]

Yet clear patterns of change mark the reflections of people like Poley. Americans wandering the ethical and emotional minefields of human reproduction expressed new doubts, new aspirations, and new visions of the past and future. Seeing birth control through their eyes, as the gradual, furtive, decentralized movement of women and men who were not necessarily outspoken, feminist, progressive, or politically engaged, helps us understand the birth control movement's enduring foundation of support. It helps us understand Americans' reproductive interests as *they* understood them, and the potential connections of everyday moral action to profound historical consequence.

The Outlines of Legitimacy

Few domains of human experience escaped the attention of citizen-moralists pondering reproductive ethics. Money, time, divinity, nature, health, self-fulfillment – these topics and many others continually bubbled to the surface. Boundaries between them were indistinct. Observers contradicted themselves or settled on sweeping moral-historical shorthands. "Don't ask me why they practice birth control," declared one population expert in 1935, "but they do."[14]

For all that, a definite core of ideas concerning economic self-interest, spiritual alignment with divinity or nature, and self-placement in cosmic and historical time underpinned Americans' gradual justification of ever-greater family limitation. Popular adoption of more material, this-worldly, present-minded, and self-consciously modern outlooks formed the essential basis for the birth control movement's success. Other priorities – notably women's pursuit of physical and mental well-being – were also important, but no class of legitimating ideas was as essential as the interlocking triad of economic, spiritual, and temporal modernism, applied by men and women alike. Over the course of the nineteenth and early twentieth centuries, Americans considering childrearing assigned progressively greater moral priority to rewards they could see and enjoy in their own lifetimes. Their motives for family limitation were not simply "selfish"; the welfare of living children was an essential point of concern. But the erosion of binding transcendent and eternal orders was indispensable to birth control's legitimation.

In terms of sheer frequency, moralists found two points on the triad – spiritual intuition and economic calculation – more relevant to explaining fertility decline than all other factors. Economic explanations were especially common. In reality, though, economic and "cosmic" explanations *together* dominated Americans' thinking. Because all parties assumed reproductive decisions were of basic moral and existential importance to any adult, speakers rarely viewed those decisions as merely rational or adaptive. Instead, economic self-interest was inextricably bound up with spiritual and emotional judgment. Whether fertility limitation was rational *per se* was less important than whether personal and cultural norms would allow for such rational action.[15]

But this moral economy of birth control was closely bound up in observers' ideas about the third point on the triangle, modern historical time. Recognizing family limitation as a long-term trend, many citizens spoke as amateur historians, measuring their own generational norms against those of their parents and grandparents. The reweighting of economic and moral priorities formed part of an irresistible historical logic. Recent history seemed to *want* smaller families. How much one resisted or accommodated this telos was a matter of acute relevance for individual reproductive outcomes. Should one adopt the old ways, with their worldly inconveniences but clearer view of eternal and natural orders? Or did recent flux demand a new "modern" approach? In asking these questions, moralists used history to make history, acting within intergenerational narratives of their own making.

Notably less important to American commentators were many of the ideas that animated outspoken activists, such as egalitarian feminism, eugenics, sexual liberation, and access to contraceptive technology. Though all those issues concerned Americans living during the fertility transition, they were considerably less prominent than moral-economic questions, and sometimes took a back seat to issues like mental health and landlord discrimination that have received little attention in the birth control story.

The significance of the citizen commentary, however, lies less in fixing an exact hierarchy of motives than in understanding these categories together, as they might have appeared in the mind of someone deciding on a course of reproductive action. Americans did not go to chalkboards to diagram their family size preferences, dividing and rank-ordering motivations from, say, "economy" down to "natural order" and "health." Their acting ideas were hazy and impressionistic. Collectively, however, they shared many ideas – or clusters of ideas – about the place of birth control in a good life. Those patterns of thought never amounted to a unitary mentality, but they allow us a better understanding of modern Americans' ethical worlds and the changing place of childrearing within them.

BACKGROUND TO A MASS MOVEMENT

Birth Control Methods

1 "birth control" was coined in 1914 by the journalist Otto Bobsein and popularized by Margaret Sanger. From the start it has meant two things: first, specific technologies for controlling fertility before conception, such as condoms or diaphragms; second, the broader phenomenon of controlling births. These twin meanings create confusion. Many people equate the phenomenon with the technology, and vice versa. We often assume that birth control's story is one of growing access to revolutionary devices and techniques, culminating in "the pill."[16]

The story is actually much older and more complex. A 4,000-year-old Egyptian papyrus recommends "crocodile's dung cut up on *auyt*-paste" as a means of preventing conception. Another ancient scroll suggests lint tampons saturated with honey and "tips of acacia." Early Jewish rabbis permitted the use of "cup of roots" and *mokh*; some even recommended coitus interruptus despite God's slaying of Onan for that sin. Ancient Greeks "anoint[ed] that part of the womb on which the seed falls with oil of cedar, or with ointment of lead or with frankincense, commingled with olive oil," noted Aristotle, and the early gynecologist Soranos of Ephesus wrote at length on contraceptives and abortifacients. Family limitation was sufficiently common among the Romans that multiple laws sought to encourage childrearing. *Lex Papia Poppaea* (9 A.D.) allotted tax breaks, promotions, and better theater seats to citizens with three or more children.[17]

Methods of family limitation need not be technically sophisticated to be effective. Early twentieth-century anthropologists found women using seaweed (Easter Island), seed pods (Suriname), grass (East Africa), tannic acid (Sumatra), and half-lemons (the Caribbean) as means of preventing sperm from reaching the ovum. Men across many places and times have practiced withdrawal, and couples around the world have long understood the family-limiting effects of periodic abstinence, noncoital sex, and prolonged breastfeeding.[18]

This is not to say that cheap modern contraceptives such as latex condoms or the pill have failed to make fertility control safer, simpler, and more reliable. Among the many "folk" techniques prevalent before the twentieth century were ineffective and sometimes dangerous amulets, potions, and spells. When magical or unreliable methods failed, millions resorted to risky abortions or infanticide. Birth control has gained popularity, in part, as it has become surer and less dangerous, and technical innovation has lowered rates of unintended pregnancy, maternal mortality, and child neglect.

Yet the spread of birth control is far from a story of technical progress catching up to latent demand. The U.S. fertility transition was a half-century old by the time it was assisted by any significant technological advance (in the form of rubber condoms, which gradually replaced animal-membrane "skins" over the course of the late nineteenth century). There were sporadic advances later in the century: diaphragm design improved, for example, and scientists gained a better understanding of spermicides. But these advances neither revolutionized the contraceptive marketplace nor dislodged older techniques such as withdrawal, periodic abstinence, and the use of abortifacients. Nor have new technologies made contraception an exact science. Even today about half of all pregnancies are unplanned.[19]

For Americans mulling family size, in other words, technological leaps were less decisive than moral and motivational ones. Like other peoples, Americans with strong motives to control reproduction typically found ways of doing so, even in the absence of advancements in contraceptive science. Fertility outcomes hinged less on techniques than norms and motives.[20]

The importance of any particular technique was minimized, too, by the fact that many Americans used multiple methods in tandem or sequence, never knowing for certain which method or combination of methods was ultimately effective. Partly as a result of this practice, moral and practical distinctions between methods were often blurred. This was true even of abortion. Though late-term abortions carried a strong stigma throughout the nineteenth and early twentieth centuries, Americans did not consistently distinguish between pre- and postconception methods of fertility control. Women self-administered abortifacient drugs and herbs after a missed period, or used them as precautions in the event that other methods (like withdrawal) failed. "Bringing on the menses" in this way was generally considered no more (or less) objectionable than other common methods.[21]

More fundamentally, the veil of privacy over reproductive decisions, the awkwardness of discussing them, and the hypocrisy surrounding them made it difficult for moralists to know who controlled fertility and by what means. Americans' judgments concerning birth control's status therefore tended to focus on the general acceptability of family limitation rather than on the legitimacy of any one method. Though abstinence was considered noble in moderation and abortion frequently demonized, amateur moralists were less interested in methods than motives. Whatever the exact means of control, more important was the *result* in terms of numbers of children, born to whom, under what moral pretexts. A common assumption was that as one method gained acceptance, so would all the others.[22]

This book therefore uses "birth control" to mean any deliberate effort to prevent unwanted childbearing, regardless of method – and including abstinence and abortion unless otherwise specified. Birth control activists used (and still use) a narrower definition, excluding abstinence, abortion, withdrawal, and other folk methods. This definition reflected abstinence's difficulty and abortion's stigma, danger, and illegality. It suited activists' future-facing goal of distributing reliable, legal contraceptives, and their rejection of "unscientific" methods. But understanding birth control's rise to popularity and legitimacy requires a broader and longer-term view. The movement's success was built in consciences more than laboratories.

Methods nevertheless varied significantly in their popularity, reliability, risk, and the extent to which one sex or the other could control them; and these variations helped shape the popular movement. Abortifacients were among the most popular "female" methods, especially in the nineteenth century. Some recipes were dubious, such as those recorded by folklorists in Adams County, Illinois: "nine rusty nails in some whiskey and senna tea"; "a half glass of sweet milk and two teaspoonfuls of black gunpowder." But the real abortifacient properties of common herbs and fungi such as savin, tansy, pennyroyal, cotton root, apiol, and ergot were widely known. From the colonial period onward, would-be birth controllers gathered these plants themselves, obtained them from midwives, or bought extracts in pharmacies. Women used them at considerable risk, since the active chemicals induced miscarriage by poisoning the whole body, not just the uterus. Large doses could be fatal. Despite the risk, herbal remedies were widely and even casually used. Even in rural, high-fertility areas such as the early twentieth-century Missouri Ozarks, tansy was a "well-known abortifacient" and women brewed "character sp'ilin' tea" more or less in the open. Some smoked pennyroyal pipes. By the mid-nineteenth century these home remedies competed with a growing variety of commercial abortifacients – sometimes packaged as medicines designed to clear menstrual "obstructions" – sold in stores and by mail order.[23]

Assisted abortions, meanwhile, were available from midwives and doctors. Some practitioners limited this procedure to conditions that threatened the mother's life, while others operated on a more commercial

[handwritten margin note: popular methods – 1800s – early 1900s]

basis. These surgical abortions generally carried a greater stigma than self-administered abortifacients, and operations were performed in secret. All types of abortion or deliberate miscarriage, however, were considered more defensible if they occurred before "quickening" – the moment at which the mother begins to feel fetal movement. Perhaps a third of all early-term pregnancies were terminated in the early twentieth century.[24]

Another prevalent female-controlled method was postcoital douching. After sex, women immediately sought to rid themselves of live sperm using a wide variety of solutions, from untreated water to citric acid to Lysol. Studies conducted in the early twentieth century found douching to be very widespread but less effective, on average, than similarly popular methods like condoms and withdrawal. More reliable but less popular were suppositories, commercial or homemade – the most common of which used a base of cocoa butter and quinine. Later, in the first few decades of the early twentieth century, fitted rubber pessaries and diaphragms became more prevalent as "regular" doctors and dedicated clinics began to play a larger role in contraceptive provision. Finally, many women sought to space their pregnancies with prolonged breastfeeding and the rhythm method.[25]

Unreliable as some of these methods were – even in combination – they could be controlled by women, and women's social networks were important in disseminating them. Knowledge passed between mothers and daughters, midwives and patients, neighbors, friends, and co-workers. "Usually when a girl was going to be married ... old ladies would tell them," recalled a Leadville, Colorado, woman who married in 1907, noting that Leadville's women "used Vaseline a lot," as well as rock salt, the rhythm method, and prolonged lactation. Women tended to feel the need for adequate control more acutely than men, since their bodily and mental health – not just economic standing or personal freedom – could be jeopardized by unwanted childbearing. Often women took the lead in family limitation.[26]

Birth control was not, however, widely considered the natural and exclusive domain of women, as it would be in later decades. Not only did men possess strong motives to control fertility – notably the economic burden of a large family – husbands or lovers were often more comfortable obtaining contraceptive products and services on the grey market, asking for information from friends, and suggesting those methods to their spouses. Men pursuing better birth control techniques were apt to be considered virile and street smart. Women performing the same task risked seeming prurient and calculating.[27]

Crucially, too, popular birth control relied heavily on three methods – withdrawal, condoms, and periodic abstinence – that demanded strong male commitment. This commitment is sometimes framed as "cooperation": the husband acceding to his wife's naturally greater interest in controlling fertility. But there is little reason to suspect that American men were mere accessories to the widespread adoption of birth control.

In the case of withdrawal, indeed, men had to remember their contraceptive intent exactly at the moment of climax. This inconvenience did not prevent withdrawal from maintaining its age-old popularity in America. "I fucked her once, but I minded my pullbacks," protested a Massachusetts man fighting a paternity suit in 1771. Withdrawal appealed "due to its simplicity," as the sex researcher Havelock Ellis observed in 1913. "It requires no forethought or preparation, and it costs nothing." Ellis' fellow sexologists agreed that it was "the commonest of all methods." In polls conducted in the 1920s and 1930s coitus interruptus was consistently among the three most common techniques used by U.S. couples, alongside condoms and (female-controlled) douching. Beneath the surface of polite discussion, it was laughingly euphemized: in France one would "leave the dance before it's over"; in Sicily, "go in reverse gear"; and in Scotland, "get off at Paisley" – the station before Glasgow. Coitus interruptus remains popular throughout the world today, and can be highly effective.[28]

Condoms enjoyed a similar popularity, particularly after "rubbers" became cheaper and more reliable in the late nineteenth century. The major obstacle to condoms' popularity was their association with prostitution, which inhibited husbands and wives from suggesting their use. That taboo was weakened by military antivenereal disease campaigns during the First World War, and by sheer availability and ease of use. By the early twentieth century, condoms' effectiveness over time was comparable to withdrawal and significantly better than douching: one 1935 study showed a "ratio of effectiveness" of 83 percent for condoms, 72 percent for withdrawal, and 52 percent for douching over a nineteenth-month period, as compared to a baseline of couples who used no recognized birth control technique.[29]

Whatever the merits of withdrawal, condoms, abortifacients, or other common methods, the idea of either male or female "control" over family limitation can be misleading. Most techniques would have been subject to conjugal discussion and some level of mutual consent. A wife might insist that her husband practice withdrawal, or a husband that his wife induce

abortion. Concealing contraceptive intent from a spous[e]
impossible for men, and difficult for women.[30]

In the case of a final popular method, indeed, mutual v[ill]
had to be quite strong. Periodic abstinence was sure, sin[ce espe-]
cially, did not necessarily mean going without sexual [...]
Abstinence could be sporadic, meant to space children o[r...]
likelihood, not foreclose their possibility. And the inconveniences of
avoiding sex with one's spouse could be eased by masturbation, noncoital
sex, or visits to prostitutes – all additional means of separating sexual
gratification from reproduction.[31]

Where abstinence differed most from other methods, however, was
that it was publicly acceptable – even laudable – in many forms. Other
methods allowed for the expression of unrestrained passion. Abstinence
demanded self-restraint – republican civilization's foundational virtue.
Virtually no American objected to a mid-sized family carefully spaced
and limited through abstinence. Husbands were expected to "protect"
their wives by abstaining from sex when a pregnancy might be injurious.
Unmarried men were supposed to remain chaste until they could support
a household. Poor men with large, hungry families were disparaged for
their lack of "self-control."[32]

To some Americans, then, the debate over birth control appeared to be
a referendum on the legitimacy of sexual pleasure for its own sake, not
family limitation. Could men and women set out to achieve bodily pleasure and not return to an animal state? At the intellectual poles of debate,
conservatives and radicals sparred over this question with great force.
Popular moralists, however, were less concerned with the abstract value of
sexual expression than with end results in the form of children. All but
fanatics could accept great sexual ardor so long as it was discrete, spousal,
and suitably reproduced families and communities. Americans took
sexual desire for granted, used the fertility control methods they could
justify in private, and assumed their peers did the same. Given low
expectations for exact compliance with sexual norms and the difficulty
of knowing how one's fellows controlled fertility, the key questions
became: are the right number of children being born? Was a given couple
exercising too little reproductive control? Too much? Did their decisions
make appropriate contributions to the future of humanity, family, clan,
nation, and moral community?[33]

The partisans of chastity accordingly worked within narrow limits.
Lifelong singletons of both sexes were patronized, ridiculed, and even
legislated against, despite their presumed purity. Celibacy was "false to

God, false to country, and false to self." The marginalization of the chaste hardened in the decades around 1900 as many middle-class men, and some women, began to see primal sexuality as an antidote to "over-civilization" rather than a threat to civility. "Self-control" took on shades of sexlessness, domestication, and impotence. Even before that hardening of masculine ideals, however, middle-aged bachelors and old maids faced contempt as weaklings and egotists, as did many well-off parents of just one "spoiled" child. How one avoided unwanted children was persistently less important than why one did so.[34]

one child

Regulating Birth Control

By the mid-nineteenth century, deliberate fertility control was approaching universality in American households. Devices and information were available on the open market. This state of affairs struck some observers as obscene – notably Anthony Comstock, a vice crusader who devoted his life to uprooting sexual impropriety. Comstock had been raised on a farm in Connecticut, the son of a devout mother who died when he was ten years old. As a garrison soldier during the Civil War he was shocked by the behavior of his fellow troops. He boldly scolded them, preached to them, and made himself unpopular by pouring his ration of whisky on the ground rather than passing it to the regiment's readier drinkers. After the war, working as a clerk in New York City, Comstock was scandalized anew by the city's open vice markets. He began moonlighting as a volunteer enforcer of the state's obscenity law, eventually gaining the attention and support of prominent local citizens. They supported his formation, in 1873, of the New York Society for the Suppression of Vice, and in the same year Comstock persuaded Congress to pass a national anti-obscenity statute that outlawed (among other things) mailing or importing contraceptive devices and information. Most U.S. states passed similar laws around the same time.[35]

Both state and federal laws tended to be enforced sporadically or not at all, however. Enforcement of the federal statute fell largely to Comstock himself, operating as a deputy U.S. postal inspector. What prosecutions he was able to pursue often ended up being thrown out by unsympathetic courts in his home state of New York. Meanwhile the national market for contraceptive products thrived. Manufacturers of patent abortifacients and douching solutions largely ignored the "Comstock laws," selling their products under lightly euphemized titles such as "French powder." The ubiquitous Sears catalog displayed "ladies' cup-shaped silk sponges"

enforcement failed

next to an array of douches. Peddlers sold contraceptives door to door. Doctors and pharmacies remained largely exempt from the restrictions, or unaware of them. One observer of the condom market in 1890s New York predicted that if the trade ever suffered, it would be due to glut rather than effective suppression. "A very large amount of knowledge is already abroad among the people," as one contraceptive advocate wrote in 1886, "and the general complaint is not a lack of knowing some way, but a desire to know which way is least objectionable."[36]

Methods such as withdrawal and abstinence, meanwhile, remained policeable only in the realm of conscience, which was where a large and growing share of Americans thought birth control decisions should reside. Comstock's *New York Times* obituary, in 1915, noted that he had been the subject of frequent ridicule, particularly after 1906, when he seized 1,000 copies of an art students' gazette depicting five nudes. George Bernard Shaw referred to "Comstockery" as "the world's standing joke at the expense of the United States."[37]

Courts began formally voiding the Comstock laws in the 1930s. The federal anticontraceptive statute was largely nullified in 1936 when an appellate court ruled that mailing birth control devices and information was not inherently obscene, and legitimate when done by physicians. The following year the American Medical Association released a qualified endorsement of birth control.[38]

These developments have been hailed as watershed moments, but in practice few Americans had been intimidated by the Comstock laws. In thousands of letters soliciting contraceptive advice from activists like Sanger – advice which was illegal to mail – only a handful of petitioners evinced any knowledge of the ban, or their addressees' efforts to overturn it. Legal restrictions had little discernible effect: by the 1920s, Americans reported contraceptive use rates of 70–95 percent (excluding methods respondents did not consider "birth control"). Barriers to birth control's spread were not primarily legal, material, or public. The significance of the Comstock laws lay in the informal stigma they expressed.[39]

Population Thought in America

Public concern over reproductive control, however, had a very long history among elites prior to the emergence of a broad popular debate in America. "This evil grew upon us rapidly, and without attracting attention," complained the Greek historian Polybius in the second century B.C., "by our men becoming perverted to a passion for show and money and the pleasures of an idle life, and accordingly either not marrying at all, or, if they did marry, refusing to rear the children." Tacitus excoriated his fellow Romans in a like manner. Polemics of this kind circulated among classically educated Americans, and few historical topics evoked more interest in this group than the decline of ancient empires. Many civic leaders took for granted – with Polybius, Tacitus, and other ancient moralists – that sexual virtue and civilizational integrity were closely tied up in one another.[40]

Early American colonists took pronatalism for granted, leaving largely unspoken the assumption that "a fruitful progeny" was desirable. Colonial New Englanders saw their large families and related territorial expansion as a sign of divine favor. "Children are a heritage of the Lord," read a widely repeated Bible verse, "and the fruit of the womb is his reward." A small brood was a "personal and social misfortune" through the time of the American Revolution and after. Rapid natural increase reflected America's prosperity, geopolitical destiny, and the fundamental superiority of republican government. "If in Europe they have but four Births to a marriage," boasted Ben Franklin in his *Observations Concerning the Increase of Mankind* (1751), "we may here reckon eight." With land cheap, young men "not afraid to marry," and the population doubling every twenty years, Americans could look forward to a continental destiny.[41]

As early as 1843, however, George Tucker, a professor at the University of Virginia, detected a decrease of "nearly 10 percent" in the country's ratio of children to women of child-bearing age. This decline, traceable in the censuses of 1800 and 1820, boded poorly for population increase – "the surest index of the nation's present abundance and comfort." So did the growth of cities and wealth, which brought "other checks to natural multiplication, those arising from prudence or pride." "It is even probable," Tucker wrote, "that these checks operate sooner in this country than they have operated in other countries, by reason of the higher standard of comfort with which the American people start, and of that pride of personal independence which our political institutions so strongly cherish."[42]

What Tucker detected was initially a northeastern phenomenon, and a mild one. But as early as the revolutionary era, various "forerunner" groups had begun consciously limiting their families: Quakers in Nantucket, farmers in New England's interior, Virginia gentry. By the early nineteenth century that trend had become substantial enough to affect national averages. The United States then became, alongside

France, one of the first two modern nations to enter sustained fertility decline.[43]

This trend inspired reflexive condemnation in most of the social critics who became aware of it. Two freethinkers nevertheless took up birth control as a cause in the 1830s. One was Robert Dale Owen, better known for his utopian colony in Indiana, the other Charles Knowlton, a country doctor from Massachusetts. Each man authored a euphemistically titled tract (*Moral Physiology*; *Fruits of Philosophy*) defending family limitation and providing practical advice on methods. Both works circulated widely, and Knowlton's efforts resulted in an obscenity case which aroused considerable local interest. Neither tract, however, became a national sensation or ignited widespread civic debate. This was partly because Americans were reluctant to discuss sexual topics in the public forum. But it was also because medical manuals and some almanacs – the second and third books literate Americans typically acquired, after a Bible – already supplied similar information.[44]

Even the more sensational trial of two English reformers, Annie Besant and Charles Bradlaugh, for distributing Knowlton's manual in England in 1877, failed to ignite much popular interest in the United States. In public consciousness reproductive shortfalls remained an abstruse and foreign phenomenon: largely the domain of the decadent French, whose lax sexual mores and low birthrates, it seemed to many Americans, had played a key part in the country's humiliation and territorial loss in the Franco-Prussian War. Americans' own falling fertility remained "scarcely perceptible" to them, one population theorist complained in 1883, even as French depopulation was "well understood." Mass public debate over American population trends was around the corner, but it awaited improved vital statistics, decreased sexual reticence, and increased public concern, all of which converged at the turn of the twentieth century.[45]

1800s

Improvements in local record-keeping after the Civil War gradually made the American demographic picture clearer, and sociologists grew increasingly alarmed. Their alarm concerned not only the small-family trend itself, but the parallel growth of large-scale immigration from all corners of Europe. Critics measured the fertility of "new" immigrants against that of "old stock" natives, finding to their dismay that immigrants had considerably larger families. There was "no increase of the strictly native population" in most parts of New England, the demographer Nathan Allen deduced in 1868. Only "a large foreign element" that was "wonderfully prolific, having nearly three times as many children as the Americans," staved off population decline. The implications were obvious: if native New Englanders – "the best stock that the world ever saw" – did not soon renounce "single life ... it is evident that the native stock must rapidly diminish and, at no distant day, comparatively *must run out!*"⁴⁶

Partly in response to these pronatal alarms, a counter-current of "voluntary motherhood" activism arose in the 1870s. Respectable middle-class feminists painted smaller families as emblems of enlightenment and progress, particularly for women. They affirmed a wife's right to deny sex when a pregnancy might threaten her health or her family's welfare, grounding their claims in a noncontroversial, caretaking "motherhood mystique." Women would always bear and nurture children, but honoring that sacred role required practical control over family size. This message was warmly received by America's growing women's rights movement. Like the period's population alarmists, however, voluntary motherhood advocates ultimately found themselves marginalized in the wider civic forum – not just by popular indifference but by the fact that they were women.⁴⁷

By the 1890s, as successive censuses confirmed the long-running trend towards lower fertility among the old stock, elite discussion grew broader and more sophisticated. Francis Amasa Walker, a census superintendent, economist, Civil War hero, and president of the Massachusetts Institute of Technology, wrote a widely noticed article arguing that America's "vast numbers" of poor immigrants were collectively *causing* falling native fertility. Native-born Americans, "increasingly unwilling to bring forth sons and daughters who should be obliged to compete in the market for labor and in the walks of life with those whom they did not recognize as of their own grade and condition," were not bringing them forth at all.⁴⁸

Walker's "shock theory" rejected other writers' instinct to blame the native-born for their own demographic demise, preferring to frame low fertility as an unfortunate but understandable means by which prudent, independent Americans maintained their dignified living standards in the face of competition from ignorant and indigent Europeans. Walker made this point defensively, however, and most writers continued emphasizing Americans' own moral failings. There had been a "great increase in the use of things which were formerly considered as luxuries," opined John S. Billings in 1893, "but which now have become almost necessities."⁴⁹

Elite alarm reached a crescendo in the years immediately before Roosevelt's pronouncements. Edward A. Ross, an influential sociologist, strongly endorsed Walker's anti-immigrant position. Americans would be either "displaced" or impoverished if they did not stem the tide of poor migrants. Writing from California in 1901, he was particularly concerned about Asian immigration:

The American farm hand, mechanic and operative might wither away before the heavy influx of a prolific race from the Orient, just as in classic times the Latin husbandman vanished before the endless stream of slaves poured into Italy by her triumphant generals. For a case like this I can find no words so apt as "race suicide." There is no bloodshed, no violence, no assault of the race that waxes upon the race that wanes. The higher race quietly and unmurmuringly eliminates itself rather than endure individually the bitter competition it has failed to ward off from itself by collective action.[50]

This sort of pronouncement helped shift elite attention from low fertility among the native-born middle classes to high fertility among the immigrant poor. Walker, Ross, and others would bolster doubts about America's assimilative powers and help lay the foundations for strict immigrant restriction laws.

But as the new century dawned, reproductive habits *within* America's dominant culture still inspired the most vigorous examination. In particular, a 1903 study of Harvard graduates' fertility commissioned by the college's president, Charles Eliot, drew wide attention. Eliot's statistics showed that six classes of Harvard men from the 1880s had fallen 28 percent shy of reproducing their number. This figure, announced with scorn by a widely respected public intellectual, touched off a small furor of its own. Scholars and newsmen conducted follow-up studies and found similar results at Yale, Princeton, Brown, and Bowdoin (men's colleges); Holyoke, Bryn Mawr, and Vassar (women's colleges); and among other classes at Harvard. The *Chicago Tribune* went so far as to publish the names of eighty-nine randomly selected members of the city's elite University Club alongside the (generally low) numbers of children they had fathered. Susan B. Anthony and other proponents of voluntary motherhood protested the crudity of the whole exercise.[51]

Just days after Eliot's warnings, Roosevelt (a Harvard graduate and father of six) began beating the same drum. Appropriating Ross' term "race suicide," the president began painting a vivid picture of near-term civilizational death. The fate of democracy and progress, he argued, rested on present citizens' willingness to raise enough children to perpetuate themselves and their values. Intentionally "shirking" one's reproductive debt to society was not just selfish; it betrayed a profound spiritual myopia – a "failure to appreciate aright the difference between the all important and the unimportant." Roosevelt's campaign lasted throughout his presidency and life, raising uncomfortable moral questions about the relationship of private reproductive behavior to the public good and personal fulfillment.[52]

Power in the Birth Control Movement

As essayists and professors weighed family limitation's causes and consequences across the nineteenth century, quieter moral action gradually undermined the large-family ideal. Eventually this "quiet revolution" gained prominent spokespeople with the arrival of Margaret Sanger and allies in the 1910s and 20s. To many Americans these activists heralded a new day. They would give voice, at last, to deep and broad sentiments that had long gone unspoken.[53]

To some extent activists served that role, effectively representing the citizen movement. Activists helped push birth control onto the public agenda and established an unapologetically reformist wing in debates over reproductive ethics. They initiated test cases against the Comstock laws, lobbied doctors and lawmakers, and provided practical contraceptive services to the neediest Americans. Their efforts, however, ultimately complemented a mass movement that greatly exceeded the activist movement in age, scope, and power. Though each movement helped the other expand and gain legitimacy, only the citizen movement was indispensable to making America safe for birth control.

This disparity of power is rooted in the peculiar political dynamics of birth control. Unlike other social movements in whose image it has been cast, like suffragism or civil rights, birth control's ultimate success required virtually no access to police power or public space. Key decisions could be made behind closed doors, by otherwise powerless people, for closely-held reasons that were awkward for outsiders to inquire about, discuss, or surveil. Restricting "folk" and grey-market methods of family limitation was nearly impossible. Birth control was thus able to gain great popularity and widespread tacit legitimacy with hardly a public word spoken on its behalf or a public deed committed in its name. The foundation of its support, and most of the superstructure, was built in an environment where no leaders formulated demands, no advocates represented aggrieved parties, and no policies changed.

While the physical privacy of reproductive decisions made them difficult to police, their universality and intimate importance made them difficult to influence. Nearly all adults must *act* on their ideas about the reproductive good, and these acts tend to feel significant. They form identities. They have definite near-term ramifications outside the realm of principle. As a result they resist easy suasion. "Most men can manage to live without ever attempting to decide for themselves any fundamental question about business or politics," as Walter Lippmann wrote in 1929,

But they can neither ignore changes in sexual relations nor do they wish to. It is possible for a man to be a socialist or an individualist without ever having to make one responsible decision in which his theories play any part. But what he thinks about divorce and contraception, continence and license, monogamy, prostitution, and sexual experience outside of marriage, are matters that are bound at some point in his life to affect his happiness immediately and directly.

"The affairs of state may be regulated by leaders," Lippmann concluded, "But the affairs of a man and a woman are inescapably their own."[54]

Whatever the abstract strengths of "bottom-up" or "middle-out" history, then, birth control demands investigation that reaches below even "grassroots" activism and into everyday assumptions about how to live a good life. Walled off literally by bedrooms and figuratively by reticence and privacy, citizens who wished to limit their families neither required nor developed a strong central leadership. There was no tangible, public-world objective to unite them with leaders, no space to conquer, and little need to confront state power. People who wanted to limit their families did not even necessarily require basic freedoms of body, movement, and speech, as Caribbean slaves' sub-replacement birthrates suggest. Instead, would-be family limiters required a minimum of folk knowledge, a willing spouse in most cases, and a motive drawn from their own peculiar moral worldview.[55]

Birth control, in other words, was a radically *social* social movement, but not a simple adjustment to vast structural changes. Leaderless as it was in a traditional political sense, it was composed of millions of moral agents with self-consciously new and shared ideas. Though units of influence were small – often no larger than a few acquaintances or family members – these units were connected endlessly to other small cells, and to common moral clearinghouses such as gossip networks, religious communities, and eventually the press. Private observation of reproductive behavior, meanwhile, afforded limiters a conscious sense of agency in social change. Keeping the family small, relative to past generations, was the mark of modern and forward-thinking people, for better or worse. A small family seemed well adapted to chancy times. It eased worldly concerns. The new ethic could be easily observed and discussed. After 1900, it could even be read about in newspapers, debated on stages, and discussed at kitchen tables. Centerless as this moral shift was, its agents acted on similar ideas, at similar times, in self-consciously modern and innovative ways. Ultimately they formed the decisive force in one of recent history's fundamental upheavals.[56]

Birth control's privatized politics limited the reach of family limitation's enemies as well as its friends. Though critics like Roosevelt spoke from a position of time-honored respectability, pronatalists were no more capable of convincing any wide public to prioritize transcendent reproductive duties over more immediate and worldly concerns. "No doubt every one in society discussed the subject," Henry Adams recalled of the race suicide controversy, "and the surface current of social opinion seemed set as strongly in one direction as the silent undercurrent of social action ran in the other."[57] *limitation*   " *pronatalism*

Rather than suffragism, antislavery, or civil rights, the birth control movement is better analogized to the folk movement that effectively nullified prohibitions on alcohol. Prominent Americans organized an Association Against the Prohibition Amendment (AAPA) in 1918, lobbying lawmakers until the U.S. repealed its alcohol ban in 1933. But we tend to remember Prohibition's failure as a more popular phenomenon – a de facto nullification rooted in mass action. Birth control's path to power was much more gradual, but broadly similar. Indeed, the two mass movements' shared qualities were not lost on Americans during the interwar years. Birth control's enemies, one newspaper reader complained, possessed "a psychology akin to the drys during prohibition."[58]

For prospective leaders of all descriptions, power in the birth control movement was maddeningly dispersed. It had no location, no offices, no central ideology, and virtually no hierarchy outside tiny spheres of indirect local example and influence. Reproductive action seemed poised to sway the destiny of nations, and perhaps to dignify human freedom, or demonstrate freedom's fragility – and yet there was no specific person or body to address. Even close friends and family members would do as they pleased. None of this dissuaded leaders from approaching birth control as a political question. But obstacles to their effectiveness were formidable. In the birth control movement, political power was cultural power, and more fundamentally, individual existential power vested in basic ideas about the worthiness of human life over time.

The Story of Birth Control: Historians and Gender

The challenge of birth control history is to expand the story beyond the most visible activists without losing sight of individual moral action. This challenge has been met, in part, by historians of nineteenth-century America's sprawling contraceptive marketplace. The "tale of physicians, lawmakers, and political activists," as Andrea Tone writes, conceals the dominance of informal commerce in meeting contraceptive needs, "irrespective of the legal and medical status of birth control." Historians of contraceptive supply have not, however, set out to explain the sources of contraceptive demand. "What changed the motivation and attitudes of ... couples or individuals remains mysterious and complex," Janet Farrell Brodie writes, "perhaps more in the realm of the poet or novelist than the historian."[59]

Major surveys of birth control history have hazarded explanations for birth control's underlying popularity: a "women's rebellion"; "social ambition," and an "increasingly manipulative attitude toward nature"; a "modern confluence of scientific confidence with romantic optimism." These assessments are asides, however, in works focused on the words, deeds, and influences of birth control's would-be leaders and representatives. We do not know much about the social history of these ideas, or others like them.[60]

To the extent that historians have paid attention to the popular movement, many have framed it as an extension of the women's movement. Family limitation gained popularity, in this view, as women asserted a right to equality and self-determination. The birth control and feminist movements progressed in tandem and complemented one another. Whether feminists worked within the prevalent gender norms as maternalist reformers, or outside them as egalitarians and radicals, the spread of birth control relied on their growing assertion of a right to be free, secure, and well.[61]

This emphasis reflects the greater urgency with which women pursued birth control and the prominence of women among birth control activists – but also, inevitably, latter-day concerns. History is a moving dialogue between past and present, and antifeminists' ongoing threats to reproductive self-determination have encouraged historians to examine birth control as a women's issue. At times, however, this initiative has flattened family limitation's history into what Kate Fisher, a historian of birth control, calls "a teleological progression from the 1870s through to the 1960s," in which "the era of the Pill becomes the end point in a narrative of women's desperate attempts to control their own bodies and divorce sex from reproduction." The connection between reproductive control and women's agency has become so naturalized that many scholars of birth control assume they are addressing a women's issue before formulating research questions.[62]

Fisher's research suggests that women, as a sex, were of less singular importance. In several hundred interviews with elderly men and women, Fisher uncovered an unambiguously "male-dominated culture of contraception" in early twentieth-century England. "Both husband and wife saw contraception as part of the male world, and a man's duty." Husbands determined why and how the couple would use birth control in most households. Wives shied away for fear of appearing immodest. "It was husbands, not wives, who rooted out birth control information, framed contraceptive strategies for the family, and put these into practice," Fisher writes. "Women were not incrementally taking control of contraception."[63]

Early twentieth-century Americans lived in a similar world. Contraceptive exchanges were at least as much male as female domains. Though women were often physically desperate for birth control information, men feared and resented their breadwinner's responsibility to provide for additional children, and longed for sex without consequences. They blamed themselves when their families suffered as a result of failed attempts to control births, and half-jokingly ridiculed their wives' desire for children.[64]

That said, Americans did not live under a truly male-dominated culture of contraception. Women were much more likely than men to solicit contraceptive advice by mail, and many argued fervently that birth control *should* be considered a women's issue, even when it *was* male-controlled. Women bore the day-to-day strain of risky pregnancies, overcrowded homes, or childrearing in poverty. Women spoke of birth control in a more urgent tone. All this suggests that in households where both spouses where ambivalent about additional children – as was often the case – women may have done more to push for family limitation.

This is not to say that ordinary Americans saw birth control as a women's issue to the same extent as activists and their historians. Instead both men and women, and amateur social critics of all political stripes, tended to frame birth control as a world-historical phenomenon driven by moral changes that transcended gender. Pronatalists rarely blamed women for popularizing birth control. Liberalizers rarely singled women out as an essential constituency. Commentators routinely failed to designate either women or men as primary initiators or beneficiaries of contraceptive action, even in passing. If gender was a dominant nexus of concern in fertility limitation, a large majority of commentators neglected to mention it, despite widespread contemporary debate on the rights and duties of women and men.

Rather than drawing lines from "woman" to demand for birth control to legitimation, as activists often did, amateur critics tended to see gender as a messier tangle of motives and sex-specific natures. Men might be vectors of birth control's popularity not just because of their economic responsibility or privileged access to contraceptive exchanges, but because masculine "nature" seemed amenable to family limitation. Men were morally pragmatic, selfish, footloose, lusty, and greedy, pronatalists complained. They were rational and attuned to societal progress, affirmed birth control's defenders. Women, meanwhile, had their own strong and particular reasons for seeking birth control: vanity, covetousness, ostentation; or attention to the welfare of the young and to their own health and sanity. At the same time women possessed a stronger sense of childrearing's immaterial rewards, and a stronger resistance to the heartless ethics of the market.[65]

All these gendered variables might influence birth control decisions, but none of them appeared so singularly essential as to rise above the cross-currents in gendered motivation, or overshadow larger questions about a good life. As a result, for Americans surveying the reproductive scene, sex-specific characteristics rarely rose to the fore. More important were moral and spiritual questions that challenged "us," "souls," or "folks," rather than men or women as such.

In a more abstract and mystical sense, however, gender was an important concern to American reproductive moralists. As a "natural" and even divine binary that *united* men and women and imposed on them the shared burden of sexual reproduction, gender difference was an important category among nonactivists. Strong or "animal" feelings of manhood or womanhood predisposed people to relatively large families, for better or worse. But as a divider of reproductive motivation, gender difference did not appear uniquely significant in explaining the small-family trend. Gender – in the sense of women or men acting and thinking *as* women or men, constrained by norms of femininity or masculinity, and challenging those norms – was one issue in a crowd, certainly not a trivial factor in the minds of observers surveying their communities, but just as certainly not a dominant one. This sidetracking of gender issues in popular debate does not invalidate the prevailing gender-based approaches to birth control history, which focus on the roles of women and feminists. But it does suggest that historians have partly mistaken the importance of birth control to women and feminists for the importance of women and feminists to birth control.[66]

The Story of Birth Control: Demographers and Modernization

As historians have told one story of birth control, demographers have told another. For generations of demographers explaining historical fertility decline has been a central preoccupation – a sort of holy grail. In America the quest focused initially on explaining domestic "depopulation" in Theodore Roosevelt's time. After the Second World War demographers redoubled their efforts, hoping that improved understanding of American and Western fertility declines would allow social engineers to defuse the world's ticking "population bomb." From this effort emerged "demographic transition theory," which attributed lower fertility to a broad array of modernization indicators drawn from the American and European experience. "Development" was the best contraceptive: as people moved to cities, became wealthier and better educated, eschewed religious fatalism, competed for social position, relied less on their children for labor, trusted that more offspring would survive into adulthood, and generally abandoned premodern pronatalist and patriarchal customs, they would have fewer children.[67]

No sooner had demographic transition theory become the dominant paradigm, however, than demographers began to question its predictive power. The United States provided a key foil. Early nineteenth-century Americans were not "modern" by any indicator except perhaps literacy. Even in the 1860s, 80 percent of Americans lived in rural areas, child mortality rates ran around 20 percent, secondary education was rare, and churches and patriarchs remained strong. Further complicating matters was the mid-twentieth-century U.S. baby boom, which inexplicably persisted even as the postwar demographers wrote, defying America's superlative modernity.[68]

From this conundrum emerged a linchpin idea in U.S. historical demography: the so-called "land availability hypothesis." A nation of farmers might lead the world in fertility decline because farm parents' fondest wish, typically, was to establish their progeny on nearby farms. As land prices rose along the Atlantic seaboard, fertility declined alongside fathers' optimism about their sons' prospects. In the west, where land remained cheap, fertility remained high. Later studies confirmed this correlation, but scholars also found variables such as ethnicity that appeared more predictive of differential fertility than land prices. Ultimately, land availability appeared to have been important, if not singularly important, in determining Americans' desire for children.[69]

Other scholars focused on urbanization. Children who had been economic assets on farms became liabilities in growing towns and cities. In the words of one demographer, wealth flowed "up" from children to parents on farms, but "down" from parents to children in cities. Both farm and city parents responded rationally to children's economic status.[70]

But even after setting aside the question of whether farm parents assessed children's value in rational, future-oriented terms, the U.S. fertility transition is hard to explain in this way. Children have not always been obvious "assets" on farms – even the family farms of nineteenth-century America, where population density was low, hired hands expensive, and labor-saving machinery rudimentary. The economist Lee A. Craig, seeking to put a figure on the labor value of antebellum American farm children, sampled 20,000 rural northern households in 1860 and determined that an average child's net economic worth at birth was between -$100 and -$200. Young children, after all, not only required food and lodging, they needed care from an otherwise productive adult. Worse, older children typically left home just as they became fully capable farmers, and adult children were not reliable income sources in old age. The economic demographer Ronald Lee, in a study of studies, concluded that net transfers between generations in agricultural societies are "invariably downward from older to younger when we consider the whole life cycle." This is true even after accounting for the care children might provide their parents in old age. "On average," Lee writes, "a parent recovered in old age about one tenth of the net cost of raising a child." Non-economic values appeared to be in play.[71]

Partly as a result of the continuing lack of any empirical consensus on the origins of fertility decline, demography as a discipline began to move away from rational-actor models over the course of the 1970s and especially the 1980s. At the center of this shift was the Princeton European Fertility Project (EFP), which saw dozens of demographers analyze over a century's worth of socioeconomic data for several hundred European provinces. Seeking to isolate underlying factors in fertility declines across time and space, researchers discovered none: not literacy, urbanization, religious affiliation, economic development, mortality rates, nor any other measurable metric of modernization. Fuller explanation of fertility decline awaited research into "cultural factors."[72]

The EFP has since been criticized for working at too wide an angle to detect small-scale socioeconomic variation. But the broader importance of "culture" has not been challenged, and has inspired new research into issues like religious sentiment, media and kin influence, and the diffusion of moral innovation. Second Demographic Transition (SDT) theory, a benchmark scheme for explaining historical fertility decline, brings many of these strains together, emphasizing moral shifts in attitudes towards the family, money, and self-fulfillment.[73]

Even after this cultural turn, however, historical demographers still struggle with "vexing problems of absent quantitative data," and with the complexity of the data that does exist. Cultural analysis has brought more variables to an already daunting list. As a result, fertility transition has "perhaps too many formal theories, none of which seems wholly satisfactory," as Karen O. Mason writes, and many demographers have decided to forsake grand theories entirely, arguing that causation is too variable to be intelligibly theorized. The resulting "trend toward particularistic explanations" has led to "confusion" – even "epistemological crisis" – within historical demography, as findings have piled up in isolation from one another. "One may argue that the more we know about the past the less we can say about it," one demographer observes.[74]

The American birth control debate suggests ways of integrating some of this profuse data from a more existential perspective: from the vantage points of people forced to act on complex information without categorizing and scrutinizing every detail. No demographer would confuse the birth control debate's documentary record for a traditional data set. But that record offers connective tissue for demographic data, and a reasonably diverse and detailed view of fertility change from the perspective of several thousand people who witnessed and enacted it.

FERTILITY AND IDEAS ABOUT TIME

Subjective Modernization

For decades, making sense of popular fertility control meant gathering all possible causes under the big tent of "modernization." Every change associated with the West's long industrial age seemed to favor small families. Even today – as modernization theories have fallen from favor due to presumed sidelining of human agency and privileging of recent Western experience as the moving endpoint of world-historical progress – scholars who have jettisoned the formal language of modernization struggle to find another explanatory rubric. "Nearly all ... theories treat demographic transition as a consequence of modernity under some guise."[75]

The American case suggests a new way of understanding the role of macrohistory in fertility change. "Modernization" was never just an analyst's retrospective category; it was also a central idea to Americans making reproductive decisions during the fertility transition. In 1905 or 1935, in Chicago or Santa Barbara, to have a small family was to be modern. Embracing modern reproductive logic was "forward-thinking" or "progressive" to some. To others it was "decadent" or "unnatural."

2 sides of the same coin

For a majority it was somewhere in between. This moral-historical grayscale – to what extent was modernity good or bad, and to what extent were smaller families *part* of that goodness or badness? – exercised a direct influence on Americans' attitudes towards family limitation. Far from being a remote abstraction, modernization was a lively, front-of-the-mind presence in Americans' acting ideas about reproduction.

A sense of open-ended social and economic change made challenging eternal orders easier. If people were fundamentally reorganizing and subjugating their worlds – vanquishing diseases, stringing railways across continents, reforming politics and culture, and creating new uncertainties and opportunities in the process – was it wrong to reexamine the claims of timeless orders? Though divine or natural law was a real enough presence in the lives of Americans living in the industrial age, so too were the risks and responsibilities of new human mastery. The modern world seemed to punish trust in providence, or even community. It rewarded individual control, skepticism, economic rationality, and careful risk mitigation. Children born under the new regime were best considered individual material responsibilities, rather than a sort of spiritual property held jointly by parents, the community, and the cosmic order. Even Roosevelt conceded that the "tendencies of the times … unavoidably discourage large families," objecting only to the "regrettable disposition to yield too much to them."[76]

Reproductive dispositions, American moralists thought, tended to draw on the whole spirit of a person and his or her age. They were existential rather than categorical – shaped by sweeping changes in moral conventions across the generations. Birth control had become popular because of shifting views on life's final purposes; the spirit of modernization and that of family limitation were hard to separate. Though a person might yet denounce the logic of modernity and raise "the good old-fashioned family," progressively fewer parents did so as it became more apparent that abundant procreation put one outside the main stream of relentless social development. One's most modern-seeming neighbors and friends all seemed to have small families, by past generations' standards. Birth control appeared to have time on its side.

Acting on this sort of historical vision required no special interest in history or factual knowledge about the past. As humans we continually construct and reconstruct meaning-giving narratives for our lives without recalling life events systematically or even accurately. In the same way, intergenerational memory shaped acting ideas about reproduction.

"Progress may be slow" as a Kansas man wrote of birth control in 1927, "but changes must come."[77]

Rather than consciously calculating pros and cons, virtues and transgressions, better birth control methods or worse, three children or four, Americans tended to form acting reproductive ideas in an existential haze – acting on intuitively blended moral, economic, and spiritual ideas without really examining them individually or developing a clear endgame. What many had, instead, was a feeling – often a strong feeling – for what was right in the present moment, based on personal and community ideals that were difficult to articulate but nonetheless real. Because those ideals were very often rooted in ambient attitudes about the course of social history, the degree to which people embraced or rejected modernization had an acute effect on reproductive action.[78]

There is no reason to suspect that this subjective modernization influenced fertility behavior more strongly in the United States, in the early twentieth century, than other places and times. In Kenya's Nyanza province, for example, a large family was long associated with wealth. Over the course of the twentieth century, however, small families gradually came to be seen as "progressive" – associated with wealthy British expatriates in Nairobi, upward mobility via urban migration, education, and with other markers of a new social order. Migrants returning to Nyanza from the growing cities "stimulat[ed] those who had remained at home to imagine the 'possible lives' that were now available and to consider how they might be achieved." Among Palestinian women in late twentieth-century Israel, similarly, "the discourse that sorts people as reproductively modern or primitive is unmistakably dominant" and "arguments for and against modernization define, shape, and limit the debates on gender, nation, class and religion." Victorian-era English couples adopted gender roles and educational expectations that "offered their children explicitly 'modern' advantages," while Sicilian artisans "characterized French people as *più evoluto* (more evolved) than Italians, and France as 'orienting Italy' toward the small family." A "unique form of Bengali 'modernism'" allowed parents "to question the old ways"; educated Cameroonian women "characterize their rigorous management of motherhood as an expression of their modernity, discipline, and honor"; Bangladeshis attribute smaller families to "change over the last few decades or the previous generation."[79]

Subjective modernization does not comprehensively explain recent global fertility decline. Great modernizing changes have occurred *without* corresponding declines in fertility. England's industrial and agricultural revolutions, for example, recreated that country's social order but preceded its fertility transition by a half-century and more. And historical self-perception may also favor larger families, as perhaps occurred during the early European settlement of North America or the mid-twentieth-century baby boom. Lags between broad-gauge social change and local action, meanwhile, make it difficult to definitively establish links between social history and demographic shifts.[80]

Nevertheless, Americans' acute feeling for modernity's demands appears to have been a singularly potent force in legitimating family limitation. Allusions to modern change saturated their observations on the small families in their midst, regardless of the speaker's opinion of reproductive control. Birth control's friends viewed this sensibility as their greatest ally. Activists who appealed to "modern" pragmatism evoked enthusiastic responses. Contraceptive advice-seekers sensed that "progress" entitled them to greater control over reproductive circumstance. The semblance of sweeping, open-ended change allowed ordinary people to tie together countless worthy but not quite self-evident challenges to eternal orders – like economic need, health risk, or higher expectations for happiness – into a dense, intuitive nugget.[81]

Reproduction is far from the only field where "reflexive" modernity has allowed people to "use history to make history." Self-conscious "historicity" is "intrinsic to the processes which drive modern social life away from the hold of tradition." More than other domains, though, reproductive ethics invited non-intellectuals to use history to make their everyday lives. For washerwomen, ranchers, or doctors across America, questions about the goodness of birth control and modernity existed in tandem. Because the causes of the small-family trend were considered so disparate, slow-moving, and reflective of recent moral history, the birth control debate was also a modernity debate. Judgments of one invited judgments of the other. The debate opened windows not only on reproductive ethics but on the meanings of modernity for people who did not ponder it for a living.[82]

"Developmental idealism," as the social demographer Arland Thornton terms it, has been especially powerful in shaping family norms. It has created a self-consciously modern family in which pride of place is given to "individualism, mature and consensual marriage, independent living, personal freedom, high status for women, and controlled fertility." This developmental idealism "may be the single most powerful explanation for many family changes in many places inside and outside

northwest Europe" over the past two centuries. Thornton traces this ideal
to the Enlightenment, early industrialism, and especially the age of
exploration, when European thinkers encountered foreign peoples who
they quickly judged materially and morally inferior. Having placed
Europe at the "pinnacle of history," men like Hobbes, Locke, and
Rousseau assumed that non-Europeans' ways of life approximated those
of the primitive European past. By "reading history sideways" in this way,
they established a durable paradigm where Europe's present represented
other places' future. The paradigm reached its fullest extent in the post-
1945 decades, as mass education, media, and various agencies carried
a Euro-American development ideal to all corners of the world. Giddens
sees the postwar period similarly, arguing that modern historicity then
became "global in form with the creation of a standardized 'past' and
a universally applicable 'future.'"[83]

For Americans debating birth control, however, modernity's relevance
was more local and organic: rooted as much in informal observation and
intergenerational folklore as cross-cultural comparison or global vision.
Of key importance for reproductive ethics were quasihistorical vernacu-
lars that compressed community memory into actionable ideas.
Modernization provided a shorthand for the observable moral and socioeconomic changes that appeared to demand smaller families than in
generations past. The "old-time" families were noble, perhaps, but also
careless and innocent.[84]

Understanding modernization's subjective importance to family limiters does not permit a simple revival of objective modernization theory.
Nor does it provide a substitute for existing theories of fertility transition.
Moral-economic factors can be important outside any shared vision of
historical flux. A woman might avoid a third child because she feared
another pregnancy would kill her, or the child would go hungry – never
reflecting on her place in any larger scheme. But so prevalent were compressed modernization narratives in Americans' discussions of birth control that this sense of flux would have been hard to avoid even for the most
isolated and least reflective Americans. Part of what made hedging against
a dangerous third pregnancy justifiable was the backdrop idea that new
circumstances demanded new responses.

Ultimately subjective modernization opens up a variant of the "multiple modernities" paradigm in which modernity-as-actor's-category
defines and shapes a new kind of modernity-as-analyst's-category.
It furnishes a loose, flexible, individual-level way of tying together the
profusion of moral-economic changes that, mixed by degrees, allowed

birth control to become popular and legitimate in the United States and elsewhere.[85]

Being across Time

At the widest angle, however, subjective modernization was important not only as a shared sense that modern people had smaller families, but as justification for a fundamental reshaping of ideas about morally relevant time – about the competing claims of transcendence and immediacy.

For industrial-age Americans the felt power of eternal orders formed the highest barrier to birth control's legitimation. To perpetuate any human fellowship across time was to align oneself with God, nature, and the infinite. Transcendent chains of being such as families, clans, nations, creeds, and cultures gave meaning and grace to fleeting existence. Each chain was morally powerful in itself, and even more powerful when entwined with the others, intuitively and emotionally, in death-defying orders that dignified short and suffering lives.[86]

Other means of self-transcendence existed, of course, such as religious asceticism, social service, learning, or the pursuit of beauty. But the sanctified biological continuum had a unique universality, both in the sense that it was an act of self-transcendence available to all – and expected of full community members – and in the sense that it appeared to offer anyone a connection to the fundaments of the universe. Reproduction commanded universal moral attention and allowed every person, no matter how humble, to act as caretaker of an immortal body. Insofar as Americans felt themselves strongly, rightfully, and inevitably sublimated in these eternal chains, birth control faced a long road to legitimacy.

This vision of sanctified continuum did not simply perish in nineteenth- and twentieth-century America. If anything, its apparent peril made it seem more valuable, and inspired impassioned defenses of the eternal community. But these defenses reflected weakness: whatever the poetic value of the eternal chain, other priorities made greater gains in the domain of action. Worldly, progressive, and pragmatic approaches to reproductive ethics eclipsed otherworldly, infinite, and mystical ones.

Those gains happened first in the realm of private morality – in the acts people could justify to themselves and their immediate communities – as birth control gained popularity across the nineteenth century and beyond. Then came a mass public reckoning with this private acceptance, mostly in the decades after Roosevelt's campaign. These two phases – popularization = private and legitimation – worked on different timescales and at different levels of

"public

visibility, but shared similar themes. They overlapped and cross-fertilized, so that the story of either one substantially echoes that of the other. In both cases, the essential underlying questions had to do with the immediacy of one's moral vision: did one award moral priority to welfare in the present material world – in the "modern" way – or did one stand with the old and eternal?

It is tempting to think of birth control's popularizers and legitimizers as defiant revolutionaries confidently unclasping the dead hand of the past. But more often they were uncertain and ambivalent. Because most people respected, by degrees, both eternal orders and modern prerogatives, only a small minority of America's citizen-moralists were categorically for or against birth control. Staunch opponents could imagine cases where limitation was justified; diehard supporters could imagine cases where it was abused. The real dispute was between moderates over the definition of moderation. Should a worthy citizen have as many children as God or nature sent? If not, how much willful action was too much? Should one only have as many children as one could reasonably feed, clothe, and shelter? If so, what standard of living was reasonable? Should a good person aim for a specific number of children? Or simply err towards having more rather than fewer? And under what specific circumstances might one excuse oneself, entirely or partly, from that standard?[87]

In the American case, only ideas as capacious as modernity or immediacy offered credible challenges to similarly commanding ideas about divine, natural, or eternal orders. Later in the twentieth century, many Americans would assume without much reflection that childrearing was preeminently a question of moment-to-moment adult tastes and preferences. But in the early twentieth century, children were more likely to be seen as community and cosmic property. If life was worth living, it was worth perpetuating, and excusing oneself from the chain of life – even partly – required a reckoning with some higher power. One was born into reproductive debt. Against this logic, modernization provided an exemption. Birth control gained popularity and legitimacy as the claims of history superseded those of eternity.[88]

Note on Parameters and Methods

Fertility control remains as contentious an issue today as it was a century ago. No topic so effortlessly renders the personal political and the political personal. Every adult feels qualified to speak from experience on

reproductive ethics, and we struggle to address the subject dispassionately. "Vital processes are the true playground of moral systems," one
observer writes.[89]

Within this context it is important to note that this study was not
conceived or written with a political lesson in mind. Though I support
reproductive rights and believe I have personally benefited from the legitimation of birth control, I did not set out to demonstrate anything in
particular about the historical foundations of that legitimacy. My initial
inquiries into this topic, indeed, were motivated less by specific interest in
birth control than a general interest in the intersections of philosophical
principle with everyday action. Birth control in America provided
a window on the social history of ideas.

Any study of popular ideas opens questions of knowability and repre-
sentativeness. "Getting at the interior thought of a friend, or a spouse, or
one's own child is hard enough; trying to catch the mood of strangers in
the present ... is harder," as Andrew Delbanco writes. "But retrieving
something as fragile and fleeting as thought or feeling from the past is like
trying to seize a bubble." In the case of reproduction, this difficulty is
compounded by secrecy, emotion, and kneejerk moralism. How much can
we know about Americans' inner lives based on the dashed-off words of
a few thousand literate citizens? I am optimistic: with appropriate circum-
spection I believe we can know a lot, and I believe this study offers an
unusually close view of Americans' working ideas about the reproductive
good. A few limitations nevertheless warrant brief discussion.[90]

First, these are amateurs' voices: observers based their conclusions on
fragmentary information they could gather quickly or summon intuitively, acting briefly as sociologist-historian-moralists before resuming
life as newspaper editors, housewives, doctors, or farmhands. Their
assumptions about reproductive motivation were not always carefully
considered, nor their conclusions sophisticated. If we indiscriminately
trusted this group's conventional wisdom, we might learn that myriad
physical ailments could be cured by dry air and mineral baths, that some
European "races" were inherently superior to all others, or that anarchist
infiltration posed an existential threat to the United States.

That said, amateur observers made few outlandish claims in light of recent
historical and demographic research. And "experts" were hard to distinguish
from amateurs in the early twentieth-century's birth control debates.
The universality, secrecy, emotional resonance, and existential importance
of reproductive action tended to blur that divide. Many Americans rejected,
with some reason, the idea that better-credentialed peers might possess any

special claim to understanding the complexities of reproductive motivation. "Everyone is an authority in this field," as one columnist wrote.[91]

Second, because observers tended to see birth control's liberalization as a complex moral-historical process, decades or centuries in the making, their perceptions of the past were subject to distortions of collective and individual memory. "The old ways" became a conveniently flat baseline: either a golden age of abundant, vital, simple, happy families or a dark age of ignorance, repression, squalor, and unwanted children. "Memory is knowledge from the past," Avishai Margalit observes. "It is not necessarily knowledge about the past." For the most part, this book treats Americans' memories as knowledge from the past – fungible, quasihistorical ideas intended to shape or comment upon the present. But I also assume some basic underlying validity in Americans' memories of earlier reproductive codes. In early twentieth-century America, moralists of all stripes tended to agree on a basic historical narrative in which previous generations, for better or worse, had been more communitarian, less willing or able to master arbitrary nature and risk, and more impressed with transcendent bodies and cosmic mysteries – all with definite consequences for family size. I accept this general outline without claiming that descendants remembered past generations' values with the same fidelity as latter-day historians – though those two groups' viewpoints often intersect.[92]

Finally, many commentators discussed only abstract public ideals, not specific private actions. They operated in the realm of moral-emotional intuition, middlebrow cultural criticism, and practical self-justification. Their comments rarely allowed for direct correlations between professed ideals and actual behavior. But reproduction blurs the rhetoric-reality divide. Even when citizens did not live up to the ideals they professed, those ideals helped set the conditions of their action, and social action around them. Community idealism helped determine paths of least resistance for citizens contemplating the reproductive good.

This study's strengths and drawbacks tend to invert those of better-established historical approaches. Most demographers favor wide cross-sections, and many historians prefer to deal in distinctive personalities and events. I do not dispute the relative advantages of demography in statistical replicability or narrative history in storytelling. But both approaches have limitations, and on the question of why past people have had children or not, I believe those limitations are great enough that neither approach offers a full complement to the other. So I have tried to open a new window on an old question, mining the sprawling richness of both traditions while also seeking to venture between and beyond them.

2

Race Suicide

The Moral Economy of Birth Control, 1903–1908

Be fruitful, and multiply, and replenish the earth, and subdue it.
                    Genesis 1:28

I have not that strong obligation that they say ties men to the future, by the children that succeed to their name and honour . . . I am but too much tied to the world, and to this life of myself; I am content to be in fortune's power by circumstances properly necessary to my being, without otherwise enlarging her jurisdiction over me.
                    Michel de Montaigne[1]

** **

In 1901 a young journalist named Bessie Van Vorst visited Perry, New York, a small and muddy mill town near Rochester. She planned to live among Perry's seamstresses for several weeks, document their working conditions, and write about her experiences as a "lady" among workers. She rented a room and took a job in the local shirt-making factory.

Perry's "mill girls" worked long hours and lived in crowded, slapdash boardinghouses. But they did not exhibit the same hopelessness Van Vorst had encountered during an earlier stint at a pickle factory in Pittsburgh. Many of the young seamstresses, Van Vorst wrote with surprise, were not in Perry out of hardship. Instead they worked eleven-hour days out of a desire for independence from their modestly prosperous families, toiling at least partly "for pleasure" – for weekends and evenings of shopping, lakeside amusements, and dalliances with young men. Many of them appeared happy.[2]

But what seemed a very American "triumph of individualism" in youth quickly became a less admirable disregard for "the important decisions of life," Van Vorst warned. Some of the girls married, but all deferred motherhood in favor of greater financial and domestic freedom. "I never saw a baby nor heard of a baby while I was in the town," she wrote of her three weeks in Perry. Instead she heard gossip, occasional tales of heart-break, and many appreciations of recently purchased velvet ribbons or lace. What a shame, lamented Van Vorst, that fleeting material concerns were taking the place of "tenderness, reverence, gratitude, protection . . . the feelings which one generation awakens for another."[3]

Van Vorst's magazine article would have passed quickly into obscurity had it not found its way to Theodore Roosevelt's desk. The young pre-sident, an anxious student of demographic matters, read it and promptly dispatched a reply to the author:

I must write you a line to say how much I have appreciated your article . . . But to me there is a most melancholy side to it, when you touch upon what is fundamentally infinitely more important than any other question in this country – that is, the question of race suicide, complete or partial.[4]

Roosevelt continued for several paragraphs, moving from melancholy to anger. Seeing the letter, a publisher asked Van Vorst to quickly compile her magazine work on laboring women into a book prefaced with the president's note. In February 1903 the book was ready, and Roosevelt's message reached the press. One passage in particular echoed across the country:

If a man or woman, through no fault of his or hers, goes throughout life denied those highest of all joys which spring only from home life, from the having and bringing up of many healthy children, I feel for them deep and respectful sympathy . . . But the man or woman who deliberately avoids marriage, and has a heart so cold as to know no passion and a brain so shallow and selfish as to dislike having children, is in effect a criminal against the race, and should be an object of contemptuous abhorrence by all healthy people.[5]

Roosevelt's words caused a sensation among Americans more accustomed to hearing presidents address such issues as tariff rates, railroad regulation, or the navy. To Roosevelt, however, statesmen's typical concerns were of "wholly ephemeral importance, compared with the questions that go straight to the root of things." "It goes without saying that, for the race as for the individual, no material prosperity, no business growth, no artistic of scientific development, will count, if the race commits suicide."[6]

For the youthful "cowboy president" to introduce such an earthy topic, intruding himself on the homes and bedrooms of his constituents, struck many Americans as barbaric and crude, others as eccentric or comic. For the most part, though, Roosevelt's outcry inspired respectful, earnest, and sympathetic consideration, notably in the period's preeminent public forum, the daily press. "Anyone can discuss it," one editor wrote in 1903, "It is a matter that concerns every family and is of universal interest; no wonder it is profusely considered."[7]

Ongoing public interest in "race suicide" was partly the result of Roosevelt's long personal crusade, which lasted until his death in 1919. More important, however, were the knock-on efforts of journalists and citizens who, Roosevelt aside, felt qualified to speak to the matter by virtue of their own life experience. Letters to the editor, editorials, sermons, speeches, and miscellaneous commentary rebounded through the press and the culture at large. Where reproductive practices had previously been too obscure or too delicate a topic to merit wide public attention, now debate flourished. Following Roosevelt, cultural observers felt sanctioned to contribute to a new body of social thought – to speak aloud on subjects previously hushed.[8]

PUBLIC OPINION BEFORE POLLING

To survey that body of thought this chapter uses 605 newspaper articles – editorials, letters to the editor, and reportage – published in nine major U.S. newspapers between 1903 and 1908. Each article deals directly and primarily with questions of reproductive ethics.

Why this medium? During the 1900s newspapers saturated American culture. More circulated per day than there were households to consume them. Before radio, television, or the internet, with the media market largely to themselves, big dailies acted as clearinghouses for popular conventions and ideals. "Organized gossip" was papers' stock in trade, as the sociologist Charles Horton Cooley wrote in 1909: "the sort of intercourse that people formerly carried on at cross-road stores or over the back fence."

This enlargement of gossip ... promotes a widespread sociability and sense of community ... It also tends powerfully, through the fear of publicity, to enforce a popular, somewhat vulgar, but sound and human standard of morality.[9]

Editors avoided straying too far from the presumed opinions of their readerships, particularly in charged matters of everyday morality. Newspapers served as "narrators" and "advocates" but most importantly "as weathercocks," observed the early public-opinion theorist James Bryce. "They indicate by their attitude what those who conduct them and are interested in their circulation take to be the prevailing opinion of their readers. It is ... as an index and mirror of public opinion that the press is looked to. This is the function it chiefly aims at discharging."[10]

Newspapers' "back fence" and "weathercock" functions have long inspired attempts by sociologists to mine them for social data. In 1910 Max Weber, and in 1912 Alvan Tenney, proposed large-scale press-monitoring projects to record what Tenney called "social weather." These projects were frustrated by logistical constraints. In the twenty-first century, however, large text-searchable databases have vastly reduced the time costs of compiling thematically focused media materials. This chapter takes advantage of that development by working from samples gathered in one large database for the period 1903–1908; Chapter 3 uses the same method for 1927–1935.[11]

Each article was coded for the presence of any of twenty-three "frames" on fertility decline, such as "economic rationality" or "religiosity" (Figures A.1 and A.2; see Appendix). The frames measure simple frequencies, usually without tracking commentators' degrees of emphasis on, or approval for, the idea in question. So if an editorialist elaborately disparaged religious dogma, then briefly argued that small families allowed for better education, the "religion" and "education" frames would be marked equally, as single mentions. Frame frequencies are thus intended to reflect the raw prominence of various ways of thinking about birth control, especially as they changed between the 1900s and 1930s. Nuances of opinion I address qualitatively.[12]

The newspapers (Table A.1) were "establishment" broadsheets and papers of record. The people who wrote for these papers, or had their views aired in them, were predominantly white, middle class, native born, and city based. They were overwhelmingly male (85 percent), as were most readers. Few women wrote for newspapers in the 1900s, sent letters to editors, or occupied public positions that made their views newsworthy. This gender disparity biased the sample towards Roosevelt-style pronatalism, since female moralists were more likely than their male counterparts to support birth control.[13]

Finally, observers held vague and mostly unspoken assumptions about who composed the endangered "race" in "race suicide." In the decades around 1900 "race" could designate almost any group of people – or all humankind – and Roosevelt was markedly nonspecific in drawing racial borders. What he and other commentators meant by "average men and women," however, was the country's dominant majority: white; nonindigent; civically engaged; native born or "the self-respecting son or daughter of immigrants." Tacitly excluded from this "us" were three large but marginalized populations – African-Americans, poor recent immigrants, and the white native indigent – who together made up roughly one-quarter of the country's 76 million people. Those groups, for their part, largely ignored race suicide or treated it as a dominant-class issue. Though birthrates were falling among African-Americans, the poor, and immigrants' descendants, no equivalent moral panic ensued in those communities. W.E.B. Du Bois, for example, spoke of race suicide as a problem of "modern European culture nations," and speculated that "the Negro race may teach the world something" on "mother-love and family instinct."[14]

EXPLAINING FERTILITY DECLINE: SELF AND SOCIETY

For years Roosevelt wondered if his pronouncements on race suicide were unbecoming of a president. Ultimately he excused himself – in part because his ideas were popular. A majority of all newspaper commentators supported the president's pronatalism (55 percent), while just 15 percent dissented; the remainder took neutral or ambivalent stances (Figure A.3). At the poles of opinion pronatalism was even more dominant: 26 percent of writers expressed strong support, just 6 percent strong dissent. This support would decline dramatically in the two decades that followed, but in Roosevelt's time, it held sway.[15]

American observers tended to see falling birthrates as a complex moral-historical issue concerning the changing relationship of self to society. Most commentators assumed, regardless of personal opinion and before assigning specific causes, that the driving force behind falling birthrates was "the modern spirit of individualism," as one editorial board put it. For the pronatalists whose views provided a baseline for public discussion, it was obvious that "selfishness" drove the small-family trend, and that this moral failure constituted a fundamental near-term threat to the nation's survival. Families were half the size they had been in the early republic. If fertility rates continued on their apparent trajectory towards zero, American institutions would not be transmitted through the family, new immigrants would not assimilate, and the culture would fail.[16]

For some pronatal moralists this disintegration was a tragic paradox of progress. There was nothing to be done: Civilizations rose and fell in unbreakable cycles of death and rebirth. More often, though, it was a call to the barricades. "All important general laws bear hard at times on the individual," chided a Boston clergyman. Calls to subordinate vain selfhood to the timeless collective were legion. "Starting with the race which is all race and no individual at all," wrote a physician of post-protozoan evolution, "we may end up with the individual which is all individual – the race thus coming to an end." Other moralists condemned their "small-souled" peers for transgressions such as avoiding children in favor of leisure, career, wealth, or adventure.[17]

Differences of degree, not kind, separated pro-Roosevelt stalwarts from birth control's defenders. "All the readers will agree with me," a woman wrote to her newspaper editor, "when I say that race suicide in the eyes of the Almighty God is a terrible sin. On the other hand, improper treatment of innocent children when better can be had is another." Everyone objected to cultural extinction, and everyone objected to a tenth child being born into a family where nine went hungry.[18]

The dissenting minority, meanwhile, saw reproductive individualism as a benign trend, in line with Americans' time-honored genius for practical self-improvement and intergenerational striving. The immediate-term welfare of individuals or nuclear families, rather than the permanence of the social body, was the most appropriate unit in evaluating reproductive ethics. "Large families are not the salvation of the nation," a New York milliner told a reporter. "Better one child well brought up than a dozen neglected."[19]

Birth control's strongest defenders trusted that conscientious individual action would not harm society, much less extinguish it, and indeed might strengthen America in the long run. Where Roosevelt and his allies assumed a need for strong moral standards that would check human depravity, birth control supporters looked optimistically and pragmatically to the observable good nature and well-being of small families around them. "The two sons of the well-to-do New York business man, whom he can feed with the best cuts of beef, rear with intelligent discipline, and prepare for useful careers," one editorialist observed, "will be physically, morally, and mentally superior to the whole dozen children in the fecund family of the Italian laborer of the tenements." The Italian, too, would "in time become a section boss, and his son a contractor, who will in turn send his comparatively few children to college."[20]

Reproductive liberalism of this kind mimicked the economic and political liberalism that permeated respectable American opinion. Though reproductive liberals were aware of their minority status and quick to acknowledge the biological continuum's importance, they eagerly played on their fellow citizens' devotion to individual liberty. Self-interest had to be trusted to serve the common interest. Just as individual economic or political decisions might seem shortsighted and yet produce a system preferable to any other, reproductive decisions could be made on short time horizons, for selfish motives and based on mundane concerns, yet result in a better overall social outcome.

Critics of all opinions could agree that reproductive control was an individual right, the legal restriction of which would be undesirable even if it were possible. But whereas pronatalists viewed that right's exercise with regret, liberalizers emphasized with remarkable uniformity birth control's positive effects on the population's "quality," if not "quantity." Over a third made this quality-quantity argument explicitly; most others did so implicitly. Smaller families, far from threatening the nation, civilized it. Rather than plunging inexorably to zero, birthrates would reach a self-governing equilibrium point where quality was maximized and quantity adequate to replace population. Somewhere in human nature or instinct, an invisible hand ensured this balance. Rather than an existential menace, mass birth control was another modern triumph of rational liberalism over the blind inertia of nature, patriarchy, or clerical fatalism. Believing in one's fellow citizens' ability to act responsibly in this way was akin to believing in the promise of democracy.

Distinctive as this position was in the public forum, birth control's defenders were few and cautious. Only a handful of speakers overtly challenged the idea that individuals owed a reproductive debt to society – asking, for example, "if people do not want to have children, whose business is it but their own?" and proposing that Roosevelt "ought not make such an old woman of himself." Arguments such as these antici-pated a more private view of reproductive ethics that would become common later in the century, and eventually win formal acceptance in the U.S. Supreme Court in 1965. But in the 1900s radical reproductive liberalism remained unusual. By consensus, children remained a form of community property, and childrearing remained a legitimate interest of the collective. The question was how parents could best serve the social organism.[21]

In the absence of many voices denying any reproductive debt to society, citizen moralists divided over exactly how many children constituted repayment. Nearly all parties considered zero- or one-child families self-ish, except in unusual circumstances. Two-child families were considered small, though some liberalizers defended them as adequate for high-quality social reproduction. Roosevelt and most of his allies wanted more: "all that I have ever said," the president wrote to E.A. Ross, "was that here in America, if the average family able to have children at all did not have three or four children, the American blood would die out – which is a statement not only of morals but of mathematics." A family standard of at least three children seemed necessary to replace population, given high rates of child mortality and the permanent minority of childless people.[22]

Precise accountancy of this kind was a side issue for most commentators, however. More important were fundamental moral divides that predisposed some couples to accept children at *any* number, while disposing others in the opposite direction. The key question was how to interpret intergenerational shifts in these divides – whether to call the new ways selfish or conscientious, spiritually shortsighted or practically farsighted.

MORAL ECONOMY

Within this broad self-society framework, moralists had many ideas about what caused their peers to have one number of children or another (Figure A.1). Economic factors were most important: 43 percent of commentators thought economic calculation depressed fertility, and/or associated large families with poverty. By comparison, 23 percent mooted the next-most common frame: changes in perceived divine or natural order. Insofar as the declining birthrate was a specific sort of social problem, rather than a generalized moral upheaval, it was an economic question before all else.[23]

In reproductive matters, however, economic reasoning was inextricable from moral intuition. For citizen moralists, lines between healthy economic "prudence" and malignant greed or selfishness were fluid, unclear, and ultimately drawn by feelings for the right more than deliberate calculations of cost and benefit. Reproductive questions demanded reflection on money's rightful purposes, not the most rational ways to use it. Virtually no one disputed the small family's rationality, but one moralist's enlightened foresight and self-respect was another's pettiness or cowardice.[24]

Half of all "economic" commentators made explicit, disapproving connections between economy and morality – framing small families as an outgrowth of luxury or decadence. "What were formerly the luxuries of the rich have become the necessities of the poor," one complained. "Commercialitis," "money-love," "the siren calls of fashion," "the patent leather life ... the universal climb on the social staircase": all these tempted the selfish, particularly in cities. "Where money makes for self-indulgence," one aphorist wrote, "children make for self-denial."[25]

The other half of economic-minded observers were less overtly moralistic. For some, a small family was an adaptive means of maintaining or advancing one's economic position (the "rationality" frame). For others it was a way of avoiding becoming poor or behaving like the poor ("poverty"). These observers took some measure of moral responsibility from the individual and placed it on "society" or "the times." Uncertain economic circumstances pushed modern people to protect themselves by limiting their families. Just a quarter of "rationality" or "poverty" commentators, however, saw socioeconomic pressures as sufficient to explain the small-family trend. For the remainder, decisions about fertility occurred at the nexus of economic self-interest and equally essential contingencies concerning God, natural order, modernization, or some other definitive realm of experience. Just one in ten commentators framed declining birthrates as the simple result of individual-level rational economic choice, without disparaging "love of display and luxuries" or otherwise complicating the context in which such choices were made.[26]

Even the strictest rationalists, meanwhile, often took a moral tack – heaping scorn on the all-powerful economic systems that encouraged small families. "For the capitalists to condemn the masses because they limit their families is like blaming a man for being prostrate when we have knocked him down," wrote one editorialist. Until the "strenuous rush for wealth" was moderated, another observer wrote, well-intentioned Americans would remain "victims of circumstance": "race suicide must continue until the economic problem is solved."[27]

For all the importance Americans attached to economic calculation as a factor in fertility decline, then, it would be less accurate to say that economics dominated the conversation than to say moral economy did so. Fertility decline was not the product of changing economic structures per se, nor of people comprehending birth control's rationality for the first time. It arose as people rethought life's end purposes, including standards of material comfort and security.[28]

The Rooseveltian majority thought moral priority should go to eternal orders, not material comfort, except in extreme circumstances. The dissident minority saw dignity in their peers' higher economic expectations and careful planning. For neither group were parents mere economic actors; they were moral agents whose departures from past standards would reinforce themselves over time. Their actions seemed destined to bring about a radically new climate of belief about the place of children in a good life, for better or worse.[29]

WORLDLINESS AND TRANSCENDENCE

If the moral economics of self and society underpinned many Americans' understandings of why families had become smaller, a second overarching frame on fertility decline concerned the interplay of worldly pragmatism and transcendence. "Pragmatic" and "transcendent" were not common terms in the race suicide debate, but they capture two ubiquitous ideas from it. Transcendent-minded people's first references were to otherworldly objects such as God, natural order, or imagined timeless continuums like the family or society. Pragmatists focused on the present material world and the individual's mastery of it. Family size was determined in part by parents' orientations towards the immediate here and now, on the one hand, or the eternal and universal, on the other.

The transcendent-minded had more children. They were less likely to see their life's primary meaning in terms of observable rewards accumulated in a lifetime. Rather than regarding themselves as cosmic end-products, they found meaning in mystical chains of being that fulfilled the intentions of a higher power. Their view to eternity helped them glide over the day-to-day concerns of raising children in any number.

Pragmatists had fewer children because they weighed risk more carefully and doubted the reality or authority of invisible moral orders. They might have transcendent or quasi-transcendent goals in other realms, such as career, learning, art, social service, or mystical discovery, but were less likely to express their desire for self-expansion in the irreversible, costly, physical form of a biological family.

Regardless of approval for birth control, most commentators assumed that Americans were becoming less transcendent-minded in general, less likely to steer transcendent impulses into children, and consequently less inclined to take existential pride in a large family. This trend chafed pronatalists despite the fact that many of them, Roosevelt included, would not have hesitated to call themselves pragmatists and include pragmatism among American culture's signal virtues. The same skeptical practicality that made Americans self-reliant democrats and tradesmen was petty and graceless when applied to the family. It showed a lack, Roosevelt argued, of "devotion to high ideals, a proper care for the things of the spirit."[30]

In reproductive matters at least, pronatalists encouraged their peers to cast their gaze on the infinite horizon rather than matters of the day. "Do not sell your soul for a few earthly desires," one moralist warned parents. "This life is short, and will soon fade away." A humorist mocked childless couples' pettiness and myopia with a fifty-item list of points over which a divorcing husband and wife had quarreled: " . . . because the Mormons are not Indians; because pineapples do not grow in Canada; because he fell in the creek; because he shot the pig; because he sat down on his hat; and BECAUSE THEY HAD NO CHILDREN."[31]

Liberalizers framed worldly pragmatism favorably. Family limitation was a rejection of "blind fatalism," a recognition of "sin, disease, distress, and . . . uncertainty," and an embrace of the modern duty "to perfect the practical comfort and well being of the world." A new millennium would occur exactly when people ceased to "believe everything is in the hands of Providence, that the Lord alone is responsible and that the Lord will provide." No holy spirit demanded, sent, educated, or provided for children. It was no longer the fashion, thankfully, "to let . . . children take the common chance in life." Instead, reproduction presented a series of complex but solvable technical problems, the end of which could be a "better world." The president was "right" about race suicide, conceded the *Chicago Tribune*'s editors, but they could not fault parents for acting pragmatically: "Beneath all exaggerations there exists the big fact that children are no longer casual happenings. Every new human life is more and more a problem and a responsibility."[32]

Questions of worldliness and transcendence pervaded discussion of the role of God and nature in family size. Though the Bible offered contradictory messages on family size, most Americans assumed the Christian God wanted his flock to bear children abundantly. God had commanded his people to "be fruitful" and killed Onan for "spilling his seed on the ground." Clergy and devout laypeople mixed these common scriptural references into cloudier evocations of Christians' obligation to perpetuate a species God had created in his own image.

Theology interested few commentators, however. Formal religious teaching was worth little in the face of slackening religious or mystical *feeling* – a key variable in the small-family trend. "The evil is deep seated," wrote one pronatalist citizen, "and the harder to combat that its votaries fall into it of their free will, require no organization, supply their own public opinion, and are beyond the reach of the law. The only law that can affect it is the law of God; the only tribunal that can check it is in the individual soul." Invocations of declining religious *obedience*, such as a doctor's insistence that previous generations had "heeded the injunction of the Bible to 'multiply on the face of the earth,'" were comparatively rare.[33]

If traditional theism seemed less important than general transcendent-mindedness, it also took a back seat to informal sensibilities about nature and natural law. Whatever a person believed about divine commandment, a sense that transcendent Nature "wanted" or demanded reproduction was uniquely important for action. A couple was more likely to have any number of children if a new birth provided them a sense of connection to the universe and a feeling of doing its work. Mystical naturism thus paralleled formal theism and complemented its attention to eternal order. But naturism also held special power in a self-consciously modern and material world, since it required no belief in God, knowledge of doctrine, or acceptance of specific prophetic teachings.[34]

Naturist arguments flourished in tandem with criticism of urban vice and corruption, a common trope of the period. Race suicide was "nature's protest against the unnatural town life." Childless urbanites had lost touch with "the delights of life where one can observe the beauties of nature." "The cities and the rush of things" were "breaking up the home or making it unfruitful." Some critics believed race suicide was inevitable unless more families could be kept on the land, in contact with wild nature – or at least moved to "suburban cottages inhabited mainly by children." Prospects for this sort of reform appeared grim. "What with shortened lives, bachelorhood, late or childless marriages, and small families," E.A. Ross wrote in an op-ed, "the cities constitute so many blast furnaces where the talented rise and become incandescent, to be sure, but for all that are incinerated without due replacement."[35]

Compounding cities' inherent moral deficiencies was the practical problem of landlord discrimination against large families. Most American city-dwellers rented their homes, and landlords had both the right and inclination to turn away tenants based on the number and unruliness of their children. With Roosevelt's campaign, this practice came under fire. Landlords were ridiculed for posting signs prohibiting "Dogs and Children" and levying surcharges on large families. Stories circulated about a Brooklyn woman with five children who had been turned down by eighty-seven apartment houses despite her husband's steady job. Illustrious inventors, businesspeople, and political leaders had received similar treatment. "The penalty of raising a family," reported *The Washington Post*, "is banishment to a section of the city where the streets are unpaved and ill-lighted, and the quarters squalid." Antichild landlords seemed to incarnate the spiritual myopia of city life.[36]

The matter of family housing inspired a few social entrepreneurs to construct apartment buildings designed for families. One in Alton,

Illinois, featured multiple playgrounds, "sand heaps," and perks for new parents like baby carriages and three months' free rent. The owner received an invitation to the White House. Housing discrimination also inspired most of the few traditional policy proposals to emerge from the race suicide debate. Chicago, Boston, Cleveland, Denver, Los Angeles, and other cities considered restricting landlords' ability to discriminate against families. None of the laws passed, however, and most observers continued to see cities' problems as primarily moral rather than legal and residential. "The landlord who insists on barring the Rooseveltian family may bring down on his selfish head the opprobrium of the anti-race suicide clubs," wrote the *Chicago Tribune*, "but he has the law with him ... It is impossible, by mere legislative fiat, to cause the milk of human kindness to well forth from the barren paps of the perverted soul whose only god is self." The basic problem, given that cities seemed set to grow indefinitely, was to infuse the new Babylons with the godly naturalness of the countryside and the past.[37]

In this quest, naturism and religious teaching often melded together. American Protestants had long detected in "nature" both dangerous wildness and earthly clues to divine intent. As modernist Protestants adapted their teachings to science and abstracted their God, the idea that semidivine nature demanded reproduction remained one belief that united them with traditionalists. Among educated Catholics, meanwhile, natural law was an oft-cited underpinning of formal theology. "All violations of the laws of nature are violations of God's laws and must ultimately be punished," declared one Catholic clergyman. God's will and nature's demands merged into one another.[38]

More than a complement to religious belief, however, moralists invoked natural order as an alternate cosmic force, omitting any reference to formal theism. The advice writer Mary Terhune skewered bloodless city women who refused to nurse their children, since that act demoted them from "refined intellectual beings" to "mammal females." Elite writers, summoning the common association of the working classes with natural vitality, used the innocent-spirited, outdoor-living poor as foils for the conniving, velvet-walled rich. One writer recounted the parable of three brothers in Philadelphia: a corrupt official without children, an anxious postman with two, and a boisterous oyster seller who lived happily in a shanty with his sixteen children. "A wealthy lady, childless ... offered to take any one of the sixteen and make him her heir," whereupon the peddler's wife indignantly "drove her from the house with a broom," her "rage aroused at the idea that she could be asked to spare one when she only had sixteen." Race suicide was a disorder of the denatured – men and women who had mastered their animal natures to the point of losing them entirely, and lived in and for an "artificial world" of bricks, crowds, business, refined tastes, and social anxieties. Valuing life across generations seemed to require that survival itself remain a struggle, as it was in the animal kingdom, among the working classes, and on the land. To invest oneself completely in the super-fluities of human creation was to die completely.[39]

Many naturists were secular Protestants who had been influenced by Charles Darwin and his interpreters. Roosevelt himself was typical of this group. Lambasting a New Jersey preacher who advised his flock to confine themselves to two children so they could "taste a few good things," the president thundered:

The people who had acted on this base and selfish doctrine would [soon give] place to others with braver and more robust ideals. Nor would such a result be in any way regrettable; for a race that practiced such doctrine ... would thereby conclusively show that it was unfit to exist, and that it had better give place to people who had not forgotten the primary laws of their being.

Roosevelt's disingenuous endorsement of nature over nation was tarter than other moralists' naturism, but no less convinced that natural law demanded a new kind of piety.[40]

In the discussion of nature and procreation were echoes of old theological debates within Protestantism. Some commentators believed "nature" demanded that morally free humans conform to its dictates; others considered it a predestinatory force. The former position was more common, but a smaller group of naturists took the more fatal-istic view, declaring that American civilization, as a body, was aging and entering organic decline. "Civilization has always carried within itself the seeds of its own decay," one columnist wrote. "We cannot escape the penalty that every dominant race has paid to nature." From this perspective the passing of civilizations was bittersweet, inevitable, and perhaps even romantically beautiful. E.A. Ross called it the "the-ory of national afternoons."[41]

For the majority who wished to believe in freely willed agency, appeals to nature-religion were not always the answer. Roosevelt's naturism struck some respectable people as "animal" or sensual, and the president faced occasional criticism as a "pagan." More than once the president was compelled to clarify that he was not calling for unrestrained sexuality or nihilistic biological competition among peoples. Rather than "an instigation to a riot of physical forces in mankind," an administration surrogate wrote in 1903, the president was making "an appeal to the moral being." His efforts were "merely a protest against a form of selfishness which robs nature of her perfect work."[42]

Regardless of their exact views on nature and God, most pronatalists agreed that the central question in the race suicide debate was how to instill transcendent-mindedness in urbanizing, secularizing Americans. Whether this vision was rooted in naturist mysticism, divine revelation, or both was less important than whether *any* vision of the eternal could remain viable in places "where the sky is seen only as a rift between solid walls of masonry." No one wanted a full reversion to the "old times," but nearly everyone hoped that children would retain some hold on the transcendent imagination – enough, at least, to provide reasonable continuity to the American experiment.[43]

TIME

Moral time formed the final major dividing line between parents of small and large families. For citizen moralists, anyone who rejected modernity, wholly or in part, tended to have more children. So did people whose sense of relevant time extended beyond their lifetimes and far into the past and future. Pronatalists thus pleaded for expansive views of relevant time. "Individuals," scolded one, were "deliberately, in their own persons, putting an end to the process – millions of years in duration – which has produced them." Parents, lamented another, seemed to see children as "mere chattel" rather the fulfillment of a sublime rite. "There are lots of people that do not like children, won't have any, and do not care whether it's race suicide or not; they are living for themselves and their generation and are not lying awake at night thinking about posterity."[44]

Religious commentators amply supplemented this line of thought, asserting that life was purposeless without a clear commitment to eternal laws and enduring institutions like family, nation, or church. By the 1930s this sort of religious traditionalism would dominate the much-reduced ranks of American pronatalists. In Roosevelt's time, however, many "baby boosters" made their case in secular terms, as a defense of America's democratic progressivism. Roosevelt and his allies hoped that Americans who no longer felt bound to divine or natural continuums might respond to an alternate call to eternalize republican civil religion. The licentious French may be "indifferent to the future," as one patriot argued, but more should be expected of Americans, who "build their greatness for posterity." "Without family, without the loves and cares and responsibilities of family, what is a man's work worth? Without a noble future, without a magnificent posterity to inherit the fruits of its endeavors and to build upon them a yet nobler state – what is the nation's life worth?"[45]

Weaker views to eternity were especially dangerous in republican America, where the nation depended on the self-reinforcing virtue of its citizens. In other domains, rights might replace duties to noble effect, but in reproduction, that transition threatened to undermine the rights-granting society. "The current of public sentiment," as one critic wrote, "is in most serious danger of cursing its blessings."[46]

The baby boosters' reproductive traditionalism sat awkwardly with the progressivism of many of their number. The progressive ethos was neither mystical nor indebted to eternal orders. Progressives wanted open-ended social improvement through technocratic leadership, scientific discovery, and continual moral reform. Perpetual adaptation was necessary for survival. "The worst evils we have to combat have inevitably evolved along with the evolution of society itself," as Roosevelt wrote, "and the perspective of conduct must change from age to age."[47]

The progressive view of history created a series of apparent para-doxes for secular republican pronatalists. Even as they asked one another to adopt eternal time horizons, progress itself appeared to spring from (and reinforce) the shortening of those horizons. Progressives criticized Americans' attention to the practical present world, then turned and asserted that the same practicality was the driving force of the country's world-leading progress. They questioned the sustainability of modern societies, then argued that modernity made them worth saving. Though "modern times" and the spread of "human will and choice" had caused the falling birthrate, one critic observed, "this power to control" now appeared to work against "social welfare and progress."[48]

Birth control's defenders, also progressives, seized on these contradic-tions. They worked to shift the focus away from the *scope* of personal time (did a person perceive binding commitments outside the immediate term?) towards the *direction* of historical time (was a person modern?). Birth control was good, they argued, because by common acclamation it was associated with innumerable modern improvements. People with small families were freer, wealthier, healthier, better educated, less dogmatic, and better able to control their worlds and contribute to progress. The decline of mystical eternalism was a good thing for everyone – not least the relatively few children born into prudent families. Practical immediate-term outlooks and limited families, far from threatening progress, were preconditions of it.

This proved a strong argument, and one that would grow rapidly in the decades to follow. Because everyone could agree that birth control's spread reflected "modern ideas," "modern life," "modern civilization," or "the modern spirit," every perceived advancement in medicine, or engineering, or wealth, also became a potential credit to birth control's legitimacy. Small families were an expression of "modern conditions" which "all tend to discourage matrimony," as one letter-writer put it. Couples with few children might be "calculating," but they also expressed a fundamentally American skepticism in the face of arbitrary antiquity or dogma. "It is a thoroughly American belief that a life that is merely existed is not worth living."[49]

For most citizen observers, the spread of smaller families was an expression of every change that separated the present world from the half-remembered ancestral one. Older generations had been more awed by the claims of eternity than those of history. Now people had a clearer picture of the chancy and shifting worlds in which they lived. There were obvious benefits to this clarity, but also a danger of spiritual myopia. Hundreds of moralists thus tried to spell out the eternal's value to individuals, society, and even to progress. They believed such a campaign might bring basic moral reform. A generation later they would be less hopeful.

GENDER

With some exceptions like landlord discrimination, Americans tended to explain the small-family trend in terms of sweeping intergenerational moral-economic change. Narrower-gauge explanations seemed insufficient. Virtually no one attributed falling birthrates to growing availability or knowledge of contraceptive methods, for example. Surprisingly few saw educational costs or content as a major factor. High fertility among immigrants and the poor was not seen as a cause of low fertility among the native middle classes, as in Francis Walker's "shock" theory. The idea that children were once economic assets (on farms) but had since become liabilities (in cities) was virtually absent.[50]

Most notable in its absence was a clear conception of birth control as revolution for and by women. The mostly male newspaper commentariat did not see the small-family trend as strongly motivated by women or associated with their interests (see Figure A.4). Pronatalists seeking culprits for race suicide generally addressed themselves to both sexes, as did liberalizers pinpointing beacons of progress. There was scant panic over women's escape from domesticity, pursuit of education, or special susceptibility to luxury. There was little celebration of women's gradual emancipation from domestic drudgery.

Instead, a majority of commentators never alluded to gender in any way, even briefly, while another 11 percent specifically mentioned *both* men and women as contributors to falling birthrates. The remaining third associated falling birthrates with one sex or the other, often weakly. Of these, three in five framed birth control as a women's issue, two in five as a men's issue.

Male moralists of the period had little compunction about criticizing specific faults in women's behavior, including deficiencies of femininity or maternal "warmth." But critics saw men as well as women as culprits in race suicide. Women had much to gain from a small family. But men were understood as the original sinners in the sexual regime. More than women, they sought out nonreproductive, nonmarital, recreational sex. Men were more likely to be calculating individualists. They controlled marriage proposals, and many critics saw declining birthrates as a result of men's reluctance to marry. Major contraceptive techniques were under men's physical control. As heads of household, husbands were liable for their families' material welfare. Censure for hungry or ragged broods fell on them more than on their wives. "The responsibility for the neglect and nonsupport of the children rests, in the great majority of cases, upon man while the labor, privations, and pain fall upon the woman," explained the *Chicago Tribune.*[51]

Women commentators often sought to assert their sex's special interest in reproductive reform. Whereas just 18 percent of men spoke of women's agency – actual or deserved – in fertility decisions, 46 percent of women did so. But whether these observers believed their fellow women *were* the key determiners of fertility outcomes or *should be* was not always clear. For example, when a female speaker derided "women who remain at home, attend to domestic duties, and rear large families" as "primitive squaws," she clearly framed fertility as a women's issue. But it was not clear if she was making an observation about who controlled family size, or who ought to do so. By contrast, few commentators seemed to think men *should* govern family size, though many believed they *did*, at least in part.[52]

This ambiguity regarding female agency stemmed partly from the disparity between women's heavy domestic responsibilities and limited power. The hour-to-hour rewards of a small family were greater for the women, in terms of tasks and anxieties foregone. But women's economic and social dependency limited their authority over consequential household decisions. Meanwhile men, though their rewards were less immediate, exercised greater authority. That domestic power disparity, combined with the widespread presumption of men's relatively mercenary nature – their irreligion, orientation toward worldly gain, and lack of "maternal instinct" – made them no less suspect than women in the eyes of pronatalists. The same power and pragmatism made them appear as potential leaders to liberalizers.

Inattention to gender did not reflect the *absence* of gendered divides in fertility motivation, but the perception that traditional male and female roles – and their modern evolution – might influence family-size preferences *in either direction*. Neither feminine nor masculine norms provided moralists with clear, unidirectional clues as to why families were shrinking. Women, as women, were pulled in two directions. On the one hand, "the old feminine instincts" disposed even "the new woman" to appreciate children. Women's religious and moral superiority lent them a clearer vision of the family's higher purpose, and checked men's aversion to commitment and domestic responsibility. On the other hand, natural "love of children" might make mothers "anxious to have only one or two feel they could only truly nurture." Modern women also did "not believe," as one woman wrote, "that the price of motherhood should be freedom and the right to self-ownership."[53]

Men, too, were pulled in two directions. A man might wish to carry on his family name. His paternity represented sexual potency and full manhood, and he might take pride in a large family while suffering few of its day-to-day burdens. But men were also rovers rather than nesters, and avatars of the modernity's cold calculation. At worst they were serial seducers; at best, victims of "industrial conditions which render it impossible for a large portion of the young men in the community to marry." These gendered crosscurrents helped ensure that as moralists surveyed their social worlds, they made no necessary association of smaller families with either sex or with any gender-specific complex of revolutionary ideas. Both sexes had compelling reasons to want children or avoid them, at any number.[54]

Stronger than the case for women's special agency in birth control's spread is the case for women's greater urgency and sympathy in addressing family limitation – regardless of ability to act. Women newspaper commentators were much more likely to oppose pronatalism than men: just 41 percent of women supported the president's position (versus 57 percent of men) while 42 percent opposed it (versus 12 percent of men). Female reformers had already distinguished themselves as some of birth control's few public advocates, campaigning for voluntary motherhood and in a few cases, penning defiantly anti-Roosevelt defenses of their childlessness. "I am not prepared to say that I absolutely refuse to accept the charge of motherhood," wrote "A Bachelor Maid" in 1904, "but I do refuse – and I have no words to express the loathing with which I regard this idea – to be looked upon as a mere means of swelling the census report." "Such women as 'The Bachelor Maid' and I are products of modern conditions," added another anonymous reader. In the future, this writer hoped, women could have both motherhood and freedom. "Meanwhile, I deny the right of any one to criticize me who is not doing something to lighten the pressure of those social conditions which have forced this dilemma not only upon me, but upon thousands of American women."[55]

Women also differed in their views of birth control's risks and rewards, framing birth control as a health issue far more often (26 percent) than men (7 percent). The physical danger of bearing children and sometimes exhausting or dispiriting challenges of raising them gave women an extra incentive to limit their families. "Women ... are the ones most intimately and immediately concerned," as the progressive journalist Lydia K. Commander wrote in 1907, after interviewing several hundred New Yorkers for a book on race suicide.[56]

In any culture gender assumptions may become so naturalized as to go unspoken. It is possible that, just as some Americans spoke of "race suicide" without needing to clarify what they meant by "race," others spoke of smaller families without needing to specify that women were responsible for that trend. "But," Commander continued, "it does not appear that American men are more desirous than women of large families." One of Commander's interviewees, a doctor practicing among "people in comfortable circumstances," guessed that "men probably on the whole desire children more than women":

Naturally they would; they get all the pride and miss the pain. But in my experience they are usually satisfied with two or three – often with one. Sometimes men welcome a large family and will seem pleased over every additional arrival, but they are the exceptions.

Another doctor did not believe "there is any considerable sentiment in favor of large families among men. President Roosevelt would find himself in a minority even among his own sex." Commander's female interviewees backed up these accounts: "the majority of women with whom I have personally come in contact confirm this evidence of physicians."[57]

Both women and men were essential to legitimizing fertility control in America. Women might hold special power in demanding fewer children due to the risks and demands of maternity. Men might spurn domestic responsibilities or take hedonic views of sex. In most cases, however, women and men seem to have taken moderately different routes to similar conclusions about the value of children to a dignified and righteous life. They moved on separate but broadly parallel tracks. As moral priority shifted from imposing continuums to living, practical selves, children became a greater burden on both parents. Rearing them became more expensive and less cosmically valuable, not for men or for women in particular, but for millions of modern people seeking dignity within a society in flux.

CONCLUSIONS

Demographers often note how "quietly" reproductive ethics changed before the 1960s. That assessment is true of the early twentieth-century United States in the sense that few Americans openly supported fertility control as a solution to social or personal problems. And it is true in the sense that outspoken activism was less important than private action in birth control's rise to popularity and legitimacy.[58]

But fertility change in the U.S. was not quiet in a general civic sense. Particularly after Roosevelt's "trumpet-blast protest" in 1903, popular debate over reproductive ethics was vigorous. "Race suicide" became a household term. Speculation on its causes and consequences became part of the period's civic furniture. "This is a pretty hard question for 'mere man' or a mere newspaper to discuss, and it is much pleasanter to talk and to write about other subjects," as one editor wrote. But discuss it Americans did. Race suicide seemed at once important and invisible, apparent and impossible to explain. "It seems to be one of those vast, slow, silent movements which pass almost unperceived at the time," wrote one critic, "but are more potent to shape the destinies of mankind than war or policies which look so much more important to a near vision."[59]

The debate focused attention on the private evolution of moral conventions that had long been taken for granted. It produced a few halting proposals to rewrite those conventions in light of modern progress. But most reaction was more conservative. Instead of reacting to smaller families with the characteristic progressive optimism of turn-of-the-century middle classes, American moralists mostly produced a sprawling attempt to restate and reinforce "old-fashioned" virtues that appeared, paradoxically, to be a precondition of further progress. "If it were possible for the *Post* to be pessimistic as to the republic's future," the Washington daily wrote, "a cause could be readily found in our social statistics." Democratic progress required the continued biological production of democratic progressives.[60]

The mere fact that these codes had to be spelled out caused considerable consternation among the pronatal majority: "when a people begins to talk about the 'duty' of marriage," one critic commented, "it is about time to bring down the curtain." Americans nevertheless proclaimed that duty with passion, giving voice to a code that, in common memory, had formed a basic moral backdrop to life during "the simpler days of the Republic." Men and women were born into reproductive debt. They were links in a chain rather than finished products. Children were an individual gratification but also a form of community and cosmic property. Good citizens did what was necessary to perpetuate themselves, their families, and their communities. They supported and celebrated their peers in this endeavor. Without such a common view to the eternal, children would not be worth the trouble.[61]

This fragile consensus emerged in public view only because it was breaking down. With every year it seemed to hold less power to sway action. "Why should men sacrifice to plant trees whose fruit they would never taste?" one essayist asked. "I suppose we all settle the question for ourselves," wrote another, as if to answer. "And if one sins, that one, and no other, will suffer."[62]

FIGURE 2.1 Three "female medicines," early twentieth century. Courtesy Dittrick Medical History Center, Case Western Reserve University.

FIGURE 2.2 Abortifacient tablets, early twentieth century. Courtesy Dittrick Medical History Center, Case Western Reserve University.

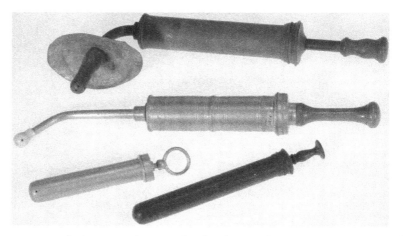

FIGURE 2.3 Syringes used to apply douching solutions. Courtesy Dittrick Medical History Center, Case Western Reserve University.

FIGURE 2.4 Box of condoms, c.1931.

FIGURE 2.5 Postcard, c.1906. Courtesy Deanna Dahlsad.

91. WHO SAID RACE SUICIDE?

1884   10-1-07   "NO RACE SUICIDE"   COPYRIGHT 1905 THE ULLMAN MFG. CO., NEW YORK

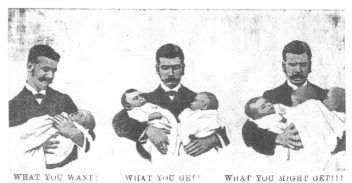

WHAT YOU WANT!   WHAT YOU GET!   WHAT YOU MIGHT GET!!!

FIGURE 2.6 Postcards, c.1905–10.

RACE SUICIDE FOILED ON THE BANKS OF THE WATAUGA

[Special to The Times-Dispatch.]

BRISTOL, TENN., October 27.—President Roosevelt is in receipt of a picture of the model anti-race suicide family, which is in many other respects a model one. It is that shown in the accompanying cut.

The family represented in this picture is a product of East Tennessee, and is an ideal representative of the "simple life." The picture is that of J. I. Reece and wife and their family of thirteen children, ten boys and three girls.

Mr. Reece is fifty-two years of age and his wife is forty-seven. They were married thirty years ago, when he was twenty-two and she sixteen years of age. In the thirty years of their married life fourteen children have been born to them, but one of the number died. The oldest of the living children is twenty-nine and the youngest five years.

This family now resides at Emmett, Sullivan county, Tennessee, ten miles from Bristol, but was reared in the Watauga Valley, near the picturesque spot where ex-Governor Bob Taylor was born, and where the music of this genial politician's fiddle was a constant source of inspiration to the young set in the childhood days of Mr. Reece and the winsome little girl who was destined to become his wife.

The Reece family is one of the happiest in all the wide world. The marriage was a happy one, and through all the years that have followed the wedding ceremony this man and his good wife have maintained a spirit of good cheer and have imparted it to their children. Indeed, the simple life has found permanent reign in the family, and home has been made so happy that not a one of the thirteen bright boys and girls would desert it for a million dollars.

In the world's goods the family is not rich, but it has ever been rich in the sunlight and good cheer of a happy home; and the death call, which summoned one of the number—a little child—from the family circle, visiting its heart-rending grief upon the household, but brought the family closer together in the bonds of a common sympathy and affection, so that the gentler and better influences have had all to do with shaping their destiny. It is easy, therefore, to understand how from the oldest to the youngest child the principles of a model rural life, in all its beauty and simplicity, have been instilled. And so it is that not a single member of this family has been addicted to bad habits of any character; every one being sober, obedient, energetic and faithful to every duty, each cheerfully accepting what they all, without exception, have received as they grew up—the advantage of a common school education.

Mr. and Mrs. Reece are naturally very proud of their children, and Mr. Reece has occasion, too, to be gratified with his success in a business way. He began his married life with $150 as his only material asset, and although ever since carrying the burden of a constantly increasing family, he has not only fed and clothed the family and given to the children a public school education, but by his industry and economy has accumulated sufficient to be the proud possessor of a fertile farm in the Watauga Valley, valued at $4,000.

The history of this bright, good-natured, cheerful family, unacquainted with the bitter disappointments of the reckless and misguided ambitions in the higher circles, strangers to practices which have blighted so many lives, is the history of a success whose price is not money, and which cannot be had for a mere cash consideration.

FIGURE 2.7 A family of fourteen from Emmett, Tennessee. Many large families sent similar photographs to President Theodore Roosevelt, who often replied with a note of congratulations. *Richmond Times-Dispatch*, Oct. 28, 1906.

FIGURE 2.8 Two-child family, Vermont, 1939.

3

Sensible as Spinach

The Moral Economy of Birth Control, 1927–1935

Desire not a multitude of unprofitable children.
　　　　　　　Ecclesiasticus 16:1

Statistics clearly show that the choice between a Ford and a baby is usually
made in favour of the Ford.
　　　　　　　Enid Charles (1934)[1]

**

All Theodore Roosevelt's lamentations were in vain. By the 1930s
Americans had just over two children on average – significantly fewer
than a generation earlier, and well below replacement due to higher
mortality. No country had ever had better reason to suspect that every
increase in modernity – in wealth, health, freedom, rationalism, and
mastery of nature – led to a corresponding decrease in human reproduction. In Germany, this "law of civilization" crystalized in the work of the
reclusive philosopher Oswald Spengler, whose dark prophecies animated
Nazi antimodernism. Across Europe and elsewhere, fear of biopolitical
decline led to explicitly pronatal and anti-birth control policies, such as
bans on contraceptive devices or cash payments to parents.

But in the early twentieth-century United States, where fertility decline
had been longer-running and more pronounced than virtually anywhere
else, attitudes towards birth control liberalized. Birth control gained widespread public legitimacy. It was a muted legitimacy – the legitimacy of
liberal tolerance and resigned acceptance, not celebration and acclaim.
"Many people are not yet adjusted to a full acceptance of birth control, yet
view it as a necessary evil," as an early chronicler of birth control wrote in
1929. "They look at the difficulties of modern life and prepare to accept
the inevitable." Nevertheless, birth control emerged from the 1920s and

'30s on a strong democratic foundation – one that would last for many decades. This chapter explores the roots of that legitimation process, contrasting the views of Roosevelt-era observers with moralists commenting on the same issues, in the same media, a generation later.[2]

FRACTURE AND THE NEW MORAL ECONOMY

By the late 1920s pronatal arguments appeared in major newspapers at half the rate of the 1900s. Support for birth control more than doubled (Figure A.5). Perceived causes of fertility decline remained largely the same (Figure A.6) but moral assessments of those causes grew more sympathetic. Where observers in Roosevelt's time had detected selfishness, luxury, and pettiness in the face of looming cosmic responsibilities, later ones saw a reasonable concern for self-preservation, child nurture, or maternal well-being.[3]

Meanwhile, overt Roosevelt-style pronatalism came to be seen as ineffective and overbearing. As fewer local moralizers actually produced "the old-time family" of four or more children, demanding an abundant brood from others invited charges of hypocrisy. "It is one thing to raise a large family of children," one letter-writer chided, "and quite another thing to sit in a comfortable easy chair by the fireside and write stories about how people should behave, and how many children they must bring into this world of sorrow." Not only did baby boosting seem increasingly tasteless – especially as European militarists and doctrinaire Catholics adopted it – pronatalism also seemed pointless. Ideals notwithstanding, visible example continued to suggest an association between small families and modern savvy. In this context, rather than shaming small families, citizen moralists made much smaller and weaker claims on each other's fertility. With a combination of invigorated liberal optimism and reluctant surrender to fate, Americans increasingly accepted parents who put self before society, worldly concerns before transcendent ones, and the immediate term before the infinite. They embraced reproductive liberalism, still fearful of race suicide but hoping for the best.[4]

Moralists still tried to ground reproduction in social norms, not just personal preferences or "the mating instinct." But by the standards of earlier generations, expectations were relaxed. Generalized calls for larger families became rare, and the number of children in a "large" family fell. For Roosevelt, "large" had meant five or six children – four being merely adequate. His constituents drew that line somewhere between three and four. By the 1930s "large families" had "more than two" children, one critic observed, while "cultured or intelligent" parents had "two, at most three, children," wrote another. When an early Gallup poll, in 1936, asked Americans their "ideal size of family," two- and three-child families each received 32 percent of the vote, four-child families 22 percent, and all other sizes tallied in the single digits. Rather than assuming that maintaining population required a strong pronatal culture, Americans hoped that human nature guaranteed a floor below which fertility would not drop.[5]

If there was a limit to the reproductive liberalism of the 1920s and 1930s, it was voluntary childlessness. Even as normative family size dropped from three or four towards two or three and pronatalists retreated from the civic stage, intentionally forgoing children remained radical. "I do not believe that any two people – a man and a maid – marry nowadays for the express purpose of propagating the race," as one columnist wrote. "And yet if any one, particularly any woman, says 'I want a husband but I do not want children,' she is put beyond the pale." Beyond that "spiritually starved" standard, however, any number of reasonably well-tended children was increasingly considered acceptable.[6]

The retreat of pronatalism emerged from pragmatic resignation to visible reality and to reproduction's ungovernability, but also ethnic and economic fracture. In a half-century leading up to the 1920s and '30s, American civic life became markedly more heterogeneous. The notion of a single organic "us" committing "race suicide" became progressively harder to uphold in a rapidly industrializing nation with growing disparities of class, creed, and ancestry. Between the 1880s and 1920s, large communities of "new" immigrants arrived from Eastern and Southern Europe. Masses of discontented, quasi-proletarian workers seethed and struck. African-Americans became increasingly visible in northern power centers. Popular science, in the form of social Darwinism and eugenics, divided society into innately superior and inferior groups. All these changes helped convince a growing share of dominant-class moralists that across-the-board baby boosting, even if it could be effective, would not be as appropriate as resigned liberalism – combined, perhaps, with eugenic engineering at the margins.

Enfranchised Americans did not give up hope that people like themselves would gain ground, demographically, on the growing populations of outsiders and others. But increasingly blurred lines between insiders and outsiders, and between more and less desirable others, made it ever more difficult to vaguely minister to an organic *volk*, as Roosevelt had

[handwritten margin notes: "2-3 children 'ideal' in 1936"; "bias asst childlessness"]

done. This weakening of the intuitively imagined "us" made it easier to judge reproductive decisions in situational and personal terms. The old middle-class pronatalism had relied on the prioritization of a commonsense collective over the reasoning individual, and the collective was losing coherence.

For this reason and others, American moralists scaled back their organic collectivism in the first decades of the twentieth century. Building on the Roosevelt era's minority liberalism, they built a majority position where children were defined more as risks and worldly things, and less as transcendent bounties. Children remained sentimentalized – all the more so as their economic and experiential costs increased. But parents' highest attainments had less to do with mystical eternities than earthly responsibilities. "The old idea of unlimited families" gave way to careful, preventative parenthood and a "new sense of the sacredness of human life." "Pending the coming of Utopia, we need birth control," a New York craftsman wrote. "Voluntary parenthood is not race suicide but a means of attaining a better, stronger family life."[7]

By the 1920s vastly fewer critics saw birth control as the vice of the prosperous and frivolous. The 21 percent of moralists who had condemned small families as an outgrowth of "luxury" in the 1900s fell to 7 percent a generation later. Men in particular ceased to strongly associate falling birthrates with decadence. Rather than chiding "lap-dog women" and "Peachtree Street swells," male moralists reframed economic birth control as "prudent," "intelligent," or at least "hard to fault." Both sexes began to favor the idea that birth control was a reasonable defensive measure against downward mobility, and one that benefited children as well as adults.[8]

Might this moral-economic shift be attributed to the Great Depression? Historians have long suspected that birth control gained legitimacy in the 1930s as more Americans faced the prospect of raising children in poverty, or hoped contraceptives might thin the ranks of the poor. If such a shift occurred, however, it failed to impress many amateur moralists. Approval for economically motivated fertility control stayed nearly constant before and after 1929 (Figure A.7) and few commentators mentioned the hard times. "Economic conditions may have something to do with it," a doctor speculated in 1933, "but I believe in the end that it is due to the desire of parents for more leisure, a desire to get about." The American economy had always been volatile, and millions who had felt insecure before the crash remained that way afterward. "The responsibilities of parenthood at which people shy are not primarily financial," observed *The New York Times* in 1932, but "psychological and social."[9]

Nevertheless, the Depression surely dissuaded many Americans from expanding their families in the short term. Even before the spiraling collapse of the early 1930s, couples courted for years without marrying. Men delayed proposals until they felt "established," and material thresholds for "starting a little family" could be quite conscious and concrete. New York University students surveyed in 1928, for example, only felt prepared for marriage (and the 2.5 children they imagined raising) after attaining a "nest egg" averaging $3,750, plus an annual income of $4,250. For couples such as these, new levels of economic uncertainty could present a major obstacle to marriage and children.[10]

More than the hard times, though, loosening stigmas on economic birth control reflected the growing perception that children, not adults, benefited most from family limitation. As children came to be seen in more practical and worldly terms, it became easier to see birth control as prudent economic altruism. "The people [want] to give their children a better chance than they have had, and to do this a man cannot be burdened with a large family," as one letter-writer argued. Even as columnists continued to jeer the childless and selfish, their critiques took on greater irony: "There is not enough room for children with a dog, two golf bags, a lunch hamper, cocktails . . . and the portable radio in the back seat," one humorist wrote. In place of the earnest contempt that had marked the 1900s, there was a mixture of dark humor and sincere pity for "the unwanted and unloved child."[11]

Refocusing public concern on living children, not social organisms, had been a goal of birth control activists since their rise to prominence in the late 1910s. Margaret Sanger and others thus peppered their arguments with pleas for suffering children, not just downtrodden mothers. Innocent children should not suffer for the circumstances of their births. Sanger in particular drew press coverage that helped redirect moral attention to helpless children, rather than calculating adults.

More important in establishing children as primary beneficiaries, however, was the gradual erosion of confidence in traditional social supports promoting the idea that, regardless of circumstance, a child's life was inherently worthwhile. By the early twentieth century, several generations of Americans had taken successively more sentimental views of childhood, replacing their ancestors' stern emphasis on original sin, filial duty, and patriarchal authority with a softer vision of children as fragile vessels of hope and innocence. As this sentimental vision flourished, so did the idea that childrearing was a risk borne by individual parents rather than a reward or duty acknowledged by God and the community. A child's life had less inherent value outside whatever privileges and comforts a parent might provide and the child might enjoy.[12]

The sense of solitary responsibility was evident in the derision with which Americans greeted the so-called "Toronto Baby Derby" – a "cradle competition" engineered by a lawyer in that city who, upon his death in 1926, bequeathed a half-million dollars to the local woman who bore the most children over the following ten years. This provision of his will was interpreted as dark satire or a practical joke, and contested in court, but upheld. A decade later, several mothers of over ten children split the prize. Where moralists of the 1900s might have found this contest amusing at worst, those of the 1920s and '30s heaped scorn on it. Gallup reported that 87 percent of American voters, and 91 percent of women, disapproved of the derby. Over three-quarters of those polled wanted no more than three children. *The New York Times* noted its doubts about the (mostly immigrant) Toronto families' earning power. A columnist asked what sort of man would wish to "inflict life and its responsibilities on a lot of innocents and their children who otherwise might not have had to be born at all."[13]

The association of children with worldly risk was rooted not only in sentimentalization, but also in a sense of social flux. Practical economic responsibility merged into more existential questions concerning parents' feelings of security in the world and the shifting thresholds below which new lives became precarious. Though economic volatility was a constant of American life, successive generations of Americans had become less inclined to trust that their children's innate resources would secure them a worthwhile life. Shame increasingly attached to those who failed to "set up" children with material and educational endowments, not those who defied divine or natural orders. "Keeping up with the neighbors is becoming nature's substitute for war and famine in limiting human populations," a college president remarked. Middle-class Americans wished to maintain their status at worst, at best to "get ahead." To act otherwise was "unfair to the children," as one critic put it, "who would be better off unborn."[14]

This growing sense of chanciness and potential shame constituted a profound antinatal force in America's dominant culture. For some critics the question of whether children would remain naturally desirable came down to the same question about life itself. Did it have an inherent value, or was it just a meaningless series of contingencies and risks? "We are living in an age of rapid transition when the old idea and established theories are being forsaken," wrote one critic. "Under these circumstances it is natural for us to question the worth of everything, and especially for us to debate concerning the abiding value of our most stable possessions."[15]

Such was the state of affairs, it seemed to the sociologists Robert and Helen Lynd, when they visited Muncie, Indiana, in 1935, to follow up to their famous "Middletown" study. "Middletown is overwhelmingly living by the values by which it lived in 1925," they observed. Despite a recent "unduly stiff bit in the road" – the Depression – people still sought to "live hopefully and adventurously into the future." They retained their defining, quasireligious faith in progress. But their sense of security was not what it had been a decade before. "Down here under our vests we're scared to death," residents told the Lynds when speaking "unofficially." They found themselves in an increasingly disenchanted, plural, dangerous world. Even as they maintained an overt faith that fortune favored them and their descendants, residents found fewer reasons to think their destiny as benevolent or providential. "One suspects that for the first time in their lives many Middletown people have awakened ... from a sense of being at home in a familiar world to the shock of living as an atom in a universe dangerously too big and blindly out of hand," the Lynds wrote:

With the falling away of literal belief in the teachings of religion in recent decades, many Middletown people have met a similar shock, as the simpler universe of fifty years ago has broken up into a vastly complicated physical order; but, there, they have been able to retain the shadowy sense of their universe's being in beneficent control by the common expedient of believing themselves to live in a world of unresolved duality, in which ones goes about one's daily affairs without thought of religion but relies vaguely on the ultimates in life being somehow divinely "in hand."[16]

This world still offered middle-class Americans the reasonable hope that life was getting better across the generations, and children's lives would be worth living. But without a sense of common sublimation in an eternal and natural order – with childrearing increasingly defined as a technical problem and material risk – growing a family was an act of faith in an environment lacking in it. "It is not a pretty social picture, this new caution, this mutual look-before-you-leap-and-then-don't-leap attitude toward marriage," wrote the novelist Fannie Hurst. "But it is as sensible as spinach."[17]

RELIGIOUS PRONATALISM

The race suicide debate of the 1900s had often pitted progressives against one another. Some argued that small families were both a precondition of progress and a result of it. More believed demographic trends imperiled progress, since timeless duties to timeless chains of being seemed, paradoxically, to underpin the ongoing conquest of timeless nature and fate.

By the late 1920s, secular progressives had largely disappeared from the shrunken ranks of American pronatalists. Beyond the many who resigned themselves to reproductive liberalism, others began supporting birth control only insofar as it might serve "eugenic" purposes by slowing the perceived growth of marginal groups. With the departure of these progressive moralists, pronatalism in America became markedly more religious. Debate pivoted away from sociological principles and towards religious ones. Moralists of all opinions became more likely to frame modernity-defying religiosity as the last great remaining obstacle to ever-greater reproductive control. Where 23 percent of commentators had mentioned religiosity in the 1900s, 36 percent did so in the 1920s and '30s. Birth control had become a "controversial religious subject," as the National Broadcasting Company explained in 1929 – and a subject too fundamentally divisive for national radio play.[18]

In the opening decades of the twentieth century, American pronatalism became not just religious, but distinctively Catholic. Well before the Vatican officially condemned most birth control methods in 1930, in *Casti Connubii*, U.S. Catholic clergy and laypeople had been prominent among birth control's opponents. But whereas earlier Catholics had been joined by at least equal numbers of Protestant and secular allies, by the 1920s Catholics dominated traditionalist positions. They were larger in numbers and less ambivalent in message. "[We] stand against all modern vagaries that threaten the integrity of the Christian ideal of the family," a Catholic women's group declared. Conservative Protestants, despite widespread distrust of Catholicism, voiced admiration of this stance. Pious Protestants were "just as zealous of guarding the sanctity of the marriage relation ... as is the Catholic Church," intoned a Baptist preacher.[19]

The Catholicization of anti-birth control sentiment, however, did help convince modernist Protestants of birth control's progressive bona fides. For centuries Protestant polemics had contrasted Catholicism's authoritarian "medievalism" with the conscientious freedom of the nonconforming churches. Decentralized religiosity was, for millions of Protestants, the foundation of American democracy and progress. As pronatalism became more Catholic, then, birth control's supporters worked to portray their opposition as an antiprogressive, anti-American, Catholic conspiracy. This tactic was adopted with special gusto by Margaret Sanger (herself a lapsed Catholic) and echoed in the public forum. "The menace of intolerant tyranny," Sanger warned, posed a direct threat to "the future of American civilization."[20]

Sanger's assertions of insurgent Catholicism contained a grain of truth. Catholic political clout in big cities made public figures wary of backing birth control, and Catholic clergy devoted substantial energy and resources to educating their flocks on the sinfulness of "artificial" birth control methods (abstinence and rhythm methods were acceptable). Catholic exceptionalism was thrown into even sharper relief as liberal Protestant clergy began publicly backing birth control in the 1920s, arguing that family limitation was a practical and Christian means of stabilizing marriages and ensuring child welfare. The Anglican Lambeth Conference, after denouncing contraception as "demoralizing to character and hostile to national welfare" in 1908, reversed itself in 1930. Questions of family limitation deserved to be "examined dispassionately from the point of view of morality and hygiene," wrote the Federal Council of Churches, "with due regard to the best means of maintaining desirable standards of living and fully discharging the fundamental obligations of parents to each other and to their children." These positions evoked little opposition from editorialists or letter writers, apart from those who identified themselves as Catholics. Sectarian divides grew further as many Protestant laypeople embraced birth control on eugenic grounds, a stance many Catholics considered elitist, illiberal, and arrogant in the face of divine authority.[21]

Mirroring wider low-boil animosity between Protestants and Catholics, both sides tended to dismiss each other's ideas as naïve, short-sighted, and destructive. Progressives foresaw a nation blinded by superstition and incapable of progress. Catholic pronatalists saw one blinded by progress and incapable of eternal vision. As in earlier intra-progressive debates, much disagreement centered on how to relate birth control to history. Progressives displayed a new confidence in pragmatic, evolutionary, scientific viewpoints. "No subject" could be "rightly shut off from scientific investigation" – "It is not primarily a question of morals or religion, but rather a question of common sense and evolution." Catholics lamented a moral collapse equivalent to that of decadent Rome. "The modern world in a determined effort to defeat the principles

[margin handwritten note: Catholics resisted birth control much more vehemently]

of the church," wrote one priest, "has formed a conspiracy which it has launched vigorously throughout the world to keep children out of God's universe." Reversing course meant rejecting a number of large and growing social assumptions, the priest argued, such as the idea "that our private lives are our own business," that earthly salvation was possible, or indeed that "modern" developments in general were leading to a fundamentally new and better world.[22]

At the heart of the Catholic objection was a belief, not just in unchanging divine law, but in original sin. Sin and corruption resided permanently in human hearts; redemption was possible only through God, not progressive self-improvement. "Be not deceived by these false arguments of practical men of the world – men of science – who speak of a new morality in terms of freedom, action, emancipation," one Catholic moralist warned. "They are rocking the foundation of civilization." That foundation was a shared sense that some realms of human experience, notably sexuality and reproduction, should not be subject to the same well-intentioned meliorism as, say, engine building or disease eradication. "There must be a 'right' and a 'wrong' side to every question," a Catholic professor argued, "and in this present discussion, that 'rightness' or 'wrongness' must be eternal."[23]

Catholics and other conservatives bridled at the term "birth control" and its implied association between contraception and other forms of benign human mastery over arbitrary nature. Birth control was not like flood control or pest control. Indeed, for conservatives the connection between "progress" and family limitation was mutually damning, not mutually complementary. Open-ended fertility decline showed definitively that earthly progress was deceptive, and that its Protestant enthusiasts had lost sight of the unyielding demands that God – or God-in-nature – made on individuals. Especially maddening in this respect were Protestant defenses of birth control on Christian grounds, which invoked a God of compassion and love rather than sacrifice and natural law. This good-natured and practical God, conservative Catholics complained, was a perfect match for a Protestant community that had ceased holding itself to even the most basic moral standard of natural self-perpetuation – preferring genial privacy to combative engagement with lurking sin and selfishness. "Tell your Protestant friends," said one anti-birth control priest, "that only Communism and Catholicism present an ordered way of life for the future. Despite the pleasant phrases of liberal Protestantism, it offers no remedy for a sick society morally, socially and economically."[24]

Not all religious commentary neatly fit the Catholic–Protestant and eternal–progressive mold. Some Catholics opposed birth control on social justice grounds. "The argument against large families," one such critic argued, "is simply an effort to shift the responsibility for poor economic systems onto the shoulders of the founders of large families." A lay Catholic excoriated the governor of Puerto Rico for suggesting that contraception, not land reform, was the answer to the island's socioeconomic problems. Rather than asking parents to adapt family size to wages, a Jesuit priest argued, employers should adapt wages to family size: "Husband and wife should in a just social order have a sufficiency of goods to support and educate the children nature gives. To this they have a moral right granted by nature and nature's God."[25]

By the same token, many conservative Protestants opposed birth control. Outspoken liberalism from the Federal Council, Lambeth, and modernist clergy spurred backlash. Denouncing and disowning "pseudoscientific" modernists, fundamentalists painted support for birth control as a crystallization of theological liberals' loss of any sense of transcendent majesty and mission. A *Washington Post* editorial skewering the Federal Council's "mixture of religious obscurantism and modernistic materialism" drew so much interest that the paper reprinted it by popular demand, then produced a series of symposia on religion and birth control. "If the churches are to become organizations for political and 'scientific' propaganda," concluded the *Post*'s editorial, "they should be honest and reject the Bible, scoff at Christ as an obsolete and unscientific teacher, and strike out boldly as champions of politics and science as modern substitutes for old-time religion."[26]

Some conservative Protestants believed, with varying degrees of regret, that the Catholic Church's unbending traditionalism assured it a dominant future position. Catholics would soon dominate the United States as the Church's pliant flocks, instructed by an antimodern clergy, kept sight of eternal orders while Protestants melted away into modern time and its distractions. Catholic leaders knew better. Their combative urgency reflected a tacit realization that lay Catholics were not far behind their Protestant peers in adopting small-family norms. Evidence from the confessional booth and the baptismal font seemed to indicate that priestly instruction was not having its desired effect. "In many cities the number of children per family among Catholics of the middle and comfortable classes is little more than half the average that obtained in the families of their parents," one priest observed in 1916. Within a few decades Protestant and Catholic fertility behavior would be indistinguishable.[27]

This put some U.S. Catholic clergy in the unusual position of urging their parishioners to adopt quasi-Protestant approaches to divine revelation, following "unsophisticated conscience" or "instinctive repugnance" to their own "natural" conclusions about God's intentions for moral beings. Ultimately, critics of all denominations and persuasions continued to underscore the importance of religious feeling, as opposed to direct teaching, in determining the size of families. Catholics espousing formal Catholic doctrine played a role similar to that of Theodore Roosevelt, or later birth control activists, in the realm of popular reproductive ethics. They articulated bold abstract ideals, helping define the terms of debate, but nevertheless stood at a certain looming distance from citizens' actionable ideas. What was important about religion was not its exact content so much as its capacity to make a person see beyond the most immediate and material worlds.[28]

NATURISM AND EUGENICS

Ideas about nature changed alongside those about divinity. In the 1900s natural law had appealed to progressives as a source of final moral authority that required no adherence to religious dogma. Nature in all its mystic grandeur wanted reproduction. By the late 1920s this form of pronatal naturism had become rarer – abandoned in favor of technocratic or eugenic arguments, or annexed by Catholic critics as a religious principle.

Indeed, some of birth control's bolder supporters began appropriating "nature" for their own purposes, arguing that contraceptives allowed for a natural expression of sex instinct. Abstinence – "unnatural continence" – was "impractical." Prostitution, venereal disease, and ill-tempered passion flourished wherever people relied on it. Sexual expression was merely inevitable; birth control softened the repercussions for public health and social stability. "The postponement of marriage until economic competence is assured is one of our chief problems," argued an Episcopal priest. "Human instincts rebel against this restraint and social irregularity is the result." A vocal and sometimes Freudian minority decried the warped and weakened psyches produced by polite society's "thwarting of the natural life."[29]

This form of naturism had a long pedigree, and did not reflect any new sexual hedonism so much as continued concern about overcivilization. Partly as a result of Roosevelt's race suicide campaign, middle-class American men had become "increasingly attracted to the idea of a natural or primitive masculinity," as the historian Gail Bederman writes. Men's latent wildness became something to be harnessed rather than repressed, an antidote to urban "softness" and feminization rather than a threat to America's nature-taming, civilization-building mission. Frank sexuality expressed a refusal to be neutered by self-restraint.[30]

Meanwhile the stern and God-like Nature that demanded abundant children – not just natural sexual expression – became less secular and more Catholic. For Catholics, nature was a foundation for theology rather than an alternative to it. Priests distinguished between "natural law" – which expressed God's will on earth – and "natural desire," which insisted only on human sense gratification. Birth control contravened "law established by nature when the world was young," a Catholic club argued. Why "attempt to trick nature (God?) by chemical and mechanical devices?" a lay believer asked.[31]

As progressives turned away from naturism, many turned towards class chauvinism and the language of eugenics. Proposals for directed human breeding were entering peak popularity in the late 1920s, and presented an appealing alternative to vague national baby boosting. If "average" middle-class citizens could not be cajoled into producing more children, perhaps their social inferiors could be coerced or manipulated into producing fewer. As a result of this shift, 8 percent of commentators in 1927–1935 supported birth control *only* insofar as its reach might depopulate socially marginal groups.

The birth control movement's success is often attributed to the combined efforts of feminists and eugenicists. For the most part, however, the "eugenics" of newspaper moralists differed from that of elite eugenicists. For the latter, the rediscovery of Mendelian genetics in 1900 had been a revelation. Gregor Mendel's experiments appeared to confirm that the "protoplasm" stayed intact from generation to generation, transmitting traits regardless of environment. If permanently inferior genes could be bred out of humans, as from livestock, irreversible human progress seemed possible.

But for centuries prior to 1900, more fluid interpretations of heredity had circulated in the general public. These included the Lamarckian idea that acquired characteristics (such as alcoholism) might be passed from parents to children, and less exact folk notions of hereditary continuity ("like father, like son"; "like begets like") that allowed for the influence of both nature and nurture. As two prominent eugenicists noted in 1918, "eugenics" for typical middle-class Americans still connoted a vague sense that good parents made good children, and that families could be improved over the generations by progressively bettering the conditions under which each generation lived. "It is widely supposed that, although nature may have distributed some handicaps at birth, they can be removed if the body is properly warmed and fed and the mind properly exercised," complained Paul Popenoe and Roswell Johnson. "It is further widely supposed that this improvement in the condition of the individual will result in his production of better infants, and that thus the race, gaining a little momentum in each generation, will gradually move on toward ultimate perfection."[32]

Popenoe and Johnson hoped this misunderstanding would vanish with time. For the moment, however, "eugenic" vocabulary mostly offered linguistic decoration for the long-standing idea that some babies and families were more valuable than others. To secular progressives it offered a way to replace the older intuitive language of paternalism, class bias, and ethnic boosterism with a pleasingly scientific-sounding scheme. Within the birth control debate, soft hereditarianism remained healthy even as the cult of eugenics reached its heyday. Just 21 percent of "eugenic" commentators evinced a "hard" or Mendelian view of heredity – only slightly more than those that held nurturist views. The remainder blended vagueness on hereditary transmission with an older tradition of nonscientific social criticism. "Control of affairs may soon be taken over by the moronic majority," wrote one disillusioned columnist. "Meanwhile, to jazz music and torch songs, more cultured communities are doing what looks terribly like a dance of death."[33]

Eugenicists' major contribution to birth control's legitimation was not to convince middle-class Americans that progress depended on deploying birth control against a genetic underclass; it was to help divert many progressives' attention away from universal natural-law arguments and towards more technical and categorical approaches to reproductive ethics. Though eugenicists were often bystanders in the use of their own terminology, they introduced a vocabulary that helped associate birth control more closely with technical social management and the objectivity of science. Under the heading of eugenics, birth control seemed less like a challenge to inherited morality and more like a practical tool for progress.

ACTIVISTS

In the 1910s and '20s, prominent birth control activists arrived on the American scene. Their message was not entirely new. Physicians like Charles Knowlton and Edward Bliss Foote, radicals like Robert Dale

Owen and Moses Harman, and various social reformers had long promoted birth control as a cause and practice. Though they promoted birth control on grounds similar to those of later advocates – including feminist grounds – they gained limited public recognition. More notable were later activists who lived in a time of franker sexual speech and were not just feminist but female. The prospect of a defiantly female-led "birth strike" brought new publicity to the cause, both elevating its profile and making it somewhat harder for moderates to endorse.[34]

The anarchist Emma Goldman arrived first. During a national lecture tour in 1915 she became "the first and last to give actual methods from the platform," as a deputy later boasted. Arrested periodically for this offense, Goldman generated substantial publicity for her cause before abruptly abandoning it, having decided birth control methods were already too "well circulated and known." Around the same time, Mary Ware Dennett founded the National Birth Control League with a group of progressive New Yorkers, including many suffragists. Across the country, small female-led leagues sprang up between 1914 and 1916, sometimes in response to the arrest of local activists for distributing birth control pamphlets.[35]

Margaret Sanger began her activities around the same time and quickly came to dominate the organized movement. Sanger was born in 1879, in Corning, New York, to Irish-American parents. Her mother bore eleven children in twenty-two years, succumbing to tuberculosis six years after the last child's birth. Her freethinking father, a stonemason, periodically struggled to support his family. Sanger eventually attended nursing school with her older sisters' support, moved to New York City, and married William Sanger, an architectural draftsman. They had three children and lived for a time in the commuter town of Hastings-on-Hudson. Growing bored with suburban life, the Sangers returned to Manhattan in 1910 and soon settled in the bohemian enclave of Greenwich Village, where "radicalism in manners, art, industry, morals, politics was effervescing," as Sanger later recalled. "The mental stirring was such as to make a near Renaissance."[36]

Sanger made radical friends and embraced various socialist and reformist causes. By 1913, however, she had determined to devote herself to just one issue, women's reproductive control. Using a combination of confrontational rhetoric and direct-action tactics, she was soon generating considerable publicity. In 1914 she was indicted, and William Sanger jailed, for distributing contraceptive advice literature. Sanger went into self-imposed exile in Europe for over a year, during which time she inspected contraceptive clinics and visited various experts on sex and contraception. Returning to New York in 1916, she opened a birth control clinic in the poor Jewish and Italian neighborhood of Brownsville, Brooklyn. Police raided and closed the clinic ten days later, arresting Sanger and other workers. This led to a high-profile hunger strike by Sanger's jailed sister, Ethel Byrne, and eventually to a court decision favorable to medical distribution of contraceptives. Having gained notoriety through this case, Sanger began a long career of sparring, eloquently and unapologetically, with birth control's enemies. She published widely circulated books and pamphlets, and spoke regularly to reformist audiences. Occasional efforts by police, politicians, and clergymen to keep her from the podium drew additional attention to her cause.[37]

By the mid-1920s, however, Sanger and the movement had assumed a lower profile. Sanger's message had become less confrontational, and she spent much of her time behind the scenes, organizing conferences and wooing influential people – especially doctors, professors, and eugenicists – to the cause. She turned over many of her speaking duties to Dr. James Cooper, an obscure obstetrician who lacked her reputation for radicalism. She was neither famous nor forgotten. When a group of Yale seminary students were asked, in 1925, if they knew of Sanger before seeing her speak in a course-sponsored lecture, ten said "no," six "yes," and seven claimed to have had "some" knowledge of her.[38]

Sanger retained some power to influence public discussion. Twelve percent of articles from the 1920s and '30s mentioned Sanger or her movement – a rate similar to that of Sanger's Catholic antagonists. Sanger's term "birth control," moreover, had gained near-universal currency by the early 1920s. Though not all Americans would have been able to connect the term to its popularizer, Sanger's replacement of older phrases like "prevention of conception" or "keeping from having children" helped reframe family limitation as positive control rather than negative avoidance. At a more fundamental level, Sanger's bold publicity, though it offended some Americans, also helped shift the respectable center of the birth control debate by pushing its margins.[39]

Some citizen observers independently judged the organized movement a relevant factor in the discussion of reproductive ethics. Columnists alluded to "Mrs. Sanger's doctrines" and dubbed her "the great pioneer of birth control." Catholics railed against "the godless, selfish and inhuman propaganda of birth prevention" and "the public attitude that designates people of Mrs. Sanger's type as 'high-minded and forward-looking.'" For the most part, however, attention to the activist movement came from publicity-generating efforts by activists themselves, such as speeches, conferences, and protests. Whereas observers often brought up the Catholic opposition independently, as an important social force, the activist movement did not command independent attention in the same way.[40]

Opinions of the organized movement were split almost evenly. Opponents often focused on the organized movement's perceived gratuitousness and poor taste. "Birth control has already been abused too much without giving license to it," complained a reader from Albany, New York. "Birth controllists" fostered the "vicious idea" that "the burden of birth control is a female function," a medical columnist complained. Favorable commentary praised the movement's role in hastening the collapse of anticontraceptive taboo and hypocrisy. "When the movement was first launched by such leaders as Mrs. Sanger there was an almost unanimous expression of disapproval," one editorialist recalled. "Many earnest men and women [still] oppose it on conscientious grounds, but these have grown steadily fewer and they have been deserted by those who at first sided with them undoubtedly as a result of lack of information or prejudice."[41]

Sanger and other activists helped bend the terms of discussion by, for example, reinforcing the links between poverty and high fertility. Sanger strategically placed clinics in poor immigrant neighborhoods; continually framed large families as a curse of the poor; and frequently told the tale of Sadie Sachs, an impoverished and dying mother who, Sanger said, inspired her crusade. Gestures such as these encouraged the idea that the prolific poor were not only a threat to the social order, but victims of prudish, irrational, outdated prejudices.[42]

Ultimately, though, the movement was not a major frame of reference for Americans considering the causes and consequences of fertility trends. Like Roosevelt, Sanger was able to stir discussion, and like him she worked in an arena where few Americans seemed to believe leaders and institutions had a large part to play. The informal movement was too large and too self-policed. "The efforts of leagues such as those sponsored by Margaret Sanger," one columnist argued, were "relatively futile compared with the hit-and-miss methods as practiced by millions of women who procure their knowledge principally from one another."[43]

GENDER

Neither Sanger's outspoken feminism nor growing legitimacy increased the popular perception of birth control as a women's issue. Neither women nor men, and neither pronatalists nor birth controllers, strongly emphasized female agency in reproductive control. "Rebuke those cautious college couples," Hurst mockingly told pronatalists: "Blame the bridge-whist wife, the delicatessen mother and the wary bachelor." George Ade, a popular chronicler of Midwestern manners, went so far as to ask, "If the birth-rate languishes, shall *no* part of the blame be put on the modernized young woman?" Ade, a lifelong bachelor, saw pronatalism as pressure on men to propose marriage and settle down.[44]

Still, the dawning redefinition of birth control as a women's movement was apparent, and not just in the pronouncements of Sanger and her allies. Women remained more likely than men to support birth control (see Figure A.8) and frame it as a women's issue (see Figure A.9). When *Country Home* magazine surveyed its readership on a variety of "public and private questions" in 1930, few topics interested the 14,000 respondents – and women in particular – more than birth control (not even "farm machinery and food production"). The editors noted two qualities in the returned surveys: first, respondents' favorability to birth control (by a margin of two to one), and second, the fact that "women were much more interested in the subject than their husbands." Husbands (40 percent of the respondents) supported birth control, but many of their wives went further, including "long letters with their questionnaires, mostly expressing in their own direct way the opinion that 'birth control is as necessary to improve social conditions in the open country as the removal of crop surpluses to a permanently improved economic condition.'" Catholic priests, who grew acquainted with private birth control practices through the confessions of their parishioners, began shifting some attention from lusty men to "the modern up-to-date girl." Whereas men had been presumed the guilty parties in the nineteenth century, women came under closer scrutiny in the twentieth.[45]

American women of the 1920s and '30s felt freer than their mothers to claim birth control as an individual benefit. In particular, women capitalized on an increasing sense that maternal suffering, exhaustion, and death were not simply the way of the world, but preventable public health problems. The mere sight of "worn-out, haggard-looking mothers" in backwoods Appalachia, one woman warned, would be enough to silence the sternest priest. The body-and-soul health benefits of prevention, combined with older assumptions concerning women's moral superiority, made women a formidable force in backing birth control. "Nature picked women to have the babies because it's the hardest and most important job there is," as the folk oracle "Aunt Het" declared. "If . . . men had to bear 'em, they wouldn't be two days thinkin' up some way to prove big families a wicked abomination in the eyes o' Heaven."[46]

Women denied community claims on their reproduction in ways that would have been virtually unmentionable a generation earlier. "I want to live my own full life" wrote a twenty-two-year-old married woman who felt it would be a "colossal, stupid mistake" for her to have children. "I want to live well and freely, to travel everywhere and see everything, to experience the many joys of life, to improve myself, to make life a rich adventure and not a longtime chore. Brutally stated, I just can't be bothered with procreation, for I am convinced that there is a tremendous responsibility involved in having children." Childless women expounded on the fulfillment they derived from careers, the unbroken companionship of their husbands, or voluntary social work.[47]

Most women, like men, remained more deferential to pronatal norms. To the extent their voices differed from those of men, it was primarily in the assertion of a connection between women's physical and moral stakes in reproduction. As bearers and caretakers of children, women offered themselves as vulnerable individuals for whom a large family might mean suffering or death, and to whom society therefore owed deference and protection. It was an old argument, but one which carried additional weight as Americans took a less organic and corporate view of their society. Women were better defined as singular individuals, not parts of a social body. Though it was "hard to say to what extent women's motivation for birth control differed from men's," as the historian Ida Blom wrote of Norway in the same period, "it is striking that while women took their arguments from private family life, men mainly considered the importance of the number of births for society as such, for the public world." A similar though subtler divide marked U.S. public commentary. In personalizing reproductive ethics – forcing the mind to individual cases – women helped privatize childrearing and weaken the primacy of the abstract collective in reproductive ethics.[48]

For all that, plenty of men took a household-level view of birth control's advantages, and plenty of women preferred social and statistical abstraction. Most assumed questions of reproductive ethics were more likely to divide couples from other couples along moral-economic lines, rather than wives from husbands along gender lines. There was "little reason to believe that a fundamental disagreement on limiting the number of births existed between spouses," as Blom wrote, despite men's fondness for the bloodless social panorama and women's for the mournful scene. Even as egalitarian feminism made gains in society at large, debating the

rights and wrongs of reproduction still did not mean weighing the interests of women against those of men.[49]

CONCLUSION: PRIVATIZING REPRODUCTION

In 1965 the Supreme Court overturned one of the last remaining
Comstock laws, in *Griswold v. Connecticut*. The landmark decision
found that "penumbras" in the Constitution guaranteed a "right of privacy." "Would we allow the police to search the sacred precincts of marital
bedrooms for telltale signs of the use of contraceptives?" asked William
O. Douglas, writing for the majority. "The very idea is repulsive to the
notions of privacy surrounding the marriage relationship." Marriage was
a sacred "way of life" rather than a political institution; it was "a coming
together ... a harmony in living ... a bilateral loyalty." The union of
a woman and a man had no necessary relationship to reproduction.
In these matters above all, Americans had a right to be left alone.[50]

Consensus on this point was already emerging in the early decades of
the twentieth century. "We are told that our private lives are our own
business," as one clergyman noted. "That is the mood of today." Though
moralists did not always specifically invoke a right to privacy, few cultural
shifts between the 1900s and 1930s were more apparent than that which
redefined the purposes and responsibilities of marriage and parenthood,
making reproductive morality less public, political, and universal, and
more private, personal, and contingent. Overshadowed by the '30s was
the idea, still popular in Theodore Roosevelt's time, of families as core
units of government – physically and spiritually reproducing a sanctified
social organism. Replacing this idea were, on one side, defensive Catholic
appeals to the "old way," and on the other, liberalism of the sort eventually codified by Douglas.[51]

Pragmatic liberals began to challenge and even mock the premise of an
organic nation. "Nothing has been more of a farce than to assume that
women bear children – or men father them – for such lofty, altruistic
motives as the good of the nation or the race," wrote one women's
columnist. "Few women are vitally concerned about what is going to
happen one hundred years from now. No more than men do they see far
beyond their own graves." Better suited to chancy modern times was
a universal self-directed rationalism. Pragmatists sought to distance ethics
from mystical revelation, while maximizing individual self-government.
In reproduction as in economics or governance, this was a core American
project. "The disparity between the 'right' and the 'good,'" a letter-writer

argued, was lost on believers in objective natural law. "I suppose it would be right for a genius to give his life to save an idiot in a fire, but it would not be good. Neither does it seem good to limit free will on the ground of 'natural' morality."[52]

Reproductive liberals grew bolder with the rise of fascist regimes in Italy (1922) and Germany (1933) that combined political repression, militarist aggression, and nationalist pronatalism. Eager for "cannon fodder," as *The Baltimore Sun* put it, each regime's "controlling idea" was to make its home country "as unpleasant as possible to live in and then to insist that unborn millions must live in it." Mockery of fascist baby boosting became a minor cottage industry, with observers making light of the Italian practice of publishing daily birth tallies "like the scores of baseball games" or the unmarried Adolf Hitler's "campaign to drag women to the altar." Liberals reveled in the futility of policies such as Nazi *kindergeld* or Italian housing assistance for families. "Population has very little to do with speeches by Cabinet Ministers [or] medals for fathers of 24 children," one editorialist observed. Across-the-board contempt for nihilistic "soldier-breeding" helped build popular associations between pronatalism and authoritarianism.[53]

As parents prioritized the welfare of living children, families became less imposing as transcendent institutions. Protestants in particular led the conversion of the Victorian "Christian home" – an "enduring, divinely ordained moral institution" into the early twentieth century's "Christian family" – "not an abstract ideal or a physical place but a set of fluid, roughly egalitarian human relationships." The immortal clan or "family name" carried less weight. Pragmatic protection carried more. "I am yet the mother of several well-spaced children, and who can doubt that they and I are better for it?" one newspaper reader wrote. "However, had I decided to bear no children at all, I cannot see that it is anyone else's business."[54]

Only the most zealous advocates for privacy denied the claims of *any* transcendent order, whether organized around family, ethnicity, nation, creed, or some intuitive composite of these ideas. Most writers hoped enduring orders would survive, and demoted them only relative to other more urgent practicalities, like maintaining or advancing social status in the next generation.

In any case, there appeared to be little to *do* about reproductive trends. Just as Douglas' objections were partly practical – would we send police into bedrooms searching for contraceptives? – so too did many interwar observers see the case for privacy as largely a matter of cultural and political realism. Even if a pronatal agenda were generally desirable, it was not feasible. "However much we protagonists or antagonists of ... birth control, with its moral, emotional and economic aspects, may air our views, it is probable that the rank and file of us will have it settled in our own notions anyway," one letter writer observed.[55]

How far a person might go in relinquishing common claims on reproduction was strongly linked to ideas about modernity. "The plain fact is that our social environment today is *better* adapted to the old ideals of marriage than ever before," protested a New York judge, George Appell, in a challenge to the consensus view that modernity demanded ever-smaller families. Americans were better educated and wealthier than their grandparents. Women were freer. "Every phase of progress has been an asset to the family, not a blow delivered against it." The basic problem, Appell argued, was that Americans had "slumped spiritually." "We have adopted jazz, speed and show as our national slogans." Rather than insisting on the right, Americans had lazily accepted the idea that the dictates of "progress" excused them from "fostering the next generation." "These cravings have not been forced upon us by exterior forces, but by an inward yielding. Are we so supine and stupid a race as to pretend that we cannot control the machine of civilization which we have been clever enough to create? No – we can easily guide it upward if we will. We lack the will."[56]

Most critics were happier to entrust themselves and their posterity to the presumed modern order. "Instinct" or "human nature" would supply enough children for social replenishment. In the meantime, modern advancements and modern risks justified smaller families. A sense of vulnerability and responsibility made Americans less willing to uphold public fertility standards that seemed impossible; at the same time, this privatization of reproductive responsibility made the public rewards of parenthood less apparent. Though children still seemed like an important cosmic and social imperative, the binding communities that supported children seemed less stable, enveloping, and authoritative.

With the rising consensus that there was no direct way to influence reproductive motivation, public pronatal standards became a burden to the moralizers as well as the moralized. Replacing such standards was an assumption that *most* people would have at least one or two children *most* of the time. "Worthy" families might still be congratulated for their three or four children, and the willful childless scorned. But pronatal preaching or policy was not a community function. "The solution will be found in the principle of 'self-determination,'" wrote one columnist, "when those most concerned write the law and define morality." More than ever, Roosevelt's "race" would have to persist or perish in the domain of private conscience.[57]

EPILOGUE: BABY BUST TO BABY BOOM

Not long after this resigned liberalism gained broad support, American birthrates unexpectedly rebounded. Family size leveled off in the mid-1930s, then began rising as that decade ended. By the mid-1950s young Americans had an average of 3.5 children, up from around two. The baby boom then ended as abruptly as it arrived, in the 1960s. Fertility rates quickly returned to the vicinity of 2.0 and stabilized. Other countries saw similar trends around the same time.

The baby boom begs the question: if the story of the popular birth control movement is one of people gradually awarding moral priority to history over eternity, worldiness over transcendence, particularism over organicism, pragmatism over idealism, and so on, how could all these ideals have suddenly reversed course?

Before considering this question it is important to note that the baby boom was largely a "marriage boom." Family size did not balloon in the postwar years. Instead, beginning in the late 1930s, more people married and subsequently had moderate-sized families of two and sometimes more children. Families became slightly larger on average, but the boom's foundation was a new desire for small to moderately sized families, not large ones. In that sense the boom is not as perplexing as it might otherwise seem.[58]

The underlying causes of this shift remain poorly understood. Most scholars emphasize the sudden uptick in economic opportunity brought about by the Second World War. Couples who had postponed marriage and childbearing in hard times began opting for a small family rather than no family at all. As these cautious cohorts began having children, they were joined by younger newlyweds for whom the rebounding economy offered security, even luxury, in relation to childhood expectations set during the Depression.[59]

Historians have noted the gendered dimensions of this economic story. After 1945 the single-earner or "male breadwinner" family – long an ideal – became economically feasible for a wider range of Americans. Husbands took pride in their ability to provide for a wife and multiple children. Though large proportions of women continued to work, many found themselves pushed or pulled into the socially prescribed role of full-time homemaker. "Experts called upon women to embrace domesticity in service to the nation," Elaine Tyler May writes. "Along with the baby boom came intense and widespread endorsement of pronatalism." Baby-boosting formed part of a postwar security culture in which settled family life, and especially motherhood, represented a contribution to national development and safety.[60]

Essential as these economic and domestic factors surely were, they have provoked searching questions. If postwar prosperity was the key to rebounding fertility, why did couples begin to "cast caution aside," as one columnist observed in 1935, in the 1930s? Why had earlier surges in prosperity, pronatalism, or gender conservatism failed to spark higher fertility? If Depression-related postponement was the issue, why did countries such as the U.S., Canada, and Australia see their booms endure into the 1960s? If the general "spread of family-centered values played an important part," as Andrew Cherlin speculates, why did these values flourish?[61]

These open questions have directed attention to the boom's origins in the prewar world. No American alive in the 1920s or '30s would have predicted a sudden, sustained increase in fertility rates. Everyone, including experts, was caught off guard by the boom. Yet Americans' ways of thinking about childbearing *before* the boom hint at possible explanations for the abrupt shift in behavior that followed.

First, memory of prewar demographic decline narratives may have played a role in the fertility rebound. Simmering anxiety about long-term fertility decline continued well into the 1940s, despite a widespread sense of helplessness before "modern" demands. It would have been difficult for any enfranchised American to live through the first few decades of the twentieth century – or have parents who did – without encountering the idea that birthrates were tending dangerously towards zero. The sense that past generations' grimly impractical survival politics had become more realizable amid rising prosperity may have contributed to the boom.

Second, the replacement of unsettling economic and social flux with the sharper existential threat of war may have produced a resurgence of social vitalism. Similar phenomena have occurred elsewhere. In Palestine during the first intifada, Marwan Khawaja observes, "intensification of the sense of collective identity, and altruism, at the expense of the individual," produced a new demand for parenthood. America was gripped by similar sentiments during and after World War Two. It may be that whereas a large family seemed dangerously out of touch with the times in the 1930s, later

decades' triumphalism made reproductive *caution* seem like a l
more fearful times. Demonstrating an ability to care for childɪ
a status symbol; an emblem of stable prosperity rather than a ɪ
Familism became self-conscious and self-reinforcing: everyone w
everyone commented on it; everyone applauded it. The perceive
of history, in other words, may have temporarily reversed.[62]

More practically, the boom coincided with mass suburbanization.
Early twentieth-century Americans saw the crowding and pressures of
"city life" as a major cause of small families. Housing costs, landlord
discrimination, weak communal norms, and the pace of urban life combined to make children less welcome in cities than in the countryside.
"Our modern cities, like ancient cities, will stand forth as the great
destroyers of men," argued a 1931 U.S. Census monograph on birth
control. "The city does not yet recognize the child as a citizen of the
community." Race suicide was actually "urban suicide."[63]

After the war, the sudden affordability of suburban bungalows, and
cars to reach them, offered families more physical space. For millions of
families, having a third child no longer meant adding a third bed to a small
room in a cramped apartment. More important, perhaps, a move to the
suburbs offered a sense of new *possibility* to millions of urban families.
"Suburbanization gave a majority of Americans for the first time ever the
opportunity to become people 'of property,'" as Lizabeth Cohen writes.
In prewar cities most families had rented homes close to their workplaces.
When government-subsidized homeownership, cheap automobiles, and
free highways made suburban living easier, many Americans felt they had
crossed a threshold into a freer and more promising life.[64]

As banal as a move from Chicago to Oak Park may seem, physical
migration can have psychic and demographic consequences. In agrarian
societies, families suddenly arriving on abundant frontier land typically
have more children than families in more densely settled areas. This
"initial frontier effect" – strong in the nineteenth-century American
west, among other places – is built on a perception of new opportunity
for both parents and children. In newly settled parts of New York state,
Mary P. Ryan writes, couples migrating from relatively crowded New
England counted themselves "blessed with abundant farmlands on which
to settle their sons," and raised larger families than their parents. This
effect faded in subsequent generations as children and grandchildren,
accustomed to their now-settled community, did not perceive the same
"bright promise [as] when it was being settled." They limited their fertility
accordingly.[65]

A parallel effect might easily have worked on Americans leaving cramped apartments for the "wholesome out-of-door life on a half-acre," as the *Los Angeles Times* put it in 1932. Families who gained that half-acre shared "a sense of security and optimism not to be found among workers cooped up in city houses or apartments." This suburban idyll appealed most to the groups whose reproductive behavior changed most with the baby boom: upwardly mobile, white, working-to-middle-class people. (Blue-collar workers who remained in cities, in laboring jobs, were less likely to join in the boom.) Meanwhile, "the move to the single-family suburban house represented for millions a great leap forward into the middle class," as Cherlin writes. Life in the suburbs meant buying into a piece of a rejuvenated American mythos, contributing to a collective project that promised a better life for oneself and as many children as one could raise.[66]

Finally, quite apart from the extra bedrooms of sprawling ranch houses and bungalows, land ownership allowed new suburbanites to feel romantically embedded in nature. The naturalness and healthiness of suburban homes with yards and gardens – particularly for children – had long been among their major selling points. Attaining this pastoral ideal may have encouraged optimism about childrearing among new suburbanites. "Most working class people," Lee Rainwater wrote of Chicagoans and Cincinnatians he interviewed in the late 1950s, "have a deep, not consciously formulated belief that nature 'wants' people to have many children and that when they limit the number of children they go against nature, although doing so may be legitimate in terms of the realities of life." It may be that ordinary naturists found in the manicured lawns and winding parkways of suburbia a happy convergence of visible flora with the natural interest in procreation. Like other promises of the new suburban life, this escape to nature may have fleetingly helped make familism seem like the way of the present and future.[67]

Evidence from the preboom years can only be suggestive. Nevertheless, it would seem that the baby boom demonstrates the malleability of historical memory. People construct narratives to describe communal pasts, and alter their behavior to enact or defy history. Those trajectories are not based on complex empirical study, and can be quickly rearranged in response to individuals' recent experience. In the case of the baby boom, many Americans appear to have done just that. The sudden convergence of crisis-based communitarianism, material opportunity, and expansion onto the land seems to have encouraged Americans to reject, for a time, the wary, risk-averse, besieged individualism of their parents and grandparents.

4

Dear Friend

Citizen Letters to Birth Controllers

Unto the woman he said, I will greatly multiply thy sorrow and thy conception; in sorrow thou shalt bring forth children.

Genesis 3:16

Whenever I am discouraged I go to these letters as to a wellspring which
sends me on reheartened. They make me realize with increasing intensity
that whoever kindles a spark of hope in the breast of another cannot shirk
the duty of keeping it alive.

Margaret Sanger (1938)[1]

**

"What are contraceptives?" a Kansas woman asked Margaret Sanger
in 1925. "I never heard of anything like that until I read your book."
The woman was twenty-one years old and raising a young daughter.
"Walking through hundreds of miles of fire could not have been as
what I suffered for her." She had considered separating from her
husband in order to avoid more pregnancies, as other women did,
but hoped she could avoid that. She distrusted abortifacient "dope."
"The doctors around here say there isn't anything that won't kill you
after you've used it for a while," she wrote. Was there a better way?
"I am writing for help," she told Sanger. "Lincoln freed the Negro
slaves, but who (if not you) is going to free women from the bonds of
slavery that hold them?"[2]

Thousands of Americans, mostly women with children, wrote similar
letters to Sanger and other birth controllers between the 1910s and 1930s.
Sanger preserved hundreds of them, publishing them in the 1928 com-
pendium *Motherhood in Bondage* and in *Birth Control Review*,
a monthly journal she edited. At the heart of most of these "client" letters

91

were simple requests for information: how can I stop having babies? What is the best way to have them less frequently? What is "the secret of birth control"? Requests were usually accompanied by an outline of the writer's circumstances, justifying the appeal.

Sanger's letters tell the story of America's contraceptive have-nots: the women (and some men) who were least satisfied with their family-limiting options and most motivated to improve them. For these Americans contraception was an immediate need rather than an abstract cause. It was neither the social panacea promoted by activists nor the fatal sin denounced by pronatalists. Right and wrong in birth control was situational – not a "social question" but one of immediate personal circumstances weighed against local community norms.

By the 1920s, when most of the letters were written, such have-nots did not represent a large part of the U.S. adult population. Though Sanger promoted the idea that untold numbers of American women were completely uninformed as to effective birth control methods, she exaggerated. Nineteen of every twenty women visiting Sanger's New York clinic in the 1920s reported prior contraceptive use, and steadily declining birthrates after 1800 indicate the raw effectiveness of marketplace and "folk" methods. Even among writers dissatisfied enough to petition Sanger in a letter, 42 percent alluded to specific methods of controlling family size already known to them. In the far more numerous letters *not* selected for Sanger's publications, meanwhile, most writers addressed themselves as they would to a simple dispensary, casually inquiring as to the availability of any new and improved method. Stark ignorance was rare.[3]

Sanger's letters nevertheless shed light on how and why Americans sought birth control information, and how the citizen movement related to the better-remembered activist one. Desperate correspondents also serve as a reminder that even as the U.S. fertility transition neared completion, Americans did not have *equal* access to convenient, effective contraception. As late as the 1930s, some young couples had no idea how to prevent births without physical separation. Others relied on dangerous abortifacients or other unsatisfactory methods. The mass movement bypassed thousands of people who, for one reason or another, never talked about family limitation with the right friend, relative, doctor, or pharmacist, or never built up the courage to talk about it at all.

Each letter stands as a testament to activists' accomplishments – if not as leaders or representative agents of the popular movement, then as its technicians and heralds. Sanger's American Birth Control League (ABCL) attracted hundreds of thousands of writers. It directed many of them to sympathetic doctors and clinics, and away from relatively dangerous, ineffective, or inconvenient methods. Mere knowledge of the League's existence fomented discontent with existing birth control options. Through publicity generated by Sanger and others, Americans were introduced to the possibility that distant experts might possess new, scientific knowledge on the old question of how to prevent unwanted children. That sort of health- and wealth-making knowledge seemed part of the promise of modern life, and a multitude sought it.

THE LETTERS

Of the 556 letters that form the basis for this chapter, two-thirds were addressed to Sanger and printed in *Birth Control Review* between 1918 and 1925. The remaining third of letters were never published and serve to contextualize Sanger's relatively dramatic selections. Of these, 103 went to Sanger's fellow activist Mary Ware Dennett, mostly between 1927 and 1931, and eighty to the Birth Control League of Massachusetts (BCLM) – one of the ABCL's independent affiliates – between 1932 and 1936. Supplementary quotations and context come from letters Sanger published in *Motherhood in Bondage*.[4]

Writers' socioeconomic self-identifications (Table A.4) and English usage suggest a population poorer, more rural, and less tutored than the middle-class moralists represented in urban newspapers. Writers also self-selected: all were dissatisfied with their existing contraceptive options; none strongly objected to contraception on principle; all were literate in English and willing to pay postage in exchange for the uncertain possibility of assistance; none balked at addressing a stranger about intimate issues; and all were sufficiently unaware of the Comstock laws, or unbothered by them, to ask for information that was banned in some states and illegal to provide by U.S. mail.[5]

Though Sanger preserved over a thousand letters in total – a likely majority of all firsthand U.S. testimony of its kind – she selected the surviving letters from a base numbering in the hundreds of thousands. Sanger claimed her selections were representative of the bulk from which they came. But so relentless was their pathos that even sympathetic *Birth Control Review* readers occasionally wondered if the letters were completely genuine. To such queries Sanger wrote: "Every letter that has ever been printed in our pages [represents] the actual and literal utterances of the woman who appeals for aid." "The records I have chosen for publication are by no means exceptional," she added in *Motherhood in*

Bondage. "I have not picked them out to harrow the finer feelings of the readers, but rather because they are typical of a certain definite phase of enslaved motherhood in America."[6]

Sanger was "never a slave to the literal truth," as Margaret Marsh has noted, and while she did not fabricate letters or significantly edit them, she certainly chose letters based on their special poignancy and ability to aid her movement. Writers who were poor, female, married, and already had multiple children were especially likely to be selected. Ill health or a professed a desire to help one's offspring (not oneself) also increased a writer's chances of inclusion. In some cases, in fact, Sanger may have solicited longer and more dramatic letters from writers whose initial queries were short and matter-of-fact. Replying to an Indiana man whose three-sentence request for "full particulars" on birth control mentioned only an unspecified "serious problem" within his home, Sanger encouraged the man to "Tell me something of your circumstances, how many children you have, etc."[7]

Unpublished letters strongly suggest that large majorities of all letters to contraceptive agencies were, in fact, brief and matter-of-fact – dashed off with an eye to bringing their writer up to date on the latest contraceptive options, not acquiring them for the first time. Few desperately required help that would secure their family's basic welfare. "Dear Friend, Enclosed you will find two dollars for which I want to ask you to kindly mail me your pamphlet on 'Birth Control.' Thanking you kindly, [redacted]," read one typical unpublished letter. After Sanger's departure as president of the ABCL, the League commissioned an analysis of the 7,039 letters it received over a one-year period in 1931–1932. "The strongest impression," concluded the report, "was the general attitude of the writers. Whether they were men or women, they assumed that the information was available and could be had for the taking." Fifty-nine percent provided no justification for their request, such as health or financial problems. The study drily noted the contrast between these writers' nonchalance and the "personal and emotional pleas" compiled in Sanger's *Motherhood in Bondage.*[8]

It is nevertheless clear that the poignant circumstances highlighted in Sanger's publications were no great rarity. Roughly a tenth of the unpublished letters would have been plausible candidates for publication, as would similar proportions of petitions to agencies such as the U.S. Children's Bureau, the Cleveland Maternal Health Association, and various European birth control organizations. Sanger probably received between 200,000 and 300,000 letters from 1915 to 1940, so if even a tenth of her correspondents registered dire need, then the published "crisis" letters could easily represent tens of thousands of letters that do not survive. How many silent sufferers in turn may be represented by *those* letters can only be guessed. There can be little doubt, in any case, that writers' predicaments were echoed in milder form by millions of people in other times and places.[9]

JUSTIFYING BIRTH CONTROL

"We ain't living – just merely existing, that's all," wrote a Wisconsin mother of ten to Sanger. "It sure is a task to bring up a large family, as you ain't able to send them to school, or learn a trade ... They have to start in life by working when they are twelve years old, to help buy their clothes. But what's a poor woman going to do?" Another mother, "doubly ruptured" and "very much run down" after five pregnancies, feared her kidney problems would not allow her to survive another child. But "as I am a married woman," she wrote, "I suppose I'll have to have more until finally I don't exist." An alcoholic's wife declared simply, "If you don't help me I will take poison and kill myself."[10]

The desperate shared with the merely curious an overriding concern with two issues: health (including mental well-being) and economic security. Two-thirds of Sanger's correspondents, and half of Dennett's, justified their requests solely on one or both of these grounds (Table A.5). No other issues were nearly so important.[11]

Practical and urgent as these rationales were, writers still faced moral dilemmas in expressing them. Even in the relatively permissive 1920s and 1930s, and even among people writing privately to sympathetic activists, unsteady income or extreme exhaustion did not constitute self-evident justification for fertility control. Many have-nots lived in socially conservative communities where taboos on reproductive control remained strong. Writers felt compelled to explain their actions in light of personal and local norms. These justifications help illuminate the shifting moral landscape around birth control.

Writers went out of their way to establish that they had at least one child: 97 percent of Sanger's writers enumerated children under their care (3.6 on average) as did 77 percent of Dennett's (2.4). Writers with four or more children tended to see their existing broods as justifications in their own right, as did some with three. "My case is not very tragic," wrote one mother of four, "but all the same I badly need Birth Control ... they are more than enough – bless 'em." Mothers enumerated stillborn and deceased children alongside their living ones, emphasizing the frequency of their pregnancies. Parents of large families, meanwhile, congratulated themselves on having done their duty to "the commonwealth," "the race," "the world," or "God and country" – then asked for advice on capping this contribution. "We were always glad and willing to bring up our share of babies and are proud of the record," wrote one man, "but we think eleven is really more than our share."[12]

Since no consensus existed on the ideal meeting point of child numbers, material circumstances, and contraceptive need, writers with families of all sizes tended to emphasize well-received justifications for birth control, especially acute physical illness and poverty. Above all, American women had come to expect more in the realms of health, well-being, and wealth. They were aware of advancing minimum standards in medicine, material life, and contraceptive technology, and increasingly expected access to those benefits.

Health

Dire health threats – physical, mental, or both – offered a particularly potent form of justification. Some of the most desperate writers were women with histories of pregnancy-related ailments: hemorrhage, paralysis, "inflammation and misplaced organs," lost legs, "milk legs," ruined posture, perpetual itches, and bloating so severe it would not allow some women to open their eyes or put on their shoes. Others had prior conditions that would complicate pregnancy: tuberculosis, gall stones, goiters, anemia, epilepsy, small stature, weak hearts, asthma, high blood pressure, "diseased ovaries," pneumonia, St. Vitus dance, kidney problems, back problems, blood problems, "poisoned milk." A farmer's wife in Oklahoma "spit up two gallons of blood" during one pregnancy; another woman was enshrouded by a "white foamy mist which I could not see through." Some wanted to avoid toxic abortifacients or impregnation by syphilitic husbands. Others – at a time when obstetric anesthesia was mostly confined to the well-to-do – found the pain of childbearing unbearable. "I think I have been down the valley of death enough times," wrote one mother.[13]

Even the healthiest women faced the possibility of death with each pregnancy. As late as 1925, one woman died for every 154 who survived childbirth in the United States – roughly twenty times the rates attained later in the century. Most Americans would have known, or heard of, a woman close to them who had died in this way. The threat of pregnancy-related death or disability was constant and produced intense physical and mental suffering.[14]

Though doctors played an important role in the organized birth control movement, it is easy to overlook the impact of rising physical health expectations among everyday birth control users. Health concerns motivated many of the most desperate writers, and more important, offered women in particular a way to shift attention from moral contingencies to physical realities. Even in cases where the condition in question was not life-threatening, mothers found it easier to defend their physical integrity than less tangible measures of well-being. This was especially true as medical advancements made bodily suffering appear less inevitable. Mothers were as socially valuable as their children, after all, and both deserved modern medicine's full array of protections.[15]

There was nothing new about women's desire to avoid pregnancy-related death or injury, of course. But before medical advances in the decades around 1900, women had been expected to accept pregnancy's risks and pains dutifully, as a fact of life. Doctors attending births sometimes found themselves "under the more or less close scrutiny of relatives" who believed "nature should be allowed to take her course unaided, and that interference of any sort is flying in the face of Providence." Stoicism in the face of pregnancy's risks seemed a basic prerequisite of social reproduction. "All honor is due the man ... who as a soldier does his full duty in war, but even more honor is due the mother," intoned Theodore Roosevelt, using a common analogy. "The birth pangs make all men the debtors of all women."[16]

By the 1920s this self-sacrificing ideal seemed outdated. The primacy of nature in childbirth was weakening. Women increasingly demanded the sanitary measures, anesthesia, and close medical attention of a hospital birth. Preventing dangerous births went hand in hand with minimizing the trauma and risk of too-frequent pregnancies. Many looked back in horror on the resigned suffering of their forbearers. "I do not want a half-dozen children," wrote a Kansas newlywed, the oldest of six siblings, recalling her worn-down mother. "I simply will shoot myself if I have to go through what she did." Repeated, ill-spaced, blindly dutiful pregnancies were the way of the past.[17]

This preventative sensibility was an important factor in birth control's legitimation. It emerged in part because of larger individualizing trends. Medical birth control became easier to justify as individual lives – women's lives in particular – gained greater inherent value. Prevention reflected higher general expectations for managing health risks, and the increasing prestige and reach of scientific medicine. Suffering and death no longer seemed like eternal preconditions of a sustainable society; this transition allowed reproduction to be framed more as a technical issue and less as a moral one. Childbirth could be managed by experts in the same way as other modern risks. Many advice-seekers accordingly framed their requests as medical inquiries – some going so far as to address Sanger and Dennett as "Doctor," though neither was a physician. About a quarter reported seeking doctors' help in their previous efforts at fertility control (Table A.6), usually without success. Patients expected not just advice, but good advice – such as a prescription they could take to a specific pharmacy. Instead, they often had doctors who refused to provide contraceptive advice or recommended expensive, difficult, or ineffective methods. These inadequacies caused patients considerable distress and annoyance. "Every time I have a baby the Dr and nurse tell me I have had enough," wrote a mother of five, "but when I ask them what I can do not to have any more, they laugh at me." A father of four from Montana complained that he had "been to the best doctors in my town and the best doctor in the nearest city, and if they gave me any advice at all it was something that did not work out." Doctors who merely referred patients to the informal market with a wink and smile, as some did, risked losing business.[18]

Requests for birth control advice, indeed, were nothing new for physicians of the 1920s and '30s. "How often have we been approached by young men on the eve of marriage," a Texas doctor complained to his colleagues in 1903, "asking us if there is not some way in which their wives can be prevented from having children; that they are not prepared to have children just now?" As long as birth control's moral status remained unresolved in their communities, however, doctors had to balance patients' demands against the desire to appear professional and virtuous. Prescribing birth control often meant delving into unofficial knowledge from the doctor's own life experience, since it was not until the 1930s that contraceptive instruction became common in medical schools. Recommending informal methods could appear inexpert. Some doctors associated contraception with hucksters, quacks, and abortionists, or confined their recommendations to "natural" methods such as continence or rhythm. Even as childbirth became medicalized – the proportion of hospital births rose from 5 percent to 75 percent between 1900 and 1939 – the combination of local moral uncertainty and wary professionalism discouraged some doctors from dispensing advice. "Maybe someday it will be 'professional' to give information on birth control," an Alabama woman complained to Sanger in 1925.[19]

As a result doctors did not monopolize the contraceptive markets in the early twentieth century; nor were they necessarily at the vanguard of contraceptive technology. "Until the FDA approved prescription-only oral contraceptives in 1960," as Andrea Tone writes, "a majority of Americans, including the most affluent, acquired birth control over the counter, not from doctors."[20]

Still, enough doctors were dispensing enough effective advice to make the medical profession an increasingly important clearinghouse for birth control information. In 1917 a pharmaceutical journal advised druggists who wished to avoid the "indiscriminate sale" of contraceptives simply to ask for a prescription, which most doctors would happily provide. A Texas doctor told the birth control campaigner James Cooper in 1927 that it was her "practice, as it is, no doubt, that of every other gynecologist and obstetrician, to give contraceptive advice to patients when your deliberate judgment indicates to you that the case requires it." When the *Medical Journal and Record* surveyed its readers on birth control in 1928 – asking their opinion of providing contraception for "therapeutic," "economic," "eugenic," or "euthenic" reasons – just 5 percent of over 300 respondents opposed providing contraceptive advice under any of these circumstances. Forty percent found birth control appropriate for at least one of the listed reasons, and the remaining 55 percent favored it for all four reasons mentioned. "Doctors more and more are willing to advise people," Dennett wrote in 1929.[21]

Birth control's "medicalization" has long been associated with Margaret Sanger: her "efforts to win over the medical establishment" helped male doctors assume duties previously performed by midwives and female social circles, causing "a loss of female control and feminist consciousness" in matters of family limitation and laying the groundwork for medical control over hormonal contraception once it became available. Letters to birth controllers suggest a more popular medicalization process. As the risks of repeated pregnancy began to seem less inevitable, Americans gained confidence in asking their doctors for birth control advice. Sensing the popularity and moral heft of this view, Sanger may actually have followed her correspondents in "medicalizing" birth control. "The letters have had a powerful effect on Mrs. Sanger," as a former ABCL field worker observed in 1929: "the impact of these stories of suffering has engendered an emphasis on the humanitarian health aspects of the problem."[22]

Well-Being

Maladies of the body and spirit were often inseparable. Physical jeopardy and anxiety about future pregnancies combined to trap women in malaise and depression: "almost broken down," "sick and worn out," "tired and nervous," as dozens described themselves. Heavy day-to-day domestic duties exacerbated physical vulnerability and mental uncertainty, causing comprehensive exhaustion. Higher expectations for holistic well-being, meanwhile, made this exhaustion too great to bear. Mothers felt unable to raise children properly or even remain sane, and begged for a foolproof way to avoid more responsibilities. "My health isn't any good, I am simply a nervous wreck," wrote a mother of six, typically.[23]

Expecting peace of mind, not just bodily health, left mothers more open to criticism. In Roosevelt's time pronatalists had sought to associate small families with neurasthenia and other ailments that straddled the line between medical problems and moral failings. A worn-out mother deserved no less sympathy than a worn-out soldier, but also no more. This idea still held considerable sway in the 1920s and '30s. "The pressure of custom and tradition combined has made me feel a coward, criminal and traitor," wrote a mother who feared death in pregnancy, "and yet stronger than this pressure is my determination to remain with the baby for whom I have paid so high a price."[24]

Even in addressing Sanger, mothers like this one felt uncomfortable complaining of mental difficulties unless they were very severe. Writers repeatedly declared themselves close to insanity or suicide. "It seems that if I were to have another one soon that death would be welcome," a farm woman wrote. "I am so nervous and these five children are even more than I can handle alone as I can't afford help. It worries me now to see them neglected." Waiting for a menstrual cycle was "mental torture" for many writers. "I just live in misery until my monthly comes around," wrote a characteristically distraught Kansas woman. "My life is just one doubt and fear after another." Writers routinely proclaimed that they would "rather die" than go through another pregnancy.[25]

Unpublished writers were less apologetic in their pursuit of personal well-being. Reproduction was to be made compatible with happiness, not the other way around. "I have been married 10 months and oh! so very happy," wrote a Los Angeles woman who "got up the courage" to write to Dennett after missing a period.

Would you tell us how to avoid children until we are ready for them? We are both very young and both working, and could not possibly afford babies right now . . .

We do want to stay happy and not end up the way a lot of marriages do. This worry is bothering me to the extent of my becoming a little nervous wreck on that subject. Right now I am doing any thing any one advises, if I am a day overdue in menstruation I doctor up immediately, until I am afraid I am really hurting my health.

The desire to *feel* well, not just physically survive, was not necessarily utopian or romantic. Many writers wanted nothing more than moderate relief from deep unhappiness. Still, rather than assuming the presence of children and dutifully building lives around their care – the traditional purpose of marriage – advice-seekers sought to build lives in which excess children would not diminish a felt sense of mental, physical, and material well-being. "Help me regain my health and enjoy life as I deserve," asked a West Virginia farm wife.[26]

Even in Sanger's published letters, writers did not confine themselves entirely to the physical threats of death or hunger. "Postmaterial" benefits like personal attractiveness, leisure, fulfilling work, or pleasurable sex crop up around the edges of letters focused mostly on dire poverty, ill-health, or debilitating exhaustion. Some women feel haggard and unattractive as a result of repeated maternity. "I am only twenty-two years old, but look thirty-two and feel about fifty." They suffered from crumbling teeth, graying hair, and varicose veins, and worried they would lose their husbands to younger-seeming women. "I am a little over twenty-four and already skinny, yellow and so funny looking and I want to hold my husband's love." "This tells the story – a radiant bride at 20; at 25 what? If you could see me you would not have to guess."[27]

Others wanted to maintain youthful freedoms. "How I would love to enjoy myself still!" wrote one. "My heart is just craving for good times, like going to dances and parties." A married couple wanted "nothing to mar our happiness." Older women regretted that they had never known youthful freedoms because of unplanned pregnancies. A widowed cotton-picker with six children "would have given worlds ... for some way to have governed the size of my family when I was young. [I] could have made something of myself, besides a child bearing machine and a drudge."[28]

Employment, too, offered a path to greater self-fulfillment. "I have ambitions too numerous to mention and a high school education for a basis to work," wrote a new bride with interests in music and mechanical drawing. A young Minnesotan had "an opportunity for marriage, but, like most girls, I dislike the possibility of having to settle down and accept the responsibilities of rearing a family." She hoped to continue her job as a teacher; a pregnancy would result in her dismissal.[29]

Finally, writers wanted sex without the penalties of abortion or abstinence. Abortions, self-administered or assisted, weighed on women physically and psychologically. "Only three weeks ago I went to a doctor and got rid of one, the second time I have been guilty of this awful crime," wrote a Missouri woman. "I have come to the point where I refuse to be tied down again, and that means doing the thing I dread for the sake of my health and the awful feeling that I am a murderer." This combination of hard pragmatism, self-recrimination, and fear of abortion-related death was typical of dozens of writers. "Every now and again they go to a doctor and get rid of one," wrote a mother of her three daughters, "and someday I think it will kill them but they say they don't care for they will be better dead than to live in hell with a big family and nothing to raise them on."[30]

Abstinence was also intolerable for some couples. Writers complained of ill tempers, quarrels, and even mutual hatred as one or both partners tried to enforce periods of celibacy. A ship's captain from Maine returned home after months at sea to find his wife "very wrought up and scared," and physically blocking their front door, having been told by her doctor that she would not survive a seventh child. "I am not going to live with you as a man and wife any longer," she shouted through the door. "You can do as you please; get a divorce or anything, but we are done." The man was able to enter his home only by agreeing to sleep apart from his wife for the few days he was home each year. This stalemate made him increasingly jealous and irritable. "I still love my wife and want to be a true husband," he told Sanger, "but as I am a still young man what can I do? . . . Will you help us to live a natural life again?"[31]

Similar scenarios encouraged other men to separate from their families for the sake of fertility control. One took work "about seven thousand miles" from his wife so that his children could be educated properly. Another wrote: "I have been separated from my dear wife and son . . . twelve months . . . in the pretense of building them a home on the Western prairies of Canada." He would move back if he could be sure his family would not grow. Some men simply abandoned their homes rather than face the prospect of continually growing family. Those who stayed sometimes turned to sex outside marriage, especially with prostitutes, as a way of easing the strain of abstinence within marriage. "There is an ill-famed house a few streets from us," wrote a distraught wife who had suffered four births and nine abortions. "Last Saturday evening . . . I took my daughters and went for a walk. I saw my husband and another man go in this house. I have never let my husband know I saw him go there, but I feel heartbroken over it."[32]

Writers who disliked abstinence did not necessarily take a romantic view of sexuality. Though Sanger and Dennett framed sexual expression as a path to emotional and spiritual rewards, writers looked to manage sex's inevitability. Though some may have hoped for deeper sexual fulfillment once their day-to-day worries were appeased, birth control's ground-level legitimation relied less on any romantic sexuality than on a more practical expectation of control over sex as a fact of life. "My husband is very kind but he is very healthy," explained one mother.[33]

Adjusting family size to happiness, not the other way around, remained morally fraught well past the 1920s and '30s. Mental trials, exhaustion, and unhappiness were not self-evident justifications for limiting the family. Conditions of the spirit commanded less sympathy than those of the body. Despite that, contraceptive have-nots claimed a right to happiness, echoing popular moralists in the press. Even in the relatively conservative communities from which Sanger's correspondents wrote, the modern order promised greater control over one's environment, relief from suffering, and the renegotiation of timeless constraints on the human will.

Living Standards

Deep poverty, like severe illness, could serve as a safe and self-evident justification for contraception, almost regardless of family size. Few moralists worried that their communities' poorest residents were not producing enough children.[34]

The majority of writers were not desperately poor, however. Even among Sanger's hand-picked unfortunates, only 20 percent professed day-to-day struggles to make ends meet. Unpublished writers were even less likely to report severe poverty. The ABCL's study of its 1931–1932 correspondence found that just 16 percent of writers appeared "not well off" – meaning their letters "seemed to indicate that economically they were or might become wards of the state" – while the rest were, by degrees, "privileged."[35]

Under the old, duty-centered pronatal ideals, it would have been difficult for most of these writers to make an economic case for birth control. With the exception of large families that struggled with essentials like food and shelter, couples could expect little moral support for any decision to prioritize additional material comforts over additional children.

"The dainty home will pass to strangers after the aged and lonely inhabitants have drained to the bitter dregs their selfish draught," as a Roosevelt-era pronatalist wrote. "Our forefathers led a simple life. They were strangers to luxury."[36]

Suspicion of economically motivated birth control persisted in weakened form through the 1920s and '30s. Many hospitals and clinics, for example, began dispensing contraceptives in the early twentieth century – but only to "medical" cases, not "economic" ones. Some clinicians interpreted medical need very broadly, to include dire poverty, but others were less bold. Though the boundaries of illegitimate "luxury" had been rolled back, nobody was sure how far. Even in letters to Sanger – known for her expansive view of birth control's moral acceptability – many writers remained skittish and defensive, elaborating on their poverty at length.[37]

Nervousness about economic birth control was nevertheless waning. In place of the old deference to "simplicity," Americans embraced two standards with increasing confidence. First, children deserved an upbringing no *less* comfortable than that of their parents, regardless of their parents' economic status. Adults might defer childbearing if they could not match the housing, education, or consumption standards they had enjoyed as children.

Second and more controversially, parents might seek socioeconomic *advancement* through family limitation – not just escape from poverty, but upward mobility within the ranks of the broad middle class. Though that idea remained associated with selfishness and luxury, a handful of writers forthrightly adopted it. Keeping the family small, a German immigrant father wrote, was "the only way to get ahead." Once a couple had two children, writers tended to award moral priority to economic advancement over the raising of additional children, when these values came into conflict. "It isn't because we are selfish or extravagant that we don't want any more children," wrote one couple. "It is because we really can't afford them, if we are to give these two a better education than we had ourselves." A father of eight wrote in a similar vein: "If we had, say, two ... I might have had a business of my own instead of having to work for someone else at fifty ... Even now we can't save anything." The man's sons were now following his example and marrying young. He hoped Sanger could spare them his disappointments.[38]

Some parents, indeed, were more concerned with appearing backward than luxurious. "What a burning shame," wrote a mother of four, "when I think how rearing children has brought us down from what we were."

A mother of eight lamented that "ignorance on this important subject has put me where I am. None of my friends ever told me anything, and I'm sure they knew for they are married as long as I am, and have only one or two children, have ideal homes and everything to their hearts' content." Mothers complained that they were not able to dress their children as well as parents who concentrated their income on fewer children. A woman in Pennsylvania declared that she would rather see her daughters "dead" than living "like others in large families."[39]

Some of the most ardent writers blamed the material deprivations of their own upbringings on their parents' excess childbearing. "I would rather die than bring as many children into the world as my mother did and have nothing to offer them," wrote an Oklahoma mother of two. Elderly mothers advised their children never to marry, and so avoid the burdens of motherhood. "Your father every time said 'In God's name it will grow up with the others, and better so than commit a sin,'" a Wisconsin man's mother told him. "My dear boy, learn you from the sufferings of your mother ... and procure for your children a happier youth than you had yourself."[40]

Looking back on youthful deprivation in a large family – and forward to a small and upwardly mobile one – was one essential way in which Americans came to associate birth control with progress. Though parents and grandparents may have been stoic and virtuous in the face of their family duties, from a modern vantage point their naturalness appeared irresponsible and inhumane. "I am the oldest of a family of eight, and my husband also comes from a family of eight," wrote a woman. "We don't want that size family ourselves, because we've seen the drudgery, the striving to make ends meet, that such a family brings."[41]

Like moralists in the daily press, advice seekers vaguely associated large families with religiosity, fatalism, and mysticism – and by extension, with a passing world in which ordinary people could expect to master fewer domains of life. Writers balked at the idea that "God wants me to have babies when I can't take care of them," as one mother wrote. A Wisconsin woman had, until reading one of Sanger's books, "believed it to be my duty to accept my fate as God's will. Now I know better." Catholic writers explicitly rejected their clergy's teachings. For writers of all faiths, the role of religion in birth control was an unpleasant legacy of a providential culture that had not always provided. "My grandmother had 12 children," explained a Pennsylvania mother of three, "and before the last three were born she was sick half the time, but she thought it was her duty [and] that God would not send more than could be taken care of some way, and that women who took things and done things to keep from having babies were to be shunned, they were the same as murderesses." Burdened with debt and anxious for "proper food and clothes," this woman and her husband had little trouble rejecting this view.[42]

For many of these writers, rising economic expectations across the generations developed in parallel with similar expectations concerning health. Thirty-one percent of writers who mentioned one of the two major justifications for fertility control – health and economy – also mentioned the other. "I do not believe God wants me to die bringing more unwanted babies to this 'all ready too full world.'" wrote a railway laborer's wife who wanted an alternative to condoms. "I love my family and I want to be well so I can help them get ahead." Just as mental and physical health worries often merged seamlessly in writers' minds, so too did health and economic anxieties.[43]

Pure socioeconomic ambition was nevertheless a major driver of fertility limitation in twentieth-century America. Parents' commitment to intergenerational prosperity was not a simple valuation of material comfort and devaluation of children. Instead, both children and comforts rose in value. Children remained a prized means of transcendence – all the more so as the perceived costs of raising them grew. The idea that they represented sublimation in nature or a "heritage of the Lord" became more popular, if anything, as alternatives grew more compelling. But there was a basic irony to this idea, since the real value of adding children to families of any size was clearly falling *relative* to other emblems of a good life.[44]

One of those emblems was the carefully tended family centered on children whose prospects for social advancement had not been unduly handicapped by their parents' irresponsibility. Giving children a tangible "leg up" was the central demand of the new parenthood. The dignities of material abundance seemed to grow more essential with each passing generation, but also harder to achieve with rising expectations. Uncertainty and the perpetual march of progress unburdened the living from the weight of eternity.

MOVEMENT CONSCIOUSNESS

Birth control activists shared the rank and file's concern with health and economic issues. "The deadly chain of misery is all too plain to anyone who takes the trouble to observe it," wrote Sanger. "Unwanted children, poverty, ill health, misery, death – these are the links in the chain." Activists promoted birth control as – among other things – a medical and especially economic panacea. They also sought to phase out family limitation by the unpopular methods of abortion and abstinence.[45]

But activists also prominently supported other goals – notably legal reform, eugenic improvement, the expansion of contraceptive clinics, egalitarian feminism, and sexual liberation – that sharply distinguished their concerns from those of the popular movement. Ordinary actors were vastly less interested in these issues than their putative leaders and representatives. Even in petitioning activists for practical advice – often after reading their literature or public statements – correspondents showed little engagement or concern with key activist themes. We would not expect writers to meditate at length on birth control's abstract social benefits, but we might expect passing allusions, particularly in the published letters. Instead, nearly all correspondents wrote with one eye to their own practical needs and the other to the moral standards of their communities.

Unpublished petitioners, indeed, often omitted even the most basic forms of moral justification. They wrote off-handedly, as if addressing a sympathetic family doctor or advice columnist rather than the leader of an embattled reform movement. They evinced little fear or knowledge of the Comstock laws, little hesitation to discuss the relative merits of birth control methods, and scant awareness of activist goals. Rather than a political movement struggling for a brighter future, they emphatically framed birth control as a present technical issue. Sanger and Dennett stood as distant urban experts who might provide useful information, or indeed might not. "I would like to obtain further information on birth control as I am a mill worker with three children and cant afford to have any more hoping for a reply, [signed]" read the entirety of a typical unpublished letter.[46]

Because many petitioners discovered Sanger or Dennett through books, pamphlets, or newspaper articles that laid out movement positions, Sanger in particular had some correspondents who evinced understanding and sympathy for movement goals. They celebrated Sanger's "brave fight for freedom," declaimed the "horrible laws" she sought to amend, and eagerly anticipated "knowledge of This Wonderful Cure of Scientific Birth Control." "If I were a millionaire I doubt if I could find any worthier philanthropy," an Iowa mother wrote. Sanger published many of their letters: 21 percent of her writers expressed some generalized moral support for the movement.[47]

Just 6 percent of the unpublished writers did the same, however. As surely as one writer thanked Dennett for addressing "this sexual problem which everybody seeks," another "had no idea so many people were interested in birth control." When it came to specific issues like legal reform or sexual freedom, overt support dwindled almost to zero. Many writers assumed *Birth Control Review* and other movement literature would consist of simple instructions on state-of-the-art techniques. When they found moral advocacy, they wrote to complain. "The enclosed paper was sold to me for 'Birth Control' and it is not what it was represented to be. What I want is 'Birth Control' explaining preventatives, etc. Kindly see that the proper paper is forwarded in its place."[48]

If writers viewed the ABCL as a dispensary rather than the embattled hub of a major moral reform movement, their practicality did not necessarily distinguish them from other rank-and-file constituencies. Social movement leaders supply an expansive vision. They translate quotidian concerns into the language of social policy, mediating between specific everyday challenges and political elites who think in broader strokes. Supporters need not articulate the cause's broadest goals. In the case of birth control, however, writers' practicality also reflected a movement where neither traditional authorities nor traditional reformers held great power or influence, and where activists and actors had different legitimating visions. The movement worked largely through undirected citizen action, and though leaders encouraged that action, the older and larger popular movement turned on its own independent axes.

Legal Reform

"Changing the so-called obscenity laws" was in Sanger's historical vision the "the third and most important of the epoch-making battles for general liberty upon American soil" (the first two were the American Revolution and the "battle for religious liberty"). Through the 1920s and '30s, Sanger became increasingly preoccupied with overturning Comstock laws at the state and federal level. Dennett too disliked the laws, though she was more forthcoming about the "unenforceable" and "unenforced" nature of birth control legislation. "Most people manage in various ways to avoid the law, in much the same way that they do in regard to the prohibition law," she told one advice seeker. Comstockery was for Dennett an embarrassment more than an obstacle. A "clean repeal" would be "dignified" and lessen political hypocrisy.[49]

There were nevertheless some practical reasons to seek the obscenity laws' repeal. The federal statute made it difficult to send specific contraceptive information to thousands of needy petitioners, and local laws sometimes caused puzzlement and hesitancy among doctors, pharmacists, and sympathetic public figures. In the 1910s a doctor named G. Alfred Elliot spent six years in federal prison for a violation of the postal law, and as late as 1913, a federal judge fined several hundred pharmacists between $200 and $500 for "advertising and sale of medicinal agents intended to produce abortion or prevent conception." Such incidents were notable for their rarity – the *Bulletin of Pharmacy* drily noted that the guilty pharmacists were "Sunday-school superintendents, church elders, and men of light and leading generally" – but sporadic strict enforcement created uncertainty. "One of the charming features of this law," wrote Upton Sinclair, "is that they will never tell you in advance what you may say, but leave you to say it and take your chances!"[50]

The obscenity laws' formal repeal, beginning in the 1930s, helped make birth control easier to discuss and distribute publicly. Sanger had an important role in that process. She convinced privately sympathetic doctors to support ongoing legal reform in public, lobbied state and federal lawmakers, and initiated important test cases. News of repeal created a safer environment for contraceptive exchange and facilitated the eventual development of oral contraceptives.

The laws nevertheless presented a greater problem for public advocates than private citizens. Correspondents were resoundingly unintimidated by the Comstock laws. Less than 10 percent showed any awareness or concern with them, despite the fact that responses to their requests would have been illegal. "I would like to know if the little rubbers that so many use are what is next by use of prevention," wrote one unpublished writer (Milan, Tennessee, five children); "I have the contraception methods of control but would like to known something to do to bring on the period" (Crossware, North Carolina, no family details); "I have heard of a few methods of prevention but none of them have appealed to me as being safe and practical" (Holdingford, Minnesota, no children). If anything, Comstockery appears to have cast less fearsome a shadow than Prohibition.[51]

Even for licensed businesses and medical practices, the laws provoked little fear. Pharmacists stocked myriad contraceptive devices and formulas, often in their front windows. The federal law "may not be generally known," one physician noted in 1921, and in any case belonged to a class of laws "pernicious as far as they are, or can be, carried out," and "foolish, in proportion to their measure of being a dead letter." When Francis Vreeland, a sociologist who conducted his field work as an ABCL

volunteer, asked himself why the movement received such "scant attention," he speculated "perhaps this is because, in practice, drug stores,
doctors and other available media have actually forwarded the movement
itself, while the League, more recent and with a more remote educational
and legislative task, has been less emphasized."[52]

Clinics and Contraceptive Provision

In 1923 Sanger set up her first permanent contraceptive clinic on Fifth
Avenue in New York City. Local leagues built similar facilities in other
cities. The clinics had several purposes. They would circumvent the postal
laws by providing on-site medical advice. They would promote female-
controlled contraceptive technologies like diaphragms, empowering
women. Finally, leaders hoped, they would serve a poor and overbur-
dened clientele, providing eugenic benefits. Sanger predicted the clinics
would precipitate a "remarkable increase in the wealth, stamina, stature
and longevity of the people."[53]

Legal reform and clinic-building consumed much of the organized
movement's resources in the 1920s – so much that some activists conceived of their mission as a series of trade-offs between these two goals.
After Sanger left the ABCL and formed a Committee on Federal
Legislation for Birth Control, for example, the League told supporters
that while amending or repealing the law was "desirable," because the law
did not "actually interfere" with the League's clinics, it was preferable to
focus on that "practical, constructive work."[54]

Clinics directly improved thousands of American women's lives.
Sanger's Manhattan clinic alone advised tens of thousands of patients in
the 1920s and '30s. By 1937 approximately 320 clinics were performing
similar services across the United States – though most were independent
offshoots of existing medical institutions. Between 1916 and 1939 these
several hundred clinics served approximately 300,000 women, some of
whom were deeply ignorant of any method of family limitation and had
borne children at an uncontrolled and punitive rate. The clinics' purpose
was to reach women like a "very weakly" mother of fifteen who wrote to
inquire about "the secret of how to control the birth rate," stood "in
deadly fear of more children," and did not "know of any way to prevent
pregnancy."[55]

Activists' emphasis on clinical provision nevertheless placed them at
a remove from the popular movement. "Birth control activists portrayed
their patients as ignorant of contraceptives," as Cathy Moran Hajo writes

in a history of the clinics, "but this was simply not true." A study of 714 patients at Sanger's clinic found that 93 percent had used some form of contraception before arrival: "most frequently ... coitus interruptus, condom, and douche, in the order named." Unpublished writers often alluded to the same popular triad, along with abortifacients and assisted abortions (Table A.7). Just 8 percent professed complete ignorance of any method of birth control. Some writers apologized for somehow failing to gain knowledge of contraceptive methods in adolescence or young adulthood. Many more weighed their options as knowledgeable consumers. "These patients were real women," Hajo writes of clinic visitors, "women with their own ideas, often strong ones, about birth control."[56]

The "scientific" birth control method prescribed by the ABCL's medical staff – a diaphragm with spermicidal jelly – was more effective over time than coitus interruptus, condoms, and especially douching. Used correctly and consistently, the diaphragm's effectiveness rate was over 90 percent over a given period, whereas in a study group of women from New York City, common folk methods decreased couples' chance of conception by 72–83 percent.[57]

Popular methods often won out, however. Diaphragms required fitting by a specialist, were expensive to replace, and often irritated both women and men. More than half of ABCL "clients" abandoned their diaphragms within two years of their clinic visit, usually because wife or husband found it bothersome during sex, or otherwise distasteful. Many women wanted advice on a simpler method "that could be purchased in drug stores or through the mail." Birth control advocates needed to make their prescriptions "less dissatisfying," wrote the author of a study on contraceptive provision in late-1930s West Virginia. "Most birth control services are fated to have little influence upon their patients because of the rigid restriction of advice to a single prescription. The present need is for more diversified contraceptive service."[58]

Some writers went to Sanger and Dennett with the specific intent of finding a worthy pharmacist. A New York woman wanted the address of a "reliable chemist" selling the "ProRace" pessary. From Albany, Georgia, another complained that "it certainly must be far easier to have prescriptions filled in New York than in these southern cities!" Contraceptives were available in Albany, but in "drugstore after drugstore" she could not find Mizpah pessaries, and her preferred pharmacy did not stock Aseptiken suppositories.[59]

Like doctors, pharmacists had an ambivalent relationship with birth control. Pharmacy associations sought to distance themselves from cheap and dangerous abortifacients in the late nineteenth and early twentieth centuries. But pharmacists continued selling profitable items like condoms, douches, antiseptics, and emmenagogues that had – in theory at least – medical purposes which shielded them from Comstock laws. Even abortifacients were not subject to strict condemnation: some pharmaceutical manuals cautioned against selling large quantities of well-known abortifacients like ergot, savin, and apiol without a doctor's prescription. But others simply noted the substances' potency in provoking menstruation, making no recommendations on the conditions of sale.[60]

More than a question of locating a clinic or doctor, writers tended to see access to contraception as a more basic question of modern know-how. They were sorry to trouble Sanger and Dennett with problems other people seemed to solve so easily. "My wife is of a modest and shy nature, which keeps her from obtaining any information from other sources, such as neighbors or woman friends," explained a father of four. An Iowa woman was afraid to "impose on" her nurse friends by asking for advice, and unable to "be plain to my doctor."[61]

Others were simply baffled by their inability to locate good information. "We tried very hard not to have any of the children, but luck or something seems to be against us," wrote a New York woman. Perhaps the impediments were related to class barriers, writers speculated. "Most rich women," wrote a woman who had been pregnant thirteen times, "know what to do because they can buy the information; it is poor things like myself that has to bear it all and then have sickly children." Rather than victims of unjust laws which barred them from high-quality clinical contraception, writers were more likely to see themselves as failed consumers who had not mastered modern contraceptive markets.[62]

Sanger was aware that the marketplace already provided many contraceptive services. Her first publication, the practical advice pamphlet *Family Limitation* (1914), noted the availability of many methods at drugstores. Clients at Sanger's short-lived Brooklyn clinic, in fact, were discharged to a nearby pharmacy after being told which kind of diaphragm and jelly to buy, and how to use them. But in her later capacity as an activist in need of donations and support, Sanger strove to paint effective contraception as a rarer phenomenon than it was. Clinics would fill this void. "When [a woman] is not given such information," Sanger wrote, "she is plunged blindly into married life and a few years is likely to find her with a large family, herself diseased and damaged, an unfit breeder of the unfit, and still ignorant!"[63]

Even within the organized movement, this sort of dramatization raised eyebrows. "The need for special birth control clinics is often questioned," wrote Caroline Robinson, an ABCL donor and author of a 1930 study of contraceptive clinics. "Is not every dispensary equipped with this knowledge?" In researching her book, Robinson had politely but pointedly asked Sanger if the clinics – some of which Robinson had helped fund – were not closing for lack of patients. Finding Sanger's answers obfuscatory, Robinson speculated that two of ABCL's New York clinics had in fact shuttered for this reason. Others certainly struggled to draw patients. A Baltimore clinic's annual report indicated that it had drawn 168 patients in the 104 days since it had officially opened. In Santa Fe, New Mexico, a Sanger-affiliated clinic drew almost 1,400 patients in its first year, but only 4 percent came for contraceptive consultations; most sought general health advice or other forms of charitable assistance. Across the country, too, clinic patients often seemed poor cases for philanthropy. "It is easier to obtain wide-awake upper-class clients merely seeking a safer or more comfortable contraceptive than the one they already know," Robinson reported, "than it is to obtain the lowest class clients for whose own sake and the race's sake birth control is most imperative."[64]

Clinics, finally, were located in cities, while many of the most desperate women lived in rural areas. Partly in response to this problem, the ABCL developed one of the organized movement's most important services – a medical referral program that matched advice-seekers with sympathetic nearby doctors. This program, though less heralded than the clinics, was probably at least equally effective in reaching needy cases.[65]

Friendly doctors' names came to the League in three ways. The ABCL sent circular letters to medical societies seeking information on physicians who might cooperate with the movement; it asked correspondents and ABCL members to send the names of "doctors in your area" then ascertained via correspondence whether those doctors provided contraceptive services; and beginning in 1925, Dr. James Cooper began collecting the business cards of sympathetic doctors during his transcontinental speaking tours. By the mid-1920s the League's growing "Doctors File" contained several thousand names. The program grew gradually throughout the 1920s, and may eventually have provided over a hundred thousand referrals.[66]

The referral program had limits. The League sometimes informed writers that referrals could "only be given to League members" and suggested they purchase a "life enrollment in the League" (for one dollar) or a year's subscription to *Birth Control Review* (two dollars) if they wished to receive further information. This may have dissuaded poor writers from pursuing the matter. Among those who *did* receive a referral we must assume that many never used it. Some were not in the habit of consulting doctors, particularly on birth control. Others suspected they could not afford medical services. Of those referred to clinics or doctors, Robinson wrote, "it is suspected that many never summon the courage to go."[67]

At other times, however, the League referred writers immediately and free of charge, or forwarded their letters to local leagues like the BCLM, which performed the same function. If even a fraction of these writers reached helpful doctors, many thousands would have received practical advice. And because doctors referred patients to specific products and pharmacies, doctors' most effective recommendations probably diffused quickly among laypeople. The referral program was thus one of the organized movement's major accomplishments.

Many writers, indeed, received exactly the advice they sought from Sanger, Dennett, or the BCLM, and came away satisfied. Tens of thousands ventured to movement clinics. Though these dispensaries did not reach as many unfortunates as their founders hoped, their mere existence may have emboldened some have-nots. "The very publication of the news that a birth control clinic exists, is a signal drawing all persons' thoughts to the desirability and possibility of limiting their families – to which end they then direct their own ingenuity without applying to the clinic," as Robinson wrote. As with the broader activist movement, the clinics' symbolic value at least equaled their practical effect.[68]

Eugenics

Many activists supported eugenics with only slightly less conviction than they opposed Comstockery or supported clinical expansion. From its inception in 1917, Sanger's *Birth Control Review* consistently promoted legal contraception as means of thinning "inefficient" populations. Sanger was personally wary of eugenicists' racism and elitism, but ultimately decided their influence was too important to ignore. "Birth control," she wrote in 1920, "is nothing more or less than the facilitation of the process of weeding out the unfit, of preventing the birth of defectives or of those who will become defectives." Eugenic language bulked large in many activists' appeals to respectable citizens uncomfortable with birth control "radicalism" but even less pleased with the perceived expansion of the unfit.[69]

Here again the organized movement represented the citizen movement poorly. While Sanger and company may have convinced some elite clinicians to provide contraceptives to needy patients due to perceived deficiency, the poorest cases were relatively unlikely to consult medical experts in the first place. Nor were impoverished advice-seekers eager to excuse their limitation as a benefit to society. Three writers emphasized their desire not to produce children who would, in the words of one, "become a public burden," but eugenic terminology occurred in just one letter (from a woman who had taken a course on the subject). As an ABCL member in Minnesota complained, people jumped at the chance to get literature on "finer cattle or better chickens," but not "better babies and happier family life." "No one is interested," she told the birth control advocate Ben Lindsey. "They have yet to learn."[70]

Feminism

For Sanger, men could not be full and trustworthy partners in fertility control. "Despite the sympathy sincerely expressed for the suffering of the wives," there was "a vast contrast between the psychology of fatherhood and motherhood." "His experience is fundamentally vicarious in character, never at closest grip with the great biological drama of reproduction." This was evident from letters: women petitioned for advice in such large numbers, Sanger argued, because they were "confident that I might extend help denied them by husbands" – or by clergy, doctors, or politicians.[71]

Not all birth control activists supported Sanger's feminist conception of the movement. Dennett thought "nothing is gained by emphasizing sex exclusion or antagonism" and called on her better-known colleague to reimagine birth control as a civil liberties issue. Sanger declined. "My own convictions are very decided," she wrote. "Birth control is a woman's problem ... hers and hers alone."[72]

Sanger's view has since become influential. And some of her correspondents shared it. "It is certainly up to us women to take care of ourselves," a working-class mother wrote. A substantial 12 percent of Sanger's writers framed birth control as a women's issue (Table A.8) or told of unsupportive men. Some sensed women's shared suffering as they read Sanger's books or the letters in *Birth Control Review*. "It brought tears to my eyes to even notice that other mothers are just like me," wrote a Kentucky woman. "You are the savior of women," declared another.[73]

Many of Sanger's writers had hard experience with men. "My husband is ... one of them mean men and likes to keep me tied down with a little baby all the time," wrote one woman. A young woman knew her father liked to "go to town and tell people what he has done, 'raised eleven children' . . . He ought to be at home under the bed with his head hung down. He never done no such of a thing; mother did, and cared for him besides. Sometimes I can hardly keep from hitting him to save my neck." Women compared their status to that of livestock. One of Sanger's most avowedly feminist petitioners had "thought for several years that a woman has almost ceased to be a woman but a brood sow or something of the kind, with the difference that the animals are given more care and consideration."[74]

Unpublished letters leave little doubt that women felt the need for expert birth control more urgently than men. Over 80 percent of those writers were female. Women's strong motivation to avoid unwanted childbearing, however, generally seems to have been backed by strong support from their husbands. No unsupportive husbands are mentioned in the unpublished letters, and even in Sanger's published letters, ten supportive husbands were mentioned for every one unsympathetic or uncooperative one. "My husband is just as interested in my writing as I am myself," wrote one woman. Female writers were more likely to identify their need with that of their husbands – by using the marital "we," for example – than to make common cause with other suffering women. Even among writers who directly mentioned Sanger's books, emulation of her woman-centered style was unusual. Less than 2 percent of the unpublished letters contained even subtly feminist language, such as a personal plea from a "woman in need."[75]

Husbands, for their part, blamed themselves for failing at withdrawal or for their inability to procure reliable contraceptive information. Since women often had limited social or professional networks outside their extended families, the street-smart task of finding the right contraceptive, doctor, or abortionist often fell to the man. A naval officer told Sanger of the guilt he had felt watching his wife "writhing in agony" during the birth of their son five years earlier. "She trusted me, and I fumbled the ball – through ignorance." A poor Minnesota farmer repeatedly went to town to "ask the druggist if there were not some medicine that would prevent conception," but was frustrated. "So there we were."[76]

Men's underlying concerns mirrored those of women even as they were framed in less personal and urgent terms. Husbands worried about living standards and their wives' health. A tailor wished to avoid "adding any more to a family that I cannot take care of properly." A New York man, "surprised at not seeing any [letters] from husbands," in *Birth Control Review*, wrote that "it is just as much the business of a father to know how many children he can bring up as it is of his wife. He is the one who is bringing in the daily bread, and should know how much he can bring in, and should see that the stop is made at the proper time." A *Review* street vendor in Buffalo reported that "men bought as eagerly as women – in fact I thought more eagerly."[77]

Men's relative comfort in publicly pursuing birth control made them less likely to use the private medium of a letter to a distant expert. The anonymity of correspondence, inversely, made it attractive to women. A letter to a friendly stranger did not risk the scorn or pity of relatives, friends, doctors, or storekeepers. "One hardly enjoys discussing methods of contraception with any drugstore clerk," as a Brooklyn woman wrote Dennett. For women, discussing contraceptive methods was not evidence of virility or worldly know-how, but an unpleasant necessity.[78]

This is not to say men were the essential actors in spreading birth control. Though customary male privileges often afforded men greater practical power over family limitation, women's less tangible moral pressure was at least equally important. Both sexes, in any case, acted in a moral landscape unmarked by crisp boundaries between male pronatalists and female birth controllers, but instead by subtle cross-sex mixing of moderate pronatalism and moderate reproductive liberalism. "It now seems possible to theorize," as the historian Katherine Lynch has written, "that the increasing limitation of births within marriage, particularly among couples using methods mainly within the control of the husband, did not require a modern revolution in the ways that husbands and wives communicated with one another, but only the sort of consideration that has characterized happy marriages for centuries." Not all marriages were happy, of course, and not all methods male-controlled, but on balance, letters to birth controllers suggest that spouses were more likely to agree than disagree on family size. The importance of gender to birth control lay less in women's new consciousness of a female interest in small families than in an array of subtle differences between the paths men and women took to similar conclusions about family size.[79]

Sexual Liberation

Activist and citizen viewpoints diverged, finally, on sex. "The greatest central problem [is] the shame and fear of sex," Sanger argued. "Through sex, mankind may attain the great spiritual illumination of the world, which will light up the only path to an earthly paradise." On this issue, Dennett agreed: "Sex emotion is an unsurpassed joy, something which rightly belongs to every normal human being, a joy to be proudly and serenely experienced."[80]

Conservative feminists resisted the idea of sexual liberation through contraception. They believed women stood a better chance of expanding their freedom – and avoiding unwanted childbearing – if they asserted a right to refuse unwanted sex. They worried that greater sexual license would hurt women by allowing men to enjoy sex without making lasting commitments. But to leading voices like Sanger and Dennett, this abstinence ethic was antiquated, unhealthy, and miserable. Obscenity laws hampered "frank, unashamed" sexual enjoyment, wrote Dennett. Even withdrawal and condoms, Sanger argued, deprived women of "sacred closeness or spiritual union." Only free access to "scientific contraception" would truly emancipate human sexuality.[81]

For centuries leading up to the twentieth, marriages had gradually become more "companionate": less focused on household economy, more on emotional and sexual connection. Men supported and women oversaw homes built on affection and altruism. For men who increasingly worked for wages in large, impersonal firms, such homes provided a haven from the pitiless world of work. There men could expect comfort, including sexual comfort, from warm and loving wives. By the mid-nineteenth century, romantic companionship became a quasireligious imperative for many middle-class Americans. To the extent such people accepted sexual compatibility as a domestic virtue, the companionate ideal helped lay the foundation for birth control's legitimacy.[82]

Some advice-seekers looked forward to this sort of romantic breakthrough. "Of course 'abstinence' would be the answer to my problem," a New York man wrote, "but both my wife and I are of an affectionate nature and we could hardly apply abstinence with any kind of success." "The old standby, rubbers," complained another, "is a preventative that is hard to keep using when you are in love and the love for each other is still growing." Women who disliked sex, often due to fear of pregnancy, sensed that their loathing was no longer necessary. "I have always thought of sexual union as something to endure," wrote an Oklahoma mother, "but you have given me a beautiful thought of love which I shall give to my girls."[83]

Most petitioners' motives were less romantic, however. In keeping with the commonplace view of sex as merely present and inevitable – an innate drive – writers tended to be more concerned with accommodating sex than discovering themselves through it. If women or men wanted greater sexual-to-spiritual satisfaction within marriage, they rarely mentioned it, even in the euphemisms available to them. This was partly because Sanger's desperate writers had more pressing concerns, and because health and economic concerns had greater social legitimacy. But it was also because Americans were not as sexually stunted as Sanger and Dennett imagined, and their erotic desires were not necessarily neglected under the existing reproductive regime.[84]

Marital abstinence, for instance, was neither universally despised nor synonymous with chastity. For the least sophisticated writers, bouts of abstinence could be lengthy, quarrelsome ordeals. But many Americans deployed periodic "continence" alongside other techniques without great distress. Young people usually entered marriage with experience in abstinence and the expectation that they might sometimes deploy this method within marriage as well. And crucially, coital abstinence within the marital couple did not necessarily mean a lack of sexual pleasure. Effective separation of sex from reproduction was possible (and common) via prostitution, masturbation, and noncoital or "unnatural" sex acts.[85]

Because these forms of nonreproductive sexual expression were considered shameful and kept secret, their scale can only be estimated. But the New York Bureau of Social Hygiene counted 14,926 "professional prostitutes" working in Manhattan in 1912, and assumed the presence of many additional part-time sex workers. The professionals alone attracted as many as 150,000 paying clients every day, the Bureau calculated. Vice commissioners in Chicago found a similar market in their smaller city, which supported at least 5,000 full-time prostitutes in 1911.[86]

Masturbation was also common. In 1924, in a group of 1,183 unmarried, educated American women – average age 37 – two-thirds admitted to having masturbated at various times in their lives, and one-third were doing so actively. Robert Latou Dickinson, a gynecologist and early sexologist, reported in 1931 that his female patients masturbated not only with their hands, but with "slipper heel on foot, keys, roll of blanket, pillow, towel . . . banana, sausage, candle, bottle, vinegar cruet." Men, too, masturbated privately while remaining abstinent publicly. "The great majority of men who remain 'pure,'" a minister from Maine told Ben Lindsey, "have done so (1) in fear of parental displeasure; (2) in fear of syphilis or gonorrhea; (3) and knowing that they may give themselves the delights of sexual connection with their own hands, unseen and unheard." "For both men and women," the historian Thomas Laqueur writes, "masturbation loomed in adulthood or late adolescence as a deeply guilty pleasure."[87]

The extent to which Americans engaged in other forms of nonreproductive sex can only be guessed. Dickinson recorded a remarkable variety of practices among the mostly middle-class patients he treated between the 1880s and 1920s. Some reported a history of homosexual activity prior to marriage, and many opposite-sex couples used their hands, thighs, and mouths to bring their partner to climax. Oral sex was common in brothels, and it is possible that this practice, like condom use, gradually lost its association with prostitution in the early twentieth century. Among Alfred Kinsey's interviewees from the late 1930s and '40s, about sixty percent of college-educated respondents admitted to engaging in oral sex – fewer less-educated Americans did so, but Kinsey speculated this was due to "cover-up" and associations of oral sex with homosexuality. More common in respectable marriage and courtship was manual sex, or "petting" to the point of climax. Kinsey's subjects preferred manual to oral sex regardless of educational level. Ninety percent of male respondents with college education, and 75 percent of the least educated, "frequently" stimulated their wives' genitalia with their hands. Wives reciprocated at a similar rate. As Kinsey noted, ordinary marriage manuals had long encouraged petting as a means of sexual "adjustment."[88]

The prevalence of prostitution, masturbation, and noncoital sex made interludes of coital abstinence tolerable for those Americans who did not trust other methods of fertility control. Abstinence from vaginal intercourse with one's spouse was not the same as sexual deprivation, and did not necessarily result in emotional and spiritual distress. Nor was abstinence necessary for the majority of Americans who had settled on a working contraceptive regime. "Fear of pregnancy appears occasionally but is not characteristic," Dickinson wrote of his patients. "The general attitude takes both contraception and child-bearing for granted." Patients' romantic complaints centered as much on inadequacies of sexual technique – especially male technique – as on inadequate birth control.[89]

Though Americans did not await the liberation Sanger and Dennett foresaw, birth control activists helped break down sexual taboos. Their mere presence in newspapers and public speech contributed to a sense of the old sexual restraints' vulnerability. Discussion of birth control made sex easier to talk about. In a more intentional way than Theodore Roosevelt, Sanger in particular challenged Americans to reckon with the disparities between their sexual ideals and practices. To be a "professional shocker of the bourgeoisie," as H.L. Mencken labeled Sanger, was also to shape the middle ground of respectable sexual discussion.[90]

For the most part, however, Sanger's romanticism was not representative of the reigning sex ethic as birth control become legitimate and popular. Where Sanger saw sexual-spiritual liberation on the horizon, most Americans approached sexual desire as a fact of life. Birth control's legitimacy rose alongside that of marital sexuality, but it did not rely on a new appreciation of sex's higher-order pleasures, made possible by new birth control knowledge. For petitioners the promise of expert birth control was incrementally better mastery over the realities of sex, not a new millennium.[91]

CONCLUSIONS

The birth control movement looked different from the standpoint of its ground-level agents than that of its most prominent avatars. The two dominant goals of Americans seeking contraception – economic advancement and better health – were also important to vocal activists. But many of the activists' other ideas attracted little sympathy or attention from ordinary family limiters – even highly motivated ones who were familiar with the organized movement's literature and wrote to prominent leaders.

Legal reform and eugenic goals were least relevant to contraceptive agents. Feminism and sexual reform were more important, though it is not clear that these ideas were essential to the mass movement's success. Clinical and medical outreach programs were acutely helpful to relatively few people. Activists saw their movement as a groundbreaking reform that would bring about a happier future. Agents understood it as a possible aid in longstanding and present problems.[92]

5

Missionary Work

Touring America for Birth Control

Man must begin, know this, where nature ends. Nature and man can never be fast friends.

Matthew Arnold[1]

A life process which consists only in a series of sacrifices – the present generation sacrificing itself for the next, and so ad infinitum – is an absurd conclusion for a race of supposedly rational human beings.

Warner Fite[2]

**

Early in 1925, Dr. James Fryer Cooper, an obstetrician and longtime advocate of birth control, appeared before eighty-five members of the Camden County Medical Society in New Jersey. He told them that legitimizing contraception would foster progress in six specific ways. It would prevent overpopulation, lessen poverty, and improve maternal health. It would boost child welfare, foster women's freedom, and promote eugenic improvement. It would *not*, he vigorously protested, exterminate the middle classes, foment sexual immorality, or violate natural law. After speaking for half an hour, Cooper opened the floor for discussion. The doctors shifted silently in their chairs. Eventually a local health officer offered "vague" objections: large families always seemed to get along somehow; there was no need to "agitate the matter." But no one seconded the officer, and generally, Cooper reported, "the message was well received," though "there were many present who were naturally conservative."[3]

A few weeks earlier Margaret Sanger had hired Cooper as medical director of the American Birth Control League. Cooper did not actually direct the League's clinical operations. Instead, from the beginning, he did what he called "missionary work," taking "the gospel" of birth control to all corners of the United States, and especially to doctors. Between 1925 and 1927 he completed five extended tours of the country, speaking in 46 states, 199 towns and cities, in front of over 280 assemblies.[4]

Sanger hired Cooper in the hope that he would convince his fellow physicians to support her cause, and thus accelerate the repeal of legal prohibitions and informal taboos on birth control. In the short term she wanted to convince more doctors to prescribe birth control devices; in the longer term she hoped their cultural power would undermine law and taboo. "I have long felt the necessity of having with us a physician whose special work would be to open the doors of the medical profession," wrote Sanger in 1925.[5]

This strategy had Cooper as its centerpiece through much of the 1920s. "Tall, blond, distinguished, a fine combination of missionary and physician," as Sanger remembered him, Cooper was the son of English Quaker immigrants to Massachusetts. After training for the ministry as a young man, Cooper gradually left his parents' faith. He attended medical school in Boston, graduated in 1910, and accepted a position as a physician with a Congregational medical mission in south China. Cooper's interest in fertility control emerged in that country, where he lost his wife of two years, Ruth Quimby, to preeclampsia during pregnancy, and "had ample opportunity to study and appreciate the significance of an unrestricted birth rate," as a friend later recalled. After Ruth's death Cooper left China, serving first as physician to a Chinese labor battalion during the First World War, then establishing a medical practice on Boston's North End, a predominantly poor and immigrant neighborhood, in 1919. Soon he began conducting contraceptive "experiments of various kinds" on dozens of patients who requested or "required" birth control advice. He met Sanger while presenting the results of these experiments at a conference in Chicago.[6]

Cooper was one of only two paid employees of the ABCL, and his $10,000 salary represented a significant expense for the small and struggling organization. But his activities promised to overcome some of Sanger's limitations. He would reach audiences that Sanger, as a nonphysician with radical antecedents, could not. Once among other doctors, he would offer them expert technical instruction on contraceptive techniques. "Propaganda can be made by others," wrote Sanger's second husband and primary financial benefactor, Noah Slee. "I only pay his entire expenses so he educates the medical profession, who will accept nothing except from their own. Greatest Trust in USA."[7]

Cooper proved adept at this task, overcoming considerable "shyness" about his topic and addressing at least 150 medical meetings, most of them friendlier than his early audience in Camden. He also, however, energetically ignored Slee's instructions and sought out lay audiences wherever he could find them, speaking to men's and women's clubs, civic and church groups, social workers, college students, hospital staffs, and mere "curiosity seekers" – often on very short notice – so that non-medical listeners eventually made up more than two-thirds of his total reported audience.[8]

Once at the podium, Cooper's approach was expansive. Both lay and medical audiences heard thirty to forty-five minutes of unapologetic "propaganda" for the cause, beginning with the six-point argument for birth control then moving to the three-point preemptive rebuttal of common criticisms. At the end of medical meetings, doctors got fifteen minutes of technical instruction on the use of various pessaries, and instructions on how to order them. Both audience types then had a chance to question and comment.

Cooper directly reached at least 20,000 people, including 5,500 physicians. Because he was a male medical doctor with no radical reputation, because his campaigns convincingly framed birth control in scientific as well as moral terms, and because he was able to address large numbers of the unconverted, Cooper may have been a more effective propagandist, speech for speech, than his better-remembered employer. Rather than focusing on Cooper the operative, however, this chapter examines his audiences – their responses to Cooper's mission and message, and the ambivalent process of local birth control legitimation.[9]

After each of his meetings, Cooper dispatched a field report to ABCL headquarters in New York. The 274 reports, mostly handwritten onto standardized forms, concisely addressed several questions, including: How many doctors and/or laypeople attended that day's meeting(s)? What was their affiliation? Who (if anyone) expressed opposition to birth control, and why? Who would "cooperate" with the ABCL by joining the mailing list, taking patient referrals, or helping to found a local chapter or clinic? What general remarks did Cooper have on the tenor of the meeting? How was his message received?[10]

The reports and related correspondence open a window on the moral status of birth control in mid-1920s America among the sort of middle-class, politically unadventurous doctors and laypeople whose opinions – thought Sanger, Cooper, and other reformers – collectively exercised an outsized influence on contraception's social acceptability. For these civic worthies of the 1920s, few of whom would have otherwise left a trace of their views, birth control was fitfully gaining legitimacy alongside the perception that it was scientific and technocratic, socially desirable for eugenic or class purposes, and aligned with a progressive direction of history.

Cooper's fieldwork also suggests new ways of understanding the *process* of birth control legitimation. Rather than strong supporters or opponents, Cooper typically found ambivalent in-betweens. For most groups birth control was not an obvious blessing or curse. It had wide but qualified support. Diffuse social movements like birth control, as Francis Vreeland later put it, were "made up of numbers of people, each one but slightly involved," but collectively decisive. "We find the movement functioning through flickers of persons."[11]

THE PROCESS OF CONTRACEPTIVE LEGITIMATION

Attendees at Cooper's talks were generally well-educated and well-off. At least three-quarters were male, including nearly all the physicians. They came from across the United States and were somewhat more urban than the country at large. The great majority attended Cooper's meetings as members of groups devoted not to birth control or any other reform agenda, but to relatively conservative goals like medical professionalism or civic improvement. Very few audiences had a prior collective commitment to the birth control movement, and after hearing Cooper speak, only a quarter of attendees agreed to have their names added to the ABCL mailing list. An even smaller proportion agreed to provide active support by, for example, taking referrals. Birth control, in short, was of no special interest to most of Cooper's listeners. It was neither the panacea touted by Sanger nor the impending social cataclysm foretold by her most zealous opponents.[12]

These respectable townspeople, Cooper found, almost without exception had already privately and locally legitimized family limitation at some time before his arrival, *despite* the efforts of Sanger, whose perceived radicalism made her cause harder for some upstanding citizens to accept By the time Cooper toured the United States, the major stumbling block to public acknowledgment of birth control's benefits was a cautious and formal reluctance to outwardly associate oneself with "a tabooed subject," as Cooper put it, before one's peers did so.

Cooper's experiences in Detroit illustrate this dynamic. His first talk in that city, sponsored by the progressive Penguin Club in the summer of 1925, drew an overflow crowd of 350 listeners. Its favorable reception led to a hastily arranged follow-up speech in which 150 physicians packed a hall on "one of the hottest nights we have had in Detroit," as an organizer recalled. "His personality, training and knowledge had a most gratifying effect on the doctors," wrote the organizer of Cooper. "He has aroused their interest in a direct professional way."[13]

But when Cooper returned to Detroit the following year seeking officially sponsored medical meetings, he saw a different side of the city. The president of the Women's Hospital regretted that such a meeting might jeopardize her fundraising drive. Henry Ford Hospital's chief surgeon informed Cooper that his address would have to be approved by Ford himself, "for fear of sensational publicity." The county medical president pleaded illness. Even the ABCL's local delegate was "conservative" and "cautious not to offend his medical colleagues with the semblance of anything unethical." Across the country, local leaders encouraged Cooper in private conversation but balked, at least initially, at the prospect of formally sponsoring his talk.[14]

In his struggles with formal opposition, Cooper traveled in the footsteps of the early birth control advocate Charles Knowlton, who issued a similar report from his home state of Massachusetts in 1834: "In my travels I have introduced the work promiscuously," he wrote of his short contraceptive manual. Four-fifths of his listeners approved, Knowlton claimed, but "people won't speak out for it in public – they are too afraid."[15]

Cooper, however, had the good fortune to tour the country at a breaking point in these taboos' credibility. His successes in Dallas represent his overall experience better than his frustrations in Detroit. Three hundred forty Dallasites stood outside in hard rain to hear Cooper speak from the steps of city hall, in a talk sponsored by the county medical president. Over 150 doctors, "a record attendance," turned out for a medical meeting. He addressed the entire senior class at a local medical school, and the state medical president agreed to help Cooper arrange meetings in the state's more conservative cities. There was "plenty of favorable publicity in all the papers."[16]

As Cooper crossed the 48 states he believed he was witnessing in real time the eclipse of the "hidebound," "mossback" ideas that had long made birth control unmentionable. "Only a few years ago," he told a Montana newspaper in 1925, "it was impossible to hold a public meeting for the discussion of the subject" of birth control. "At present it is almost impossible to fill all the speaking dates arranged."[17]

He was exaggerating. Though taboos were declining in the 1920s – as Cooper well knew after ten frustrating years in support of his cause – formal "shyness" about contraception was still strong enough that he often had to go to great lengths to convince local leaders to allow him a forum. Cooper's difficulties in Detroit and elsewhere, he thought, might be attributable to a "large Catholic population." But even in "very progressive" and largely Protestant California, just two county- or city-level medical societies (Santa Monica and Fresno) replied affirmatively to the ABCL's circular letters requesting bookings for Dr. Cooper. As a result, in California towns as elsewhere, Cooper often arrived with no prior appointments and had to spend hours or days personally cajoling reluctant local leaders into sponsoring meetings. "Often much running about and much diplomacy is necessary," he wrote. "To ... get influential doctors to take the initiative of sponsoring a stranger on a mooted question is not easy." The same was true of civic groups.[18]

No matter whom he addressed, Cooper was more likely to find weak resistance and weak support *in the same person* than strong partisans for and against his cause. The doctor nevertheless discovered that after a time most potential sponsors (or committees) could be persuaded. Despite their keen awareness that an invitation could be construed as an endorsement; despite their suspicion that Cooper's talks would be covered by local newspapers (as they usually were); and despite pervasive unease about "what might be said by outsiders," Cooper ultimately succeeded in addressing groups with no explicit social reform agenda in nearly all the towns and cities he visited. Over the course of three years during which he addressed close to three hundred officially convened audiences, less than thirty times was Cooper reduced to chatting with a few local sympathizers or cutting his losses and moving on.[19]

Once he succeeded in winning a sponsorship, Cooper could expect large audiences and responses ranging from ecstatic celebration to grumbling acquiescence. He was favorably received by a great variety of groups including doctors, medical students, college students, PTA members, Protestant clergy, social workers, college faculty, clubmen, and clubwomen. Occasionally he encountered "violent and emotional" objections. But opposition of any kind – even from a single person – emerged in just 10 percent of Cooper's meetings, and from less than 1 percent of all attendees.[20]

OVERCOMING THE STIGMA OF RADICALISM

Though Cooper admired Sanger, he did not believe his good fortune owed much to her prior work. In towns and cities across the country he discovered widespread ignorance or misunderstanding of the organized movement's goals. "Many heard of Birth Control Movement for [the] first time," he reported from a meeting of 150 clubwomen in Wyomissing, Pennsylvania. In Greensboro, North Carolina, townspeople wanted to "know exactly what it is all about" before "taking a public stand." Other towns were similarly ill-informed. Even in the medical hub of Philadelphia, "conservatively interested" doctors "knew so little" of birth control clinics "that they could take no intelligent action." "Doctors as well as many other groups," Cooper wrote to headquarters, "do not realize what it is all about and therefore need educating."[21]

This sort of obliviousness was less common, however, than a sort of half-ignorance consisting of a few "perverted ideas" about birth control activism. From all quarters of the country, from doctors as well as lay-people, Cooper reported on groups who before his talk had "known little of the movement" except that birth control's publicists had sometimes offended established notions of the good. "Usually those opposed have wrong ideas," wrote Cooper after being refused a meeting in South Dakota. "This is one great difficulty everywhere . . . Wrong ideas of what B.C. means."[22]

Cooper had to tread lightly in discussing these misconceptions, since his employer was the organized movement's central figure. Over the years Sanger's message had become less confrontational as she pursued main-stream support, not least from doctors. But the press was less interested in moderation than sensation, and by inertia Sanger's reputation remained radical. Even after her adoption of eugenic and medical rhetoric, Sanger struggled to reach mainstream and conservative groups. Women's clubs occasionally extended her an invitation, but she had difficulty spreading her moderate message much further among the respectable middle classes. "The best ground received the most cultivation," Vreeland remarked of Sanger's outreach efforts. "It seems everyone knows all that I can say!" Sanger herself complained to a friend in 1928.[23]

For this reason, and because of problems with her health, Sanger spent much of the 1920s focused on coordinating a number of U.S. and inter-national conferences on birth control. As late as 1937, a polling firm found that Sanger's name still hindered popular acceptance of her move-ment. The recent founder of a birth control clinic in Detroit, after neglect-ing to thank Cooper and the ABCL for their support, explained that she had feared associating her upstart facility with any doctor not "*entirely outside* of the organized propaganda for birth control." When Sanger attempted to introduce herself to a North Carolina health officer,

Dr. George Cooper, after he started a contraceptive clinic in the late 1930s, the doctor replied that Sanger "did not have a dad-blamed thing to do with it and we don't want any part of Margaret Sanger's advertising and controversy."[24]

Sanger was hindered, too, by her sex, her lack of a medical degree, and her refusal to observe gendered taboos on sexual speech. Early in her career these qualities had helped Sanger gain more publicity than earlier male and medical activists, since she projected disempowered defiance rather than ameliorative authority. But as Sanger tried to move to the center in the 1920s, the same outsider status held her back. Women had long since seated themselves at the table of respectable social reform – pushing to end slavery, child labor, or drunkenness – but the minefields of sex-tinged reform campaigns (such as that against venereal disease) were more easily navigated by men who claimed the dispassionate language of medicine and science.[25]

As a result Cooper was often at pains to hide his connection to Sanger. He seems never to have mentioned his employer's name to potential sponsors, to audiences, or to the newspapermen with whom he spoke in most towns. He presented himself as an independent medical speaker sponsored by the American Birth Control League – a name most people could not connect to Sanger. Though even the League could be a burden: "to the doctors the League seemed far away," Vreeland reported. "They had heard many slurs on the movement and were afraid of radicals."[26]

All this caused Cooper frustration, even as he worked assiduously for the movement and maintained close personal ties to Sanger. At least once, the traveling doctor spelled out the handicaps under which he believed he labored as the movement's agent. He was upset with Noah Slee, who in mid-1926 instructed him to stop making so many last-minute appointments with medical societies. A "more dignified" approach, thought Slee, would be for Cooper to allow his schedule to be set from ABCL headquarters.[27]

This suggestion, as Cooper saw it, would jeopardize his entire mission precisely because doctors, like laypeople, would not respond to a letter from the ABCL in the way they would to a personal visit, note, or telephone call from a traveling medical expert. To help Slee and the home office understand this, Cooper dispatched an air-clearing letter from Butte, Montana. First, he noted, "the League is not known to most doctors" – thus some of their initial wariness. Second, Cooper wrote, "the League is a lay organization interested in propaganda" – if the ABCL were better known, such recognition would likely *hurt* the cause. Why?

Because, third, "much birth control work in the past has been emotional and sentimental. Therefore does not appeal to the scientific group."[28]

POPULAR SCIENCE

Cooper was successful, in large part, to the extent he appealed to this scientific group. At every stage of arranging and delivering his talks, he presented himself as a man of science. He would bypass the hysterics of birth control's most zealous friends and enemies, treating the matter instead as a matter for dispassionate technical consideration. He would rationalize superstitions and demystify moral phobias. "A common expression everywhere," he boasted in one report, "[is] 'That is the first time I have heard the subject discussed from a scientific viewpoint.'"[29]

Cooper's scientific credentials and real technical expertise made such an approach credible. He had ten years' experience as a clinical instructor and practitioner, and his empirical knowledge of birth prevention was unsurpassed in 1920s America. During his tours he completed *Technique of Contraception*, a pioneering book that would soon become the definitive American medical text on contraception. His talks to doctors, in particular, contained abundant statistical and technological details. By all accounts his manner was calm and dispassionate. The fact that he was a man made the task of broaching contraception with male doctors easier, and doubtless afforded him additional scientific mystique.[30]

Yet to a great extent Cooper's "scientific viewpoint" was rhetorical. Long stretches of his stump speech differed little from those delivered by Sanger and other "sentimental" propagandists. Only one of his six talking points was unambiguously medical: birth control would lessen maternal mortality. Three others might have seemed loosely connected to public health: preventing overpopulation, improving child nurture, and bolstering eugenic fitness. The doctor's final two points were both nonmedical and marked by a history of public controversy: couples might improve their economic status though limitation of offspring, and "modern woman" could claim "the right to be the mistress of her own body and to decide her own maternal destiny."[31]

What Cooper offered – more than a newly scientific view of birth control – was a Sanger-like message delivered *in the name* of scientific objectivity by a physician who could credibly claim science's cultural power. In Cooper's hands, birth control was preeminently a question of progressive expertise, not moral compromise. Rather than an emotional flashpoint, a rebellion against coercion or an omen of race suicide, it was a technical tool appropriate for an increasingly anonymous, heterogeneous, demystified society.[32]

Before moving from scientism to other causes of Cooper's success, it bears asking whether Cooper's message benefited from audience self-selection, or Cooper's coziness with his fellow physicians, rather than wider popular sentiment. Cooper only spoke when some locally prominent person agreed to sponsor his speech, making dissent costlier for individual members. And occasionally his meetings were boycotted by anti-birth control factions or sponsored by pro-birth control splinter groups. This sort of division was rare, however, and audience size alone suggests that Cooper rarely spoke to a self-selecting minority. "Increased attendance at a Birth Control meeting is typical of meetings all over the country," Cooper wrote, and at local medical meetings, audiences averaged two-thirds of the hosting society's total membership, far more than usual. These audiences consisted of "serious" physicians but also the merely "curious." Lay groups, too, were large and drawn by curiosity as much as sympathy.[33]

Not even curiosity was a prerequisite for attendance, however. Because about two-thirds of Cooper's talks to physicians' groups occurred during scheduled monthly meetings, many doctors were present for reasons unrelated to Cooper's appearance. Far from being filled with enthusiasts, some audiences were lethargic and unresponsive. "Indifference" characterized the thirty-seven doctors who heard Cooper's talk in Wilmington, North Carolina (though after the talk they asked "many questions . . . mostly as to the ethics of B.C.," and eventually came to "a more favorable attitude"). Doctors in Muskogee, Oklahoma, skipped Cooper's meeting because the circus was in town; in Aberdeen, South Dakota, because hunting season had just begun; in Jonesboro, Arkansas, because of a "big religious revival in nearby Baptist church." Cooper had so much trouble gaining attention in California's Central Valley during the hot summer months that he gave up trying.[34]

Not everyone was bored. Some audiences were enthusiastic about Cooper's scientific message from the start. In Fresno the thirty-three assembled doctors voted to send their entire membership roll to the League's doctors file, and at Williams College, Cooper was "very enthusiastically received" by no less than 75 percent of the student body. Even in friendly groups, however, Cooper was regularly disappointed with the results from his postspeech requests for movement volunteers. He was not simply preaching to the converted. His message's success reflected widely shared middle-class values.[35]

A second question is how much Cooper's *personal* qualities – especially his M.D. – might have swayed listeners to tolerate him even when unsympathetic to his arguments. Medical collegiality probably made doctors more likely to accept Cooper's pitch. Cooper used his medical credentials as an ideological passport, working to create a confidential atmosphere with his fellow physicians. His speeches suggested that he and his listeners were gathered to weigh difficult and important matters which medical men of their sort – rational, progressive, public-minded – were uniquely qualified to consider. He dismissed race suicide hysteria ("let us not be deceived by the cradle competition for big battalions") and mystical naturism ("to be vaccinated against disease is unnatural"). Doctors, he argued, ought to act as birth control's public trustees, deploying safe scientific techniques in morally and sociologically appropriate cases. Support for Cooper was therefore not simply support for birth control, but for the moral competence and progressive bona fides of the medical profession.[36]

It would nevertheless be a mistake to attribute Cooper's success with medical audiences entirely, or even mostly, to his medical degree or his support for doctor-controlled contraception. Fellow physicians had to take Cooper at his word when he presented his medical credentials, and often did so grudgingly. Audiences then had to accept Cooper as the emissary of a lay organization that was either unknown or hazily associated with radicalism. They had to trust that he was not a quack or – because he displayed mail-order pessaries – a salesman. Most significantly, Cooper asked his fellow doctors to accept an essentially nonmedical message pitched to them as progressive citizens. Even for physicians who could condone technical instruction on measures to prevent dangerous pregnancies, Cooper's very broad interpretation of the nonmedical indications for contraception might have rankled.[37]

For all these reasons, Cooper's "propaganda" duly irritated many doctors. Robert Latou Dickinson, the pro-birth control obstetrician, told Raymond Pearl, an ABCL board member and population scholar, that some of Cooper's "statistical claims" were "obvious nonsense." Pearl agreed that Cooper was not "in the least degree scientific" and suggested revisiting "the whole question of Doctor Cooper's activities." His address at Johns Hopkins medical school, Pearl reported, had created "the general impression . . . that Doctor Cooper will never be allowed again to speak on the subject . . . in this city."[38]

In other words, Cooper's message was not sufficiently "medical" or "scientific" to satisfy doctors on those grounds alone. But combined with private moral sentiment, it was scientific enough to attract support from doctors (and laypeople) with no necessary prior commitment to the cause. Cooper – rather than a simple guest of the medical fraternity – was the beneficiary of gradual changes in medical opinion that echoed wider shifts among millions of educated Americans. "Here is a considered statement," Cooper noted in his dispatch from Rutherfordton, North Carolina, one year into his tours. "I have never seen a city or town yet where there is not a doctor who will give B.C. information in proper cases. Of course these doctors do not advertise the fact but they are 'carrying on.' Physicians everywhere are recognizing more and more the importance of considering Social, Psychic, and Economic circumstances in life as causative factors in illness." "With proper understanding of the movement," Cooper later wrote from Walla Walla, Washington, "most doctors are favorable."[39]

Doctors, indeed, may have been taking moral cues partly from their own patients. As more patients and acquaintances approached birth control as a modern necessity, asking for it without shame, doctors' fear of appearing unprofessional may have lessened. "Conversations with thousands of physicians," as Cooper noted, "show an increasingly large number of women applying to physicians for contraceptive advice." Word that respectable doctors prescribed contraceptives, meanwhile, lent reciprocal scientific credibility to family limitation. In this way and others, birth control became more a technical tool and less a moral compromise, and transcendent continuums lost some of their imagined force.[40]

REPEALING RETICENCE

For Cooper's tours to succeed, however, he needed more than just a credible appeal to scientific rationality. He also needed a more open sexual culture – one in which respectable people could attend a birth control lecture without undue fear for their reputations. The problem was not just radicalism but older associations with prostitution and sexual licentiousness.[41]

Taking sexual desire for granted, as most Americans did, was not the same as permitting its free expression. The pervasiveness of sexual temptation made taming it essential. In the nineteenth century, respectable Americans had insisted that sex be subordinated to marital and reproductive duty. Sexual pleasure might gratify and bond married couples, but its core purpose was procreation. This ideal of dutiful sexuality was so central to everyday moral calculation that many Americans used "morality" as a synonym for sexual morality. Transgressors risked social isolation, particularly if they were women. The intimate intensity of these norms made them difficult to question or even discuss.[42]

In private, most Victorian-era Americans held their strictest ideals at some distance. Mid-nineteenth century contraceptive advice manuals, of which there were many, presented practical birth control techniques without embarrassment. Ubiquitous domestic medicine books often contained anatomical drawings and rudimentary information on avoiding pregnancy. "Nature is nature," observed a New York writer in 1861. "You may as well try to suppress the sense of hunger and thirst by abstaining from food and drink, as to attempt to appease the equally imperative demands of sensual desires by some other method than the natural indulgence of the sexes." But such books were "kept in many households on a high and forbidden shelf." Whatever nineteenth-century Americans may have done in private, few had been willing to speak of contraception in public, much less defend it as an abstract good. This silence made it harder for nonradical couples to think of reproductive control as a normal activity, even as they practiced it.[43]

In the decades around the turn of the century a convergence of factors had made sexual norms easier to discuss in the open. Popular scientism relieved sex of some of its mysterious horror. Companionate marriages expanded alongside the industrial economy. Social science and anthropology made sexual codes appear more arbitrary and changeable. Inherited faiths ceded some ground to skeptical inquiry. More practically, the old unspoken rules seemed incapable of restraining sexual vice or convincing "normal" citizens to reproduce themselves. Venereal disease – a substantial cause of involuntary childlessness – and especially "race suicide" persuaded many progressives that sexual topics were too important to be left decorously unspoken. "Traditionally, voluntary control of parenthood is strongly tabooed in this culture," wrote the Lynds of Middletown in 1925, "as is all discussion of sexual adjustment in mating, but this prohibition is beginning to be somewhat lifted."[44]

Opening discussion of sexual topics had not been Theodore Roosevelt's intent in sparking the race suicide debate, but it was an important consequence. Roosevelt and his sympathizers had attempted to imbue traditional sexual morality with scientific authority (effectively inverting James Cooper's later use of "science"). Drawing on Darwin, census data, and the new science of sociology, Roosevelt and his allies had proposed a secularized natural-law theology or sacralized Darwinism, where organically reproducing the dominant culture ("the race") was a good citizen's first and fundamental duty. And for a time birth control had been credibly framed in these terms, as a symptom of civilizational decline arising from self-serving violations of natural law. The result was a country where, as birth control activists liked to point out, legislators and doctors maintained conspicuously small families while the former outlawed contraception and the latter often refused to prescribe it. "The larger number of men and women living within the orbit of the Great Society," as Walter Lippmann wrote of the sexual mores of the late 1920s, "are no doubt aware that their inherited beliefs ... do not square entirely with the actual beliefs upon which they feel compelled to act."[45]

As Cooper toured the states he witnessed hundreds of Americans confronting the gulf between their inherited and actual beliefs, nervously abandoning the old culture of sexual reticence and formal deference to duty-based standards. He witnessed the creation, not of a new sexual ethic, but a new willingness among respectable citizens to acknowledge and normalize birth control. His accounts of pre-meeting "diplomacy" and "salesmanship," in particular, suggest the tipping point at which many Americans found themselves. Before agreeing to sponsor a talk, local leaders typically asked "for time," Cooper reported, to consult with colleagues and friends. Normally this process took between 24 and 48 hours, though sometimes much longer. Some potential sponsors remained suspended indefinitely in indecision, forcing Cooper to move on to another town. Others backed out at the last minute, or agreed to hear the talk only after reading it in outline. "Medical societies fear publicity on tabooed subjects," Cooper noted, "unless that publicity is approved first by them."[46]

A doctor in Hamilton, Ontario, for example, was "much interested" but "conservative": he provided contraceptive advice for "marked health reasons" but feared legal action and "criticism of colleagues" if he expanded his ambit. Another "fine ... progressive" physician was "very much interested in [the] general program as carried out by medical profession," but complained that a local "lay group of radical women" had been "continually asking his cooperation for wide open dissemination of Birth Control methods, which program he will not endorse." Selling *Birth Control Review* on the streets stuck the doctor as crude.[47]

In St. Louis Cooper encountered a mixture of instinctive caution and practical reformism. A minister would cooperate "if the movement is dignified" and "associates itself with the influential people of St. Louis." The head of obstetrics at Barnes Hospital, a Catholic, would not do "contraceptive work himself" nor "permit unlimited work done on economic cases," but allowed his assistant to give advice in medical cases. And the president of the League of Women Voters would work for the cause but thought "unwise to introduce the B.C. subject in some of the present organizations for fear of disruptions." A medical professor would "cooperate in a general way but does not want to be conspicuous."[48]

Cooper understood much of this hesitancy as inarticulate sexual fear. For some waverers the issue was specific: race suicide, violations of natural law, the failure to properly channel innate sexual desire into procreation. For others, however, there was only the less examined sense that sexual ethics was morally risky territory. In rebutting the idea that birth control would "make immorality safe," Cooper first made a liberal case: "We cannot withhold the good from the many because of the evil that might result to a few. We do not take the franchise from our citizens because some man sells his vote." Then, at greater length, Cooper made a maternalist case. Not only did women deserve control over their own bodies and destinies, they deserved public confidence as moderators of male lust and guardians of sexual virtue. To imply that birth control would lead to promiscuity was "to say that womanly virtue is only a sham." "Women can be trusted. Character counts."[49]

As Cooper came to expect friendly audiences, he grew increasingly impatient with prudery and moral caution. "These men don't dare to say their soul is their own," he wrote of four skittish professors in Nashville. Most waverers eventually gave way, however. After consultations with trusted friends or colleagues, their verdict was typically positive, and a well-attended meeting took place sometime in the following two days. Though local leaders did not feel comfortable assessing by themselves the residual strength of the old sexual codes, larger communities overwhelmingly answered "yes."[50]

On the one hand then, Cooper's reports illuminate the extent to which the twenties' "revolution in manners and morals" quietly reached beyond jazz clubs and petting parties and into the sexual morality of stalwart citizens across the United States. These citizens remained wary of the old sex taboos, and sensed danger in violating them. At the same time they sensed their weakness.

On the other hand, Cooper's experiences underscore the essential ambivalence of birth control's long legitimation process. Popular acceptance did not emerge from a victory of zealous reformers over equally zealous traditionalists. Instead the decisive conflicts played out within small communities and even within individuals, among people only dimly aware of the most strenuous disputants. What these citizens lacked in decisive conviction they made up in a sense that the old sexual morality was newly open to question. This unsettledness bred hesitation and fear but also possibility.

PROGRESS, EUGENICS AND NATURISM

Cooper closed every speech with an attempt to refocus his listeners on the moral claims of progress rather than those of nature. "The statement has been made that Birth Control is unnatural," he told his audiences:

Of course it is. All of our life is unnatural ... Why will a man speak of Birth Control as unnatural and use a safety razor? ... It is the glory of our civilization that we are continually improving on the conditions of nature, and we are urged to build for our souls more stately mansions and leave the worn-out abodes of the past ... Birth Control is necessary if we are to adjust ourselves to the ever-changing circumstances of human progress.[51]

Of all his messages, Cooper expected this one to be best received. Even in rebuffing Cooper, many listeners assented to the now time-honored view that history favored birth control. "I do not think the time is quite ripe," demurred a Minneapolis doctor who Cooper hoped would sponsor a clinic. "Let us hope it will be before long." Cooper, seeing the progress–nature divide as his primary battlefield, classified audiences and individuals by how "progressive" or "backward" he found them to be.[52]

Virtually all the specific feedback Cooper reported – positive or negative – pertained to this divide. Broad affirmations aside, many progressives particularly liked Cooper's eugenic arguments – especially in the western states. Cooper's listeners were characteristically vague, however, about the means of inheritance: New Mexico eugenics supporters were concerned about "poor Mexicans, poor white trash, and many tubercular people"; in the Missouri Ozarks it was the "very prolific ... poor American whites"; in Washington state "inskilled" lumbermen. Listeners appeared less interested in genetic engineering than in enlisting scientific language in local class politics. Even for doctors, Cooper acknowledged, the prospect of eugenic sterilization was a novelty; this group needed to be "educated to the facts."[53]

Cooper's other substantial strain of feedback came from natural-law conservatives skeptical of his appeals to progress. Here he faced criticism on two fronts: from remnant Rooseveltians who feared race suicide, and from religious antagonists of the sort Cooper labeled "Daytonian" – after the site of the recent Scopes trial, which had mired the town of Dayton, Tennessee, in a tea-kettle *Kulturkampf* between the forces of secular progressivism and those of biblical literalism. One otherwise sympathetic doctor was "not interested in helping the 'idle rich' to escape all responsibility," while another felt the ABCL "should do more to help arouse public sentiment in favor of fairly good sized families among the rank and file of normal people." From California in 1926, Cooper reported that many doctors in the otherwise progressive state had been "prejudiced" by Edward N. Ewer, a recent state medical society president who lamented to his fellow doctors that the U.S. birthrate had declined 30 percent in thirty years "with the assistance of clinics or other birth-control ballyhoo." Rather than convincing the poor to have fewer babies, Ewer had argued, doctors should push for better maternal and infant care so that poor children became fitter citizens.[54]

By the mid-1920s, however, only religious conceptions of natural law inspired much *public* opposition. In Cooper's meetings, as in newspaper commentary, religious law continued to fuel fiery indignation even as Roosevelt-style secular communitarianism faded. Like Sanger, Cooper tended to see religious objections as, in his words, "vague," "pointless," "emotional," and strongly tied to "R.C. [Roman Catholic] influence." The state of New York earned Cooper's special enmity on this score. After encountering tepid support in Rochester, Buffalo, and Niagara Falls, then paralyzing fear of Catholic opposition among backers of a birth control clinic in Syracuse, Cooper wrote off the nation's most populous state "on account of the R.C.'s," his "greatest hindrance" in the urban north. Across the country, in San Antonio, St. Louis, New Orleans, Detroit, and elsewhere, Cooper attributed his failure to secure sponsors to shadowy Catholic influence.[55]

Religious opposition was more remarkable for its stridency that in frequency. In Tacoma, for example, "Catholic doctors stirred up trouble" and "offered violent and emotional objections after [the] address" but the "vast majority [were] very favorable and want supplies." In Sacramento, when a Dr. Frank Topping rose to pronounce birth control "unnatural, nasty, against religion," the fifty other doctors mostly ignored him. Topping "was the first and only speaker who opposed" while "7 others spoke favorably." Opposition was "fortunately very rare."[56]

Even so, Cooper found defiant religious conviction difficult to dismiss. Only three of the fifty-one Sacramento doctors agreed to cooperate with the ABCL. "One rabid one such as Topping has a bad influence on a meeting," Cooper reported. Vague as theological or naturist appeals may have seemed to the progressives in the room, they seeded moral doubt. Happily for Cooper, though, neither natural or divine law was deterring many Americans from supporting birth control. They were simply the last objections standing.

REGIONAL AND RURAL–URBAN DIVIDES

James Cooper considered himself not only a herald of the scientific progress but a conqueror of space. He enjoyed analogizing his work with that of missionaries and early settlers, writing repeatedly "I like this pioneer work." Though acceptance varied more by the audience than by region, some areas were more amenable to Cooper's mission than others. In the western states, especially, there was "no opposition to speak of." "Economic conditions are recognized as almost of equal importance with medical conditions as indications for contraceptive advice." Sanger too found the west congenial. West of St. Louis, she recalled of her first speaking tour, in 1916, "the atmosphere changed." As she approached the Rockies she was able to reach more and more respectable audiences. "A similar attitude of liberality prevailed on the far side of the Rockies."[57]

Sanger and Cooper doubtless attributed this to the relatively sparse Catholic population in the west. But Protestant towns in the southeast and northeast also presented Cooper with overt opposition and long wait times before his talks were approved. In Alabama there was "a lot of shyness ... about the movement" and throughout the south it was "very difficult getting up a meeting and getting on a program." These difficulties were often merely formal, however, and eased once Cooper was behind closed doors. Overall the south was "conservative but not indifferent," and southerners were generally "sympathetic" after getting "an intelligent idea what the movement is, what it stands for, and what it hopes to do."[58]

Least receptive were the northeastern states – not only cities with large Catholic populations like Hartford or Bridgeport, but also the Protestant hinterlands. "Tough work in conservative New England," wrote Cooper after a tour of small-town Vermont in 1926. Doctors in Middlebury were "cordial and cooperative but conservative and slow." In St. Albans conservative doctors acrimoniously fought the meeting. The mayor of Burlington and a local medical school dean were both sympathetic "but for political reasons non-cooperative."[59]

Cooper was twice as likely to face opposition in the country's hundred largest cities than elsewhere, due in part to Catholic opposition. But rural Protestants all over the country could be recalcitrant. Doctors had to "be very careful on account of the small town gossips," Cooper reported from Pawnee City, Nebraska, since the "uninformed laity" often did not "differentiate between a man who does abortions and one who gives B.C. advice." Country doctors nevertheless went out of their way to attend Cooper's meetings, and once there, seemed eager to demonstrate their forward thinking on birth control. Doctors traveled over seventy miles to see Cooper's talk in Devils Lake, North Dakota, explaining that birth control was needed in their location as much as in cities. "Demand for B.C. [is] just as evident in rural as in city life."[60]

CONCLUSIONS

Cooper's mission ultimately covered 40,000 miles. With his medical degree, courtly manner, and persistence, Cooper was able to insert himself into hundreds of groups that would not otherwise have sought out a speaker on his topic. Perhaps no other person gained so comprehensive a picture of middle-class, middle-of-the-road opinion on birth control in America during its critical period of public legitimation.

Cooper pressed the worthiness of birth control on thousands of people who would have preferred to dodge the issue. He prodded locally influential people to challenge their inherited ideals. He made it easier for doctors to feel that they worked in communities that supported birth control as a tool of scientific medicine. He helped associate his cause with a confident, forward-looking vision of history's march.

For the most part, though, as Cooper moved from town to town every few days, he found that most of the groundwork for his success had been laid before his arrival. Few middle-class people recoiled at the mere thought of associating themselves with birth control's liberalization. They were uncertain how much the local moral consensus had changed, and needed time to meditate and consult. But all over the country, these consultations resolved themselves in Cooper's favor. Already more and more people acknowledged the good or inevitability of birth control. It did not seem like a much greater step to welcome a traveling speaker on the subject.

Cooper's middle-class audiences appreciated his ability to separate birth control from the emotion and fear surrounding sexuality. Birth control at its most palatable was neither liberation nor perdition. It was a settled fact of life. It was also a technical tool that might help consolidate progressives' control of society, perhaps improving health and welfare along the way. It betokened a world with fewer illusions and fewer problems.

For respectable burghers across America, family limitation was an expression of several of the characteristic features of their self-consciously progressive society. Rather than heralding moral decline and national death, mass birth control held out the possibility of further mastery of the material environment. For a nascent majority of 1920s middle-class Americans, to sanction birth control was to think scientifically rather than superstitiously, to be frank rather than hypocritical, and to recognize the need for a pragmatic social engineering if progress was to endure. To deny this, as James Cooper would have said, was to live in abodes of the past.

6

Marriage as It *Is*

Birth Control on the Radio

All lasting reforms are derived from within.
Ben Lindsey[1]

**

Last Sunday night, at nine o'clock, I spoke for exactly one hour over KOA Radio Station here in Denver ... They told me I talked to over a million people ... KOA invited its listeners to write letters and ask questions, if any of them cared to. We have been getting a bushel of letters all this week.[2]

On March 13, 1927, Judge Ben Lindsey became the first American to support birth control in a national radio address. Speaking loudly and anxiously, Lindsey asked Americans to support loving marriages between spouses who wanted each other's companionship, including sexual companionship, but did not immediately want children. He called these marriages "companionate." "What is 'companionate'?" Lindsey asked: "IT IS present marriage just as it exists now ... because of certain privileges that so many of these modern married people are claiming. The most notable of these privileges is birth control."[3]

Lindsey argued that as long as companionate couples remained childless, they ought to be entitled to a second privilege: simple, no-fault divorce, "if it is impossible for them to get along together." This would prevent unhappy homes, improve child nurture, and eliminate fraudulent divorces. So long as couples remained diligent in controlling births, they could stress-test their marriages before having children. Rather than "steel trap" obligation and hasty childbearing, marriage would be built on a solid foundation of mutual affection.

Lindsey presented birth-controlled companionate marriages as a reality awaiting recognition, not a reform awaiting execution. Neither law nor stigma actually prevented young people from obtaining birth control or divorce, he noted. They did so freely but deceitfully. Better than piously maintaining hypocritical standards would be to acknowledge and rationalize these practices – birth control in particular. In a society where no shadowy disrepute attached itself to contraception, couples would sooner "give up their liaisons outside of legal marriage and get married," he told KOA listeners. Young people would find legitimate sexual outlets, grow in mutual affection, and build up "financial ability" during the birth-controlled phase of their marriages, *then* enter "permanent family marriages for the procreation of children." Everyone would benefit.[4]

At the time of his KOA speech Lindsey was nationally renowned as spokesman for progressive causes, and particularly as a founder of juvenile courts. His life story made him a sympathetic figure. His father, a telegraph operator from Tennessee, had committed suicide when Lindsey was eighteen, forcing Ben and his brother to leave school and work odd jobs. At nineteen Lindsey himself attempted suicide. The gun jammed, and he found purpose. He studied law, established a practice in Colorado, and entered local Democratic politics. Soon he was a magistrate in Denver. Physically small but fearless in the courtroom, he soon gained a reputation as a protector of children and families. When he subsequently began advocating for separate juvenile justice, he earned national fame as "the children's judge." A 1914 poll of *American Magazine* readers ranked him eighth among the "greatest living Americans," in a three-way tie with Andrew Carnegie and the preacher Billy Sunday.[5]

The first few months of 1927 saw the end of Lindsey' uncomplicated reputation for progressive beneficence. After the KOA speech and a barrage of similarly themed efforts around the same time – including a series of articles in *Red Book* magazine, a *Companionate Marriage* book, and a speaking tour – Lindsey came to be better known as America's leading champion of "modern marriage" – or for his many detractors, "trial marriage" and "free love."[6]

KOA's request for comment drew at least 258 letters from twenty-six U.S. states and three Canadian provinces. Most correspondents lived in the rural Great Plains, in a broad fan extending north, east, and south of Denver. Unlike Sanger's petitioners, few of Lindsey's correspondents sought practical contraceptive knowledge. Just 6 percent did so, despite Lindsey's "kindly offer to give advice to anyone who writes," as a Montana homesteader put it. Like most Americans, KOA listeners took birth control *methods* for granted. Their interest was in ideals governing their use. Rural dwellers tended to discuss birth control "as simply as they would the limitation of crops and the breeding of live-stock," as a contemporary magazine put it.[7]

Lindsey's pragmatic realism better suited this group than Margaret Sanger's utopian futurism. Though Lindsey knew Sanger and James Cooper personally – hosting them when they passed through Denver, helping arrange meetings, and maintaining friendly ties – he did not paint birth control as a dawning social panacea, as Sanger tended to do. Instead he emphasized its universality. At worst there was "drug-store birth control" for "the poor and the ignorant"; at best, "scientific" medical advice for the "educated and intelligent." "Legal, recognized, controlled and directed companionate marriage," Lindsey told his radio listeners, "WOULD SIMPLY BE RECOGNIZING AND MAKING LEGAL WHAT ALREADY EXIST IN PERFECTLY RESPECTABLE SOCIETY." Lindsey saw himself as a herald rather than an agitator. "We already have 'companionate' marriage ... Why do we keep up the pretense?"[8]

Lindsey thus asked Americans to accept a different set of premises than Cooper or Sanger. Cooper, above all, wanted his audiences to accept birth control as a matter of scientific social management. Sanger emphasized women's ongoing struggle to free themselves from servitude and drud-gery. Lindsey, by contrast, primarily wanted Americans to accept birth control's mass adoption as a matter of moral pragmatism, sincerity, and liberal social optimism. Rather than a promise, family limitation was a fait accompli with observably benign results. It made Americans happier and more secure. There was no need for hypocrisy. People could be trusted to do what was best for themselves and society. Whether these results could be squared with inherited first principles was beside the point at best. This message was well received.[9]

THE RESPONDENTS

KOA ("Klear Over America") had been founded three years earlier, in 1924, by General Electric Company. Its 15,000-watt transmissions reached a vast expanse of sparsely settled land. Listeners responded to Lindsey from as far afield as California and Pennsylvania, though other signals created interference east of the Mississippi River and the Rocky Mountains limited reception to the west. As a result, 78 percent of KOA's respondents came from the band of fifteen states that form United States' longitudinal midsection (map). Another 12 percent came from the three Canadian "prairie provinces" directly north of this band. Just 25 percent of writers lived in towns of more than 5,000 inhabitants. Letters from urbanites came mostly from Denver and its suburbs.[10]

Radio sets were common by the late 1920s. In 1922 Americans spent $60 million on radio sets and parts; by 1927 that figure was $446 million. Mass-produced sets like the Crosley Pup cost less than $10, roughly equivalent to one week's rent in a medium-sized urban apartment, or – more to the point for many of Lindsey's listeners – the price of a hog at market in Chicago. A Pup would have been a mild extravagance for working-class people, but well within reach of the middle classes. Close to half of American homes contained a receiver by 1930.[11]

Respondents who declared their occupations were farmers and ranchers, but also small-town professionals and middle-class Denverites. Nearly all used standard grammar and spelling. Half were identifiable by name as male, 23 percent as female. Nine percent signed their letters as a couple. Finally, because KOA was a radio station and not an advocacy organization, Lindsey's writers tended to encounter his ideas unintentionally. KOA broadcast standard advance promotions for the talk, but most listeners would have heard the judge by accident, on one of the few radio stations available to them that Sunday evening. One couple had "already taken in two sermons and a short anti-evolution lecture before your hour arrived." Many expressed surprise, delight, or dismay at hearing Lindsey address birth control over the radio. As a result – and because KOA *solicited* comments – letters tended to be blunt expressions of all manner of personal philosophies, rather than practical petitions or careful essays.

THE WIDER CONTROVERSY

Many KOA listeners would have been familiar with the companionate marriage controversy before hearing Lindsey speak. For over a month leading up to the KOA address there had been "so much interest in Judge Lindsey's views that any expression of them is news," as one newspaper exclaimed. Discussion of companionate marriage never reached the fervid pitch of the "race suicide" debate during Theodore Roosevelt's presidency, but Lindsey's respondents, like Roosevelt-era social critics, tended to write with one eye to the judge's actual words and another to a wider press-fueled controversy.[12]

In Lindsey's case that controversy began shortly after he published the fifth article in his series for *Red Book*, a popular general-interest

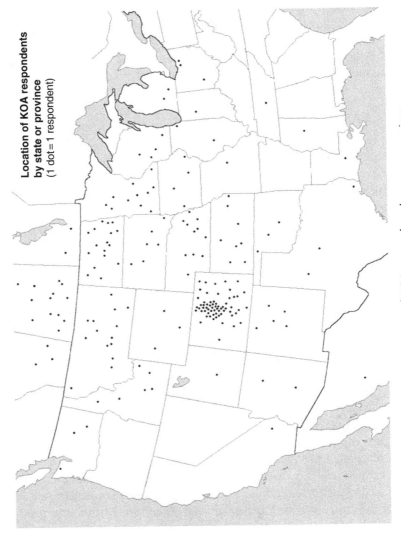

Location of KOA respondents
by state or province
(1 dot = 1 respondent)

FIGURE 6.1 Location of KOA respondents by state or province.

FIGURE 6.2 Ben Lindsey speaking on KOA, c.1927. Courtesy History Colorado.

magazine, in January 1927. Before this "fatal Fifth," as Lindsey later dubbed it, his series on "moral revolt" among American youth had attracted little attention. This changed when Lindsey introduced two characters from his courtroom: "Fred," 20, and "Inez," 17 (with "bobbed head"). Fred and Inez were loving newlyweds who nevertheless wished to annul their marriage and thus avoid the risk of conceiving children they could not afford. Lindsey argued that couples like this should be allowed to "put off the birth of babies till the groundwork of the home had been laid." How would they do this? Not via the "traditional puritan" method of abstinence, "which is against nature," but with "the assistance of modern science, it almost goes without saying."[13]

Anticipating his critics, Lindsey reminded *Red Book* readers that he was "not responsible" for the practice of birth control "among young people in every class of society." But he closed his article with unabashed moral pragmatism: "I have been receiving a good many letters of late asking me how I reconcile some of the views I am expressing in these articles with the Bible," he wrote. "I don't reconcile them with the Bible." Modern morality, he said, required consideration of "matters which were not factors in the speculative thought of the ancient Jews." "A custom must produce in terms that are practicable and measurably good, or I am done with it, and so, in the end, is everyone else."[14]

With these words Lindsey suddenly found himself under close national examination. Journalists first fixed on a group of Baptist preachers in Knoxville, Tennessee, who sought to prevent Lindsey from making a planned address to the local Optimists Club. When Lindsey responded defiantly, promising to schedule even more speeches in Tennessee and calling the preachers "pulpit pounding peewees," attention grew more intense. The ensuing press circus fed partly on Lindsey's incendiarism, partly on the sexual titillation inherent in the subject matter, and partly on fresh memories of the Scopes trial.

Early coverage was largely negative. Of 123 original editorials and articles gathered by Lindsey's clippings service in the two weeks following the *Red Book* article, 63 percent painted the judge unfavorably. Just 20 percent supported him. More negative publicity poured in via wire service and syndicated columns. Lindsey's treatment might have been even harsher had not many observers softened their criticism in deference to his previous work with juvenile offenders.[15]

Lindsey's perceived stridency turned many critics against him. He was accused of petulance, fame-seeking ("Lindsey ... loves the front page as a cat loves new milk"), and detachment from extrajudicial reality ("There is a sane, wholesome strata of society in American life with which Judge Lindsey appears to have little contact"). His apology for the young couple's marriage and immediate divorce struck many critics as flippant and deliberately sensational. Many writers who could accede to Lindsey's views on birth control could not condone other of his positions or tactics.[16]

This uproar caused Lindsey to take a more defensive tack, telling anyone who would listen that he was "opposed to trial marriage" and wanted all companionate relationships to end in "procreative or family marriage." Still, the effect of the press criticism was to transform Lindsey's public image from reliable progressive to incipient radical. If his proposal would encourage marriage, critics argued, it was the wrong kind of marriage. "Flitting from flower to flower" in volatile, self-serving relationships would undermine civilization. Lindsey was a positive danger to the youth he ostensibly sought to help: a "godless," "undecent," "pathetic," "Bolshevistic" "nut" – or, at best, "a good man gone wrong." "Imagine a world without marriage, without the moral code, without any God except animal impulse," cried an Iowa editorialist, "with Lindsey dancing in the street hand in hand with Phyrne in defiance of the experience and the wisdom of the ages!"[17]

FAVORABILITY

The *Red Book* uproar made KOA's directors wary of allotting Lindsey airtime. Advance publicity distanced the station from the judge's views, and just before he took the air, an announcer nervously assured listeners that the *Red Book* articles in fact contained "nothing of free love." Lindsey opened his speech by reminding listeners of his unexceptionable work in juvenile justice and denouncing "exaggerations in newspapers" and other "abuse." Listeners described Lindsey's tone as staccato and loud, as if he "sat too close to the 'mike.'"[18]

It was thus a surprise when KOA listeners decisively supported Lindsey. Sixty-five percent responded approvingly. "You have opened up a real, big and vital subject," wrote a married couple from North Dakota. Listeners praised the judge and the station for their "bravery" and "moral courage" in airing the program. Much of the praise was mild and qualified, but decisive nevertheless, and detractors were few. Just 25 percent disapproved in any way, while the remaining 10 percent of listeners declared neutrality or found themselves perfectly unable to decide if Lindsey was right.[19]

The strongest critics attacked not only Lindsey but KOA, berating the station for intruding on their living rooms with its "rotten propaganda." "You may count upon my petition to the Radio Commission to eliminate your station from the air," wrote a Kansas man. A smaller group of conservatives found themselves unsatisfied that, in "clearing the air," Lindsey had not been more contrite. They had expected the judge to explain how he had been unfairly victimized in the press and renounce the radical views attributed to him. Instead they were shocked to hear confirmation that Lindsey had in fact morphed into a prophet of debauchery. "I am almost ashamed to call myself a woman and acknowledge at the same time that I listened to such an address," wrote a Mrs. E.A. Williams. "I have lived in Denver for almost thirty years, have worked for Judge Lindsey's cause, have done all that I could to help keep him in office. It is very discouraging to find after all these years that one's idol should fall and crumble into decay." Another former supporter called Lindsey's arguments blasphemous and arrogant: "Our religion he mentions in a slurring sarcastic way ... Anyone with other views is ignorant and out of date."[20]

Lindsey's many supporters effectively rolled their eyes at the uproar over his ideas, expressing the patient confidence of a moral majority in waiting. One "violently" anti-Lindsey newspaper editor was "a dirty hypocrite who left his wife," a Fort Collins man noted. "You have been 'razzed' so much," a college student wrote. "One lady said you were trying to legalize a crime, and when I asked her if she knew what your idea of companionate marriage was, she said 'Well, I know what the newspapers say.' So you see it was fortunate that you had a chance to personally explain your ideas."[21]

PRAGMATISM

Lindsey's talk touched briefly on all the major activist arguments for birth control, promoting women's rights, poverty alleviation, sexual freedom, eugenic reform, and the repeal of Comstockery. Those arguments, however, were overshadowed by Lindsey's attention to the "measurably good." More than anything, the KOA speech was a referendum on listeners' moral pragmatism. Lindsey focused relentlessly on birth control's present benefits for living people. Unapologetically skeptical, practical, and "modern," Lindsey wanted listeners to prioritize observable results over inherited first principles. He asked them to join him in a plural and evolving universe where morals, like animals or civilizations, adapted in order to survive. Times were changing, and the family's survival depended on innovation.

In a way traditionalists found exceedingly difficult to digest, Lindsey therefore pitched himself as a guardian of traditional values, even a "conservative." Without the dead weight of hypocrisy and cynicism, marriage would become less "rigid" and imposing, more vibrant and appealing. Marriages would be stronger and last longer. Sexuality would be contained. The alternative to companionate marriage was not traditional marriage, but no marriage all. The way to realize "the highest ideals ... as to fidelity, monogamy, morality, permanency AND THE PRODUCTION OF CHILDREN," Lindsey argued, was counter-intuitive. It was to relax those ideals, replacing absolutism and attendant hypocrisy with flexibility, understanding, and sincerity.[22]

To Lindsey's least sympathetic listeners, the judge's claims to conservatism were a blatant smokescreen – "sordid and secret warfare against the laws of nature and the laws of God." They lent his campaign an air of conspiracy and deceit. "He said companionate marriage is not trial marriage," wrote one woman: "I suppose he does not call a highwayman a robber but just merely a gentleman in reduced circumstances."[23]

But Lindsey's opponents and supporters did not diverge on the desirability of stable and reproductive families, only on how best to achieve that goal. Supporters wanted to prioritize realizable ideals; opponents preferred aspirational standards. Should the community maintain an age-old ideal of pristine sexual forbearance, shunning the sinful but tacitly accepting the inevitability of sin? Or should it adopt more pragmatic standards, working incrementally towards realizable earthly goals?

Lindsey's preference for the latter, his critics thought, reflected a wider social failure to understand the function of public idealism. "It's like taking the top bar off to protect the fence," wrote a Wyoming rancher. "We sure expect better from any citizen of the U.S." Precisely where Lindsey saw cancerous hypocrisy, his opponents saw the hard path of the righteous. "I never have been able to see very worthy motives in marriage that coldly determines there shall be no children," wrote a Methodist pastor from Memphis. "I know you will say that we are not dealing with an ideal but a present situation. But you can never remedy a condition by deserting our ideals for a lower level. The way of Jesus is to set the ideal high and challenge humanity to aspire to it."[24]

Like James Cooper, Lindsey found religious idealism heartening his strongest critics. Writers invoking religious principles were more than twice as likely to oppose Lindsey as those who did not. Though the odd liberal Christian supported Lindsey on religious grounds, arguing that a merciful and loving God did not want unrelenting childbirth, the devout more typically found his confidence in moral evolution debasing. "He absolutely ignores the existence of moral law ... which has for its authorship the Divine and Infinite God," complained one writer. A North Dakota couple patiently reminded Lindsey that God had "said 'be fruitful and multiply.'" "We might just as well repeal the prohibition law and legalize intemperance as to legalize fornication and adultery just because they are practiced so much."[25]

More secular-minded idealists saw in Lindsey a figure out of "the later Roman Empire." Just as the gradual erosion of stern idealism had undermined past greatness, it promised to undo American achievements and return the country to "pre-society." "When you propose to legalize prostitution and birth control you strike a blow at the very heart of our national strength," wrote a Nebraska man. "Your act should be construed as treasonable." Lindsey's offense was especially great because America stood as an emblem of virtuous democracy in a benighted world.[26]

For Lindsey, as for James Cooper, secular republicans often lacked the absolute conviction of the religious. "I am heartily in favor of birth control properly applied for the good of society," wrote a typically ambivalent critic, "yet the universal practice would present grave dangers." What both republican and religious critics tended to share, however, were cyclical views of history. Civilizations, especially republics, rose and fell with the virtue of their citizens. That had been the conclusion of the classical writers and later of Edward Gibbon in *Decline and Fall of the Roman Empire*. The United States now seemed to be reckoning with similar moral degeneration.

More than the keenest republicans, the devout tended to view this sort of decay as inevitable. Though it was good to struggle against sin and vice, man was inherently sinful and his works corrupt, so the goal of a progressively more perfect republic was chimerical. History worked in cycles of convergence and divergence from unitary moral truths rooted in nature and divine revelation. The United States was in a divergent cycle, and recognition of this unfortunate reality was as important as stubborn action against it.

For both these groups, inspired by Gibbon or the doctrine of original sin, ideals needed to be persistently insisted upon in civic discussion. Only "the old-fashioned method of character building" based on "God given moral law" promised salvation, a Denver man warned Lindsey. It was a "colossal conceit" for any "weak, puny, finite unit of humanity" to attempt amendments to eternal law. Even in a doomed effort, individual virtue was godly.[27]

Birth control's legitimacy rose, in part, alongside the weakening of these Gibbonian or Augustinian visions. For Americans who saw human history as a series of deviations and rapprochements with eternal virtues, Lindsey's reformism was short-sighted and naïve. It trusted too much in human nature. These critics could understand birth control's social logic, and perhaps tolerate it in some cases, but sanctioning it publicly was a different matter.

More than other activists, Lindsey understood that countering this sort of argument did not require a competing idealist edifice, but might subsist on a pragmatic distaste for hypocrisy, superstition, and puritanism. Americans may not have been unreservedly enthusiastic about the spread of birth control, but they practiced it, and knew their peers did too. The observable benefits were apparent. Rather than deviants from hallowed standards, parents of small families were more like models for an uncertain but promising future. "Why not pull for a thing that most all married people are practicing?" one man asked. "It is only a matter of time before Birth Control must be inforced by law as well as society."[28]

PROGRESS

In addition to his unmistakable pragmatism, Lindsey supported an unusually radical progressivism. Alongside standard modernization arguments, Lindsey predicted that the state would soon maintain a "House of Human Welfare" or "Temple of Venus" where married couples could receive free sexual and marital instruction from "specialists, biologists, psychologists, scientists." The "youth revolt," moreover, was a good thing. Far from being degenerate or "flaming," young rebels were showing the way to sustainable progress. "Happily, this younger generation, so much wiser, franker, cleaner-minded and more moral than the older generation, will soon be in command," Lindsey told his listeners. Already "most of the intelligent people in modern Christian church marriages are probably using birth control," and though there were "plenty of witch-burning, sixteenth-century-minded people still with us," new generations would reject "the dead hand of superstition" and older generations' "Freudian complexes." "Priestly threats of hell terrorize no longer." Hypocrisy would give way to honesty. "No wholesale rebellion against the ancient conventions of sex has ever been known before in the history of our civilization," Lindsey concluded in *Red Book*. "*The reason is that this present civilization is the first of its kind.*"[29]

Lindsey's many sympathizers saturated their letters with support for this kind of optimistic, anti-clerical modernism. "Just as the present custom took the place of the ancient custom of having to kill two alligators before one could be married," wrote a Nebraska woman, companionate marriage would triumph. Leaders would "catch up with modern customs," declared another Nebraskan, "and these things which are today universally practiced will be legalized." The church "with her ... mother goose fables and her pre-civilization laws and codes," added a Minnesota man, was already "making her last stand against progressive idear's."[30]

Lindsey's detractors, meanwhile, sensed that the tides of opinion were against them. Sixteen percent requested anonymity in the event that KOA broadcast their views in a follow-up program the next Sunday. Far fewer of Lindsey's supporters – just 5 percent – wished to conceal their names. On reproductive ethics, moralists across the Great Plains were more concerned about appearing out of date than ahead of their time.[31]

LIBERAL OPTIMISM

Lindsey's final inescapable argument was libertarian and optimistic about human nature. Here again, the judge proved himself an adept populist. Recognizing that support for reproductive self-determination was stronger than support for birth control per se, Lindsey appealed to the fundamental American belief in "freedom of choice." Then, characteristically, he pushed further. "Dark age" moralists failed to appreciate the "inherent goodness of mankind when given a decent chance to choose for itself." Humans in a state of nature were not selfish and sinful. They required no special monitoring by their peers. "I speak from experience with thousands of cases," he said over KOA, "when I say that marriage is a greater success ... in proportion to the amount of personal liberty it allows."[32]

Human nature, in any case, precluded race suicide. Even in the absence of pronatal doctrine, people would still have children. "The mating instinct with the natural, biological preference of most married couples for children" was a "sufficient guarantee" that modern marriages would produce enough children to sustain society.[33]

This optimism was fantasy for the judge's detractors – republican and religious, realist and idealist. Unless society continued taking a skeptical view of birth control, birthrates would be "alarmingly small" because people would never overcome their "financial and social" hesitation to bear children. "In most young people the parental instinct awakens only coincident with the birth of a child," noted a "disappointed" Coloradan. Lindsey seemed to think every expansion of the individual will would have a corresponding social benefit, but – a New Mexico judge instructed him –

society is a state of obligation and duties to others, so that we ourselves may enjoy a reasonable degree of freedom. This is not a Utopian age, and neither in marriage nor in any other relation can we hope always to be floating on silvery clouds, the reputed honeymoon condition, but should learn and practice tolerance, and be happy and contented in less than perfect state.

Virtue within limits was a worthier pursuit than indefinite individual happiness.[34]

Most KOA listeners nevertheless shared some of Lindsey's libertarianism. "Decency cannot be legislated into a people," an otherwise skeptical Coloradan observed. "It is the product of long training and largely due to a condition of environment." The idea of reproductive oversight was a legacy of the meddlesome "old arrangement of 'endure the better or worse, and obey,'" wrote a Denver woman. A soldier regretted that his wife had received "a very pious home training on a farm in Mo.," and acquired "some backward ideas about marriage" – including "the idea that about the only time for intercourse was when there were to be children." Now she was using contraceptives. "For after all whose business is it outside the ones who have to supply the milk and shoes?"[35]

Lindsey's libertarianism evoked somewhat less sympathy than his progressivism. KOA listeners were more confident in declaring that Lindsey was on the right side of history than in supporting unrestrained reproductive individualism. Very often, though, these ideas fused in listeners' minds, and opinions reflected the difficulties and ambiguities of assessing whether the twin forces of modernization and liberal individualism were desirable and sustainable, or decadent and fleeting. "It spells the dawn of a new order in society," wrote D.S. Todd of Williston, North Dakota, of ideas like Lindsey's. "Ecclesiasticism has too long cursed humanity with its dogma and must heed the cry of love for love's own sake. It is absurd to believe that any curse rests upon couples who desire to maintain a home for themselves alone." But Todd was reluctant to abandon entirely the idea of a social claim on reproduction, and closed his letter with a postscript: "Lest I be misunderstood, let me say that two sons and two daughters now approaching maturity constitute our principal source of happiness."[36]

By the same token, E.G. Lauckner of Starkweather, North Dakota, found himself generally unsympathetic but reluctant to commit himself. "I will admit that you were saying facts about conditions of today, but why do they exist?" he asked. "Because God the Almighty Saviour is left out of every thing that is modern . . . And furthermore you exalt yourself as far as to call the Law of God silly, narrow and inefficient to meet these narrow modern times which will only last a few days, so to speak." Lauckner closed by noting that he was only twenty-six years old: "Do not think that I am an old narrow fool because I write thus."[37]

Todd decided hesitantly that modernity and reproductive liberalism were good; Lauckner leaned the opposite way. Both subscribed to the idea of reproductive debt, but whereas Todd optimistically believed that payment into continuums could be entrusted to innate conscience, Lauckner believed ideals needed continual reinforcement in the face of inborn selfishness and sin. For both men and dozens of their fellow respondents, Lindsey's speech crystallized the abstract forces that had made birth control popular: not just the privileging of liberal optimism over darker visions of human nature, but progress over eternity, pragmatism over idealism, and skepticism over dogma, and freedom over limits.

GENDER, FEMINISM, AND COMPANIONATE MARRIAGE

"Companionate marriage" has stuck in the lexicon in the years since Lindsey popularized it. Under that name, historians have outlined the emergence of marriage as an exchange of sympathies more than duties and services, and charted a series of important changes in the way men and women understood marriage and gender. Some Americans "recognized that companionate marriage could promote women's sexual emancipation," as one historian has written. Others saw the new standard as dangerous to women's perceived interest in restraining male sexuality. Companionate marriages encouraged expressive female personhood and even sexual liberation, on the one hand. On the other, they did nothing to address women's economic dependence, and indeed continued to define a woman by her husband's needs.[38]

Characteristically, however, gender questions remained in the background for Americans assessing Lindsey's companionate vision. This was partly because Lindsey, though himself a feminist, did not emphasize the feminist case for birth control. He excoriated "the brutal men that so often make women mere breeding machines," and argued that "voluntary parenthood ... promotes the freedom of women instead of the slavery of women," but he generally left his cause's gender implications to his listener's imaginations. Some had their imaginations duly sparked, especially when Lindsey contrasted women's physical danger with the comfortable moralizing of celibate Catholic clergy. "Yes indeed it's a women's question only," wrote a Colorado woman. "'The women bear the children – the priests do not.'"[39]

But female KOA listeners were only slightly more likely to approve of Lindsey's message (71 percent) than men (63 percent). Less than 3 percent

of all writers implied that the judge's proposals had any special significance for women. A slightly larger proportion specifically framed companionate marriage as a problem for both men and women. "Every boy
(almost) of the 'dangerous age' knows at least one method of preventing
conception, not to mention the girls," a college student wrote. Issues like
secularization (22.8 percent), rising living standards (11.2 percent), or
modernization (14.7 percent) received more attention. Lindsey tormen-
tors in the daily press were no more focused on female (or male) agency.[40]

The feminist organized movement likewise remained obscure.
Newspapers viewed Lindsey as an independent social radical, drawing
no connection to Sanger, her League, or any other activist or organization.
Respondents made that connection just twice: a Minnesota woman noted
that she was an ABCL member, and an Idaho doctor had "read about
a society in New York advocating birth control." Both in the press and the
correspondence, writers were much more likely to mention Bolshevism as
an antecedent to companionate marriage than Sangerism.[41]

WESTERN AMERICANS AND BIRTH CONTROL

The remarkably favorable reception Lindsey, Cooper, and Sanger enjoyed
in the western U.S. invites a final question: why might westerners have
been friendlier to fertility control than other Americans? Whatever the
importance of the west's relatively sparse Catholic population, westerners' patterns of migration and settlement also seem to have been significant. Migrants to the edges of neo-European settlement, the family scholar
Göran Therborn has written, have consistently acted as "institutional
innovators." Shedding the established social controls of village or town
life in favor of an "unknown expanse of land," they have built new laws
and customs. For U.S. historians, who have long debated the significance
of westward expansion for American norms and institutions, this thesis
has peculiar resonance. "The frontier is productive of individualism,"
Frederick Jackson Turner wrote in 1893. "The peculiarity of American
institutions is the fact that they have been compelled to adapt themselves
to the changes of an expanding people."[42]

Turner saw frontier mobility – geographic and economic – as
a wellspring of signal American virtues such as self-reliance and egalitarian democracy. His idea whitewashed the resistance and displacement of
native peoples, overlooked the fact that many "frontier" settlers arrived
from nearby semifrontiers, and helped paint the United States as morally
exceptional on the world stage. But families, at least, do appear to work

differently on Therborn's global frontiers. First-generation settlers on cheap "new" land often have *large* families, in what is sometimes called the "initial frontier effect." In the United States, some families moved west with the specific intent of acquiring enough land to support a large family. Others, on arrival, abandoned the fertility controls of their native places.[43]

In later generations, however, the same relative unsettledness may have afforded birth control a quicker path to legitimacy. Migrants to the west typically left behind settled communities and extended kin groups. Farmers and ranchers lived on large, dispersed landholdings, rarely forming concentrated villages. Within this scattered patchwork of homesteads, heterogeneity ruled well into the twentieth century. "Most settlement districts had a high proportion of strangers – people coming from everywhere, with different religions, varying ethnic origins, differing and potentially incompatible personal and familial cultures and outlooks." Isolation and "utter loneliness" were as much problems as the new "terrain, climate, and wildlife." "Each family must live mostly to itself ... shut up in little wooden farm houses," wrote a visitor to North Dakota in 1893.[44]

Westerners were also highly mobile, often viewing their homes as interchangeable locations to "accumulate property that could be transferred somewhere else." Drought, railroad expansion, boom-and-bust commodity cycles, land speculation, new farming techniques, ongoing in-migration, and federal policies all encouraged western mobility. By 1910 "a mosaic of instant country neighborhoods" covered the Great Plains amid a "continual churning of population." As much as a quarter of the population decamped for a new locale every year. This mobility may have weakened westerners' sense of reproductive debt insofar as that debt was most credible when owed to a specific place-people continuum.[45]

Westerners' isolation and mobility likely decreased the moral costs of embracing fertility control. Outside relatively fixed and self-conscious communities, birth control was easier to accept as a practical benefit to immediate family – especially in cases where opportunity appeared to diminish, relative to expectations, after the first generation of settlement. Though western mobility and isolation could not have been more than contributing factors to the west's friendliness to birth control, the social conditions of frontier life seem to have made fertility control appear less a threat to settled communities and more a benefit to living families.[46]

CONCLUSIONS

Late in 1927 Lindsey met Bob Shuler, a famed evangelist, in a debate on companionate marriage in Pomona, California. The moderator, a Judge Hilton, introduced Lindsey and Shuler by noting that the two men had drawn an "immense audience" the previous night at an auditorium in Los Angeles. After their debate there, "enthusiasm was so great" that Hilton had been forced to call off a planned vote to determine the winner. "I really believe that if the question had been left to a vote," Hilton told the Pomona audience, "that every other man and woman in the audience would have had his neighbor by the hair."[47]

Hilton then ceded the floor to Lindsey, who told the crowd of several thousand, "I am happily not coming here to propose any change, practically, at all. The change is already here. The change is in our midst. The change has been here a while." He made his familiar arguments for loving, birth-controlled marriages. Shuler responded, "I have never yet taken a stand for the lesser of two evils. I stand for the right," and assailed Lindsey as an apostate, opportunist, crowd-pleaser, corrupter of young people, underminer of national virtue, and wolf in sheep's clothing. When Lindsey finished speaking the debate stenographer recorded "applause." Both speakers won "great applause" for their final rebuttals. Again Hilton forewent a vote.[48]

In private deliberation, Lindsey's views provoked similar emotion, though perhaps less certitude. Americans divided over Lindsey's views, in part, because the judge dealt in real and present conditions rather than hopeful visions. Rather than asking for faith in birth control's future promise, Lindsey wanted to ratify the visible, imperfect status quo. The future of the family had already arrived. It was not without faults, but better than the past and improving with each passing generation. All that was now required was recognition that citizen action was leading to a healthier future. "Our people are moral," Lindsey told Americans. "Customs change." The youth revolt would "liberalize and rationalize" marriage to an even greater extent, making it "fit modern conditions."[49]

Ultimately this pragmatic progressivism appealed to Americans in a way that Sanger's future-facing idealism did not. Birth control was not a new millennium, perhaps, but it appeared inevitable and mostly beneficial. Engagement was preferable to prohibition. Reproductive morality might be judged by its "fruits" rather than it "roots," and by evolving standards rather than eternal ones. Amateur moralists were more willing than their grandparents to trust, with Lindsey, that loosening social claims on individual reproduction would serve the public interest as well as private self-interest. These positions and others were interwoven in the minds of KOA respondents, to the point that they represented an intuitive moral and emotional identity as much as a set of distinct philosophical viewpoints. Accepting birth control was the liberal, pragmatic act of someone who accommodated the economic and social realities of modern life. Disclaiming it was to harken back to a more heroic and communal age which existed increasingly in memory rather than reality.

For KOA listeners birth control nevertheless presented a necessary intersection of quotidian morality with far-reaching social consequence. Whether obscure people acted on pragmatic or idealistic premises, skeptical or devout, optimistic or pessimistic, would help define in perpetuity the purposes of a good life and America's moral legacy to the future. The felt force of history, it almost went without saying, seemed to favor ideas like Lindsey's. If social or religious imperative demanded individual contributions to eternal chains of being, this imperative would have to be bent to the economic and emotional well-being of the living, reasoning individual – not the other way around. "Restraints work best when they come from within," Lindsey told his audience scattered over the prairies, and perhaps no restraints were needed.

7

Conclusion and Epilogue

As social conditions become more equal, the number of persons increases who, although they are neither rich enough nor powerful enough to exercise any great influence over their fellow-creatures, have nevertheless acquired or retained sufficient education and fortune to satisfy their own wants. They owe nothing to any man, they expect nothing from any man; they acquire the habit of always considering themselves as standing alone, and they are apt to imagine that their whole destiny is in their own hands. Thus not only does democracy make every man forget his ancestors, but it hides his descendants, and separates his contemporaries from him; it throws him back forever upon himself alone, and threatens in the end to confine him entirely within the solitude of his own heart.

Alexis de Tocqueville (1840)[1]

Why do you put your pants on in the morning? Why do you walk on two feet instead of one?

(1974)[2]

Anonymous, on why people marry and have children

**

CONCLUSION

Between the 1930s and '70s, birth control activists in the United States celebrated a series of political and judicial victories. Time-honored laws fell. Practices that had been taboo for centuries became easier to acknowledge and act upon. Birth control gained public legitimacy, and this legitimacy heralded greater freedom and self-determination for millions of people, both in the U.S. and around the world. In many respects birth control advocacy deserves to be analogized with, and commemorated alongside, other major emancipatory reforms such as women's suffrage or civil rights.

The latter movements, however, ultimately required access to public institutions and public space in ways the birth control movement did not. Though birth control's formal acceptance by judges, doctors, and lawmakers made reliable contraception somewhat easier to obtain after the 1930s, birth control's growing acceptability and availability had less to do with direct advocacy than furtive reforms in private thought and practice. Over many decades, Americans converted these private acts into public values – first within small groups, locally and informally, and later on a wider and more visible scale. By the time a high-profile birth control movement emerged in the 1910s and '20s, this tide of small-scale private reforms was nearing completion. By the time most Americans had heard more than a few words about the organized movement, or developed a favorable opinion toward it, opposition to birth control already seemed outdated and naïve.

Reproduction forms an unavoidable nexus of philosophy and action. Even among self-consciously simple people this nexus often stokes complexities of thought and emotion. Motives that may appear simple at face value ("I am work out") reflect radiating webs of deeper assumptions about a good life. Individual leeway to act on those motives is wide. Choices about reproduction are not perfectly free and autonomous – pressure from spouses, families, or communities influence them – but because these pressures converge on a core of ideas that people tend to consider vitally important, even the most intimate suggestive power may not persuade. If we believe that humans have individual agency at all, one place they are likely to exercise it is in shaping their families.

This convergence of private authority, existential stakes, and public significance blurs the lines between intellectual, social, and political life. It helps illuminate the role of popular ideas and centerless moral action in shaping historical outcomes. For some historians this sort of panoramic cultural change is the only kind of change that really matters; other events are surface disturbances. I would say popular ideas matter more in some cases than others. The formal politics of the statehouse or soapbox do not merely obscure history's deep and controlling currents. But the effectiveness of formal politics is uneven, and birth control provides one example of how fundamental reform can occur outside the traditional corridors of civic life.

Birth control also affords a vantage point on "modernization" – not as a force of nature or utopian blueprint, but a complex of living ideas that mattered to nonintellectuals. Many Americans saw mass birth control as the expression and consummation of all the changes that separated their world from that of their parents and grandparents. For these people, the connection of liberal modernity to birth control was more than a rhetorical flourish. Family limitation's moral status and popularity were inextricably tied up in a direction of history – good or bad, unsettling or promising, linear or cyclical, progressive or decadent. The "modern" was not just a convenient catch-all but a nexus of ethical choice. How should a good person position oneself in relation to time and history?

Understanding the birth control movement's scope means understanding that it was (and is) a far more formidable force than many of its friends and enemies have assumed. It was neither a triumph of engaged feminism nor a conspiracy of amoral libertines. Rather than a victory for any passionate band of idealists, birth control's legitimation was the expression of a slow, ambivalent, ultrademocratic groundswell rooted in changing ideas about virtue, time, and material life. Support was not typically vocal or whole-hearted, but quiet and qualified. The key actors pushed the moral envelope in small social circles, using subtle cues. The movement was local, private, cellular, and correspondingly difficult to regulate. It largely remains that way, notwithstanding legislative attempts to restrict access to contraception in the United States and elsewhere. Birth control's enduring practical legitimacy persists as an expression of a dense network of ideas that cannot be uprooted by pulling a single stem.

Activists were not entirely on the sidelines of the mass movement. They stoked civic conversation and directly assisted many thousands of Americans seeking concrete contraceptive advice. Indirectly, their work reached millions, paving the way for safer, more reliable, and more accessible contraceptive technology. Margaret Sanger and her allies deserve a prominent place in the story of the larger movement. Nevertheless, building the birth control narrative around activists' stories may be misleading. The ideas and actions that made birth control popular and legitimate were far from being perfectly represented by activists. This is particularly true in the case of Sanger's well-remembered egalitarian feminism. Sanger believed only women could be trusted to create a future safe for scientific contraception. Many activists and ordinary women vigorously supported this idea. But most of the axes on which Americans decided about birth control tended to cut across the interests of women and men, asking both sexes similar versions of the same ethical questions.

Part of understanding birth control's wide appeal, indeed, is understanding that the movement appealed to vital human interests, not just women's interests. In early twentieth-century America, family limitation lacked the strongly naturalized connection to women and feminism that developed later in the century. By no means did men merely "cooperate" with women's latent desire to limit the family. On the contrary, men were at least as responsible as women for converting moral ideas into action. The traditional male roles of household head, breadwinner, and worldly-wise pragmatist allowed men a privileged position in enacting birth control, as surely as in other domains.

The concept of independent female personhood was an important part of the worldview that allowed Americans to adopt birth control. Women felt the need for good contraception in ways men did not. With basic bodily and mental well-being on the line, women were more likely to support birth control on principle, and some duly recognized themselves as a distinctive interest group. But the movement's overall strength was the product of a much more complex array of self-consciously modern ideas – especially ideas on the rightful relationship of material practicalities to transcendent bodies or spirits. To this day, the movement's durability rests on the delicate interplay of ideas concerning, among other things, the moral status of self and society, worldliness and otherworldliness, the present and the infinite.

Looked at one way, this complex of ideas forms a bewildering tangle. Birth control's legitimation was about liberal optimism, privacy, preventative health, the pursuit of happiness, philosophical pragmatism and materialism, uncertainty and risk mitigation, the eclipse of mystical religiosity and naturism, the rise of consumerism, the decline of an organic *volk*, the appeal of science. Looked at another way, however, legitimation was simpler. It was about moral time: how to situate oneself in relation to human continuums, and the relative importance of transcendent chains of being – as opposed to other possible priorities – in a meaningful and righteous life. Prioritizing the continuum typically required a moral imagination oriented towards self-surrender, deference to eternal law, and a sense that only modesty before an untamed cosmos would reward a person on earth or in heaven. An additional child had more value when one saw in him or her a victory of the transcendent over the immediate and the claims of eternity over those of earthly vanity. Prioritizing the immediate rarely meant foreswearing this eternal vision entirely, but it meant focusing more on the material and temporal present, as world-historical change tenuously opened more and more domains to potential human mastery.

Because birth control remains politically provocative, even as history, it is worth asking: if we tell birth control's story as a tale of popular ideas about time, transcendence, and moral economy, more than feminist advocacy, do we detract from the historical dignity of women who stood defiantly for reproductive control, or women and feminists in general? And if so, would this weaken the foundations of birth control's legitimacy? I do not believe so. Nonactivist women were indispensable to the movement's success. Even in contexts where women were unable to directly implement contraceptive action, women's immediate concern over health and welfare provided essential fuel to the popular movement. Women helped enact fundamental change in a resistant public culture still largely dominated by men.[3]

Women are likely to remain first-line defenders of reproductive rights as long as men do not face the rigorous expectation that they share substantially in the time costs of childrearing, and as long as pregnancy remains difficult and sometimes dangerous. But historically, the foundations of birth control's cultural and political power have been broader. However important fertility control has been to women in particular, it has also been a fundamental part of the liberal project to maximize individual self-determination and opportunity. "Everyone needs access to birth control," as the pioneering birth control historian Linda Gordon wrote in 2012.[4]

It is, first, a matter of public health … More fundamentally, it is a requirement of modern citizenship. I mean by citizenship not a set of documents but the power to participate in democracy, to defend and expand it. For that reason, progressives need to make the defense of contraception and abortion funding a core part of our agenda, not – as it has usually been treated by the Left – as a separate women's issue.[5]

In the United States birth control has long seemed a requirement of modern citizenship. For early twentieth-century Americans it represented, as much as anything else, everything that separated the living from the dead, and the new spiritual and material world from the old one. Modern life seemed impossible without it. This remains conventional folk wisdom today. Reproductive liberalism's opponents, as a result, face an enemy that is scarcely more eradicable than the constellation of changes we understand as modernity. Freedom of conscience in reproductive control is more than a right of modern citizenship; it is an expression of that citizenship.[6]

**

EPILOGUE: GLOBAL FERTILITY CONTROL AND LIBERAL MODERNITY

Present status is no guarantee of future standing, however. Around half the world's people now live in countries with below-replacement fertility, and that proportion is growing quickly. As small-family norms spread to nations as varied as Brazil, Vietnam, and Turkey, low fertility is losing its association with a small and exceptional group of wealthy countries and gaining an association with "development" in general. Around the world, groups as small as families and as large as transnational communities are grappling with issues similar to those America confronted at the start of the twentieth century.[7]

Now as in Theodore Roosevelt's time, the tight cultural association between reproductive control and modernity may work to the advantage or disadvantage of both. Over the past two centuries in America that association has mostly been a force for birth control's liberalization. Reproductive control was part of the promise of modernity, and modernity part of the promise of birth control. So it remains, for the most part, across the world. The freer, richer, and more modern the place or person, the smaller the family. Mass birth control is widely seen as both a cause and effect of modernity, for better and not worse.

But as below-replacement fertility spreads around the world, there is no guarantee that links between birth control and liberal modernity will remain mutually reinforcing. Particularly as the world's "modern" standard-bearers sustain decades of below-replacement fertility, this connection may make the modern telos appear vulnerable and impermanent, with fertility control its Achilles heel. Some of birth control history's enduring significance lies in these contingencies.

In this epilogic essay I ask how low fertility's globalization may affect ongoing popular support for reproductive control, and how fertility trends may affect the modern liberal order. These are not the questions this book set out to answer, and the relevance of the U.S. historical case to twenty-first-century conditions is uneven. Nevertheless, I believe the parallels are plausible enough and the question important enough to examine a few key implications directly and in detail. As a work of history this book ends here.

The Globalization of Low Fertility

Assuming the future stability of demographic trends is a risky business, but for decades birthrates in the developed world have remained low and stable. In Italy, for example, total fertility rates have hovered between 1.5 and 1.2 since 1980; in Japan over the same period, 1.8 and 1.3; in Canada, 1.7 and 1.5; in Germany, 1.5 and 1.3. Meanwhile an array of countries that mid-twentieth-century population controllers considered disastrously fecund, like India, Mexico, or Indonesia, are moving below replacement. Only one substantial pocket of semi-stable high fertility remains, in the poorest countries of central and west Africa.[8]

Not all low-fertility countries are "liberal" or "free" societies. China, Russia, and Iran, for example, all have fertility rates well below replacement. But low-fertility countries have generally adopted liberalism in some guise, if only by building economic and governance systems that minimize the influence of rooted, traditionalist, kin-based power. "Developed" liberal democracies, meanwhile, dominate the list of the world's lowest-fertility countries. Many stand to lose between a quarter and a third of their baseline population with each passing generation.[9]

From a global perspective this may appear a trivial concern. The environmental advantages of falling fertility rates are obvious. Population growth cannot continue forever without devastating our planetary ecology, particularly if per capita consumption continues to rise. Assuming consumption can be limited, global population decline should help decrease pollution, slow climate change, relieve pressure on natural resources, and ease human encroachments on the natural world. Nor are these the only global benefits of low fertility. From a planetary perspective small families seem to nurture (and reflect) long-term advancements in human prosperity, education, and self-determination. With the halting decline of mystical collectivism and binding familism has come unprecedented flourishing.

But global, humanist, progressive, and individualist viewpoints are not the only ones we should expect to encounter as low fertility spreads around the world. For all its global benefits, below-replacement fertility also creates local instability. Local economies and national welfare states rely on productive young workers to create investible and taxable surpluses. More ethereally, most people want to live in societies that will endure over time. Human mortality is easier to deal with and nihilism easier to ward off in communities that "loom out of the immemorial past, and, still more important, glide into a limitless future," as Benedict Anderson has written. We tend to hope our folkways, languages, principles, families, and creeds will persist. Such persistence provides a sense that life matters in the face of death, and that death is not complete erasure.[10]

Already popular demographic attention has begun to shift, in many parts of the world, from global high fertility to local low fertility. Popular media regularly predict the demise of pay-as-you-go welfare systems in aging societies, and chronicle the continuing stagnation of geriatric economies. More ominously, they warn of cultural obsolescence in terms largely indistinguishable from those of the American "race suicide" controversy. Europe is "slowly dying" and "needs many more babies to avert a population disaster." Germany is a "land without children." "Time is running out for Japan's dwindling population." Within and outside such countries, citizens again confront questions about whether the liberal model is sustainable over time. Can democracy, equality, and prosperity be maximized without engendering ongoing population depletion? Must liberal citizens abandon any attachments to transcendence through enduring social bodies? At the family or community level, is liberal modernity a sort of comfortable death cult?[11]

In the decades since Roosevelt-era Americans pondered these questions, the terms of debate have changed. After the Second World War, the baby boom and global "population bomb" made small families seem more virtuous than selfish. Then, in the subsequent baby bust, population aging became a serious fiscal challenge for wealthy social welfare states. Most important, the idea of dutiful subordination to social organisms lost credibility over the course of the twentieth century. The period's legacy of murderous ethno-national conflict, mass genocide, colonialism, and racism cast dark shadows over all subsequent expressions of clannishness or collectivism. These horrors nurtured a postmodern libertarian project that seeks to maximize individual autonomy: most obviously in the face of arbitrary political coercion, but also in the face of informal cultural power. This project has taken many specific forms, including one which rejects the idea of reproductive debt – particularly insofar as the burden of repayment falls more heavily on women than men.

Disgust with ethnic chauvinism and communal violence has opened some doors to the disenfranchised and bolstered cosmopolitan humanism, but it has not eradicated individuals' primary identification with groups smaller than the species and codes less than universal. Even in liberal democracies with sharp memories of biopolitical nihilism, like Germany and Japan, low fertility's entrenchment has stoked grave popular concern across the political spectrum, and revivals of official pronatalism. Though this new pronatalism is not of the maximalist, soldiers-and-settlers variety common to the pre-1945 world, it is no less fearful or earnest.

Whether the growing array of national pronatal policies can be effective is another question. To date there is little evidence that programs to incentivize childrearing – via "baby bonuses," for example – can appreciably increase long-term fertility, though they may prevent low birthrates from dropping further. Dozens of wealthy countries have devoted large shares of their social spending to programs designed to ease the financial and time costs of parenthood, with nearly imperceptible effects on stubbornly low birthrates.[12]

Expanding immigration is the most obvious remedy, but immigrants from high-fertility countries tend to quickly adopt their host countries' small-family norms – if not in the first generation then in the second. This leaves the receiving country's age structure largely intact over time, so that demand for new working-age immigrants continues unabated. The resulting prospect of indefinite large-scale in-migration poses a major political problem, especially in places where natives possess a strong sense of indigeneity. Vietnamese in Korea or Senegalese in Spain are rarely seen as fully legitimate successors to the legacy population, at least insofar as they do not assimilate. Meanwhile immigrants' frequent physical and social marginalization makes such assimilation difficult. Mutual distrust between old and new residents strains social cohesion and emboldens divisive ethnonationalist leaders.[13]

Without large-scale immigration to shore up the working-age tax base, however, low-fertility welfare states face the prospect of bankruptcy, sharp increases in taxation and retirement ages, or the drastic curtailment of social insurance programs so popular that they effectively define the state's utility to many ordinary citizens. Maintaining the status quo thus creates tremendous demand for immigrants. For Italy to maintain its 1995 "support ratio" of working-age to retirement-age people, for example, the United Nations calculated in 2000 that the country would need to attract a total of 120 million immigrants by 2050 – more than double its baseline population. A larger study of twenty-seven European countries in 2008 found that maintaining the 2002 support ratio would require "828 million immigrants by 2052, in addition to the ones that are expected to come" – tripling the overall population and making "post-2002 newcomers and their descendants ... 72% of the total population."[14]

Statistical studies like these probably do not reflect realistic ground-level scenarios, and – through no fault of their authors – energize demographic alarmists. But whether alarmists' inferences are empirically correct may be less important than whether they are plausible enough to become matters of comment and concern to nonzealots on whose conventional opinions the legitimacy of birth control and liberal modernity depend. As such I ask, first, whether modern liberal societies are threatened by liberals' tendency to produce fewer children than traditionalists, and second, if *perceptions* of persistent low fertility could undermine liberalism's long-term credibility.

Does Low Fertility Endanger Liberalism in Substance?

Humans have long assumed that demography is destiny. The prolific inherit the earth. Tribes that transmit their values and loyalties through large families are more likely to endure. Athenians feared being outbred by Spartans, French by Germans, Germans by Russians, Russians by Chinese. Marginalized groups, conversely, have hoped their superior fertility would bring them to power. Quebec nationalists dreamed of a "revenge of the cradles." Mexican officials, after losing their country's thinly peopled northern territories to the United States, declared that "to govern is to populate." Anti-Zionist Palestinians declare "the Israelis beat us at the border, but we beat them in the bedroom."[15]

To whatever extent demography is destiny, liberalism's prospects have often appeared bleak. Even before Roosevelt began lamenting the relatively low fertility of virtuous citizens, European critics warned that more children were being born to primitive peasants than enlightened democrats. More recently, sociologists have noted worldwide correspondences between political and religious traditionalism and large families, within and between countries. One study notes that non-Hispanic whites in conservative-voting U.S. states are much less likely to postpone or avoid childbearing than those in politically progressive states: in politically liberal Massachusetts fertility stood at 1.6; in conservative Utah, 2.4. Across all U.S. states, fertility differentials correlated more strongly with conservative voting patterns than with income, education, or urban residence. In Europe greater regional support for confessional political parties correlates strongly with higher fertility. Over time trends like these may increase the representation of conservatively socialized people in the larger population. One study of twentieth-century American Protestantism, for instance, found that the steep decline of liberal "mainline" denominations relative to "conservative" ones could be explained, in large part, by differential birthrates. "Natural increase" explained "over three-fourths of the observed change in Protestants' denominational affiliations." Conservatives had "grown their own."[16]

On evidence such as this, recent critics have revived many of Roosevelt's concerns about the survival of progressives. Again skeptical individualism's survival appears to demand, paradoxically, self-sacrifice in the form of childrearing. Continuing failure in this regard could result in a "return to patriarchy," warns the center-left critic Phillip Longman. "The great difference in fertility rates between secular individualists and religious or cultural conservatives augurs a vast, demographically driven change in modern societies." In earlier generations "nearly all segments ... married and had children" – secular and religious, liberal and conservative – but more recently, the scales have tilted towards the devout and traditional. For Longman this "helps explain ... the gradual drift of American culture away from secular individualism and toward religious fundamentalism." If present trends continue liberalism stands to be replaced by "a new environment ... in which a patriarchal God commands family members to suppress their individualism and submit to father."[17]

U.S. political conservatives have popularized this idea from a different angle, authoring a corpus of literature that the demographer David Coleman has dubbed the "moralizing apocalyptic tradition of popular American 'disaster demography.'" These authors predict, among other things, that secular Europe will soon submit to rule by political Muslims, leaving an aging United States "alone" as a defender of the Western liberal tradition.[18]

Demography-as-destiny literature presupposes that social reproduction happens primarily within families. Children receive and retain values like liberalism or conservatism, faith or skepticism, from their parents. Filial rebellion is more the exception than the rule. Evidence on this assumption is mixed. Children's values do tend to mirror those of their parents: "parents' attitudes, especially mothers' attitudes, are significant positive predictors of children's attitudes in adulthood," as one research group writes. And "transmission findings tend to be preserved even when family social milieu is taken into account." Such conclusions inevitably carry a string of disclaimers, however, due to the complexities of disentangling parental influence from environmental conditions – which, circularly, parents have a role in shaping.[19]

Some of the clearest evidence indicates that parents transmit certain kinds of values better than others. "Congruence is particularly high on values dealing with educational goals, career issues, and major life concerns," note two sociologists. On "political traits," another team writes that "the more concrete, affect-laden, and central the object in question, the more successful ... the transmission." Values related to religious practice and political orientations, among other things, tend to be replicated in succeeding generations. "Children adopt parental partisan orientations more so than any other political characteristics." They typically replicate their parents' churchgoing habits and beliefs about the Bible.[20]

Family size preferences, meanwhile, are highly transmissible in themselves. The emergence of entrenched small-family norms around the world has thus led some demographers to posit a self-reinforcing "low fertility trap." Children raised in small families, and among them, tend to desire fewer offspring on average than would be necessary to replace population. Even then, it is common for young people in low-fertility countries to fall short of their modest family-size goals. The trap is further compounded by economic stagnation in aging societies, which causes high youth unemployment and insecurity regarding family formation. Young people enter adulthood with high consumer expectations set in their parents' homes, only to struggle for unstable income in an environment where settling into family life is conceived as costly in both economic and experiential terms.[21]

Finally, genetic predispositions may dispose people toward political orientations. "While there may be no gene for a specific issue preference or ideological orientation," researchers write, "the biological systems built by genes seem to play an important role in mediating political attitudes." Autonomic nervous system reactions, for example, "may predispose people toward policy preferences on... affirmative action and immigration." Geneticists nevertheless assume – in line with findings on complex human traits like personality and intelligence – that attitudes and political values could only be passed down via a "polygenic architecture, with the heritable variation explained by many genetic variants with small effects."[22]

All this suggests that low-fertility populations operate at a significant disadvantage in transmitting their values over time. Yet recent cultural history – including the story of birth control in America – provides ample examples of younger generations modifying their parents' views without rejecting them entirely. Whatever the importance of conservative childhood socialization, it has not prevented decisive cultural innovations in recent times. "The notion of intergenerational transmission of attitudes and orientations becomes problematic," one team of sociologists admits, "in times of large-scale social change, when younger generations may well part ways with their elders in beliefs, values, and behavior." Continuity of values, in other words, appears never to be more than a default tendency. Same-sex marriage, unthinkable in mid-twentieth-century America, enjoyed majority public and political support fifty years later. Premarital cohabitation, interracial marriage, and recreational drug use have undergone similar transitions.[23]

But if liberalism's fate is not sealed by fertility differentials, neither are those differentials ultimately insignificant. In practical terms, they mean liberalism faces a persistent burden of recruitment. Traditional world-views – organic, kin- and clan-based, deferential to authority, divinity, and eternity – tend to reward childrearing more than progressive, individualist, secular, and present-focused ones. Though liberal societies have long accommodated both these overlapping visions, healthy liberalism probably cannot afford indefinite drift towards a more traditionalist order. Liberal visions of a good life therefore must continually appeal to tranches of young people who by inertia might otherwise reinforce the relatively illiberal views of their parents and social milieus.

To date liberal societies have been decisively successful at this task, not only winning imaginations but physically drawing people from relatively conservative and provincial communities to diverse metropolitan centers – often in distant countries or regions – where liberal values tend to thrive. Assimilation of those values on arrival is not a given, of course, especially for new migrants with a strong sense of otherness. But the liberal model still retains a strong aura of historical inevitability that bolsters acculturation. Movement towards a liberal social, political, and economic order is simply "development." Many liberals assume this model's continued viability is assured by human nature.[24]

But the globalization of low fertility may expose liberalism to cross-winds in human "nature." As surely as we seek autonomy we also seek security within and for enduring communities. Postmodern societies may eventually find substitutes for social bodies as vehicles for self-transcendence, and particularism may recede in favor of global citizenship. But until that time any perception that the liberal democratic model is unsustainable over time will weaken liberalism's aura of inevitability and compound its burden of recruitment.

Does Low Fertility Endanger Liberalism in Perception?

This perception problem, more than progressive–traditional fertility differentials, poses a threat to liberalism. Already free societies' perceived reproductive decadence provides the closest thing to a unifying animus for religious and social conservatives within and outside those societies. Religious conservatives in the United States, though supportive of democratic government, excoriate a morally permissive "culture of death" founded on widely available contraception and abortion. Political Islamists, beginning with Sayyid Qutb, the founder of the Muslim Brotherhood, have been radically repelled by contact with overtly nonreproductive sexuality in the West. Ultra-orthodox Jewish rabbis teach segregation from a sinful modern world and underscore God's command to increase and multiply. Fringe voices are joined by relatively moderate figures such as Pope Francis, who has compared Europe to "a grandmother, no longer fertile and vibrant," or Britain's Orthodox chief rabbi, Jonathan Sacks, for whom "one of the unsayable truths of our time" is that "Europe is dying." "We are undergoing the moral equivalent of climate change," Sacks argues, "and no one is talking about it."[25]

Publicity around low fertility already rebounds through public discourse, muted only partly by political discomfort surrounding the topic. "Three stylised demographic facts are nowadays taken for granted by many Europeans," the demographer Tomáš Sobotka observes:

First, European birth rates are very low and further declining. Second, the currently low fertility will inevitably lead to rapid population ageing and population decline in the future. Third, these trends are unsustainable in the long run and constitute serious threats to the economy, the labour market, the welfare system, and to the foundations of European societies.

A 2002 study of the popular press in eleven low-fertility countries found that "the consequences of low fertility were considered to be largely negative and worthy of alarm, despite the fact that the causes of low fertility – such as greater gender equity – were seen as decidedly positive trends."[26]

Demographic narratives are slow-moving and abstract, and compete for attention with more immediate and concrete stories. People tend to "live for the here and now," as two demographers observe, rather than ponder "long-term consequences beyond their immediate horizon." Yet when U.S. President Donald Trump declares "the fundamental question of our time" to be "whether the West has the will to survive," or Italy's minister of health describes "a dying country," or Japanese diaper companies report that adult diapers now outsell those for children, journalistic anecdote compresses demography's longtime horizons, making trends that are imperceptible from year to year appear immediate and relevant. "As the lagged effects of decades of low fertility accumulate, we should ... expect excessive rhetoric, scaremongering, and distortion, either intentional or based upon misunderstanding and confusion," warned Michael Teitelbaum and Jay Winter in 2013. "The fact that such fears are almost always exaggerated does not diminish their force." Public alarm is amplified by nativists' anecdotal observation of demographic change, particularly intergenerational increases in the visibility of minorities set apart by physical attributes or dress. Demographic "replacement" narratives have helped spark right-wing populist and anti-immigrant movements around the world.[27]

Even within the careful empirical world of academic demography, scholars have sounded ominous tones. "The cycle of beneficial effects of the demographic transition appears to have run its course in [developed] countries," David Reher writes, "and a darker side of the process has begun, accompanied by increasingly public concerns for the long-term social stability of many developed countries." Lant Pritchett and Martina Viarengo ask "why large parts of [Europe] have decided ... to commit gradual demographic suicide," and John Caldwell and Thomas Schindlmayer suggest that "ultimately the reproduction of the species is not easily compatible with advanced industrial society," suggesting "that a social order that does not reproduce itself will be replaced by another."[28]

In immigrant-friendly low-fertility countries, populations are indeed evolving. In Germany 35 percent of children are born to immigrant parents; in England, 25 percent. These proportions are higher in big cities. Given the continued demand for young workers in low-fertility countries it is not entirely outlandish to imagine some becoming cultural "theme parks" or "museums," as some demographers have speculated – presenting glassed-in versions of their indigenous legacies to tourists, with economies "dominated by the hotel and restaurant and entertainment industries along with hospitals and nursing homes, both sectors increasingly staffed by immigrant labour." Such an outcome would harm no one but could hurt the credibility of the social model that produced it.[29]

Still, it is not a given that the globalization of subreplacement fertility or its entrenchment in wealthy countries will weaken liberalism. It is possible to imagine a future in which people build eternal visions around universal rather than particularist principles. Global labor markets and space-erasing technologies may atomize identity to the point that membership in ethno-national continuums (like Italian-ness) ceases to provide people with essential sources of meaning and purpose. Already the United States and other immigrant societies provide reasonably functional models of multiculturalism. Migrant groups once considered unassimilable into America's dominant culture, like Sicilian peasants or Eastern European Jews, have in the space of one or two generations effectively lost their radical otherness. Surveys of Asian and Hispanic immigrants suggest similar trajectories. Outbreaks of ethnic populism notwithstanding, a majority of Americans take multiculturalism for granted and accept its gradual increase over time. Little excitement greets statisticians' periodic projections that the United States' non-Hispanic white majority will soon become a minority. It is possible to imagine low-fertility populations with stronger senses of indigeneity, like Czechs or Thais, gradually if fitfully adopting similar outlooks as successive generations become more accustomed to the presence of "new" immigrants and their children.[30]

Sustaining multiculturalism is easiest in societies that hold out a credible promise of indefinite progress, especially economic progress, and liberal societies' relative wealth and security is the greatest reason to remain optimistic about their recruitment prospects. Maintaining economic vibrancy becomes more challenging as populations grow old, however. At best, aging economies and welfare systems are squeezed for resources by their pensioners – even when they welcome working-age immigrants. At worst, their age structure causes deflation and economic contraction. In the extreme case of low-immigration, low-fertility Japan, where the population is old (46 on average), growing older, and falling by several hundred thousand people every year, the elderly consume an increasing share of resources that cannot be allocated to the working- and school-age population. Capital becomes less productive amid a shortage of workers; government debt increases as politicians defer difficult social welfare decisions; investors and lenders lose confidence. The result is a society that offers less, economically, to both young and old. Rapid population aging makes it difficult to maintain the economic status quo, much less create the impression of continual progress.[31]

We can't be sure how economies, media, or political nativists will respond to population aging, but we can be reasonably sure who will resolve questions of low-fertility liberalism's viability: obscure, self-appointed moral guardians who make their judgments mostly in shades of gray. In America at the start of the twentieth century, nonzealots easily imagined themselves as parts of great social bodies. Just as easily, they subordinated those imaginary bodies to more worldly concerns. Without ever developing specialized demographic understanding or adopting the falling-sky prophesies of population alarmists, political moderates imagined and reimagined connections between themselves and transcendent chains of being. Stomach-churning moral emotionalism combined with mild and ambivalent action. Now as in the American past, great social movements may function in flickers of persons.

Free societies face less of an existential threat from overt radicalism, such as far-right nationalism or religious zealotry, than from the slow and partial erosion of popular ideas that legitimize both the modern liberal order and reproductive control, in tandem, within the broad political center. In a worst-case scenario based on the conditions outlined above, local low fertility could move towards the front of popular consciousness, becoming a folk issue in the way high global fertility did in the late twentieth century. Nonradicals might then view "development" as a lose-lose choice between population decline and economic stagnation (in a low-migration scenario) or population replacement and cultural obsolescence (in a high-migration scheme). Citizens could begin to *believe* that liberals were being replaced by conservatives through gradual intergenerational erosion, even if that were not the case. This would work to create an alternate sense of historical momentum, with fewer citizens seeing liberal and egalitarian ideals as the way of the future, and more as the way of the past.

Liberal Pronatalism?

American historical experience suggests the difficulty of doing anything to foreclose such a possibility. Setting aside feasibility for a moment, though, we might ask whether pronatal objectives are compatible with liberalism. Can liberals concern themselves with quasi-organic populations, not just individual rights, and still call themselves liberals? Many critics would say no. "Allowing any collective deliberation on future population size and make-up is widely seen to be denying the individual rights of citizens," Geoffrey McNicoll writes. "This position is so familiar that its sociological distinctiveness is not noted." Women's rights in particular are widely understood to be threatened by population-level social morality. "Family planning . . . is part of a progressive ideology that is often associated with the liberation of women," as Reiko Aoki writes of Japan. "It would follow that pronatal policies . . . are antiprogressive."[32]

Nor have memories of rabid ethnonationalism dissipated. "The shadow of an oppressive fascist regime hovers over demographic science" in Italy; in Germany, "since the time of the Nazis, birth regulations have been discredited." The German example in particular has cautioned liberals around the world against promoting social reproduction. "It is precisely because of Germany's past that pronatalist policies had been seen as racist and as an infringement on civil liberties in the West," as Laura Stark and Hans-Peter Kohler write.[33]

By the same token, much recent pronatal policy and rhetoric has been distinctly illiberal. In Iran, where total fertility stands around 1.9, the Supreme Leader has criticized contraception as a self-indulgent Western contrivance, called for a doubling of the population, and successfully lobbied to end state support for vasectomies. In Russia, where ongoing population decline is a major state concern, government posters show mothers of three under the banner "Love for your nation starts with love for family." Russian mothers, in 2007, began receiving bonus payments of around $12,000 for second-and-higher births, a sum equivalent to a year's salary for many in the middle classes. Russia's "gay propaganda" law is premised on the deficient "social value" of homosexual relationships. Pronatal policies such as these threaten to revive, in inverted form, the frantic social engineering of the "population bomb" era.[34]

At the same time, however, pronatalism has regained respectability in liberal democracies. The European Commission, for example, has lamented its member states' "demographic decline" and argued that one "essential priority" for Europe should be a "return to demographic growth." Mainstream leaders across the developed world have adopted similar positions, and followed them with policy: tax breaks, subsidized child care, parental leave, child allowances, and so on. As a political goal, liberal pronatalism is already a reality. The question seems to be how to keep that goal liberal in spirit, which in democracies it largely has been, while making it pronatal in effect, where the record is mixed at best.[35]

For pronatalism to be liberal it must work primarily through citizen action. If lawmakers involve themselves they must look first to the harm principle, as William Butz argues, "consider[ing] only those [policies] that do no harm to couples or society." Instead of trying to convince couples to have children they do not want, legislators should enact broadly family-friendly policies "desirable on grounds other than fertility enhancement."[36]

Most promising among such policies are programs aimed at assuring gender equity and work-life balance. Despite the widespread assumption that women's emancipation has caused small families, recent evidence suggests that more gender equity may actually enable somewhat larger families in developed countries. In "familistic" cultures like Italy, Japan, or Spain, where pressure to enter traditional motherhood remains strong, many young women feel forced to *choose* between parenthood and education, career, or other individual pursuits. In the absence of widely accepted models of work–life compromise, women (like men) often choose to defer parenthood indefinitely while pursuing other avenues to fulfillment. Where work-life balances are easier to strike and men assume greater domestic responsibilities, meanwhile, fertility may rise. For this reason, policies such as subsidized childcare and paid parental leave (not just maternity leave) seem to encourage near-replacement fertility levels. Sweden's program, for example, offers a generous sixteen months of paid parental leave. Either parent can use the leave time, but three months are set aside solely for the father's use. When the leave period ends, inexpensive childcare centers ease parents' reintegration into outside work.[37]

Improved economic policy in aging countries can also have pronatal effects while serving the greater good. Present economic conditions in low-fertility countries, two demographers argue, amount to "antinatalist coercion." High youth unemployment and inflexible working hours, among other factors, prevent young people from having children they otherwise want. Since "desired" fertility in the European Union is around 2.3, significantly higher than the "achieved" rate of about 1.5, economic reforms might allow individuals to achieve "personal preferences that, luckily, seem to mirror the needs of the collective."[38]

Disentangling family policies' effects from other phenomena is difficult, however. When Quebec introduced child allowances in the late 1980s, then generous daycare subsidies and leave policies in the late 1990s, the province's low fertility rebounded modestly in relation to that of neighboring Ontario. But the province of Alberta experienced an even greater fertility bump over the same period, without policy changes. Meanwhile the United States, where family-support policies are virtually nonexistent, consistently maintains higher fertility rates than many countries with extensive support systems. Whatever the possible effects of pronatal policies, meanwhile, their expense limits them to wealthy welfare states. And even there, expensive social programs become less feasible as population aging strains welfare spending. This is especially true because current pensioners already make up an electoral near-majority in many low-fertility countries. As long as retirees vote to preserve their pensions and medical benefits, it will be difficult for politicians to subsidize relatively small younger generations.[39]

Fertility trends, in any case, remain less likely to be shaped by deliberate policy than by shifting ethical conventions within small, interconnected social circles. Now no less than in the past, every citizen is implicated in every other citizen's reproductive expectations. The role of politicians and public figures is limited, for the most part, to provoking thought within a limitless web of subjectively important intuitions and judgments. From a liberal perspective it is not only observable but preferable that things work this way.

Any liberal pronatalism therefore faces a dauntingly ethereal goal: fostering local social climates where people award childbearing a somewhat higher moral priority. In effect this is a sort of antigoal, since there is no reason to suspect that active, Roosevelt-style moralism can be effective. It is a rare person who responds to direct calls to breed for a nation, creed, community, or even family. Imperative pronatalism may even be counterproductive, insofar as it frames childrearing as a grim duty.

Liberal pronatalism would require some sort of communitarian vision, built not on the idea that imagined "societies" have rights or goals, but that they have needs. Sustainable societies require a degree of intergenerational continuity. And around the world it is becoming less tenable to assume that someone, somewhere, will provide that continuity – having children due to instinct or inertia. "The desire for children in not an innate human drive," as the historian James Reed observes, "but an acquired motive which must be reinforced by social rewards and punishments sufficient to overcome the wish to avoid the pain of childbirth and the burdens of parenthood." Summarizing the work of field anthropologists, Reed continues: "There have never been any happy savages reproducing with ease. Rather, conflict between the social need to preserve the species and the individual desire to escape the burdens of childbearing is a universal part of the human experience. Societies that survive necessarily develop pronatal values that support the process of reproduction."⁴⁰

Though it is possible to imagine a resolutely individualist society developing these values, the American case suggests that without some measure of community vision, pronatal sentiments are unlikely to lead to action. Childrearing is not easily reconciled with a postmodern vision of the good life centered on minimizing binding commitments and deconstructing shared moral systems. As a means of transcendence, childrearing is more demanding and less reversible than, say, work, art, companionship, experience, or ritual. Unless credible community norms make childrearing seem worth that additional commitment and price, less imposing forms of transcendent experience will remain more attractive.

Strong community norms can marginalize the weak, few, and nonconforming. But as generations of liberal thinkers have argued, *some* measure of communitarianism may serve individual liberty. "Democracy, by its nature, dissipates rather than concentrates its internal moral force," Arthur Schlesinger, Jr., wrote in 1949. "The thirst of democratic faith is away from fanaticism; it is towards compromise, persuasion and consent in politics, toward tolerance and diversity in society." Yet an uncompromising sense of collective mission seemed to Schlesinger essential to preserving liberalism's core tolerance and moderation:

For all the magnificent triumphs of individualism, we survive only as we remain members of one another. The individual requires a social context, not one imposed by coercion, but one freely emerging in response to his own needs and initiatives … Optimism about man is not enough. The formalities of democracy are not enough.[41]

Values like freedom and equality are better protected when they are reinforced by self-consciously peculiar moral communities marked by idiosyncrasies of custom or history, not just by abstract, global, sovereign individualism. "The therapeutically inclined are wrong to think that … moral standards are inherently authoritarian and in the service of domination," as Robert Bellah and associates observed in 1985. "Traditional ethical reflection is based on the understanding that principles and exemplars must be interpreted to be applied, and that good people may differ on particular cases." And freedom can never be an absence of moral commitments, as Howard and Kathleen Bahr argue: "the question is not whether one will or will not give of one's self, but rather of priorities, of which people, ideals, organizations, practices, or things are worth the giving. It is not whether one will be used, but what one is willing to be used *for*." The development of community-based pronatalism would not make free societies freer, but it need not make them less so, and could make them stronger.[42]

In any such communitarian compromise, pronatalism and liberalism would probably remain awkward partners. But the U.S. case suggests that as we need each other less – as feelings of basic existential security make us less dependent on arbitrary birth communities – one realm in which modern people may still fundamentally need each other is support for parenthood. A sense that childrearing serves a shared purpose beyond self-fulfillment appears essential to making the day-to-day demands of parenthood appear worthwhile.

Will to Transcendence

Even the most widely shared social-mindedness, however, may prove insufficient in itself to inspire action. Theodore Roosevelt's calls to the procreative barricades inspired wide communitarian acclaim and no perceptible action. Subsequent moralists have achieved similarly little. Japan, South Korea, and Italy, for example, possess strong familistic cultures, acute senses of national distinctiveness, and strong cultural trepidation regarding low birthrates, yet have not seen near-replacement birthrates for decades. Reciprocal community ties appear to be necessary but insufficient conditions for liberal pronatalism.

More essential are fleeting personal feelings about how to live a righteous and worthwhile life. During the American fertility decline, reproductive decisions were not made entirely – or even mostly – in the realm of examined, categorical, conscious choice. They were also made using moral-emotional shorthands and intuitive sketches of a grand cosmic order. Would additional children make life more dignified, livable, and meaningful? Would their practical costs be repaid in timeless spiritual benefits? Momentary feelings of right and wrong were at least as important as rational, articulate, outward-looking deliberation.[43]

For Americans the outstanding determinant of fertility was that form of transcendent-mindedness linking eternal orders to the material reality of children. Whether children were desirable or affordable in any number was above all a function of one's feeling of immersion in cosmic orders that reached beyond the material present. Having a relatively large family was the act of someone whose sense of relevant time stretched far into the past and future; who saw a divine or commanding intent in the nature around them; and who detected no clear dividing line between one's own mortal lifetime and a continuing life outside physical bodies and bounds.

Sublimation in the infinite allowed such people to skate over the risks, anxieties, and costs – economic and experiential – of childrearing in a shifting modern environment. It allowed people to abandon themselves. Many observers assumed fertility would only rebound in America if people returned to this honorable, though increasingly impossible-seeming, eternalist mode of viewing the world. Eternity needed to be a part of the everyday furniture of life.

Americans often believed, more specifically, that transcending the self, the material, and the present required strong *religious* feeling. Later commentators have enthusiastically taken up this baton. "It is fairly obvious that there is some direct, indissoluble bond between faith and the will to a future," writes the conservative theologian David Bentley Hart. "Against the withering boredom that descends upon a culture no longer invaded by visions of eternal order, no civilization can endure." The agnostic sociologist Eric Kaufmann agrees that "the titanic struggle between secularism and fundamentalism takes place on a battlefield tilted in favor of faith." While puritanical creeds offer an "ideology to inspire social cohesion" and childbearing, secularism does not. In the United States, women who report that religion is "very important" to them have 2.3 children on average, as compared to 1.8 among the nonreligious.[44]

But there is no reason to assume a uniquely powerful connection between theistic transcendence and higher fertility. American evangelicals – Hart's target audience – have just over two children per family, very close to the national average. Kaufmann admits that in the Muslim world, "religiosity and fundamentalism *per se* count for little." In Iran and Turkey, for example, strongly Islamist districts are not necessarily more fertile. A better indicator of high fertility is broader familist traditionalism, as reflected in the prevalence of arranged marriages, dowries, illiteracy, rural residence, and so on. Immersive faith may even provide a competing form of transcendent self-sublimation that makes childrearing appear less urgent.[45]

Steering transcendent impulses towards childbearing seems to require moral intuitions that reach beyond simple theism and into natural law. All parties to the American birth control debate could agree that a strong sense of natural order made childrearing's risks and costs easier to accept. This idea endures. "Most people, historically, have *not* lived their lives as if thinking, 'I have only one life to live,'" the satirist Tom Wolfe observed in 1976, in an apt summary of the naturist position:

Instead they have lived as if they are living their ancestors' lives and their offspring's lives and perhaps their neighbors' lives as well. They have seen themselves as inseparable from the great tide of chromosomes of which they are created and which they pass on. The mere fact that you were only going to be here a short time and would be dead soon enough did not give you the license to try to climb out of the stream and change the natural order of things.[46]

Yet for all the multitude who "long for the simplicity of what is conceived as 'natural' sexual and family life," as Linda Gordon observes, "there is no 'natural' when it comes to human society" – only social conventions about nature. Notions of what nature "wants" vary as readily as notions of what god wants. Nature may demand *sex*, not reproduction. People may lack a "natural" desire for children, or feel natural attraction to people with whom they cannot conceive a child. Manipulating nature is the closest thing to a central human project, and we have many ways of explaining this project to ourselves.[47]

Most people nevertheless would agree that nature imposes some minimum reproductive requirement on communities that hope to persist over time. Even groups that reproduce themselves entirely by recruitment, like the celibate Shakers, do not truly evade this demand so much as they work around it. How people and communities ought to approach nature's demand is open to dispute – should we try to uphold common reproductive standards? What qualities need to be replicated for the group to be said to reproduce itself? How quickly can those qualities change? – but absent fundamental biotechnological shifts, the demand itself is not.

This encounter between biological law, individual action, and social life creates a moral, existential, and emotional maelstrom. Because we live socially and define ourselves by (or against) shared norms, neglecting reproduction may seem equivalent to refusing to invest oneself in the worthiness of life itself, as we live it. It may appear to demean common dignity. This is particularly true in low-fertility societies where reproduction cannot be taken for granted: failure to embrace pronatal norms may seem like apathy before the one kind of aging and death – that of the community – over which humans may exercise control. Emotional rejections of this perceived morbidity lend naturist pronatalism much of its core strength. Even for people who never examine the issue closely, the desire to believe that life is worth continuing – in ourselves and in general – tends to lend pronatal arguments an unsophisticated strength.[48]

In the hands of philosopher-prophets like Oswald Spengler, this sort of naturism has taken on gothic nationalist associations. For Spengler, once men and women defined themselves as "intelligences, free from the plant-like urge of the blood to continue itself," civilization was doomed to enter a cycle of death. "When reasons have to be put forward at all in a question of life, life itself has become questionable," Spengler wrote. "At that point begins prudent limitation of the number of births." Spengler's vision terrified and enraptured organic nationalists around the interwar world, including Nazis in his native Germany. Similar ideas circulated in other paranoid ethnic movements.[49]

As a popular phenomenon in America, however, reproductive naturism was less brooding and savage. If anything, Americans' sense of natural law applied more strongly to individual conscience or family perpetuation than national or ethnic destiny. Now too, the anthropologist Nicholas W. Townshend observes, people around the world tend to see reproduction as a universal and foreordained need with no necessary connection to ethnic chauvinism. In children a parent receives one's "best hope for immortality" – "the assurance that others will acknowledge one's death, praise one's life, and cherish one's memory" – but also a longer-term place in a natural chain of being. "Children are also our future, our legacy, and our continuation. It is our children who will remember us, who will carry on our work, who will preserve what we have made and what we value, and who will continue our family, lineage, nation and species." Naturism appeals to self-interest as well as social interest, and to intuitive sensibilities as well as examined morality. It does not simply demand sacrifice to God or community; it offers tangible personal rewards in the form of children who ease our helplessness and insignificance in the face of death.[50]

Naturism at any scale is the most likely basis for a moderate liberal pronatalism that does not rely on divisive religious doctrine or biopolitical competition. "Nature" can be used to defend all sorts of dogmas incompatible with a liberal reproductive order, from restricting access to hormonal contraceptives to homophobia, patriarchy, and the shaming of the childless. But if we take for granted that humans continually adapt "nature" to new uses and may deploy its moral authority for good and for ill, it is one possible basis for liberal pronatalism.

If a truly liberal pronatalism ever materializes, it is likely to draw on combinations of naturist, spiritual, and transcendent ideas – more than any distinct credo – and to emerge among people who would not recognize themselves as pronatalists or thought leaders, but nevertheless mildly challenge community norms. Perhaps growing recognition of persistent low fertility in free societies will make childrearing seem less conformist and more a challenge to reigning consumerism, risk-aversion, or anomie. Perhaps childbearing in low-fertility societies will reemerge as a public act rather than private lifestyle choice, occupying an ethical space alongside charitable giving or community service – a good and useful act when possible. Perhaps liberals will recapture the politics of "family values," reimagining familism as a social interest that implies no special burden on women, no reflexive stigma on the childless, and no blind prioritization of social bodies over living individuals. And perhaps parenthood will be reimagined as a risky proposition that demands a measure of moral support, rather than a hardwired imperative automatically filled by unseen, instinctive others. These sorts of redefinitions, however inarticulate, might encourage locally influential people to risk a family somewhat larger than those of their neighbors or parents. The desirability of such a transformation would depend on ongoing world fertility trends and the ability of any new pronatalism to reinforce liberalism's durability without compromising its spirit.[51] [52]

Conclusion

Even the lowest-fertility societies will always have more pressing priorities than achieving population equilibrium. Based on what we know now, however, the challenge of creating sustainable fertility in liberal societies appears to be preeminently a problem of reconciling community- and eternity-oriented views of the good life with the abstract-free personhood of liberalism – with equality, tolerance, rationalism, skepticism towards authority, and individual self-determination.[53]

Human fertility is determined by myriad forces that are at once highly structural and highly agentive. There are hundreds of discrete reasons to have children, hundreds more to avoid them, and dozens of overlapping themes linking those reasons to one another. Decisions to defer or forego parenthood may stem from very practical, rational, in-the-moment motives – economic insecurity, lack of housing, relationship instability – and at the same time, from a sea of more intuitive sensibilities about, say, freedom, responsibility, or cosmic order.

Reproductive motives are so intertwined, varied, and guarded that traditional public-world interventions are difficult. Institutions such as governments and interest groups are less important than individuals' half-conscious perceptions of how to act with righteousness, dignity, and practical know-how. Those perceptions reflect and shape the value of money, the lessons of history, the place of self in society, and other moral abstractions which, through the crucible of reproductive decision-making, people have been forced to act upon in everyday life.

Around the world over the past two centuries, broadly similar transitions in actionable ideas about time and transcendence have resulted in birthrates too low to sustain communities over the long term. The enduring-community ideal is ultimately imaginary, like any "population" or any future, and liberal societies do not rely on physical, one-for-one "replacement" for their survival. By definition we are united by ideals which may appeal to anyone – not "blood" or arbitrary custom. But free societies' interests are not equally well served by persistent low fertility as by near-replacement. Transcendent continuums lend meaning to most human lives, and making individualist politics appear compatible with that communal ideal will be one of global liberalism's central challenges over the coming decades and centuries. Such a project appears to require, at a minimum, some broad-based reinforcement of the ties between self-transcendence and childrearing. Barring such a groundswell, there is no guarantee that the persistent close associations between birth control and liberal modernity will continue working to the advantage of both.

Spengler believed "the sterility of civilised man . . . is not something that can be grasped as a plain matter of Causality . . . it is to be understood as an essentially metaphysical turn towards death." In that dark visionary's imagination, modernity was a passing phase, a short and riotous orgy before the fall. One of Spengler's contemporaries, the obscure American sociologist Delos Wilcox, saw the situation more fluidly. "The purpose of reproduction is the renewal and improvement of human life, on the assumption that life is worth living when it is lived well," he wrote. Apart from a belief in the inherent worth of life over time, Wilcox asked, "What reason have I to assume responsibility for the perpetuation of life? How can anything be a motive to me unless it refers in some manner to my self-fulfillment?"[54]

Versions of this question are becoming part of the fabric of our era. If indeed free and egalitarian societies never reproduce themselves over time, that outcome may ultimately be taken as a just verdict on the desirability of human life as we live it. More likely, some new adaptation will arise among us to dignify and eternalize our lives and way of life. That new world could retain the best of our blessings.

Appendix

APPENDIX TO CHAPTER 2

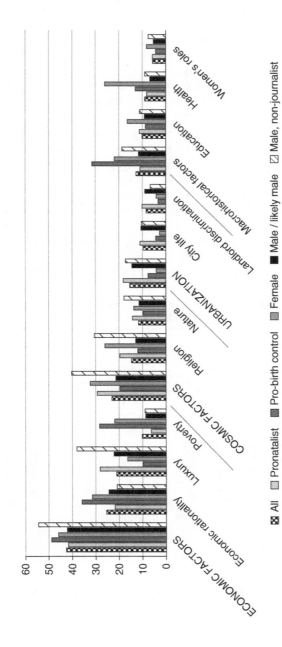

FIGURE A.1 Explanatory frames, 1903–08 (frequency in %).

All ⊞ Pronatalist □ Pro-birth control ■ Female ■ Male / likely male ■ Male, non-journalist ⊠

TABLE A.I *Explanatory frames: definitions*

Economic rationality	Economic circumstances reward smaller families
Luxury	Excessive desire for wealth and comfort motivates family limitation
Poverty	Large families as phenomenon of the poor; small families as means of avoiding poverty
Religion	Smaller families reflect secularization, materialism
Nature	Smaller families reflect detachment from natural law or biological continuum
City life	Urban moral and economic standards discourage childbearing
Landlord discrimination	Landlords exclude large families
Macrohistorical factors	Course of history (modernization, progress, decadence) encourages small families
Education	Educational expenses and/or content encourages small families
Health	Mental and/or physical health considerations encourage small families
Women's social roles	Women's emancipation or ambition discourages childrearing

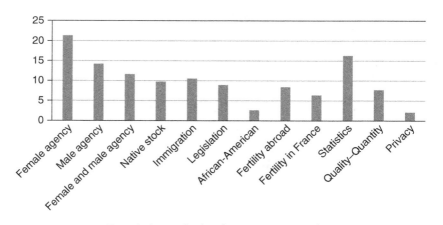

FIGURE A.2 Descriptive and other frames, 1903–08 (frequency in %).

TABLE A.2 *Descriptive and other frames, 1903–08: definitions*

Female agency	Women are/should be primary agents in childbearing decisions
Male agency	Men are/should be primary agents in childbearing decisions
Female and male agency	Both sexes are/should be agents in childbearing decisions
Native stock	Low fertility among native-born or "old stock" Americans
Immigration	Immigrant birthrates as distinct from native-born
Legislation	Birthrates potentially influenced by new public policies
African-American	African-American birthrates
Fertility abroad	Falling birthrates outside U.S. (excluding France)
Fertility in France	Falling birthrates in France
Statistics	Article cites demographic data
Quality–Quantity	Specific reference to quality–quantity tradeoff in childbearing
Privacy	Childbearing decisions not a legitimate public concern

TABLE A.3 *Newspaper roster, 1903–08*

	Chicago Tribune	Wash. Post	Boston Globe	N.Y. Times	L.A. Times	Atlanta Const.	Baltimore Sun	N.Y. Tribune	Hartford Courant
% of all articles	25.0	15.9	15.2	14.7	9.4	8.1	6.6	4.5	0.7
Political affiliation	Rep.	Indep.	Indep.	Indep. Dem.	Indep. Rep.	Dem.	Indep.	Rep.	Rep.
Support pronatalism	60.3	53.6	54.3	43.8	65.0	57.1	50.0	55.5	75.0
"Gold Marks"*	Yes	No	No	Yes	No	Yes	Yes	Yes	Yes

Rowell's American Newspaper Directory (New York, 1907) bestowed "Gold Marks" on any paper whose "advertisers value it more for the class and quality of its circulation than for the mere number of copies printed."

Political affiliation from *N.W. Ayer & Son's American Newspaper Manual* (Philadelphia, 1907).

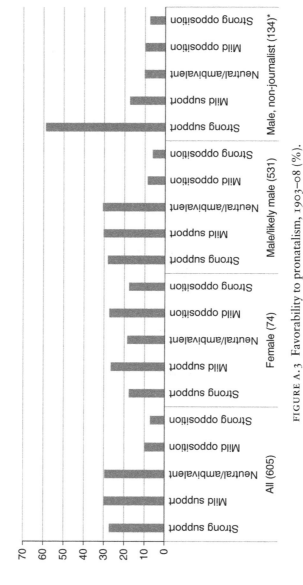

FIGURE A.3 Favorability to pronatalism, 1903–08 (%).

*Just 3% of female commentators were employed by the newspapers in which their words appeared, as opposed to 57% of men. Journalists were more likely to frame moral debates in neutral or even-handed terms, concealing significant differences in support between men commenting as private citizens ("nonjournalists") and women doing the same.

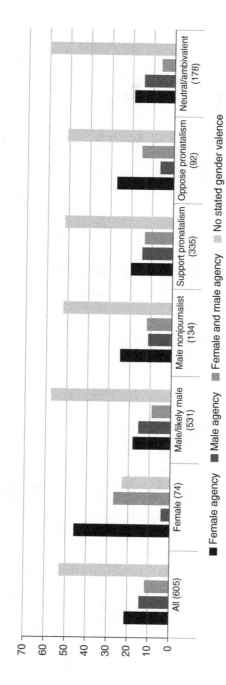

FIGURE A.4 Gender valence of birth control decisions by sex of commentators and support for pronatalism (%).

APPENDIX TO CHAPTER 3

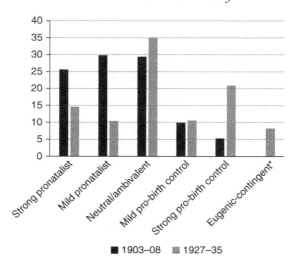

■ 1903–08 ■ 1927–35

FIGURE A.5 Favorability, 1903–08 and 1927–35 (%).
*In 1927–35 some commentators approved of birth control only insofar as it might be used as a tool for eugenic social engineering. This form of opinion was rare in the 1903–08 and not coded.

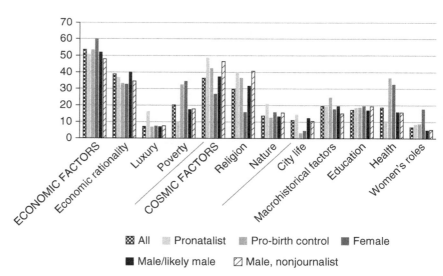

⊠ All   ▨ Pronatalist   ▨ Pro-birth control   ■ Female

■ Male/likely male   ▨ Male, nonjournalist

FIGURE A.6 Explanatory frames, 1927–35 (frequency in %).
Note: For comparison to similar frames from the period 1903–08, see Figure A.1.

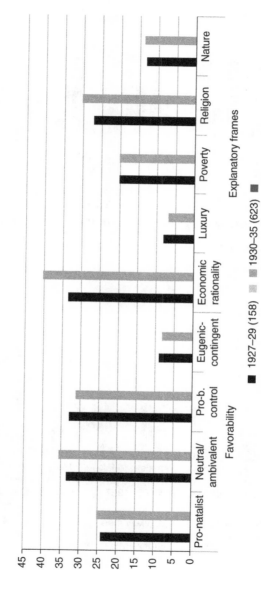

FIGURE A.7 Great Depression: Favorability and selected frames before/after December 1929 (%).

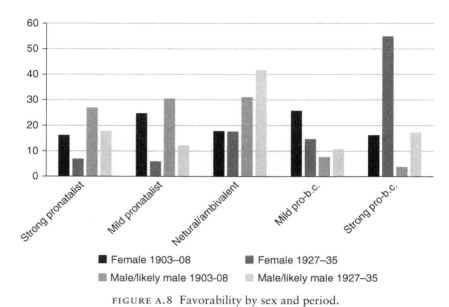

FIGURE A.8 Favorability by sex and period.

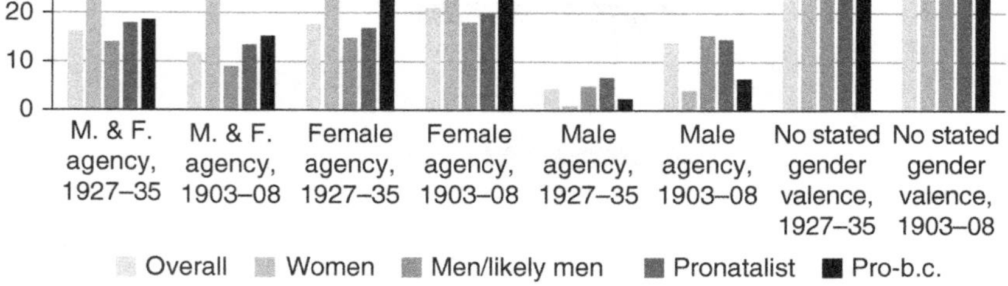

FIGURE A.9 Gender valence by period.

APPENDIX TO CHAPTER 4

TABLE A.4 *Writers' socioeconomic self-descriptions*

Sanger	Dennett	BCLM
"Poor"/"very poor": 27	"Poor": 3	"Poor": 2
Farmer: 23	Laborer: 2	Unemployed: 2
–Farmer and "poor": 7	Farmer: 2	Worker: 2
–Farmhand: 3	Teacher: 2	"Moderate means"
–Tenant farmer: 4	Pharmacist	Invalid
(*all farmers*: 37)	Businesswoman	Minister
Worker/laborer: 18	"Working class"	Nurse
–Worker and "poor": 3	"Poorly educated"	Office staff
–Day laborer: 6	Exterminator	
(*all workers*: 27)	Unemployed	
Invalid: 9		
Miner: 8		
Railroad worker: 6		
College graduate: 4		
"Middle class": 3		
Ships officers: 3		
Public works: 2		
Doctor: 2		
Unemployed: 2		
Clerk: 2		
Lawyer		
Blacksmith		
Teacher		
Salesman		
Clergy		
Machinist		

TABLE A.5 *Letter writers' terms of justification for fertility control (%)*

	Sanger	Dennett	BCLM	Definitions (B.C. = birth control)
Any justification	87.9	59.2	28.7	
Economic factors	49.6	34.9	18.8	(Composite of below)
Rationality	29.5	27.2	16.3	B.C. helps to improve or maintain economic status
Poverty	20.1	8.7	2.5	B.C. helps to mitigate effects of severe poverty
Health factors	61.1	30.1	11.3	(Composite of below)
General health*	23.1	15.5	6.3	B.C. promotes health in nonspecific ways
Physical health	21.7	6.8	2.5	B.C. prevents bodily injury or death
Mental health	7.0	4.9	2.5	B.C. prevents mental anguish
Mental & phys.	9.4	2.9	(o)	B.C. aids both physical and mental health
Education	7.2	3.9	1.3	B.C. allows education of children
Religion	6.4	2.9	(o)	B.C. is justifiable in divine law
Nature	1.3	1.9	(o)	B.C. is justifiable in natural order
Freedom	3.2	1.9	1.3	B.C. prevents overwork and allows free time
Women's work	4.3	1.0	1.3	B.C. allows women to work
Econ. and/or health factors alone	66.8	49.5	25.0	
Econ. factors alone	16.1	21.3	15.0	
Health factors alone	33.2	18.4	5.0	

Note: *Exclusive of other health categories

TABLE A.6 *Doctors' involvement in writers' pursuit of birth control*

	Sanger	Dennett	BCLM
% mentioning a doctor	24.9	8.7	23.8
% of doctors reported as:			
Ignorant of birth control	4.3	11.1	(0)
Prescribing ineffective b.c.	43.0	33.3	5.3
Refusing to provide b.c.	16.1	22.2	10.5
(Doctor mentioned, role unclear)	37.6	33.3	84.2

TABLE A.7 *Fertility control methods mentioned in letters to birth controllers*

	All (n 556)	Sanger (n 373)	Dennett (n 103)	BCLM (n 80)
	Total mentions (number also mentioning another method)			
Abortion	61	51	10	0
	(26)	(23)	(3)	(0)
Abortifacients	20	18	0	2
	(11)	(10)	(0)	(1)
Abstinence	48	47	1	0
	(22)	(22)	(0)	(0)
Withdrawal	10	9	1	0
	(6)	(6)	(0)	(0)
Douche	6	4	2	0
	(2)	(2)	(0)	(0)
Condom	6	1	5	0
	(4)	(1)	(3)	(0)
Sterilization	6	3	1	1
	(3)	(1)	(1)	(1)
Rhythm	5	4	1	0
	(2)	(2)	(0)	(0)
Suppository	4	0	2	2
	(2)	(0)	(1)	(1)
Diaphragm	4	0	1	3
	(1)	(0)	(0)	(1)

(continued)

TABLE A.7 *(continued)*

	All (n 556)	Sanger (n 373)	Dennett (n 103)	BCLM (n 80)
	Total mentions (number also mentioning another method)			
Pessary	3	0	1	2
	(0)	(0)	(0)	(0)
Non- specific	90	71	11	8
	(33)	(29)	(3)	(1)
Any alternate method	201	155	31	15
% mentioning alt. method	36.2%	41.6%	30.1%	18.8%
% declaring ignorance of any method	22.0%	14.6%	(0)	17.4%

TABLE A.8 *Letter writers mentioning gendered agency in birth control (%)*

	Sanger	Dennett	BCLM	All
Women's issue	11.5	2.9	(0)	8.3
Men's issue	(0)	1.0	(0)	0.2
Men's and women's issue	2.9	1.0	(0)	0.7
(No stated gender valence)	85.6	95.1	100	90.3

Notes

I THE LONG HISTORY OF BIRTH CONTROL

1. Margaret Sanger, "Ford Hall Forum Address," at Boston, Mass., April 16, 1929. Margaret Sanger Papers, Sophia Smith Collection, Smith College.
2. Grant Allen, *Post-Prandial Philosophy* (London, 1894), 113.
3. Elias Pym Fordham, *Personal Narrative of Travels in Virginia, Maryland, Pennsylvania, Ohio, Indiana, Kentucky; and of a Residence in Illinois Territory: 1817–1818*, edited by Frederic Austin Ogg (Cleveland, 1906), 120; Benjamin Franklin, "*Observations Concerning the Increase of Mankind*" (1751) in Alfred Henry Smith, ed., *Writings of Benjamin Franklin*, vol. III (New York, 1907); James Reed, "Public Policy on Human Reproduction and the Historian," *Journal of Social History* 18:3 (1985), 385. Total fertility rates are from Ansley J. Coale and Melvin Zelnik, *New Estimates of Fertility and Population in the United States* (Princeton, 1963), and based on child–woman ratios among white Americans, since parallel estimates are not available for non-white Americans before the mid-nineteenth century. African-American fertility followed a similar downward trajectory, albeit at a lag of several decades, and by the early twentieth century black and white total fertility rates were broadly similar.
4. Theodore Roosevelt: "Message to Congress," December 3, 1906, in *Presidential Addresses and State Papers* (New York, 1910), vol. 5. Note that total fertility rates are not equivalent to historical family size, since rates of infant and child mortality have varied across time.
5. "The Flat and Race Suicide," *Baltimore Sun*, July 6, 1904.
6. Susan Cotts Watkins, "Fertility Determinants" in Edgar F. Borgatta and Rhonda J.V. Montgomery, eds., *Encyclopedia of Sociology*, 2nd ed., vol. 2 (New York, 2006).
7. On fertility decline in Bulgaria and other agrarian European nations see John Knodel and Etienne van de Walle, "Lessons from the Past: Policy Implications of Historical Fertility Studies" in Susan Watkins and Ansley Coale, eds., *The Decline of Fertility in Europe* (Princeton, 1986), 399. On fertility decline as a plural "community"-level phenomenon see Simon Szreter, *Fertility, Class and Gender in Britain, 1860–1940* (Cambridge, Eng., 1994), esp. ch. 7, 10; John Gillis, Louise Tilly, and David Levine, eds., *The European Experience of Declining Fertility, 1850–1970: The Quiet Revolution* (Oxford, 1992). The present study investigates community-level reproductive ethics but assumes some basic congruity across the broad American middle classes. On the

continued search for commonalities among fertility transitions see Mikolaj Szoltysek, "Science without Laws? Model Building, Micro Histories and the Fate of the Theory of Fertility Decline," *Historical Social Research* 32:2 (2007); Sören Edvinsson and Sofia Kling, "The Practice of Birth Control and Historical Fertility Change: Introduction," *The History of the Family* 15 (June 2010).

8. The United Nations Population Division releases a revised version of its *World Population Prospects* every two years. See esa.un.org/unpd/wpp.

9. Theodore Roosevelt, "Address Before the National Congress of Mothers," Washington, D.C., March 13, 1905, in Alfred Henry Lewis, ed., *Speeches and Messages of Theodore Roosevelt, 1901–1905* (Washington, D.C., 1906); Roosevelt, "The Home and the Child," Earl Lectures, Pacific Theological Seminary, 1911, reprinted in Roosevelt, *Realizable Ideals* (San Francisco, 1912), 54. Before the early twentieth century, very few periodicals covered family limitation due to taboos on sexual topics. An early study of birth control coverage in magazines reported that "one or two articles appear in scattered years until 1903, which shows the first sharp thrust upward." Press taboos steadily weakened as articles became more frequent into the 1910s and '20s. "With the sudden lifting of the taboo on public discussion of the subject there was a great deal to be said at once." (Francis M. Vreeland, "The Process of Reform with Especial Reference to Reform Groups in the Field of Population," Ph.D. dissertation, University of Michigan (1929), 308, 328).

10. On the one-quarter approximation see Chapter 2, note 14.

11. Susan Cotts Watkins, "Conclusions" in Watkins and Coale, eds., *Decline of Fertility*, 435; Geoffrey McNicoll, "Legacy, Policy, and Circumstance in Fertility Transition," *Population and Development Review* 35:4 (December 2009). "We shall never get hold of mental states by making inventories of numerable things," one perceptive critic has argued. My view is that a rough numeric framework cannot *hurt* our understanding of those states, especially when used as an occasional backstop or sounding board for traditional humanist impressionism (Andrew Delbanco, *The Real American Dream: A Meditation on Hope* (Cambridge, Mass., 1999), 6).

12. Simon Szreter, Robert A. Nye, and Frans van Poppel, "Fertility and Contraception during the Demographic Transition: Qualitative and Quantitative Approaches," *Journal of Interdisciplinary History* 34:2 (Autumn 2003).

13. Ruby Poley to KOA [Denver, Colo. radio station], March 1927, Benjamin Barr Lindsey Collection, Library of Congress, box 155. "The ideas most relevant to population in Western society are of a mythic-moral character." John T. Noonan, Jr., wrote. "By ideas I mean beliefs, concepts, and valuations; by mythic I mean ideas, nondemonstrable but not necessarily untrue, of the nature of the cosmos in relation to the destiny of man; and by moral I mean prescriptions for human conduct in terms of a good" (Noonan, "Demographic and Intellectual History," *Daedalus* (Spring 1968)).

14. "Dole is Boon to Stork," *Chicago Tribune*, January 16, 1935.

15. On the dual role of intuition and rationality in moral cognition, see Joshua D. Greene, "Beyond Point-and-Shoot Morality: Why Cognitive (Neuro) Science

Matters for Ethics," *Ethics* 124:4 (2014). Greene posits based on fMRI results that a perpetual "tradeoff" mediates between the brain's reflexive, emotional "automatic setting" and its slower, rational "manual" in our resolution of moral problems. On the importance of "interaction" between material and schematic factors in fertility behavior see Jennifer A. Johnson-Hanks, Christine A. Bachrach, S. Philip Morgan, and Hans-Peter Kohler, *Understanding Family Change and Variation: Toward a Theory of Conjunctural Action* (Dordrecht, Neth., 2011), 68–73.

16. Bobsein coined "birth control" during a discussion specifically devoted to conjuring a catch-phrase for Sanger's campaign.

17. Norman E. Himes, *Medical History of Contraception* (New York, 1963 [1936]), 59, 61, 64, 73, 80, 89–90. Dozens of other writers on contraception are chronicled in Himes, which remains a definitive work. Also on the pan-historical appeal of contraception, see John M. Riddle, *Contraception and Abortion from the Ancient World to the Renaissance* (Cambridge, 1992); Angus McLaren, *A History of Contraception: From Antiquity to the Present Day* (Cambridge, Mass., 1990).

18. Himes, *Contraception*, 3–56. Another inventory of family limitation practices known to early anthropologists is contained in A.M. Carr-Saunders, *The Population Problem: A Study in Human Evolution* (Oxford, 1922), esp. 197–307. For a summary of these remedies' effectiveness, see Vern L. Bullough, "Herbal Contraceptives and Abortifacients" and "Ancient Civilizations and Birth Control" in Bullough, ed., *Encyclopedia of Birth Control* (Santa Barbara, Cal., 2001).

19. Lawrence B. Finer and Mia R. Zolna "Unintended pregnancy in the United States: Incidence and Disparities, 2006," *Contraception* 84:5 (November 2011).

20. On "folk" methods of family limitation in the United States see Andrea Tone, *Devices and Desires: A History of Contraceptives in America* (New York, 2002); Janet Farrell Brodie, *Contraception and Abortion in Nineteenth Century America* (Ithaca, N.Y., 1994); Susan E. Klepp, *Revolutionary Conceptions: Women, Fertility, and Family Limitation in America, 1760– 1820* (Chapel Hill, 2009), ch. 5; Rosemarie Petra Holz, *The Birth Control Clinic in a Marketplace World* (Rochester, N.Y., 2012).

21. On the moral status of abortifacients and assisted abortions in nineteenth-century America, see James Mohr, *Abortion in America: The Origins and Evolution of National Policy* (Oxford, 1979), ch. 3–4 and 7; Leslie J. Reagan, *When Abortion Was a Crime: Women, Medicine, and Law in the United States, 1867–1973* (Berkeley, 1997).

22. Some scholars use "birth control" to designate all forms of family limitation, as I do, while others use it to mean appliance methods such as condoms or diaphragms (excluding abortion, abstinence, withdrawal, and other long-standing methods of avoiding unwanted childbearing). The latter conception can lead to overstatements of the social impact of recent birth control technologies, as Kate Fisher and Simon Szreter have observed.

23. Harry Middleton Hyatt, *Folk-Lore from Adams County Illinois* (New York, 1935), 108–109; Vance Randolph, *Ozark Superstitions* (New York, 1947),

193–94. In colonial America "suppressed menstruation" was treated as a medical problem. Women used emmenagogues to clear "obstructions" without always knowing or concerning themselves with the cause of the obstruction. See Klepp, *Revolutionary Conceptions*, 181–87. On the popular availability of abortifacients in the nineteenth and twentieth centuries, and medical writers' views on them, see Janet Farrell Brodie, "Menstrual Interventions in the Nineteenth Century United States" in Etienne van de Walle and Elisha P. Renne, eds., *Regulating Menstruation: Beliefs, Practices, Interpretations* (Chicago, 2001).

24. Reagan, *Abortion*, argues that abortion was "widely tolerated" as a private practice in early twentieth-century America (p. 20). On the frequency of abortion in the early twentieth century, see Reagan, *Abortion*, 23; Edward Shorter, *Women's Bodies: A Social History of Women's Encounter with Health* (New York, 1982), 196–97. On the spread of knowledge about abortion, abortifacients, and other birth control methods within immigrant women's "gossip networks," see Susan Cotts Watkins and Angela D. Danzi, "Women's Gossip and Social Change: Childbirth and Fertility Control among Italian and Jewish Women in the United States, 1920–1940," *Gender and Society* 9:4 (August 1995). On the prevalence and moral status and abortion and abortifacients in colonial Pomfret, Connecticut, see Cornelia Hughes Dayton, "Taking the Trade: Abortion and Gender Relations in an Eighteenth-Century New England Village," *William and Mary Quarterly* 48:1 (1991).

25. On douching and suppositories see Tone, *Devices and Desires*, 75–77.

26. Elizabeth Jameson, *All that Glitters: Class, Conflict, and Community in Cripple Creek* (Urbana, Ill., 1998), 135; Watkins and Danzi, "Women's Gossip."

27. On nineteenth-century American men's support for birth control, see Shawn Johansen, *Family Men: Middle-Class Fatherhood in Industrializing America* (Abingdon, Eng., 2015 [2001]), 46–52.

28. Quoted in Lawrence Stone, *The Family, Sex and Marriage in England, 1500–1800* (New York, 1977), 417; Havelock Ellis, "Sexual Problems, Their Nervous and Mental Relations" in William A. White and Smith Ely Jelliffe, eds., *The Modern Treatment of Nervous and Mental Diseases*, vol. 1 (Philadelphia and New York, 1913). Euphemisms for withdrawal are noted in Jane C. and Peter T. Schneider, *Festival of the Poor: Fertility Decline and the Ideology of Class in Sicily, 1860–1980* (Tucson, Ariz., 1996), 149. Early twentieth-century studies showing the popularity of these methods include John Winchell Riley and Matilda White, "The Use of Various Methods of Contraception," *American Sociological Review* 5:6 (December 1940); Marie E. Kopp, *Birth Control in Practice: Analysis of 10,000 Case Histories* (New York: 1933); Regine K. Stix and Frank Notestein, "Effectiveness of Birth Control," *Milbank Memorial Fund Quarterly* 7:1 (January 1934). On coitus interruptus in the nineteenth-century U.S. see Brodie, *Contraception and Abortion*, 59–67. For a detailed account of popular birth control methods in mid-1920s America see James F. Cooper, *Technique of Contraception: The*

Principles and Practice of Anti-Conceptional Methods (New York, 1928), ch. 3–6.

29. Regine K. Stix and Frank W. Notestein, "Effectiveness of Birth Control: A Second Study of Contraceptive Practice in a Selected Group of New York Women," *The Milbank Memorial Fund Quarterly* 13:2 (1935). These effectiveness ratios were calculated by comparing the "ratio of avoided to expected pregnancies" with the "expected" rate based on pregnancies among women reporting no contraceptive use. On the use and effectiveness of combined contraceptives see Robert L. Dickinson and Lura Beam, *A Thousand Marriages: A Medical Study of Sex Adjustment* (Baltimore, 1931). Many of Dickinson's patients combined or alternated methods, and 24 percent had experienced contraceptive failure (p. 249).

30. On men's assumption of fertility decisions in mid-nineteenth-century America see Susan E. Klepp, "Lost, Hidden, Obstructed and Repressed: Contraceptive and Abortive Technology in the Early Delaware Valley" in Judith A. McCaw, ed., *Early American Technology: Making and Doing Things from the Colonial Era to 1850*, 105–06.

31. Chapter 4 covers alternate sexual outlets in greater detail.

32. On the nineteenth-century expectation that men avoid imposing too many pregnancies on their wives, see Johansen, *Family Men*, 50–53. On the "culture of abstinence" among English couples seeking to avoid childbearing, see Szreter, *Fertility, Class and Gender in Britain, 1860–1940* (Cambridge, Eng., 1994), 367–423.

33. See Brodie, *Contraception and Abortion*, 188.

34. "President Praises Priest," *Bryan Morning Eagle*, February 2, 1908. On the transition from restrained Victorian masculine sexuality to a more primal sensibility in the twentieth century, see Gail Bederman, *Manliness and Civilization: A Cultural History of Gender and Race in the United States, 1880–1917* (Chicago, 1996). On social attitudes towards bachelors in the United States see Howard P. Chudacoff, *The Age of the Bachelor: Creating an American Subculture* (Princeton, 1999), esp. 45–74.

35. On Comstock see Nicola Beisel, *Imperiled Innocents: Anthony Comstock and Family Reproduction in Victorian America* (Princeton, 1997).

36. Andrea Tone, *Devices and Desires: A History of Contraceptives in America* (New York, 2002), 40, 55; Brodie, *Contraception and Abortion*, 204. Comstock arrested 3,731 people in his forty-year career as a postal inspector; 55 percent of these cases ended in conviction. Many of the convicted were abortionists (Beisel, *Imperiled Innocents*, 146). See Sears Roebuck & Co. catalog no. 112 (1902), 453. One "vaginal spray" from Sears would "instantly wash out all secretions and discharges that may become lodged in the vaginal folds." Reports on contraceptive use published by the Farm Security Administration noted the presence of door-to-door peddlers (Johanna Schoen, *Choice and Coercion: Birth Control, Sterilization, and Abortion in Public Health and Welfare* (Chapel Hill, N.C., 2005), 53.

37. Shaw, quoted in James A. Morone, *Hellfire Nation: The Politics of Sin in American History*, (New Haven, 2003), 240.

38. The 1936 decision was *United States vs. One Package of Japanese Pessaries.* The prohibition on mailing contraceptive information was not fully and formally overturned until 1983, when the U.S. Supreme Court ruled in *Bolger vs. Youngs Drug Products* that the law violated the right to free speech. In Comstock's native state of Connecticut, the state law lasted until 1965, when the Supreme Court struck it down in *Griswold vs. Connecticut.* This decision – which found the law violated a constitutional "right to privacy" – would serve as a key precedent for the Court's position in *Roe v. Wade.*

39. Clelia Duel Mosher conducted the first known survey of American sexual practices between 1890 and 1920. See James Mahood and Kristine Wenburg, eds., *The Mosher Survey: Sexual Attitudes of 45 Victorian Women* (New York, 1980). Mosher's forty-five educated respondents preferred douching and safe-period methods. On contraceptive use rates see the several studies of contraceptive use (and effectiveness) summarized in Kopp, *Birth Control in Practice,* 132. Kopp's study of 10,000 primarily working-class women who sought contraceptive advice at Sanger's New York clinic in the late 1920s revealed a 93.3 percent incidence of previous contraceptive use. Another summary of studies from this period is available in Himes, *Contraception,* 335–52.

40. Polybius, *Histories,* vol. 2, trans. Evelyn Shuckburgh (London, 1889), 510. "Aristotle, Plato, Hesiod, Polybius and many other writers of antiquity discussed various aspects of the population problem, including limitation, as is well known to anyone familiar with the standard histories of economic and social thought," wrote Norman Himes in 1936 (*History of Contraception,* 79). Tacitus' appraisal of the Germans was especially well known: "no one in Germany laughs at vice, nor do they call it the fashion to corrupt and to be corrupted. To limit the number of children or to destroy any of their subsequent offspring is accounted infamous, and good habits are here more effectual than good laws elsewhere" (Tacitus, *Germania,* ch. 19). Writers like Tacitus had their ideas consolidated in Edward Gibbon's *Decline and Fall,* which attributed much of Rome's decadence to deficiencies in sexual and reproductive virtue. The ancients were closely associated with fertility control well into the early twentieth century, and Brodie writes that the "most famous" source of information on sex and reproduction in eighteenth-century America was a series attributed to Aristotle (Brodie, *Contraception,* 55). Surveys of various aspects of elite population thought include Charles Strangeland, *Pre-Malthusian Doctrines of Population: A Study in the History of Economic Theory* (New York, 1904); John T. Noonan, Jr., *Contraception: A History of Its Treatment by the Catholic Theologians and Canonists* (Cambridge, Mass., 1965); Alfred Sauvy, *Fertility and Survival: Population Problems from Malthus to Mao Tse-Tung* (New York, 1961); John M. Riddle, *Eve's Herbs: A History of Contraception and Abortion in the West* (Cambridge, Eng., 1997); McLaren, *History of Contraception.* On Aristotle's actual population writings see Philip Kreager "Aristotle and Open Population Thinking," *Population and Development Review* 34:4 (December 2008).

41. Psalm 127:3, KJV; Klepp, *Revolutionary Conceptions*, 11. On pronatalism in this period see Klepp, op. cit., ch. 5; Julia Cherry Spruill, *Women's Life and Work in the Southern Colonies* (New York, 1998 [1938]), ch. 3. On the bachelor taxes enacted in five of the thirteen American colonies, see John Gilbert McCurdy, *Citizen Bachelors: Manhood and the Creation of the United States* (Ithaca, N.Y., 2009), 50–83. Franklin's essay inspired the English cleric Thomas Malthus' famous prediction (in 1798) of famine if humans did not check the growth of their families; Malthus subsequently inspired Charles Darwin's theory of natural selection. John O'Sullivan echoed Franklin in celebrating America's "yearly multiplying millions" as the foundation for the country's "manifest destiny" in the West (1845), and Abraham Lincoln told Congress in 1862 that the union ought to be preserved, in part, so that a single population as large as Europe's might remain united.

42. George Tucker, *Progress of the United States in Population and Wealth in Fifty Years* (New York, 1843), 89.

43. On early U.S. fertility decline see Edward Byers, "Fertility Transition in an Early New England Commercial Center: Nantucket, Ma., 1680–1840," *Journal of Interdisciplinary History* 13 (1982); Helena Temkin-Greener and Alan C. Swedlund, "Fertility Transition in the Connecticut Valley: 1740–1850," *Population Studies* 32:1 (1978); Jan Lewis and Kenneth A. Lockridge, "'Sally Has Been Sick': Pregnancy and Family Limitation among Virginia Gentry Women, 1780–1830," *Journal of Social History* 22 (Autumn, 1988); Robert V. Wells, "Family Size and Fertility Control in Eighteenth-Century America: A Study of Quaker Families," *Population Studies* 25:1 (1971); Gloria L. Main, "Rocking the Cradle: Downsizing the New England Family," *Journal of Interdisciplinary History* 37:1 (2006); Klepp, *Revolutionary Conceptions*, ch. 1, 5. On regional fertility differentials see Paul A. David and Warren C. Sanderson, "Rudimentary Contraceptive Methods and the American Transition to Marital Fertility Control, 1855–1915" in Stanley L. Engerman and Robert E. Gallman, *Long-Term Factors in American Economic Growth* (Chicago, 1986), 309–13. There is some question as to whether the falling child–women ratios of the early U.S. fertility transition (pre-1840) were the product of conscious fertility control within marriage. They may also have resulted from rising infant and child mortality or increasing age at marriage (though delayed marriage may be interpreted as a form of conscious fertility control). See J. David Hacker, "Rethinking the 'Early' Decline of Marital Fertility in the United States," *Demography* 40 (2003); Michael R. Haines and Avery M. Guest, "Fertility in New York State in the Pre-Civil War Era," *Demography* 45 (2008).

44. On Knowlton's trial see Brodie, *Contraception and Abortion*, 95–96. On home medical manuals, Etienne van de Walle, and Virginie de Luca, "Birth Prevention in the American and French Fertility Transitions: Contrasts in Knowledge and Practice," *Population and Development Review* 32:3 (September 2006); Janet Farrell Brodie, *Contraception and Abortion*, 55, 181–82.

45. Nathan Allen, "Changes in New England Population" *Popular Science* (August 1883). U.S. press coverage of the Bradlaugh-Besant trial in England

was scant and euphemistic; see e.g. Vreeland, "Process of Reform," 293–4, 548–50.

46. Nathan Allen, *Population: Its Law of Increase* (Lowell, Mass., 1870 [1868]), 5–6 [italics original]. For near-comprehensive accounts of American expert discourse on falling birthrates in the post–Civil War period, see Arthur Calhoun, *A Social History of the American Family*, vol. 3 (Cleveland, 1919), 225–53; John Paull Harper, "'Be Fruitful and Multiply': The Reaction to Family Limitation in Nineteenth-Century America" (Ph.D. dissertation, Columbia University, 1975). Simone Caron writes of the post–Civil War period that "The dramatic loss of life at war's end led to pronatalist attitudes" (Caron, *Who Chooses? American Reproductive History Since 1830* (Gainesville, Fl., 2008), 119.

47. Gordon, *The Moral Property of Women: A History of Birth Control Politics in America* (Urbana, Ill., 2002), 92. On voluntary motherhood see Gordon, *Moral Property*, 55–71.

48. Francis A. Walker, "Restriction of Immigration," *Atlantic Monthly* (June 1896). Mary P. Ryan finds some support for Walker's so-called "shock" theory of fertility decline in her study of the native-born middle classes of Utica, New York. Mary P. Ryan, *Cradle of the Middle Class: The Family in Oneida County, New York, 1790–1865* (Cambridge, Eng., 1981), 155–57. Though Walker's idea is typically framed as a novel response to the "new" immigration of the late nineteenth century, Benjamin Franklin sketched out the same idea in his "Observations Concerning the Increase of Mankind" (1751), ch. 21. Concerning the breadth of elite discussion around this time, Delos Wilcox remarked in 1900: "It has now become a familiar regret of sociological writers that the sturdy old New England stock is dying out through its decreased marriage and birth rates, and giving place to the prolific and uncultured stock of French-Canadians" (Delos Wilcox, *Ethical Marriage* (Ann Arbor, Mich., 1900), 25).

49. John S. Billings, "The Diminishing Birth-Rate in the United States," *Forum* 15 (August 1893).

50. Edward A. Ross, "The Causes of Race Superiority," *Annals of the American Academy of Political and Social Science* 18 (July 1901). On replacement-level fertility during the early U.S. fertility decline, see Warren Sanderson, "Below-Replacement Fertility in Nineteenth Century America," *Population and Development Review* 13:2 (June 1987). The uptick in demographic alarm at the turn of the century was partly attributable to demographer Robert R. Kuczynski's sophisticated study of differential fertility in Massachusetts: R.R. Kuczynski, "Fecundity of the Native and Foreign-Born Population in Massachusetts," *Quarterly Journal of Economics* 16 (1901). Kuczynski's work touched off parallel concerns in Europe after he used similar statistical techniques to measure subreplacement fertility there.

51. "Finds Birth Rate Is Low," *Chicago Tribune,* February 10, 1903; "Same Way At Yale," *The Boston Globe,* February 15, 1903; "The Big Family Question Again," *The Independent,* June 18, 1903; "They Don't Marry," *The Boston Globe,* June 19, 1904; John C. Phillips, "A Study of the Birth-Rate in Harvard

and Yale Graduates," *Harvard Graduates' Magazine*, September 1916; "Quite Enough," *The Boston Globe*, February 13, 1903.

52. Roosevelt, "Congress of Mothers."

53. The idea of a quiet revolution is laid out in Gillis et al., *European Experience*.

54. Walter Lippmann, *A Preface to Morals* (New York, 1929), 285. George Bernard Shaw's preface to "Getting Married" anticipated this argument: " We may be enthusiastic Liberals or Conservatives without any hope of seats in Parliament, knighthoods, or posts in the Government, because party politics do not make the slightest difference in our daily lives and therefore cost us nothing. But to take a vital process in which we are keenly interested personal instruments, and ask us to regard it, and feel about it, and legislate on it, wholly as if it were an impersonal one, is to make a higher demand than most people seem capable of responding to" (Shaw, "Preface to 'Getting Married'" (New York, 1909), 50.).

55. Due to high mortality and low fertility, Caribbean slaves, particularly those on sugar plantations, decreased in number from year to year and had to be replaced through the continual importation of unfree labor from Africa and elsewhere. In the U.S. south, mortality was lower and fertility higher, but doctors and planters complained of slaves' low fertility. They assumed herbal abortifacients were to blame, though evidence from Louisiana (and Jamaica) suggests that overwork, poor nutrition, and disease were also important factors. When bans on the Atlantic slave trade began to take effect, many planters enacted pronatalist measures, offering cash or work-release to mothers of multiple children. For a concise review of the literature on comparative demographic trends in the Caribbean and U.S. south, see Huub Everaert, "Changes in fertility and mortality around the abolition of slavery in Suriname," *The History of the Family* 16:3 (August 2011). David Brion Davis estimates that Caribbean slave populations declined at a rate of 2–5 per cent per annum, excluding migration. Davis, *The Problem of Slavery in the Age of Revolution, 1770–1823* (New York, 1999 [1975]), 56.

56. Linda Gordon's view of social movements is somewhat more restricted: "I would say that birth control became a social movement when individuals banded together to develop collective strategies" (*Moral Property*, 3). For me the term "movement" becomes meaningful when shared ideas start to wield observable, transformative power over human action, regardless of the level of coordination among supporters with explicit public-world goals. This definition emphasizes movements' sources of power rather than their level of self-consciousness. I would argue that this model is particularly well suited to mass social movements like birth control where practical power is decentralized and primarily normative. On the importance of "non-activist types of public support" to social movements, notably environmentalism, see Paul C. Stern, Thomas Dietz, Troy Abel, Gregory A. Guagnano, and Linda Kalof, "A Value-Belief-Norm Theory of Support for Social Movements: The Case of Environmentalism," *Research in Human Ecology* 6:2 (1999). On movement away from formal politics to cultural politics in social movement theory, see Elizabeth A. Armstrong and Mary Bernstein, "Culture, Power, and Institutions: A Multi-Institutional Politics Approach to Social Movements,"

Sociological Theory 26:1 (2008). On informal social networks and fertility see John Bongaarts and Susan Cotts Watkins. "Social Interactions and Contemporary Fertility Transitions," *Population and Development Review* 22:4 (1996); Mark R. Montgomery and John B. Casterline, "Social Learning, Social Influence, and New Models of Fertility," *Population and Development Review* 22:s1 (1996).

57. Henry Adams, *The Education of Henry Adams: An Autobiography* (Boston, 1918 [1907]), 447.

58. "Excerpts from Letters on Many Subjects," *New York Times,* November 19, 1933. On the organized anti-Prohibition movement see David Kyvig, *Repealing National Prohibition* (Chicago, 1979). For overviews of disciplinary approaches to social movements and the question of culture versus organization in movement efficacy, see Bert Klandermans and Conny Roggeband, eds., *Handbook of Social Movements Across Disciplines* (New York, 2009).

59. Tone, *Devices,* xvi–xvii; Brodie, *Contraception and Abortion,* 50.

60. Linda Gordon, *Moral Property,* 241; James Reed, *From Private Vice to Public Virtue: The Birth Control Movement and American Society since 1830* (New York, 1978), x, 10; David M. Kennedy, *Birth Control in America: The Career of Margaret Sanger* (New Haven: 1970), 170. Gordon's *Moral Property* is a revision and expansion of *Woman's Body Woman's Right: A Social History of Birth Control in America* (New York, 1976). Gordon, Reed, and Kennedy's books remain essential surveys of birth control in America. Gordon's canonical work focuses on feminist activists (including obscure and conservative ones) as well as various reformers and radicals. Reed follows the careers of three prominent activists who "represented innovation or change in the birth control movement" (ix). Kennedy focuses on Sanger's leadership qualities. A notable departure from the activist narrative is Susan Klepp's *Revolutionary Conceptions* (op. cit,), which argues that the emancipatory spirit surrounding the American Revolution encouraged women to assert control over their bodies and fertility. Klepp is avowedly constrained by Americans' reluctance to discuss sexual topics openly, but nevertheless outlines important connections between elite women's private values and the spread of family limitation. Leslie J. Reagan in *When Abortion was a Crime* argues for the significance of an "unarticulated, alternative, popular morality" concerning abortion – a morality that "contradicted the law, the official attitude of the medical profession, and the teachings of some religions" (6). All the above authors were preceded by Himes' pioneering *Medical History,* which cataloged the availability and use of various methods across world history. Himes never completed a planned second volume on the cultural history of birth control use. Since Gordon, Reed, and Kennedy there have been few general surveys of birth control history. Carole Ruth McCann, *Birth Control Politics in the United States, 1916–1945* (Ithaca, N.Y., 1999) questions earlier historians' focus on Sanger, arguing for attention to a wider array of political actors. Simone Caron, *Who Chooses? American Reproductive History since 1830* (Gainesville, Fl., 2008), rejects Gordon's emphasis on feminist activism, insisting instead on the salience of "elite white officials" who sought to

demographically marginalize non-elites. Ellen Chesler, *Woman of Valor: Margaret Sanger and the Birth Control Movement in America* (New York, 2007 [1992]) is the definitive account of Sanger's life and role within the organized movement, and Jean H. Baker, *Margaret Sanger: A Life of Passion* (New York, 2011) makes the case for Sanger's enduring cultural relevance. Laura Lovett, *Conceiving the Future: Pronatalism, Reproduction and the Family in the United States, 1890–1930* (Chapel Hill, N.C., 2007) examines the "indirect" yet "coercive" gender conservatism of advocates for eugenics, maternalism, resource conservation, western irrigation, and outdoor regeneration. For all these works' many strengths, most assume that elites have been prime movers in shaping historical reproductive contingencies. Alternatives to this view come mostly from outside the United States and outside narrative history (on which more below). Within U.S. history, work on the wider culture of birth control has been confined largely to works focused on *related topics* – such as gender, the family, sexuality, or domestic economics – and on sub-specialized *aspects of birth control* in America, such as religious law or social policy. For example, on birth control in relation to: romantic love, Lystra, *Searching the Heart*, ch. 3; community life, Sylvia D. Hoffert, *Private Matters: American Attitudes toward Childbearing and Infant Nurture in the Urban North, 1800–1860* (Urbana, Ill., 1989), ch. 1; women and gender, Degler, *At Odds: Women and the Family in America from the Revolution to the Present* (New York, 1980), ch. 8–10; sexuality, Estelle B. Freedman and John D' Emilio, *Intimate Matters: A History of Sexuality in America* (New York, 1988), ch. 10–11; youth culture, Paula S. Fass, *The Damned and the Beautiful: American Youth in the 1920s* (Oxford, 1979), ch. 2; marriage's purposes, Christina Simmons, *Making Marriage Modern: Women's Sexuality from the Progressive Era to World War II* (Oxford, 2009), ch. 2–3; family life, Steven Mintz and Susan Kellogg, *Domestic Revolutions: A Social History of American Family Life* (New York, 1989), ch. 6–7; domestic economy, Nancy Folbre, *Greed, Lust and Gender: A History of Economic Ideas* (Oxford, 2010), ch. 16, 18; ethno-nationalism, Thomas G. Dyer, *Theodore Roosevelt and the Idea of Race* (Baton Rouge, La., 1980), ch. 7. Accounts of specific *aspects* of birth control history in America include: on church attitudes, Leslie Woodcock Tentler, *Catholics and Contraception: An American History* (Ithaca, N.Y., 2004) and Kathleen A. Tobin, *The American Religious Debate over Birth Control, 1907–1937* (Jefferson, N.C., 2001); social policy, McCann, *Birth Control Politics* and Schoen, *Choice and Coercion*; local organizing, Jimmy Elaine Wilkinson Meyer, *Any Friend of the Movement: Networking for Birth Control, 1920–1940* (Columbus, Oh., 2004); mass media, Manon Parry, *Broadcasting Birth Control: Mass Media and Family Planning* (New Brunswick, N.J., 2013); birth control clinics, Cathy Moran Hajo, *Birth Control on Main Street: Organizing Clinics in the United States, 1916–1939* (Urbana, Ill., 2010); fiction, Beth Widmaier Capo, *Textual Contraception: Birth Control and Modern American Fiction* (Columbus, Ohio, 2007). For a concise examination of the scholarly literature on reproductive rights, its expansion in various specialized directions, and its relationship to Gordon's definitive survey, see

Joyce Berkman, "The Fertility of Scholarship on the History of Reproductive Rights in the United States: United States Scholarly History of Reproductive Rights," *History Compass* 9:5 (2011).

61. Gordon's succession of works has highlighted the roles of women and feminists in birth control history, but see also, e.g. Rickie Solinger, *Pregnancy and Power: A Short History of Reproductive Politics in America* (New York, 2005); McCann, *Birth Control Politics*; Daniel Scott Smith, "Family Limitation, Sexual Control, and Domestic Feminism in Victorian America," *Feminist Studies* 1:3, 1973; Edward Shorter, "Female Emancipation, Birth Control, and Fertility in European History," *American Historical Review* 78 (1973).

62. Kate Fisher, *Birth Control, Sex, and Marriage in Britain, 1918–1960* (Oxford, 2006), 238–39.

63. Fisher, *Birth Control,* 189. For additional work emphasizing the importance of male involvement, see also E.A. Wrigley, *Population and History* (London, 1969); McLaren, *History of Contraception,* 203–207; J.A. and Olive Banks, *Feminism and Family Planning* (London, 1964). The latter concluded that "feminism was not a causative influence at all" in the democratization of birth control in Britain (summarized in J.A. Banks, *Victorian Values: Secularism and the Size of Families* (London, 1981), 8).

64. See Johansen, *Family Men,* esp. ch. 5. "We have wasted our time . . . if we have only sold the mother on this service," wrote a nurse seeking to interest poor farm families in birth control during the 1930s. "We are not going to get cooperation . . . unless the husband is seeing the matter in just the same light as his wife sees it" (quoted in Schoen, *Choice and Coercion,* 55).

65. Jeanne Boydston cautions against assuming "that categories of analysis" – including gender – "exist *a priori* in the sources and have merely to be revealed (like a Michelangelo sculpture imprisoned in the marble)." Rather than pre-defining gender as an "abstract and universal" "oppositional binary" which may be revealed across time and place, she advocates working *from* specific historical contexts *to* a conceptualization of gender. Boydston, "Gender as a Question of Historical Analysis," *Gender & History* 20:3 (2008).

66. Recent studies suggest that men's preferences for family limitation tend to closely approximate those of women across many social contexts. See e.g. Karen Oppenheim Mason and Herbert L. Smith, "Husbands' versus Wives' Fertility Goals and Use of Contraception: The Influence of Gender Context in Five Asian Countries," *Demography* 37:3 (2000). Mason and Smith found that when husbands wanted more children and wives did not, there was a small positive effect on overall fertility, but that this sort of disagreement between spouses was quite rare: "in the communities we studied, disagreement between husbands and wives about whether to have more children accounted for only one-twentieth of married women's total unmet need for contraception" (the five countries, selected for high levels of gender stratification, were Pakistan, India, Malaysia, Thailand, and the Philippines).

67. On demographic transition theory's formulation see Dennis Hodgson, "Demography as Social Science and Policy Science," *Population and Development Review* 9:1 (March 1983); on its application around the world, Matthew Connelly, *Fatal Misconception: The Struggle to Control*

World Population (Cambridge, Mass., 2008). On the persistence of eugenic ideas after the Second World War, Alexandra Stern, *Eugenic Nation: Faults and Frontiers of Better Breeding in Modern America* (Berkeley, 2005); Randall Hansen and Desmond King, *Sterilized by the State: Eugenics, Race, and the Population Scare in Twentieth Century America* (Cambridge, Eng., 2013), ch. 9–10.

68. Poor data precludes exact estimates of U.S. child mortality rates before the mid-nineteenth century, but infant mortality alone remained in the vicinity of 20 percent through the 1880s. By 1900 that figure was about 11 percent; in 1930, 6 percent. For a concise summary of U.S. fertility and mortality data see Michael Haines, "Fertility and Mortality in the United States" EH.Net Encyclopedia, http://eh.net/encyclopedia/fertility-and-mortality-in-the-united-states/.

69. On land availability see Yasikichi Yasuba, *Birthrates of the White Population of the United States, 1800–1860: An Economic Study* (Baltimore, 1962); Colin Forster and Graham Tucker, *Economic Opportunity and White American Fertility Ratios: 1800–1860* (New Haven, Ct., 1972); Don R. Leet, "Population Pressure and Human Fertility Response: Ohio, 1810–1860," *The Journal of Economic History* 34:1 (March 1974); Richard Easterlin, George Alter, and Gretchen Condran, "Farms and Farm Families in Old and New Areas: The Northern States in 1860" in Maris Vinovskis and Tamara Hareven, eds., *Family and Population in Nineteenth-Century America* (Princeton, 1978). An early challenge to Yasuba's work on U.S. land availability was Maris A. Vinovskis, "Socioeconomic Determinants of Interstate Fertility Differentials in the United States in 1850 and 1860," *Journal of Interdisciplinary History* 6:3 (1976). A skeptical review of land availability theories is Susan B. Carter, Roger L. Ransom, and Richard Sutch, "Family Matters: The Life-Cycle Transition and the Antebellum American Fertility Decline" in Timothy Guinnane, William Sundstrom, and Warren Whatley, eds., *History Matters: Essays on Economic Growth, Technology, and Demographic Change* (Palo Alto, 2004).

70. The idea that wealth "flows" to parents on farms is associated with the demographer John C. Caldwell, who argues that fertility transitions are primarily driven by shifting intergenerational economics, though their timing may be mediated by culture and education. Caldwell critically reviews much of the work based on this model (including his own) in Caldwell, "On Net Intergenerational Wealth Flows: An Update," *Population and Development Review* 31:4 (December 2005). Rational-actor approaches to fertility owe much to the work of Gary Becker and associates, who famously framed children as "durable goods" competing with other possible goods to provide satisfaction to consuming parents. See e.g. Gary S. Becker, "An Economic Analysis of Fertility" in Becker, ed., *Demographic and Economic Change in Developed Countries* (Princeton, 1960); Gary S. Becker and H. G. Lewis, "On the Interaction between the Quantity and Quality of Children," *Journal of Political Economy* 81, no. 2 (1973).

71. Lee A. Craig, *To Sow One Acre More: Childbearing and Farm Productivity in the Antebellum North* (Baltimore, 1993); Ronald Lee, "Intergenerational

Transfers, the Biological Life Cycle, and Human Society," *Population and Development Review* 38:s1 (February 2013). See also Schneider and Schneider, *Festival of the Poor*, 233. In an influential study, Mead Cain calculated that on average, the son of a subsistence farmer in Bangladesh "pays back" the cost of his own care, plus that of his nearest sister, by age 22 (Cain, "The Economic Activities of Children in a Village in Bangladesh," *Population and Development Review* 3:3, 1977). Karen Kramer determined that among Maya agricultural families, a male child did not recoup the cost of his upbringing until age 30, and a female until age 31 – about a decade after the children would typically leave their parents' farm (Karen Kramer, *Maya Children: Helpers at the Farm* (Cambridge, Mass., 2009), 142). Ethnographic challenges to the "farm asset" hypothesis have emphasized children's spiritual rather than tangible rewards for farming parents, e.g. Timothy T. Schwartz, *Fewer Men, More Babies: Sex, Family, and Fertility in Haiti* (Plymouth, Eng., 2009), 21–22. Viviana A. Zelizer, *Pricing the Priceless Child: The Changing Social Value of Children* (Princeton, 1985) is cited as evidence of children's declining economic value – thus smaller numbers – but the book can also be read as a testament to parents' exemption of children from rational choice. For discussion of children's value as old-age insurance see Caldwell, "Net Intergenerational Wealth Flows"; Jeffrey B. Nugent, "The Old-Age Security Motive for Fertility," *Population and Development Review* 11:1 (March 1985). Very few of the American commentators examined in this book saw non-farm children's declining economic value as a key factor in fertility decline. The same was true of Norwegian commentators chronicled in Ida Blom, "'Master of Your Own Body and What Is In It' – Reducing Marital Fertility in Norway, 1890–1930" in Angelique Janssens, ed., *Gendering the Fertility Decline in the Western World* (Bern, 2007), 68. Finally, pronatal norms and laws (such as bachelor taxes) would seem unnecessary in an agrarian society where children were widely perceived as farm assets, but early America had many such norms and laws. So while farming people surely hoped their children would provide useful labor, offsetting some of their cost, it is unlikely that this hope was ever a driving motive.

72. The EFP comprised a number of independent regional and national studies in addition to a summary volume: Ansley Coale and Susan Cotts Watkins, eds., *The Decline of Fertility in Europe* (Princeton, 1986). On the need for cultural research in the EFP's wake see also John Cleland and Christopher Wilson, "Demand Theories of the Fertility Transition: An Iconoclastic View," *Population Studies*, 41 (March 1987); Samuel H. Preston, "Changing Values and Falling Birth Rates," *Population and Development Review* 12 (1986). For a latter-day defense of DTT and its focus on economic factors see John C. Caldwell, "Demographic Theory: A Long View," *Population and Development Review* 30:2 (2004). Demography's cultural turn was innovative, but also a return to the concerns of pre-1945 population scholars who had liberally sprinkled their work with speculative assessments of changing social mentalities; e.g. Frank Notestein, "Population: The Long View" in *Food for the World*, Theodore W. Schultz, ed. (1945); Clyde V. Kiser, "The Indianapolis Fertility Study: An Example of Planned Observational Research,"

Public Opinion Quarterly 17:4 (1953). Postwar demography nevertheless generally operated on the idea that large-scale analysis of quantifiable data, especially concerning socioeconomic status, might comprehensively demystify fertility decline. For EFP-like conclusions based on American data see Maris A. Vinovskis, *Fertility in Massachusetts from the Revolution to the Civil War* (New York,1981). Vinovskis concluded that the available data was inadequate to the task of explaining fertility decline, speculating that Americans' large families shrank due to changing religious beliefs, individualization, and the "development of a modern personality" (p. 133). J. William Leasure, "A Hypothesis about the Decline of Fertility: Evidence from the United States," *European Journal of Population* 5:1 (1989) makes similar arguments for the relevance of "a greater sense of responsibility" and "the growth of autonomy" in the U.S. fertility transition, after demonstrating correlations between states with low fertility and a preponderance of liberal Protestant churches. J. David Hacker followed this research by measuring church seats and biblically named children against counties' fertility: Hacker, "Child Naming, Religion, and the Decline of Marital Fertility in Nineteenth-Century America," *The History of the Family* 4:3 (1999).

73. The EFP's downgrade of socioeconomic factors based on province-level data has been criticized by scholars working from a microeconomic perspective. See John Bryant, "Theories of Fertility Decline and the Evidence from Development Indicators," *Population and Development Review* 33:1 (March 2007); John C. Caldwell, Barkat-e-Khuda, Bruce Caldwell, Indrani Pieris, and Pat Caldwell, "The Bangladesh Fertility Decline: An Interpretation," *Population and Development Review* 25:1 (March 1999); David I. Kertzer and Dennis P. Hogan, *Family, Political Economy, and Demographic Change: The Transformation of Life in Casalecchio, Italy, 1861–1921* (Madison, Wisc., 1989), esp. ch. 8; Caldwell, "Demographic Theory: A Long View," *Population and Development Review* 30:2 (2004)." On possible conceptions of "culture" for demography see: E.A. Hammel "Theory of Culture for Demography," *Population and Development Review* 13:3 (1990); Susan Greenhalgh, "Anthropology Theorizes Reproduction: Integrating Practice, Political Economic, and Feminist Perspectives," in Susan Greenhalgh, ed., *Situating Fertility: Anthropology and Demographic Inquiry* (Cambridge, Eng.: 1995). A survey of the anthropology–demography nexus is David I. Kertzer, "Qualitative and Quantitative Approaches to Historical Demography," *Population and Development Review*, 23 (December 1997). "Diffusion" approaches to fertility decline have proliferated alongside cultural ones. Diffusionists have sometimes conceptualized fertility decline as a sort of contagion spreading from France – or from isolated, elite "forerunner" groups – to the rest of Europe and the world. However local-level evidence from what Simon Szreter calls "communication communities" ("social status groups" among the middle classes; "neighbourhood or street communities" among the working classes) renders "eminently plausible" the idea that fertility limitation was initiated via "multiple distinct innovations by independent individuals and couples" (p. 558). Szreter forcefully rejects "simple diffusion" from national or regional elites to ordinary

people. Studies of religious culture and fertility include e.g. Kevin McQuillan, *Culture, Religion, and Demographic Behaviour: Catholics and Lutherans in Alsace, 1750–1870* (Montreal, 1999); Donald H. Parkerson and Jo Ann Parkerson, "'Fewer Children of Greater Spiritual Quality': Religion and the Decline of Fertility in Nineteenth-Century America," *Social Science History* 12:1 (1988). These writers emphasize the importance of religious feeling as opposed to doctrinal instruction. McQuillan's Alsatian villagers had significantly different fertility outlooks based on their personal religiosity, regardless of denomination (Lutheran or Catholic). The Parkersons found that pietist Protestants, who emphasized personal spiritual conversion, "typically embraced a belief in spiritual free will, which nurtured a secular individualism offering women both an alternative to the domestic environment and a realistic option to limit their fertility." See also the local studies in Frans van Poppel and Renzo De Rosas, eds., *Religion and the Decline of Fertility in Europe* (Dordrecht, 2007); and Alicia Adsera, "Religion and Changes in Family-Size Norms in Developed Countries," *Review of Religious Research* 47:3 (2006). On the United States, Tomas Frejka and Charles Westoff, "Religion, Religiousness and Fertility in the U.S. and in Europe," *European Journal of Population* 24:1 (2008); Calvin Goldscheider and Wiliam D. Mosher, "Patterns of Contraceptive Use in the United States: The Importance of Religious Beliefs," *Studies in Family Planning* 22 (1991). Unlike many other social scientists, demographers have largely abstained from questioning the reality of secularization. This partly reflects World Values Survey findings concerning the decline of religious feeling in developed countries. See Pippa Norris and Ronald Inglehart, *Sacred and Secular: Religion and Politics Worldwide* (Cambridge, Eng., 2004).

74. Michael Teitelbaum, *The British Fertility Decline: Demographic Transition in the Crucible of the Industrial Revolution* (Princeton, 1984), 192; Karen Mason, "Explaining Fertility Transitions," *Demography* 34:4 (November 1997); Mikolaj Szoltysek, "Science without Laws? Model Building, Micro Histories and the Fate of the Theory of Fertility Decline," *Historical Social Research* 32:2 (2007). For extended considerations of the "malaise" and "crisis" within demography – particularly as related to the field's inability to explain fertility decline – see Nancy E. Riley and James McCarthy, *Demography in the Age of the Postmodern* (Cambridge, Eng., 2003); Stijn Hoorens et al., *Low Fertility in Europe: Is There Still Reason to Worry?* (Santa Monica, Cal., 2011), esp. ch. 3, 9. On flexible, model-based approaches to theorizing demographic variation see Thomas K. Burch, "Demography in a New Key: A Theory of Population Theory," *Demographic Research* 9 (2003). Several critics have noted the relative scarcity of gender analysis amid the profusion of demographic theories. See Susan Watkins, "If All We Knew about Women was What We Read in *Demography*, What Would We Know?" *Demography*, 30 (1993); Alison Mackinnon, "Were Women Present at the Demographic Transition? Questions from a Feminist Historian to Historical Demographers," *Gender & History* 7 (1995). In the past thirty years household-level studies by historical demographers have paid increasing attention to differing gender

interests within families and small communities. See Angelique Janssens, ed., *Gendering the Fertility Decline in the Western World* (Bern, 2007).

75. Jennifer Johnson-Hanks, "Demographic Transitions and Modernity," *Annual Review of Anthropology* 37 (October 2008); Szreter, *Fertility*, 546. Critiques of modernization theory and "grand theory" approaches in general include Greenhalgh, "Anthropology Theorizes Reproduction"; Szreter, Nye, and van Poppel, "Fertility and Contraception"; Szreter, *Fertility*, 533–558. The challenges of unifying structural factors in fertility motivation while also respecting particularity and individual initiative are evident in the avowedly high levels of "generality" in Johnson-Hanks and colleagues' still-developing theory of "conjunctural action" (op. cit., esp. ch. 3). This theory focuses more on loci of contingency than causal explanation, and in the process must consider virtually all major realms of human action. It nevertheless provides a useful general framework, rejecting culture/economy and structure/agency dichotomies in favor of flexible moral-economic, existential, and social-psychological models where hundreds or thousands of variously sized structures, material realities, and cultural ideas act together and on each other.

76. "The President," *Ladies' Home Journal*, February 1906.

77. George Colin to KOA Radio (Denver, Colorado), March 14, 1927. Benjamin Barr Lindsey Collection, Library of Congress, Box 155. On the relationship between reflexive self-consciousness about one's place in history and historical actuality, Anthony Giddens writes, "Historicity ... might be defined as the use of the past to help shape the present, but it does not depend upon respect for the past. On the contrary, historicity means the use of knowledge about the past as a means of breaking with it ... Historicity in fact orients us primarily towards the future" (Anthony Giddens, *The Consequences of Modernity* (Palo Alto, 1990), 50). The "theory of conjunctural action" (Johnson-Hanks et al., op. cit.) analogizes personal narratives with social ones, postulating that we make major decisions (such as those related to fertility) in moments when multiple subjectively important ideas intersect and must be acted upon. On the related use of "life-course" analysis in fertility studies, see Johannes Huinink and Martin Kohli, "A Life-Course Approach to Fertility," *Demographic Research* 30 (2014).

78. On the ways in which the rationality or morality of reproduction evades careful analysis, see Fisher, *Birth Control*, esp. ch. 2. On the compression of social knowledge, Walter Lippmann wrote, "The real environment is altogether too big, too complex, and too fleeting for direct acquaintance ... although we have to act in that environment, we have to reconstruct it on a simpler model before we can manage with it" (Walter Lippmann, *Public Opinion* (New York, 1922), 10). Charles Horton Cooley wrote more ominously: "To know where and how to narrow the activity of the will in order to preserve its tone and vigor for its most essential functions, is a great part of knowing how to live. An incontinent exercise of choice wears people out, so that many break down and yield even essentials to discipline and authority in some form" (Cooley, *Human Nature and the Social Order* (New York, 1902), 70). On individual-level "heuristics" in fertility decisions see Peter M. Todd, Thomas T. Hills, and Andrew T. Hendrickson, "Modeling Reproductive

Decisions with Simple Heuristics," *Demographic Research* 29 (2013). Rather than assuming that people bring "all of the available information, fully known preferences, and fully processed implications of both" in fertility decisions, this model emphasizes "simple heuristics ... built on realistic assumptions of the limited information, time, and thinking that people are actually able to bring to bear on most of their choices." Todd et al. present this as a "new approach to questions in demographics ... based on the individual-level decision mechanisms that people actually use."

79. Susan Cotts Watkins, "Local and Foreign Models of Reproduction in Nyanza Province, Kenya," *Population and Development Review* 26:4 (December 2000); Rhoda Ann Kanaaneh, *Birthing the Nation: Strategies of Palestinian Women in Israel* (Berkeley, 2002), 155, 22; Sian Pooley, "Parenthood, Child-Rearing and Fertility in England, 1850–1914," *The History of the Family* 18:1 (2013); Schneider and Schneider, *Festival of the Poor*, 223; Alaka Malwade Basu and Sajeda Amin, "Conditioning Factors for Fertility Decline in Bengal: History, Language Identity, and Openness to Innovations," *Population and Development Review* 26:4 (December 2000); Jennifer Johnson-Hanks, *Uncertain Honor: Modern Motherhood in an African Crisis* (Chicago, 2006), 2; John C. Caldwell, Barkat-e-Khuda, Bruce Caldwell, Indrani Pieris, and Pat Caldwell, "The Bangladesh Fertility Decline: An Interpretation," *Population and Development Review* 25:1 (March 1999). Also on England, Kate Fisher writes that "birth control methods were associated with a 'modern' approach to life" (Fisher, *Birth Control*, 87). Parents in the Italian Alps "talked of needing to meet the obligations of modern parenthood" (Patrick Heady, "Fertility as a Process of Social Exchange" *Demographic Research* 17 (2007). Watkins quotes a 1968 survey in which Kenyans condemned people who deliberately limit family size as "acting against custom, nature, or God," while the "small minority of respondents who explicitly approved of deliberate control described the planned family as modern, in keeping with the optimism following Independence." The study is Angela Molnos, *Attitudes towards Family Planning in East Africa* (Munich 1968). The Nyanza studies have continued in, e.g. Naomi Rutenberg and Susan Cotts Watkins, "The Buzz Outside the Clinics: Conversations and Contraception in Nyanza Province, Kenya," *Studies in Family Planning* 28:4 (December 1997). See also Arland Thornton, *Reading History Sideways: The Fallacy and Enduring Impact of the Developmental Paradigm on Family Life* (Chicago, 2005), 153–56; Bledsoe, *Contingent Lives*; Heather Paxson, *Making Modern Mothers: Ethics and Family Planning in Urban Greece* (Berkeley, Cal., 2004); Birgitte Søland, *Becoming Modern: Young Women and the Reconstruction of Womanhood in the 1920s* (Princeton, 2000).

80. Chapter 3 outlines suggestive evidence that the "marriage boom" that temporarily drove fertility back up between the late 1930s and early 1960s might have been abetted by changing popular ideas about historical trajectories.

81. Though the issue of lags complicates connections between social and demographic change, in much of Europe the onset of fertility decline has roughly corresponded with periods of capital concentration, political upheaval, or

state assumption of previously family-based roles; in East Asia, with export-driven economic boom; in Africa, with the spread of mass communication and primary education. Some historians have even suggested a connection between the early republican revolutions in the United States and France and those countries' early fertility declines. On political revolution and fertility see Susan Klepp, *Revolutionary Conceptions: Women, Fertility, and Family Limitation in America, 1760–1820* (Chapel Hill, N.C., 2009); Amy Kate Bailey, "How Personal Is the Political? Democratic Revolution and Fertility Decline," *Journal of Family History* 34:4 (October 2009); Rudolph Binion, "Marianne in the Home: Political Revolution and Fertility Transition in France and the United States," *Population: An English Selection* 13 (2001). On eighteenth- and nineteenth-century Americans' changing conceptions of time and historical development see John Demos, *Circles and Lines: The Shape of Life in Early America* (Cambridge, Mass., 2004).

82. Anthony Giddens, *Modernity and Self-Identity: Self and Society in the Late Modern Age* (Palo Alto, 1991), 17, 243–44. See also Ulrich Beck, Anthony Giddens, and Scott Lash, *Reflexive Modernization: Politics, Tradition and Aesthetics in the Modern Social Order* (Cambridge, Eng., 1994); Ulrich Beck, Wolfgang Bonss, and Christoph Lau, "The Theory of Reflexive Modernization: Problematic, Hypotheses and Research Programme," *Theory, Culture & Society* 20:2 (2003). Alex Inkeles explores the concept of "individual modernity" in *Exploring Individual Modernity* (New York, 2013 [1983]), 207–25. Inkeles sees a distinctly "modern personality" developing in novel institutions such as factories, and links this reorientation to fertility trends, arguing that "experiences with modern institutions affect psychological acceptance of birth limitation." See also the above volume's predecessor study, based on over 6,000 interviews with men in six countries: Alex Inkeles and David H. Smith, *Becoming Modern: Individual Change in Six Developing Countries* (Cambridge, Mass., 1974). Modern personality studies have been criticized for equating modernization with Americanization. With the rise of Second Demographic Transition theory, however, scholars of fertility decline have again reckoned with notions of modern personality, this time in globally-oriented frameworks built around World Value Surveys and the spread of "postmaterial" attitudes—meaning feelings of basic existential security (food, shelter, etc.) that persist despite income inequality.

83. Arland Thornton, "The Developmental Paradigm, Reading History Sideways, and Family Change," *Demography* 38:4 (2001); Thornton, *Reading History Sideways*, 133; Anthony Giddens, *Modernity and Self-Identity: Self and Society in the Late Modern Age* (Palo Alto, 1991), 243–44. The American case provides strong support for Thornton's assertion that developmental idealism is among the strongest shapers of modern family structures, including their characteristic low fertility. Thornton notes that the idea of developmental idealism was also present in C.K. Yang, *The Chinese Family in the Communist Revolution* (Cambridge, Mass., 1959) under the name "family idealism." Giddens' reflexive modernity includes not just self-consciousness about one's place in modern history, but a "more generic reflexive monitoring of action," such as in self-narratives people

construct for themselves and others. Giddens, *Modernity and Self-Identity: Self and Society in the Late Modern Age* (Palo Alto, 2013 [1991]), 76. The latter sort of developmental reflexivity is familiar to demographers from studies of the "life course", i.e., the disposition to imagine oneself developing according to a socially valued progression through life stages. In anthropology the literature on "social evolution" engages similar issues. For demographic work that engages Giddens' reflexive modernity see Rosalind Berkowitz King, "Women's Fertility in Late Modernity" (Ph.D. dissertation, Univ. of Pennsylvania, 2000); Jay Winter and Michael Teitelbaum, *The Global Spread of Fertility Decline: Population, Fear, and Uncertainty* (New Haven, 2013), esp. ch. 2; Bongaarts and Watkins, "Social Interactions"; Peter McDonald, "Low Fertility and the State: The Efficacy of Policy," *Population and Development Review* 32:3 (September 2006); John C. Caldwell, "Three Fertility Compromises and Two Transitions," *Population Research and Policy Review* 27:4 (2008).

84. Thorton sees developmental idealism spreading through many channels, including schools, churches, media, government campaigns, and even clothing styles. But perhaps because Thornton focuses on family change in general, not just fertility, his vision is ultimately rooted in a contagious set of ideas that spread from European explorers, to intellectuals, then through various elite agencies to ordinary Europeans and the rest of the world. Various forms of resistance and accommodation marked its spread, but the ideal's origin story is basically singular and "sideways"-looking, rather than local and backwards-looking.

85. In response to criticism of modernization as overly unitary and teleological, some theorists define modernity as inherently multiple and contingent. In this view modernity, like "postmodernity," can be understood as a loose constellation of outlooks and structures that retain coherence despite variation in the phenomena grouped under the term. See, e.g., Dominic Sachsenmaier, S.N. Eisenstadt, and Jens Riedel, eds., *Reflections on Multiple Modernities: European, Chinese and Other Interpretations* (Leiden, Neth., 2002). Thomas Welskopp and Alan Lessoff, "Introduction" in Welskopp and Lessoff, eds., *Fractured Modernity: America Confronts Modern Times, 1890s to 1940s* (Munich, 2012) offers helpful amendments to Eisenstadt's multiple modernities paradigm, reframing the plurality of "fractured" modernity as varieties of *individual experience* as opposed to varieties of linear, structural civilizational development. Other pluralizations of modernization are laid out in Ronald Inglehart and Wayne E. Baker, "Modernization, Cultural Change, and the Persistence of Traditional Values," *American Sociological Review* 65: 1 (February 2000) and Alberto Martinelli, *Global Modernization: Rethinking the Project of Modernity* (Thousand Oaks, Cal., 2005).

86. In classical philosophy the "chain of being" divided the different orders of existence and life. Here it links people across generations.

87. Fertility limitation need not be tied to predetermined family size goals, but can instead revolve around ad hoc norms concerning healthy spacing of pregnancies. Such methods may allow couples to restrict births without feeling that

they have interfered with divine or natural orders. See Caroline Bledsoe, *Contingent Lives: Fertility, Time, and Aging in West Africa* (Chicago, 2002); Jennifer Johnson-Hanks, "On the Modernity of Traditional Contraception: Time and the Social Context of Fertility," *Population and Development Review* 28:2 (2002); Etienne van de Walle, "Fertility Transition, Conscious Choice, and Numeracy," *Demography* 29:4 (1992).

88. On anthropological findings regarding the value of children to society, and specifically the idea that "an individual repays what he owes to older members of his descent group by producing new members for the group," see Heady, "Fertility."

89. Philip Kreager, "Demographic Regimes as Cultural Systems" in David Coleman, ed., *The State of Population Theory* (Oxford, 1986), 131.

90. Delbanco, *Real American Dream*, 6.

91. "Care of the Body," *Los Angeles Times*, December 25, 1932. On the relationship of values and attitudes to behavior, and varying sociological approaches to this question, see Steven Hitlin and Jane Allyn Piliavin, "Values: Reviving a Dormant Concept," *Annual Review of Sociology* 30 (2004). "Values do not act only as internalized schemata," they write. "Values play an important, if unarticulated, role in action ... Values operate as guiding mechanisms. As [Hans] Joas puts it, the 'state of nature is not one of apathy'" (Quotation from Hans Joas, *The Genesis of Values* (Cambridge, Eng., 2000), 106).

92. Avishai Margalit quoted in David Blight, "The Memory Boom: Why and Why Now?" in Pascal Boyer and James V. Wertsch, eds., *Memory in Mind and Culture* (Cambridge, Eng., 2009), 238).

2 RACE SUICIDE

1. Michel de Montaigne, *Works*, ed. and trans. William Hazlitt (London, 1845), 463.

2. The idea that single young women labored for "pin money," not subsistence, was a common trope in Gilded Age America. Van Vorst's reports from other towns took a darker view of women's industrial work.

3. Mrs. John [Bessie] Van Vorst and Marie Van Vorst, *The Woman Who Toils: Being the Experiences of Two Ladies as Factory Girls* (New York, 1903), 82, 85.

4. Ibid., vii. On Roosevelt's concern with falling birthrates from 1892 onwards, see Thomas G. Dyer, *Theodore Roosevelt and the Idea of Race* (Baton Rouge, La., 1980), 142–45.

5. Van Vorst, *Woman Who Toils*, viii.

6. "To Bishop Doane," *Boston Globe*, January 27, 1905.

7. *Life*, March 12, 1903. Light humor about race suicide was common in newspapers' column-fillers, and in some towns and cities groups of schoolchildren watched Roosevelt speak from beneath giant banners reading "No Race Suicide Here." Other issues remembered solemnly by historians were similarly subject to newspaper wits: Anne Ruggles Gere observes that "the 'new woman,'" for example, became a "comic icon" in the popular press between

1890 and 1920. (Gere, *Intimate Practices: Literacy and Cultural Work in U.S. Women's Clubs, 1880–1920* (Urbana, Ill., 1997), 141)

8. "What is there in marriage that makes thoughtful people so uncomfortable?" asked George Bernard Shaw in 1908. "The answer to this question is an answer which everybody knows and nobody likes to give. What is driving our ministers of religion and statesmen to blurt it out at last is the plain fact that marriage is now beginning to depopulate the country with such alarming rapidity that we are forced to throw aside our modesty like people who, awakened by an alarm of fire, rush into the streets in their nightdresses or in no dresses at all." George Bernard Shaw, "Preface to 'Getting Married'" (New York, 1909), 12. Public discussion of fertility control was difficult enough throughout the nineteenth century that many respected doctors and sociologists entertained the idea that lower fertility might be the result of physiological degeneration rather than voluntary action. See, e.g., Charles F. Emerick, "Is the Diminishing Birth-rate Volitional?" *Popular Science*, January 1911. Social critics used physiological explanations for falling fertility as arguments against the education of women, whose alleged over-involvement in "nervous" or "brain" work led, they thought, to the underdevelopment of their reproductive capacities. On Victorian medical advice regarding fertility decline and "limited vital energy," see Anita Clair Fellman and Michael Fellman, *Making Sense of Self: Medical Advice Literature in Late Nineteenth Century America* (Philadelphia, 1981), 75–87.

9. Charles Horton Cooley, *Social Organization: A Study of the Larger Mind* (New York, 1911), 84. On newspaper circulation per household see Melvin L. DeFleur and Sandra Ball-Rokeach, *Theories of Mass Communication* (New York, 1975). The "ritual" view of communication interprets media content not simply as a means of transmitting information but as a forum where readers construct and practice life rituals. See James Carey, "A Cultural Approach to Communication" in Carey, ed. *Communication as Culture: Essays on Media and Society* (New York, 2009 (1975)). For a review of subsequent developments in the field, see John J. Pauly, "Ritual Theory and the Media" in Robert S. Fortner, P. Mark Fackler, eds., *The Handbook of Media and Mass Communication Theory*, vol. 1 (Chichester, Eng., 2014). In order of frequency, the 605 articles came from the *Chicago Tribune* (151), *Washington Post* (96), *Boston Globe* (92), *New York Times* (89), *Los Angeles Times* (57), *Atlanta Constitution* (49), *Baltimore Sun* (40), *New York Tribune* (27), and *Hartford Courant* (4).

10. James Bryce, *The American Commonwealth*, vol. 2 (London, 1888), 263. Bryce's analysis has since been endorsed by contemporary scholars of public opinion: "One thing is clear," write Carroll Glynn and coauthors: "Bryce understood – as no one before him really did – the very critical role of newspapers in the communication of public opinion." Carroll Glynn, Susan Herbst, Garrett O'Keefe, and Robert Y. Shapiro, *Public Opinion* (Boulder, Colo., 1999), 45; see also p. 93–102, 381–415. Scholars have sometimes emphasized newspapers' role in "manufacturing" public opinion – rather than ratifying it – but we should not underestimate the press's reflective and populist role. "A text corpus is the representation and expression of a community

that writes," Martin Bauer argues. "Content analysis allows us to construct indicators of worldviews, values, attitudes, opinions, prejudices and stereotypes, and compare these across communities. In other words, content analysis is public opinion research by other means." Martin W. Bauer, "Classical Content Analysis: A Review" in Martin Bauer and George Gaskell, eds., *Qualitative Researching with Text, Image and Sound: A Practical Handbook* (Thousand Oaks, Cal., 2000), 133–34. The view of newspapers as manipulators of public opinion (on behalf of a capitalist class of advertisers) owes much to Edward S. Herman and Noam Chomsky, *Manufacturing Consent: The Political Economy of the Mass Media* (1988); Ferdinand Tönnies, *Critique of Public Opinion* (1922); and to a lesser extent, Walter Lippmann, *Public Opinion* (New York, 1922). Lippmann noted, however, that "a newspaper can flout an advertiser, it can attack a powerful banking or traction interest, but if it alienates the buying public, it loses the one indispensable asset of its existence … Patronage of the advertisers depends upon the editor's skill in holding together an effective group of customers. These customers deliver judgment according to their private experiences and their stereotyped expectations." (Lippmann, *Public Opinion*, 324, 333). On the tendency of historians to focus on newspaper's biases and inaccuracies, Robert Darnton writes that "newspapers should be read for information about how contemporaries construed events, rather than for reliable knowledge of events themselves." Darnton, "The Library in the New Age," *New York Review of Books*, June 12, 2008.

11. The database is ProQuest Historical Newspapers. My primary search term was "race suicide" – the phrase commonly used on all sides of the debate to introduce the subject of birthrates and birth control. I supplemented this search with another – "birth rate (and) family (or) children" – to rule out the possibility of thematic or other anomalies. From the combined results I excluded duplicates (such as wire service stories), very short items such as column fillers, and over 100 short articles documenting the great size of a local family but lacking analytic content (these articles often included a family picture, plus caption, under the headline "No race suicide here"). On Weber, Tenney, and other predecessors of content analysis, see Klaus Krippendorff, *Content Analysis: An Introduction to Its Methodology* (Thousand Oaks, Cal., 2013), 4–7. Some of the difficulties of using newspapers for this sort of project before optical character recognition are spelled out in Cynthia Goldstein, *The Press and the Beginning of the Birth Control Movement in the United States* (Ph.D. diss., Pennsylvania State University, 1985), ch. 1. For a synopsis of elite magazines' reaction to Roosevelt's race suicide pronouncement, see Gail Bederman, *Manliness and Civilization: A Cultural History of Gender and Race in the United States, 1880–1917* (Chicago, 1996), 202–5. Bederman argues that the Roosevelt-catalyzed race suicide discussion "made it possible, for the first time since the eighteenth century, for respectable American men to publically celebrate male sexuality" and "probably facilitated the development of modern ideologies of gender, in which sexual expressiveness became a hallmark of healthy manhood or womanhood" (p. 205).

12. I developed each frame using a "grounded theory" approach, refining categories as I notated the source documents, then returning to the documents and notes for coding. Eleven frames I classified as "explanatory," meaning they implied a cause for fertility decline (Figure A.1). The remaining twelve were descriptive or "other" (Figure A.2). Cases where this divide was not clear-cut included gender language, which could be explanatory, and the "poverty" frame, which included descriptions of large families as a phenomenon of the poor *and* explanations which cast fertility control as a means of avoiding poverty. Because the latter predominated, I classified "poverty" as explanatory. On the use of frames in historical demography, see John R. Wilmoth and Patrick Ball, "The Population Debate in American Popular Magazines, 1946–90," *Population and Development Review* 18: 4 (December, 1992); Laura Stark and Hans-Peter Kohler, "The Debate over Low Fertility in the Popular Press: A Cross-National Comparison, 1998–1999," *Population Research and Policy Review* 21:6 (December, 2002); Stark and Kohler, "The Popular Debate about Low Fertility: An Analysis of the German Press, 1993–2001," *European Journal of Population* 20: 4 (December, 2004). A notable application of ProQuest-based newspaper content analysis to American cultural and gender history is Estelle B. Freedman, "'Crimes which Startle and Horrify': Gender, Age, and the Racialization of Sexual Violence in White American Newspapers, 1870–1900," *Journal of the History of Sexuality* 20:3 (2011). One application of content analysis to U.S. gender history is Joanne Meyerowitz, "Beyond the Feminine Mystique: A Reassessment of Postwar Mass Culture, 1946–1958," *Journal of American History* 79:4 (March 1993).

13. Of the 605 articles analyzed, 304 primarily record the views of editors, columnists, or reporters. Though these articles were usually unsigned, we can assume male authorship for a large majority. The 301 remaining articles record the views of non-journalists, such as public speakers or writers of letters to the editor. Among working-class Americans, "the more sensational newspapers … are the ones universally read," observed one student of 200 working families in 1907 (Louise Bolard More, *Wage-Earners' Budgets: A Study of Standards and Cost of Living in New York City* (New York, 1907), 141).

14. Roosevelt to Albert Shaw, April 3, 1907, *Presidential Addresses and State Papers* (New York,1910), vol. 6; W.E.B. Du Bois, *The Negro Family* (Atlanta, 1908), 42. The same inattention to in-group birthrates prevailed among England's working classes – see Sian Pooley, "Parenthood, Child-Rearing and Fertility in England, 1850–1914," *The History of the Family* 18:1 (2013) – and in rural U.S. papers, which, like African-American papers, gave "race suicide" minimal coverage, the term confined mostly to wire service reports or reprints from big urban papers. In a sample of ten small-town newspapers from a dairy-farming county in northern New York state, for example, 130 articles on race suicide and birthrates were printed between 1903 and 1908, but just eight were produced locally: four editorials, three articles about large local families, and one about county school enrollments. Over the same period the German-language immigrant press largely ignored the issue, though it covered the militarist cradle competition between

Germany and France. Spanish- and French-language dailies were nearly silent. Regarding the "one-quarter" estimate, the *Twelfth Census of the United States* (1900) enumerated 8,883,991 "Negroes" (Census Bulletin 8, p. 19), 1,471,332 non-English speakers (Vol. 2, p. 490), and 1,916,434 native white illiterates over ten years of age (Vol. 2, p. 413). I use illiteracy as a rough proxy for indigence because the U.S. government did not establish a standard measure of poverty until the 1960s. Some commentators believed Roosevelt and his allies addressed themselves only to "the better class" or "old Americans" while others thought he was encouraging indiscriminate breeding across the board – "mustangs" rather than "thoroughbreds," as one columnist wrote. Historians have generally characterized Roosevelt's race suicide campaign as patriarchal and racist, and that is partly true: Roosevelt expected more domestic self-sacrifice from women than men, and reflexively addressed his concerns to the enfranchised white majority. Roosevelt nevertheless looked askance at many of his period's prevailing racial theories, mocking, for example, the "unconscious and rather pathetic humor in the simplicity of half a century ago which spoke of the Aryan and the Teuton with reverential admiration" (Theodore Roosevelt, "Biological Analogies in History," Romanes Lecture, Oxford, England, June 7, 1910). He called the racial designation "Anglo-Saxon" "meaningless," and was appalled that "many of the European races which come to this country with traditions of large families soon fall into the 'American way'" ("The President," *Ladies' Home Journal*, February 1906). Roosevelt's racial liberality seems to have extended only to people of European descent – not to "race differences as fundamental as those which divide from one another the half-dozen great ethnic divisions of mankind" – though he noted that it was "easy to forget how brief is this period of unquestioned supremacy of the so-called white race." Even a "barbaric race" could "suddenly develop a more complex cultivation and civilization" (Romanes lecture, 1910). On women's domestic roles, Roosevelt held both conventional and progressive views. He believed "the primary duty of the husband is to be the home-maker, the breadwinner for his wife and children, and that the primary duty of the woman is to be the helpmate, the housewife, and mother" ("Address before the National Congress of Mothers," Washington, DC, March 13, 1905). But he also supported a variety of women's rights causes throughout his life, and framed falling birthrates as a failure of "men and women," rather than mothers alone. On Roosevelt's racialism see Dyer, *Roosevelt*; Gary Gerstle, "Theodore Roosevelt and the Divided Character of American Nationalism," *Journal of American History* 86:3 (December 1999). On the intersection of race and gender in Roosevelt's thought, see Bederman, *Manliness and Civilization*, ch. 5.

15. On Roosevelt's doubts see Dyer, *Roosevelt*, 153. "It is very well to talk race suicide, but there is a place for such talk, and that place is not in the columns of a public newspaper," one reader warned the *Boston Globe* (November 3, 1907).

16. "President on Race Suicide," *The Baltimore Sun*, March 15, 1905.

17. "New Books," *The Washington Post*, November 12, 1904; "No Race Suicide – Gibbons," *The New York Times*, October 20, 1907.
18. "Everybody's Column," *The Boston Globe*, October 14, 1906.
19. "The Question of Race Suicide," *New York Tribune*, April 13, 1903.
20. "Race Suicide," *The New York Times*, September 25, 1905.
21. "Children Cost Too Much," *Los Angeles Times*, December 9, 1905. The Supreme Court decision was *Griswold v. Connecticut*.
22. Roosevelt to E.A. Ross, July 11, 1911, quoted in Ross, *Seventy Years of It: An Autobiography* (New York, 1936), 243. On the emergence of two- or three-child norm among northeastern Americans before 1900, and the demographic validity of Roosevelt's concerns, see Paul A. David and Warren C. Sanderson, "The Emergence of a Two-Child Norm among American Birth-Controllers," *Population and Development Review* 13:1 (1987).
23. Throughout this book quantitative measures are meant to read comparatively against parallel figures in this book, not as stand-alone indicators of public opinion.
24. Notable economic theories of fertility include Gary S. Becker, "An Economic Analysis of Fertility" in Becker, ed., *Demographic and Economic Change in Developed Countries* (Princeton, 1960), Richard Easterlin, "The Economics and Sociology of Fertility: A Synthesis" in Charles Tilly, ed., *Historical Studies in Changing Fertility* (Princeton, 1978). A cogent review of economic theories is included in Dov Friedlander, Barbara S. Okun, and Sharon Sega, "The Demographic Transition Then and Now: Processes, Perspectives, and Analyses," *Journal of Family History* 24:4 (1999).
25. "Race Suicide," *The Baltimore Sun*; "Race Suicide in Fact," *Atlanta Constitution*, January 24, 1904; "'Immorality' in Best of Menus," *Chicago Tribune*, January 22, 1905; "Discerns Causes of Race Suicide," *Chicago Tribune*, August 5, 1905; "Chicago Now Presents Race Suicide Problem," *Atlanta Constitution*, January 24, 1904.
26. "Some Great Problems," *Los Angeles Times*, August 20, 1905.
27. "Race Suicide," *The Baltimore Sun*; "Stork Not in Dollar Race," *Chicago Tribune*, January 4, 1907.
28. This "moral economy" was less overtly political than that described in E.P. Thompson, "The Moral Economy of the English Crowd in the Eighteenth Century," *Past & Present* 50:1 (1971), where the same term helps explain the actions of subordinate groups in response to economic changes they consider unjust.
29. Arguments for integrating economic and ideational factors, rather than opposing them, include David Kertzer, "Religion and the Decline of Fertility: Conclusions" in Frans van Poppel and Renzo Derosas, eds., *Religion and the Decline of Fertility in the Western World* (Dordrecht, 2006); John Casterline, "Introduction" in *Diffusion Processes and Fertility Transition: Selected Perspectives* (Washington, DC, 2001), 1–22. On the self-replication of fertility behavior see Julia A. Jennings, Allison R. Sullivan, and J. David Hacker, "Intergenerational Transmission of Reproductive Behavior during the Demographic Transition," *Journal of Interdisciplinary History*, Volume 42: 4 (Spring 2012).

30. Theodore Roosevelt, "Address to the General Conference of the Methodist Episcopal Church," May 16, 1908, in *Presidential Addresses and State Papers* (New York, 1910), vol. 7.

31. "Everybody's Column," *The Boston Globe*, October 14, 1906; "A Georgia Domestic Tragedy," *Atlanta Constitution*, June 1, 1905.

32. "Mankind to Fly," *The Los Angeles Times*, September 13, 1908; "A Woman on the Race Suicide Question," *The New York Times*, March 1, 1903; "Children of Ghetto District," *Chicago Tribune*, February 14, 1903; "Topics of the Times," *The New York Times*, May 13, 1908; "What People Talk About," *The Boston Globe*, October 6, 1906; "The President and the Babies," *Chicago Tribune*, March 17, 1905.

33. "A Plea for the Child," *The New York Times*, September 28, 1902; "Old Stock Will Disappear," *The Boston Globe*, February 15, 1903. Demographers' attention has increasingly turned to this sort of "inner-light" religious feeling, as opposed to more formal indicators like church attendance rates. Second demographic transition (SDT) theory, for example, attributes persistent post-1960 subreplacement fertility in the West to "the reduction in religious practice, the abandonment of traditional religious beliefs (heaven, sin, etc.), and a decline in individual sentiments of religiosity (prayer, meditation, etc.)." Using values surveys, SDT theorists have correlated relatively high fertility with, for example, their trust in churches or belief in "the importance of God in life." Ron Lesthaeghe and Johan Surkyn, "Value Orientations and the Second Demographic Transition (SDT) in Northern, Western and Southern Europe: An Update," *Demographic Research* 3 [2004], 51, 64. On the importance of shared cultural outlooks within and between religious groups, as opposed to religious doctrine per se, see Kevin McQuillan, *Culture, Religion, and Demographic Behaviour: Catholics and Lutherans in Alsace* (Montreal, 1999) and Ernest Benz, "Family Limitation among Political Catholics in Baden in 1869" in Renzo Derosas and Frans van Poppel, eds., *Religion and the Decline of Fertility in the Western World* (Dordrecht, 2006).

34. Philippe Ariès, "Two Successive Motivations for the Declining Birth Rates in the West," *Population and Development Review* 6:4 (December, 1980) – the essay that inspired for SDT theory – posits "immutable Nature" rather than codified religiosity as the indispensable element in the "traditional beliefs" which before the 1960s prevented Westerners from limiting fertility more widely. In France, "even the atheists of the eighteenth century condemned [contraceptive practices] as a violation 'Natural Law,' the new divinity," writes Alfred Sauvy in *General Theory of Population* (London, 1969), 362. On naturistic pronatalism in early twentieth-century America see Laura L. Lovett, *Conceiving the Future: Pronatalism, Reproduction, and the Family in the United States, 1890–1938* (Chapel Hill, N.C., 2007).

35. "Is Race Suicide Economic Agent?" *Chicago Tribune*, April 2, 1905; "Col. Monroe's Doctrine," *The Washington Post*, March 18, 1903; "Marriage Makes Men Brave," *Chicago Tribune*, March 10, 1907; "City and Children," *Chicago Tribune*, March 26, 1905; "American Race Has Reached Its Zenith, Educator Says," *Chicago Tribune*, August 4, 1905. On cities, overcivilization, and race suicide see T.J. Jackson Lears, *No Place of*

Grace: Antimodernism and the Transformation of American Culture, 1880–1920 (New York, 1981), 26–34.

36. "Aid to Race Suicide," *Chicago Daily Tribune,* June 8, 1904; *The Washington Post,* Mar 8, 1903. Landlords largely retained the right to decline families with children through the 1970s.

37. *American Architect and Building News,* September 3, 1904; "A Great Man," *The Boston Globe,* November 15, 1905; "Childless Flat Is Legal," *Chicago Tribune,* June 7, 1905. Proposals to tax bachelors and childless couples also came before various lawmaking bodies in early twentieth-century America – including at least nineteen state legislatures – though few passed and perhaps none were effective. See Marjorie E. Kornhauser, "Taxing Bachelors in America, 1895–1939" in John Tiley, ed., *Studies in the History of Tax Law,* vol.6 (Oxford, 2012).

38. "Little Talks with Big Men," *The Washington Post,* December 3, 1905.

39. Janet Golden, *A Social History of Wet Nursing in America: From Breast to Bottle* (Cambridge, Eng., 1996), 138; *American Journal of Clinical Medicine* 13: 7 (1906).

40. Roosevelt, "Mother's Congress Address."

41. Theodore Roosevelt, "Message to Congress," December 3, 1906, in *Presidential Addresses and State Papers* (New York, 1910), vol. 5; "Race Suicide Inevitable," *The Washington Post,* December 7, 1903; E.A. Ross, "Recent Tendencies in Sociology," *Quarterly Journal of Economics* (May 1903).

42. "Large Families or Small?" *The Washington Post,* May 1, 1903; "The Characteristics of Theodore Roosevelt, the Man," *Washington Post,* March 5, 1905. Another Roosevelt surrogate noted that the White House received countless photos of large families, often with a "jocular inscription," from readers of "the comic weeklies." The president was glad to receive these "playful evidences of popular interest in what he has tried to say, although in some cases they reflect painfully a misapprehension of what he really means." ("The President," *Ladies' Home Journal,* February 1906.)

43. "City and Children," *Chicago Tribune,* March 26, 1905.

44. "Reviews of New Books," *The Washington Post,* November 12, 1904; "Little Babe Bartered Off," *Los Angeles Times,* July 17, 1904. In a popular 1905 advice manual for young men, Senator Albert Beveridge wrote "Your father made the old home. Prove yourself worthy of him by making the new home . . . What abnormal egotism the attitude of him who says, 'This planet, and all the uncounted centuries of the past, were made for *me* and nobody else, and I will live accordingly. I will go it alone.'" (Beveridge, *The Young Man and the World* (New York, 1905), 152).

45. "France's Race Problem," *The Washington Post,* December 6, 1907.

46. "Roosevelt to the Mothers' Congress," *The Independent,* March 23, 1905.

47. Roosevelt to E.A. Ross, September 19, 1907, quoted in Ross, *Sin and Society, An Analysis of Latter-day Iniquity* (Boston, 1907), ix–xi.

48. "Too Few Children in World," *Chicago Tribune,* November 25, 1908.

49. "What People Talk About," *The Boston Globe*, March 30, 1906; "Race Suicide," *The Boston Globe*, February 14, 1903; "Trusts Bar to Babies," *The Washington Post*, January 5, 1907.

50. Though education fees surely factored into broadly "economic" rationales for limitation, overall, commentators only mentioned education at the rate of less heralded factors like housing discrimination.

51. "If Poor, Avoid Children," *Chicago Tribune*, December 23, 1907. On men's breadwinning role and ambivalence about entering it, see Stephen M. Frank, *Life with Father: Parenthood and Masculinity in the Nineteenth Century American North* (Baltimore. 1998), 83–112. When a son of Lydia Pinkham tried to pass out flyers for his mother's "Vegetable Compound and Uterine Tonic" to passers-by in New York City, he found that men would accept the offer but women would decline in embarrassment(Janet Farrell Brodie, *Contraception and Abortion in Nineteenth Century America* (Ithaca, N.Y., 1994), 192).

52. "Primitive Squaws," *Chicago Tribune*, March 8, 1903.

53. *The Washington Post*, September 25, 1904; "State Babies Advocated as a Mercy to Mothers," *Atlanta Constitution*, May 28, 1905; "Why I Have No Family," *The Independent*, March 23, 1905.

54. "Race Suicide," *The Boston Globe*, February 14, 1903.

55. "Why I Do Not Marry," *The Independent*, June 30, 1904; "Why I Have No Family," *The Independent*, March 23, 1905. For a similarly themed essay from a man's perspective, see "'Race Suicide' and Common Sense," *North American Review*, June 1903.

56. Commander, *The American Idea* (New York, 1907), 32. Also on women's differing interest and agency in family limitation see Carl N. Degler, *At Odds: Women and the Family in America from the Revolution to the Present* (New York, 1980), ch. 8.

57. Commander, *American Idea*, 35.

58. E.g. Ron Lesthaeghe, "The Second Demographic Transition in Western Countries: An Interpretation," in Karen Oppenheim Mason and An-Magritt Jensen, eds., *Gender and Family Change in Industrialized Countries* (Oxford, 2003 [1995]), 21. Lesthaeghe is a key developer of the benchmark theory of Second Demographic Transition (SDT), which uses large-scale values surveys to describe a sea change in reproductive attitudes and behavior in the 1960s. Before that decade (during the "first" demographic transition) parents across the West altruistically focused greater economic resources on fewer children, leading to below-replacement fertility. From the 1960s onward (the "second" transition) this economic altruism was overlayered with a more hedonic, existentially secure, spiritually questing moral regime, ensuring that fertility stayed below replacement into the present. Sexual and gender revolutions, plus generalized antiauthoritarianism, replaced child-centered "rationaliza-tion" with self-actualizing "individualization." SDT theory's basic historical narrative receives some support from early twentieth-century U.S. qualitative testimony, but on a different timescale. In American moralists' eyes familistic altruism and "self-fulfilling" individualism were longstanding and overlap-ping phenomena rather than sequential developments with a pivot point in the

1960s. Observers saw both trends clearly in both the 1900s and 1920s–30s. In arguing for two successive demographic transitions Lesthaeghe argues that "the 'one transition' view simply blurs history," but blurriness may be a good metaphor for the attitudinal shifts in orientations towards self, society, and the cosmos that abetted fertility transition. Though the "two transitions" schema may be fundamentally valid as a broad cultural narrative, a messy, ambivalent, reversible blur divides these two ideal types. On SDT and American qualitative testimony see Trent MacNamara, "Why 'Race Suicide'? Cultural Factors in U.S. Fertility Decline, 1903–1908," *Journal of Interdisciplinary History* 44:4 (2014).

59. "Has the Small Family Become an American Ideal?," *The Independent*, April 14, 1904; "Mrs. Frake on Babies," *The Los Angeles Times*, December 9, 1905; "General Decline of Human Fertility in Western Nations," *Current Literature*, March 1906.

60. "Warning by Two Presidents," *The Washington Post*, February 15, 1903.

61. "History from the Standpoint of a Biologist," *The Independent*, April 30, 1903; "The President," *Ladies' Home Journal* (February 1906).

62. "Mr. G.H. Wells: The Prophet of The New Order," *The Arena* (August 1906); "Everybody's Column," *The Boston Globe*, October 13, 1907.

3 SENSIBLE AS SPINACH

1. Enid Charles, *The Twilight of Parenthood* (London, 1934), quoted in Jan Van Bavel, "Subreplacement Fertility in the West before the Baby Boom: Past and Current Perspectives," *Population Studies* 64:1 (March 2010).

2. Francis M. Vreeland, "The Process of Reform with Especial Reference to Reform Groups in the Field of Population," Ph.D. dissertation, University of Michigan (1929), 323. On newspaper opinion between the 1900s and 1930s, see Engelman, *A History of the Birth Control Movement in America* (Santa Barbara, Cal., 2011), ch. 2, 4.

3. *Note on chapter sources and methods.* This chapter is based on a sample of 781 articles retrieved from the same database using similar search terms. Fertility decline remained a subject of persistent press attention in 1927–1935, but the absence of a catalyzing figure like Roosevelt or a singular catchphrase like "race suicide" reduced the issue's prominence. Perhaps because commentators could no longer assume the same familiarity with the terms of debate, fewer articles dealt in broad-brush moralizing, and more in social analysis. As a result, classifiable causal explanations of any kind became 22 percent more common. This chapter therefore does not emphasize increases in one casual frame or another unless they significantly exceed this across-the-board rise. Though race suicide's eclipse as a catchphrase was partly made up by "birth control" (popularized in the late 1910s), article retrieval required broader search terms in 1927–1935 – namely, at least one term from each of the following two sets: (1) "birth control"; "birth rate"; birthrate; contraception; "race suicide"; "prevent conception"; (2) children; reproduction; procreation; family; families; motherhood; maternity;

fatherhood; paternity; posterity. Despite the differing search terms, articles' basic subject matter remained similar. The most important framing shift emerged from the popularization of eugenic ideas. About 8 percent of observers made their approval for birth control contingent on policies that would check undesirable groups (such as the poor or "feeble-minded") without further limiting the desirable. In what follows, this category of opinion is labeled "eugenic contingent." Finally, two newspapers that made up nearly 20 percent of the 1903–1908 sample, *the Boston Globe* (15.2 percent) and *New York Tribune* (4.5 percent), were not available for the period 1927–1935. The *Tribune* was generally pronatalist in 1903–1908, and its absence may have slightly skewed the 1927–1935 sample towards approval for birth control. All newspapers, however, showed significant and similar drops in favorability towards pronatalism.

4. "Letters," *The Washington Post*, February 8, 1934.

5. "Sidelights on Current Scenes," *The New York Times*, March 31, 1935; "Women Have Decided," *The New York Times*, June 10, 1931; "Voters Call 2 to 3 Children Ideal," *The Washington Post*, December 13, 1936. Four was "large by modern standards" in 1907 ("No Children Allowed in These Flats," *Chicago Tribune*, May 5, 1907), and Roosevelt considered it "obvious that unless the average married couple capable of having children has four children the race will not increase" ("A Premium on Race Suicide," *Outlook*, September 27, 1913). Four additional 1900s observers implied that four-child families were considered large.

6. "I Have Said in my Heart," *The Atlanta Constitution*, February 28, 1928

7. "Urges Facing Facts About Marriage," *The New York Times*, November 25, 1929; "Say Birth Control Gains Public Favor," *The New York Times*, January 22, 1932.

8. "Stork a Welcome Visitor in Archer Street, Nicetown," *Chicago Tribune*, May 4, 1908.

9. "Parents' Desire for Leisure Blamed for Birth-Rate Drop," *The Baltimore Sun*, October 27, 1933; "Bigger and Better Families," *The New York Times*, May 1, 1932. On the Depression and birth control see, e.g., Steven Mintz and Susan Kellogg, *Domestic Revolutions: A Social History of American Family Life* (New York, 1987), 147–48; Linda Gordon, *The Moral Property of Women: A History of Birth Control Politics in America* (Urbana, Ill., 2002), 223. The period's small corps of population scholars mirrored the focus on moral as well as economic factors. "The spread of birth control was typically seen as connected to the sweeping process of modernization and the concomitant rise of urban lifestyles," writes Jan Van Bavel of the interwar period. "More specifically, the factors cited most often as being behind low fertility were secularization and rationalization, individualization, changing (more liberal) attitudes towards marriage and sexuality, conflicting pressures on time of work, family, and leisure, and rising consumerism" (Jan Van Bavel, "Subreplacement Fertility in the West before the Baby Boom: Past and Current Perspectives," *Population Studies* 64:1 (March 2010)). On the Depression's influence on eugenicists and other population scholars see Gordon, *Moral Property*, 211–23.

10. "As Youth Sees Marriage," *The Atlanta Constitution*, May 20, 1928.
11. "The Birth Rate Drops" *Hartford Courant*, March 14, 1931; "The Once Over" *The Washington Post*, June 16, 1933.
12. On children's sentimentalization in late nineteenth-century America see Paula S. Fass, *The End of American Childhood: A History of Parenting from Life on the Frontier to the Managed Child* (Princeton, 2016).
13. "Voters Call 2 to 3 Children Ideal," *The Washington Post*, December 13, 1936; "Stork Derby Field Scorns Split Prize," *The New York Times*, September 15, 1935; "Fair Enough," *The Washington Post*, August 30, 1935.
14. "Cites Theory Of Declining Growth Rate," *The Baltimore Sun*, August 2, 1931; "Voters Call 2 to 3 Children Ideal," *The Washington Post*, December 13, 1936. On the beginnings of middle-class parents' uncertainty about "put [ting] their progeny on a sound economic footing" in a plural and industrializing society, see Mary P. Ryan, *Cradle of the Middle Class: The Family in Oneida County, New York, 1790–1865* (Cambridge, Eng., 1981), 145–184. On the U.S. child labor debate and the rising "moral value of the economically useless but emotionally priceless child," see Viviana A. Zelizer, *Pricing the Priceless Child: The Changing Social Value of Children* (Princeton, 1994 [1985]), 56–72. On the interrelationship of risk perception and modernity see Ulrich Beck, *Risk Society: Toward a New Modernity*, trans. Mark Ritter (London, 1992).
15. "Shall We Abandon Religion?" *The New York Times*, April 15, 1928.
16. Robert S. Lynd and Helen Merrell Lynd, *Middletown in Transition: A Study in Cultural Conflicts* (New York, 1937), 489, 493, 496.
17. "Changing Marriage," *The Atlanta Constitution*, March 11, 1928. Suggestive evidence on links between anomie, pessimism, and lower fertility is gathered in Dimiter Philipov, Zsolt Speder, and Francesco C. Billari, "Soon, Later, or Ever? The Impact of Anomie and Social Capital on Fertility Intentions in Bulgaria (2002) and Hungary (2001)," *Population Studies* 60:3 (2006).
18. "Birth Control Urged for Improving Race," *The New York Times*, November 21, 1929.
19. Catholic Women Rap Birth Control," *The Baltimore Sun*, October 8, 1931; "Letters to the Post," April 5, 1931. On *Casti Connubii* and its relation to the American church, see John T. Noonan, Jr., *Contraception: A History of its Treatment by the Catholic Theologians and Canonists* (Cambridge, Mass., 2012 [1965]), 423–32.
20. "Mrs. Sanger Calls Catholics Bigots," *The New York Times*, April 25, 1928. Sanger went so far as to address a women's auxiliary of anti-Catholic Ku Klux Klan, to her later regret (Sanger, *Autobiography* (New York, 1938), 366).
21. "Council Delays on Birth Control," *The New York Times*, December 9, 1932; Leslie Woodcock Tentler, "'The Abominable Crime of Onan': Catholic Pastoral Practice and Family Limitation in the United States, 1875–1919," *Church History* 71:2 (2002). On the preponderance of liberal Protestants among clergy who supported eugenics, see Christine Rosen, *Preaching Eugenics: Religious Leaders and the American Eugenics Movement* (New York, 2005). On the philosophical underpinnings of Catholic positions and

their reception among lay Catholics see Tentler, *Catholics and Contraception: An American History* (Ithaca, N.Y., 2004), 43–72.

22. "Birth Control Report Indorsed by Ministers, Women," *The Atlanta Constitution,* March 22, 1931; "Health Talks," *The Atlanta Constitution,* December 18, 1934; "Priest Asks Fight on Birth Control," *The New York Times,* July 23, 1934; "Birth Control Plea Called Illogical," *The New York Times,* December 12, 1932.

23. "Birth Control Report Indorsed By Ministers, Women," *The Atlanta Constitution,* March 22, 1931; "Favors Birth Control," *The Washington Post,* Feb. 28, 1934; "Opposes Birth Control," *The Washington Post,* February 28, 1934; "Birth Control Plea Called Illogical," *The New York Times,* December 12, 1932. Religious and macrohistorical frames were disproportionately likely to appear in the same article: 28 percent of "religion" articles also mentioned macrohistorical factors (versus 20 percent of all articles); 42 percent of "macrohistorical" articles also mentioned religion (versus 30 percent of all articles).

24. "World's Hope Seen in Catholic Dogma," *The New York Times,* February 4, 1935. In 1910 the English Jesuit Bernard Vaughan, famed "castigator of the smart set" in London, made news during a tour of the United States by predicting "Catholic Rule by Force of Numbers," as a headline in the *Trenton Evening Times* put it. "The battle for possession of the world will soon be narrowed to the Roman Catholic Church amid the destructive forces of paganism. Protestantism is disappearing."

25. "Condemning Birth Control," *The New York Times,* December 27, 1933; "Social Justice Suggested as Puerto Rico's Chief Need," *The New York Times,* October 30, 1932; "Mgr. Ryan Assails Sterilization Aim," *The New York Times,* February 19, 1934.

26. "Forgetting Religion," *The Washington Post,* March 22, 1931; "Letters to Post Express Varied Views Inspired by Article on Birth Control," *The Washington Post,* April 5, 1931.

27. Tentler, *Catholics and Contraception,* 57–61; John A. Ryan, "Family Limitation," *Ecclesiastical Review* 54 (1916), quoted in Tentler, "Abominable Crime"; Charles Westoff and Elise Jones, "The End of 'Catholic' Fertility," *Demography* 16:2 (1979).

28. John Montgomery Cooper, *Birth Control* (Washington, D.C., 1923), 10–11.

29. "Everyday Questions," *The Atlanta Constitution,* January 17, 1928; "Urges Facing Facts About Marriage," *The New York Times,* November 25, 1929; "Birth Control Report Indorsed by Ministers, Women," *The Atlanta Constitution,* March 22, 1931. Sanger's romanticism, sexual and otherwise, is a central theme in David M. Kennedy, *Birth Control in America: The Career of Margaret Sanger* (New Haven: 1970).

30. "No Race Suicide in America," Chicago Tribune, January 29, 1905; Gail Bederman, *Manliness and Civilization: A Cultural History of Gender and Race in the United* States, *1880–1917* (Chicago, 1995), 72–73. See also E. Anthony Rotundo, *American Manhood: Transformations in Masculinity from the Revolution to the Modern Era* (New York, 1993).

31. "Birth Control Plea Called Illogical," *The New York Times*, December 12, 1932; "Birth Control Deplored," *The New York Times*, August 20, 1933; "Opposes Birth Control," *The Washington Post*, February 28, 1934; "Church Studies New Theory of Birth Control," *Chicago Tribune*, January 30, 1933.

32. Paul Popenoe and Roswell Johnson, *Applied Eugenics* (New York, 1918), 2. Popenoe and Johnson provide a detailed account of divergences between elite eugenic thought and popular understandings of heredity on p. 31–43.

33. "Are we a Vanishing Race?" *Los Angeles Times*, July 15, 1934. "Science alone never fully controlled the definition of 'heredity' or the scope of 'eugenics,'" writes Martin Pernick. "Although scientists' technical terminology distinguished between 'hereditary' and 'congenital' conditions ... scientists and lay people still shared a much broader language in which 'heredity' encompassed everything inherited from one's forbearers, no matter how they conveyed it." (Pernick, *The Black Stork: Eugenics and the Death of "Defective" Babies in American Medicine and Motion Pictures since 1915* (New York, 1999), 48, 53.) Pernick's assessment is based on his reading of 333 responses to the case of Harry Haiselden, a Chicago surgeon who allowed a newborn baby with severe birth defects to die, in 1915, for eugenic reasons. Whether the failure to embrace hard heredity was a result of obliviousness or conscious resistance is not clear. One newspaper observer called eugenics "a rare word," while another suggested that eugenics had once been popular but now seemed a poor "disguise for race prejudice, ancestor worship and caste snobbery." Eugenicists' own comments to reporters seem to indicate that they could not expect friendly receptions from the general public. From a eugenics convention in 1932, one eugenicist "termed absurd the popular accusation that eugenics is 'half-baked.'" Others denounced "detractors who have gibed 'Eugenics is good for cows but not for humans'" ("Changes Front On Birth Control," *Chicago Tribune*, January 20, 1933; "Genes And Eugenics," *The New York Times*, August 24, 1932; "Eugenists Ask Special Clinics On Marriage," *Chicago Tribune*, August 24, 1932). On the preponderance of "less-eye-catching moderate positions" within the eugenics movement, see also Kathy J. Cooke, "The Limits of Heredity: Nature and Nurture in American Eugenics Before 1915," *Journal of the History of Biology* 31:2 (1998).

34. Peter Engelman, *A History of the Birth Control Movement in America* (Santa Barbara, Cal., 2011) chronicles the careers of many early, medical, and lesser-known advocates for birth control. On freethinkers and sex radicals, as well as physicians, see Gordon, *Moral Property*, ch. 2–7.

35. Ben Reitman quoted in Vreeland, "Process of Reform," 68. "The fact of the matter is that methods of birth control were so well circulated and known in America that all earnest seekers found them," Goldman wrote in 1916. "In many cities these pamphlets were distributed openly at meetings, in shops, and on the streets. Some of the birth control advocates who sold the pamphlet complained that it was impossible to sell it for more than ten cents a copy." Quoted in Vreeland, "Process of Reform," 62.

36. Sanger, *Autobiography*, 68–69.

37. On Sanger's life and work see Ellen Chesler, *Woman of Valor: Margaret Sanger and the Birth Control Movement in America* (New York, 2007 [1992]).
38. Vreeland, "Process of Reform," 538. Despite Sanger's popularity as a speaker on college campuses, Vreeland reported in 1929 that "almost no college students know her, at least as the leader of the American Birth Control League" (p. 538). On the organized movement's stalled development in the 1920s, see Chesler, *Woman of Valor*, 226.
39. "Birth control" was not quite a household term until it was applied to hormonal contraception ("the pill") in the 1960s, a half-century after the phrase was coined. James Cooper, the traveling speaker, found confusion on the term's meaning among doctors in the late 1920s, and *Country Home* magazine tried to survey readers' opinions on the subject in 1930; "it was found necessary to print an explanation of the phrase on the ballots, because 'hundreds of farm wives' had written in to ask what it meant when the subject was previously discussed in the magazine." An account of the survey is in "A Few Rugged Individuals," *The New York Times*, September 19, 1930.
40. "'Her Unborn Child' Comes in from Road," *The New York Times*, March 7, 1928; "Care of the Body," *Los Angeles Times*, January 12, 1930; "Slump Man-Made Bishops Declare," *The New York Times*, June 8, 1933; "Opposed to Birth Control," *The Washington Post*, February 2, 1934. The 12 percent of commentators who mentioned (or were part of) the organized movement was comparable to the 10 percent who mentioned the role of doctors in shaping contraceptive behavior, and somewhat more than the 7 percent who referred to Ben Lindsey's ideas on "companionate marriage" (see Ch. 6).
41. "Letters to Post," *The Washington Post*, April 5, 1931; "The Care of the Body," *Los Angeles Times*, January 22, 1933; "Mrs. Sanger Named for Women's Prize," *The New York Times*, November 10, 1931.
42. For a critical but ultimately positive assessment of Sanger's overall contribution to the movement, see Kennedy, *Birth Control in America*, 269–71.
43. "Care of the Body," *Los Angeles Times*, June 28, 1931.
44. "Changing Marriage," *The Atlanta Constitution*, March 11, 1928; George Ade, "The Joys of Single Blessedness," *American Magazine*, June 1921.
45. "A Few Rugged Individuals," *The New York Times*, September 19, 1930; Tentler, "Abominable Crime."
46. "Letters," *The Washington Post*, February 8, 1934; "Aunt Het" *The Atlanta Constitution*, September 8, 1929. On expanding faith in the medical profession and preventative public health measures, see John C. Burnham, *Health Care in America: A History* (Baltimore, 2015), 223–52.
47. "Should Wives Have Children? No!" *Los Angeles Times*, September 29, 1935.
48. Ida Blom, "'Master of Your Own Body and What Is In It' – Reducing Marital Fertility in Norway, 1890–1930" in Angelique Janssens, ed., *Gendering the Fertility Decline in the Western World* (Bern, 2007), 82.
49. Blom, "Master," 77. Blom's study draws on primarily female sources: women's publications and letters to the Oslo Mothers' Clinic. Sofia Kling comes to a similar conclusion for Sweden in the 1930s. See Kling, "'I Think I'd

Rather Die Than Go through with a Pregnancy Again.' Experiences of Childbearing and Birth Control in Sweden in the 1930s" in Janssens, ed., *Gendering the Fertility Decline* (Bern, 2007), 186n.

50. *Griswold v. Connecticut*, 381 U.S. 479 (1965).

51. "Birth Control Plea Called Illogical," *The New York Times*, December 12, 1932. On twentieth-century U.S. debates over how public an institution marriage should be, see Nancy Cott, *Public Vows: A History of Marriage and the Nation* (Cambridge, Mass.), ch. 7–9.

52. "Birth Control," *The New York Times*, May 14, 1933; "Motherhood Is a Prerogative Safe From National Decrees, Dictator of Italy Learns," *The Washington Post*, March 15, 1935; "Disparity Found In Right and Good: Basic Viciousness of Contraception is Disputed," *The New York Times*, October 14, 1934.

53. "Ballyhooing Birthrate," *The Baltimore Sun*, June 30, 1933; "Italy Goes in for Statistics in a Big Way," *Chicago Tribune*, August 14, 1932; "Hitler and Mussolini Woo a Warlike Stork," *The Washington Post*, November 18, 1934.

54. Margaret Lamberts Bendroth, *Growing Up Protestant: Parents, Children, and Mainline Churches* (New Brunswick, N.J., 2002), 61; "Birth Control," *The New York Times*, May 14, 1933. On the development of a "new family ideal" built around "sheltered childhood," see David I. Macleod, *The Age of the Child: Children in America, 1890–1920* (New York, 1998). Rebecca Jo Plant places a similar transition later in the century: "Particularly after World War II, mainstream American culture ceased to represent motherhood as an all-encompassing identity rooted in notions of self-sacrifice and infused with powerful social and political meaning. Instead, motherhood came to be conceived as a deeply fulfilling but fundamentally private experience and a single (though still central) component of a more multifaceted self" (Plant, *Mom: The Transformation of Motherhood in Modern America* (Chicago, 2010), 3).

55. "Birth Control as a Privilege," *The New York Times*, April 12, 1931.

56. "An Answer to Judge Lindsey," *The Baltimore Sun*, April 22, 1928.

57. "The Woman Pays the Fiddler," *The Atlanta Constitution*, June 21, 1929.

58. Jan Van Bavel and David S. Reher, "The Baby Boom and Its Causes: What We Know and What We Need to Know," *Population and Development Review* 39:2 (June 2013).

59. See, e.g., Richard Easterlin "The Conflict between Aspirations and Resources," *Population and Development Review* 2:3/4 (1976).

60. Elaine Tyler May, *Homeward Bound: American Families in the Cold War Era* (New York, 2008 [1988]), 98, 132. Other examinations of changing gender norms in the baby boom era include Jessica Weiss, *To Have and to Hold: Marriage, the Baby Boom, and Social Change* (Chicago, 2000), ch. 1; Joanne Meyerowitz, "Beyond the Feminine Mystique: A Reassessment of Postwar Mass Culture, 1946–1958" in Meyerowitz, ed., *Not June Cleaver: Women and Gender in Postwar America, 1945–1960* (Philadelphia, 1994).

61. "The Marriage Mart Is Up," *Los Angeles Times*, January 20, 1935; Andrew Cherlin, *Marriage, Divorce, Remarriage* (Cambridge, Mass., 1992 [1981]), 35.

62. Marwan Khawaja, "The Recent Rise in Palestinian Fertility: Permanent or Transient?" *Population Studies* 54:3 (2000). Mohammad Jalal Abbasi-Shavazi, Peter McDonald, and Meimanat Hosseini-Chavoshi, *The Fertility Transition in Iran: Revolution and Reproduction* (Dordrecht, Neth., 2009) speculates that rising fertility after Iran's Islamic revolution was "motivated in part by the impacts of the Iran-Iraq war and the more generalised sense of threat from beyond its borders." This model may help explain the profusion of short baby booms which often coincide with wars and their immediate aftermath. On the question of why booms may persist for years afterward, some authors have posited an enduring sense of insecurity and desire for stability through domesticity. Glen Elder, Jr., *Children of the Great Depression: Social Change in Life Experience* (Chicago, 1974) studies a group of Oakland, Calif., children who were adolescents during the Depression and young adults during the war. Subjects who suffered most during the Depression were most likely to value stable family life afterwards. Ron Lesthaeghe and Johan Surkyn, "Cultural Dynamics and Economic Theories of Fertility Change," *Population and Development Review* 14 (1988) offer a similar analysis: "an older familial model whose achievement had been frustrated by depression and war" revived alongside widening "social integration via the acceptance ... of institutional regulation."

63. "Government Issues Monograph Dealing With Birth Control," *The Washington Post*, December 6, 1931. The monograph's author was Warren S. Thompson, whose work was also published under the auspices of the President's Research Committee on Social Trends.

64. Lizabeth Cohen, *A Consumer's Republic: The Politics of Mass Consumption in Postwar America* (New York, 2003), 196. Rapid and widespread suburbanization also marked the mid-century development of other countries with the strongest postwar baby booms, like Canada and Australia.

65. Mary P. Ryan, *Cradle of the Middle Class. The Family in Oneida County, New York, 1790–1865* (Cambridge, Eng., 1981); Richard A. Easterlin, "Population Change and Farm Settlement in the Northern United States," *Journal of Economic History* 36:1 (1976). On the initial frontier effect in the western U.S. see Lee L. Bean, Geraldine P. Mineau, and Douglas L. Anderton, *Fertility Change on the American Frontier: Adaptation and Innovation* (Berkeley, Cal., 1990), esp. 239–42.

66. "Anchor to Windward," *Los Angeles Times*, November 27, 1932; Cherlin, *Marriage,* 35. Not all Americans had access to the suburban dream, and not all boom babies were born in suburbs. African-Americans, for example, were largely excluded from new suburbs but nevertheless saw a larger-than-average boom. However for wartime black migrants from the rural south – like European immigrants – industrial cities may have offered a new promise, much as suburbs did for whites moving into the middle class. The same location might represent possibility for a black in-migrant and constriction for a white out-migrant. What perhaps mattered most was parents' sense that they might eventually endow their children with lives better than their own – without much material sacrifice in the interim, and without a sense that large

families were historically backward or would necessarily deny them the promises of a brighter social future.

67. Lee Rainwater, *And the Poor Get Children: Sex, Contraception and Family Planning in the Working Class* (Chicago, 1960), 56.

4 DEAR FRIEND

1. Margaret Sanger, *An Autobiography* (New York, 1938), 362.

2. *Birth Control Review*, March 1925, 78. Sanger's book was *Woman and the New Race* (New York, 1920), a feminist case for freely available contraception. *WNR* sold well partly because of deceptive advertising by the book's publisher that led buyers to believe it contained practical contraceptive advice. Discovering it did not, some buyers wrote to Sanger, whose address was printed inside. On *WNR*'s reception see Engelman, *Birth Control*, 116–17. Margaret Marsh writes that *WNR* "made [Sanger] nearly a household word in the United States" (Margaret Marsh, "Foreword" in Sanger, *Motherhood in Bondage* (Columbus, Oh., 2000 [1928]). Advice books by other authors also carried the name and/or address of Sanger's American Birth Control League.

3. Marie E. Kopp, *Birth Control in Practice: Analysis of 10,000 Case Histories* (New York, 1933). "Practically, the work of the birth control movement consists in substituting better methods of limiting the size of the family for unsatisfactory or deplorable methods already in use," wrote the birth control advocate Caroline Robinson in 1930, in a study that criticized some of Sanger's tactics. (Caroline Hadley Robinson, *Seventy Birth Control Clinics: A Survey and Analysis Including the General Effects of Control on Size and Quality of Population* (Baltimore, 1930), 65.) In parts of rural North Carolina and Arizona selected by Depression-era health officials for their poverty and presumed poor access to contraceptives, Johanna Schoen shows that "women behaved as educated consumers … comparing contraceptives … demanding one birth control method over another" and insisting on contraceptives recommended by friends and relatives (Schoen, *Choice and Coercion: Birth Control, Sterilization, and Abortion in Public* Health *and* Welfare (Chapel Hill, N.C., 2005), 39–40).

4. The unpublished letters do not appear to have been selected for their usefulness to the movement (or any other characteristic). Forty-six of the BCLM letters were originally sent to the ABCL, then forwarded to Boston with the request that the BCLM provide local assistance. They were not published. An additional 25 letters were sent directly to the BCLM. The addressee was not clear for the remaining nine.

5. Working- and lower-middle-class writers were especially strongly represented in Sanger's published letters. Both self-description and English usage suggested that unpublished letters skewed more middle class.

6. *BCR*, November 1922. Margaret Sanger, *Motherhood in Bondage* (New York, 1928), xvi (hereafter *MIB*). In 1928, Sanger claimed to have received "approximately 250,000 letters from mothers" in her fifteen years as an

activist (*MIB*, 437). In 1931 she claimed in two speeches to have received a million letters (" Mrs. Sanger Named for Women's Prize," *New York Times*, November 10, 1931; Sanger, "Birth Control Advances: A Reply to the Pope," Sanger Papers, Sophia Smith Collection). The lower figure seems more likely. Incoming correspondence peaked after the publication of Sanger's two books in 1920 and 1922. *Woman and the New Race* sold around 200,000 copies, mostly to people expecting in vain to receive concrete advice, but contained "a slip saying that if the reader desired more information he might write Mrs. Sanger" (Francis M. Vreeland, "The Process of Reform with Especial Reference to Reform Groups in the Field of Population," Ph.D. dissertation, University of Michigan (1929), 273). In 1923 the ABCL reported a remark-able 71,041 letters (*BCR*, February 1924). By 1928, however, ABCL officer Mary Sumner Boyd reported lower totals: 8,388 in 1926; 8,510 in 1927. In 1931–1932, the ABCL and Sanger were receiving 609 letters per month, a 90 percent drop from the *Review*'s 1923 figure (Boughton, "What 7,309 'Mothers' Want," *Birth Control Review*, January 1933). Even so, the early 1920s deluge renders plausible Sanger's claim to have received a quarter-million letters by 1928. Why the ABCL elected to destroy most of its "client" letters is unclear. The finding aid to Sanger's papers at the Sophia Smith Collection (Smith College) asserts that the letters were treated as medical records and destroyed to protect writers' privacy. The Margaret Sanger Papers Project (New York University) knows of no specific document laying out a policy for disposing of client letters (personal correspondence with Peter Engelman, July 19, 2013). A handful of unpublished client letters survive in Sanger's papers, perhaps due to clerical error. Additional letters may survive because the ABCL forwarded them to local clinics, but my queries to several of these clinics' successor organizations did not yield any archived correspondence.

7. Client to Sanger, October 6, 1928, Margaret Sanger Papers Microfilm, Library of Congress, Washington D.C., 1977 [hereafter MSLOC], reel 22; Sanger to Client, October 16, 1928, MSLOC, reel 22. Sanger's reply letter also asked for $1 for a League membership, which would entitle the man to free literature. This style of form letter, if common, may account for some of the differences in tone and detail between published and unpublished letters, as well as for the very high proportion of Sanger's writers who specified their number of children (97 percent). Of Sanger's published *BCR* letters, 97 percent came from married parents and 95 percent from women. By contrast, the ABCL's study of incoming correspondence from 1931–1932 found that 88 percent of writers were married and 83 percent female – proportions similar to those of the Mary Ware Dennett and BCLM correspondence. See Alice C. Boughton, "7,309 'Mothers.'" Boughton was executive director of the ABCL at the time, following Sanger's resignation from that position in 1928. Boughton placed quotation marks on "Mothers" because the term was "still used within the movement to cover all requests for contraceptive advice even though such requests are increasingly from men and persons seeking premarital advice."

8. Boughton, "What 7,309 'Mothers' Want"; "Client" to Sanger, October 9, 1928, Margaret Sanger Papers, Library of Congress, microfilm edition, reel 4. The quoted letter is one of at least twenty-two original unpublished letters that survive, unorganized, in Sanger's voluminous papers. Other letters originally sent to the ABCL but not destroyed were forwarded on the BCLM, which preserved them. Short letters containing no justification or autobiographical elaboration comprised 70 percent of these 46 forwarded letters, and 72 percent of the letters addressed directly to the BCLM.

9. A few marked copies of original published letters survive in Sanger's papers; these show corrections for spelling and sometimes sentence clarity, but no significant excisions. On her treatment of these letters see Cathy Moran Hajo, *Birth Control on Main Street: Organizing Clinics in the United States, 1916–1939* (Urbana, Ill., 2010), 218n. A selection of letters to the Children's Bureau is included in Molly Ladd-Taylor, ed., *Raising a Baby the Government Way: Mothers' Letters to the Children's Bureau, 1915–1932* (New Brunswick, N.J., 1986), ch. 8. Cleveland Maternal Health Association letters are excerpted in Jimmy Elaine Wilkinson Meyer, *Any Friend of the Movement: Networking for Birth Control, 1920–1940* (Columbus, Oh., 2004), 83–109. Meyer notes that the Cleveland MHC apparently destroyed "mundane" letters (p. 84). Eleven letters to the Committee of One Hundred (a New York-based social hygiene organization) are preserved in the Margaret Sanger Papers, Library of Congress microfilm edition, reel 9. European archives include letters to the Oslo Mothers' Clinic, the Swedish National Association for Sexuality Education, and the English birth controller Marie Stopes. The Oslo letters (4,361 written between 1924 and 1929) are excerpted in Ida Blom, "'Master of Your Own Body and What Is in It' – Reducing Marital Fertility in Norway, 1890–1930" in Angelique Janssens, ed., *Gendering the Fertility Decline in the Western World* (Bern, 2007), 68. "Most of the letters were short and mainly asked to have contraceptive information sent to the letter-writer," Blom writes (p. 60). On the Swedish letters see Sofia Kling, "'I Think I'd Rather Die than Go through with a Pregnancy Again.' Experiences of Childbearing and Birth Control in Sweden in the 1930s" in Janssens, ed., *Gendering the Fertility Decline*; Sofia Kling, "Reproductive Health, Birth Control, and Fertility Change in Sweden, circa 1900–1940," *The History of the Family* 15:2 (June 2010). Letters to Marie Stopes are preserved in two edited volumes: Ruth Hall, ed., *Dear Dr. Stopes: Sex in the 1920s* (London, 1978); Stopes, *Mother England: A Contemporary History* (London, 1929); and at the Wellcome Library in London. See also Margaret Llewelyn Davies, ed., *Maternity: Letters from Working Women* (London, 1978 [1915]). Pre-Sanger U.S. activists like Emma Goldman, William Robinson, and Rose Pastor Stokes also claimed to have received many letters from advice-seekers, though these appear to be lost. The London-based Malthusian League received enough petitions from Americans that it printed an announcement explaining that it could not fill this request due to U.S. law (Vreeland, "Process of Reform," 272).

10. *BCR*, October 1923; *MIB*, 74–76, 289.

11. Of the first 500 patients treated in two Chicago clinics opened in 1925 by the Illinois Birth Control League, 263 provided "economic reasons" for their request, versus 148 who gave "definite health" reasons (Rachelle S. Yarros, "Birth Control and its Relation to Health and Welfare," Pamphlet of Illinois Birth Control League, Birth Control Pamphlets Collection, Widener Library, Harvard University). Among Rainwater's urban workers "two major reasons for limiting a family are given . . . the necessity to support the children one has, and consideration of the wife's health" (Lee Rainwater, *And the Poor Get Children: Sex, Contraception and Family Planning in the Working Class* (Chicago, 1960), 46). Rainwater's results were based on forty-six interviews in Chicago and Cincinnati. Ida Blom's working-class Norwegian commentators justified family limitation in economic and health terms; middle-class women discussed "four main problems": economic and health issues, but also children's future and women's emancipation. Blom, "Master of Your Own Body," 65. Economic and health concerns likewise predominate among the elderly Norwegians surveyed in Sølvi Sogner, "Abortion, Birth Control, and Contraception: Fertility Decline in Norway," *Journal of Interdisciplinary History* 34:2 (Autumn, 2003), and in the Lewis-Faning survey of British fertility (1949) which is summarized in Wally Seccombe, "Starting to Stop: Working-Class Fertility Decline in Britain," *Past & Present* 126 (February, 1990), 170–71. See also the letters to Sweden's National Association for Sexuality Education surveyed in Kling, "Experiences of Childbearing," 184.

12. *BCR*, April 1923. Sanger correspondents' 3.6-child average exceeded the U.S. total fertility rates for 1920 (3.17) and 1930 (2.45) despite the likelihood that many of these writers would go on to have additional children. Writers to Dennett (2.4) and BCLM (2.1) were less prolific. In Kling's Swedish letters, 40 percent of writers "supported their request" by alluding to their existing children (Kling, "Experiences of Childrearing," 196). Nine to 11 percent of published and unpublished writers emphasized their desire to *space* rather than stop childbearing.

13. *MIB*, 16. On pain in childbirth, obstetric anesthesia, and maternal mortality in early twentieth-century America, see Jacqueline H. Wolf, *Deliver Me from Pain: Anesthesia and Birth in America* (Baltimore, Md., 2009), 44–104.

14. *MIB*, 97, 177; D.L. Hoyert, *Maternal Mortality and Related Concepts*, National Center for Health Statistics, Vital Health Statistics 3:33 (2007); Maternal Mortality Estimation Inter-Agency Group, "Maternal Mortality in 1990–2013: United States of America." Available at who.int. Maternal mortality rates did not fall sharply until the 1930s. See U.S. Centers for Disease Control, "Achievements in Public Health, 1900–1999: Healthier Mothers and Babies," *Morbidity and Mortality Weekly Report* 48:38 (October 1999).

15. Linda Gordon, *The Moral Property of Women: A History of Birth Control Politics in America* (Urbana, Ill., 2002), ch. 11, documents the organized movement's use of public health rationales in the years around the Second World War.

16. Judith Walzer Leavitt, *Brought to Bed: Childbearing in America, 1750–1950* (Oxford, 1986), 169; Theodore Roosevelt, "Address to the General

Conference of the Methodist Episcopal Church," May 16, 1908, in *Presidential Addresses and State Papers* (New York, 1910), vol. 7.

17. *BCR*, November 1923. On the move toward hospital births and relationship to reproductive control, see Richard W. Wertz and Dorothy C. Wertz, *Lying In: A History of Childbirth in America* (New Haven, 1989 [1977]) 148–60.

18. *BCR*, April 1923, June 1923.

19. Transactions of the State Medical Association of Texas, vol. 35 (1903); Lara Marks, *Sexual Chemistry: A History of the Contraceptive Pill* (New Haven, Conn., 2001), 120; Wolf, *Deliver Me from Pain*, 77; Client to Sanger, n.d. 1925. By 1890 some doctors had begun arguing against "wholesale condemnation of contraception on moral grounds" (Anita Clair Fellman and Michael Fellman, *Making Sense of Self: Medical Advice Literature in Late Nineteenth Century America* (Philadelphia, 1981), 81).

20. Andrea Tone, *Devices and Desires: A History of Contraceptives in America* (New York, 2002), 81–82. By contrast, Linda Gordon asserts "those who did not have regular access to private doctors were effectively deprived of contraceptive information" as late as the 1930s (Gordon, *Moral Property*, 226). Johanna Schoen writes that "health and welfare officials regulated women's access to birth control, sterilization, and abortion for most of the twentieth century ... Women sought reproductive control, but did so within clear limits" (Schoen, *Choice and Coercion*, 3).

21. "The Sale of Illegal Contraceptives and Abortifacients," *American Druggists and Pharmaceutical Record*, March 1917; Minnie L. Maffett of Dallas to James F. Cooper, September 12, 1927, American Birth Control League (ABCL) Records, Houghton Library, Harvard University; *Medical Journal* quoted in Robinson, *Seventy Clinics*, 208; Mary Ware Dennett to Client, May 18, 1929, Papers of Mary Ware Dennett and the Voluntary Parenthood League, Women's studies manuscript collections from the Schlesinger Library, Radcliffe College: Series 3, Sexuality, sex education, and reproductive rights. University Publications of America, 1994. [Letters from the Mary Ware Dennett Papers are hereafter cited under "MWDP."]

22. Ruth Dixon-Mueller, *Population Policy and Women's Rights: Transforming Reproductive Choice* (Westport, Conn., 1993), 49; Vreeland, "Process of Reform," 276. Gordon writes: "Undoubtedly, the largest single factor drawing doctors into the birth control movement was Sanger's support for a 'doctors only' type of birth control legislation" (*Moral Property*, 183). See also Rickie Solinger, *Reproductive Politics: What Everyone Needs to Know* (Oxford, Eng., 2013), 22–23; Sheila M. Rothman, *Women's Proper Place: A History of Changing Ideals and Practices, 1870 to the Present* (New York, 1978). Sanger had once favored a "clean repeal" of restrictions on contraception but eventually backed a "doctors' bill" in hopes of merging her movement's interests with those of culturally powerful doctors. James Reed defends this decision in his early exposition of medical men's role in the movement, writing that medical control of contraception was probably inevitable and that Sanger's accommodation was politically astute (Reed, *From Private Vice to Public Virtue: The Birth Control Movement and American Society since 1830* (New York, 1978), ch. 8). Angus McLaren, *Sexuality and*

Social Order: The Debate Over the Fertility of Women and Workers in France, 1770–1920 (New York, 1983), notes that in France organized birth control advocacy "began and ended as a libertarian crusade" without being coopted by public health officers (183).

23. *BCR*, January 1919.
24. *MIB*, 80.
25. *BCR*, January 1918; MWDP, Reel 18, 764; *BCR*, November 1923; MWDP, reel 18, 871.
26. MWDP, reel 18, 709; *BCR*, May 1925.
27. *MIB*, 91, 34.
28. *BCR*, December 1924; *MIB*, 52.
29. *MIB*, 200; MWDP, reel 18, 661.
30. *BCR*, December 1918, June 1925. Between twenty and fifty percent of visitors to contraceptive clinics in the early 1930s admitted to previous abortions (Kopp, *Birth Control in Practice*, 134). On the danger of abortion relative to childbirth in general, see Reagan, *When Abortion was a Crime*, 46–79.
31. *BCR*, September 1923.
32. *MIB*, 259, 261, 96–99. For other cases of separation for birth control purposes see the letters section of *BCR* for September 1924, and *Motherhood in Bondage*, ch. 11. Enlistment in the military or aboard merchant ships may have served a similar purpose. A financially strapped Navy sailor from North Carolina wrote: "one other reason for my enlistment is to keep away from the wife a great part of the time" (Client to Rep. Frank Hancock [forwarded to Sanger], May 22, 1932, MSLOC, reel 22). To the birth control advocate Ben Lindsey (see ch. 5), an Iowa nurse wrote "The ignorant, the very poor and those of moderate means are the family producers. Frequently the father gets tired of the whole and leaves for parts unknown, or commits suicide" (Christine Hoffman to Ben Lindsey, March 14, 1927. Ben Lindsey Collection, Library of Congress, box 155).
33. *BCR*, October 1925; MWDP, reel 18, 674.
34. In one extreme case, a poor, pregnant mother killed herself and her three young children after finding herself short of food. "It's awful to be poor, and worse to have children and no way to take care of them, and I made up my mind – no!" she wrote in a suicide note. "There would have been another one before long. Don't blame George. He has always done the best he could, but he has been up against it like me. Put in the world to work – no education, no training. Nothing to do but work like dogs. I don't think I will have any worse hell in the place where I am going. Mabel." (*Denver Post* quoted in *BCR*, September 1925)
35. Boughton, "7,309 'Mothers.'" Sanger worked to downplay the middle-class banality of much of her correspondence. An "Analysis of Typical Letters," commissioned for *Motherhood in Bondage*, and conducted by a Sanger deputy, found "80% of the writers to be very poor and only 2% prosperous" based on "the appearance of letters, the father's occupation, his stated income, and the mothers' or children's work for wages." But the study excluded letters "giving too few facts," meaning it did not account for writers who did not provide biographical details, typically an account of hardship.

(Mary Sumner Boyd, "Analysis of Typical Letters" in Sanger, *Motherhood in Bondage*, 439–44). Few of Sofia Kling's Swedish writers were poor; most proclaimed the "rather humble ambition" to maintain a modest standard of living: "It was not an economic *necessity* for most families to stop having babies" (Kling, "Experiences of Childbearing," 193).

36. "Chicago Now Presents Race Suicide Problem," *The Atlanta Constitution*, January 24, 1904.

37. Physicians had "considerable latitude" in diagnosing "medical reasons" for contraception, noted the ABCL's clinical director, Dr. Hannah Stone, in 1929. Pamphlet no. 2 of the International Medical Group for the Investigation of Birth Control (London, 1929), Birth control pamphlets collection, Widener Library, Harvard University.

38. *MIB*, 33; *BCR*, September 1924; *MIB*, 210. Arsène Dumont's early theorizations of fertility decline focused on social mobility: Dumont, *Depopulation and Civilization: A Demographic Study* (1990 [1890]), ch. 6.

39. *MIB*, 53, 237; *BCR*, January 1926, September 1924. On social ambition and birth control in nineteenth-century America, see Sylvia D. Hoffert, *Private Matters: American Attitudes Toward Childbearing and Infant Nurture in the Urban North, 1800–1860* (Urbana, Ill., 1989). Hoffert quotes an Indianapolis father of seven who, in 1835, already found that "it is not fashionable to be the parents of many childrin" (p. 17).

40. *BCR*, July 1923; *MIB*, 201.

41. BCR, October 1922.

42. *MIB*, 27, BCR, December 1923, *MIB*, 40.

43. MWDP, reel 18, 856.

44. On the rising sentimental value of children relative to consumer goods see Viviana A. Zelizer, *Pricing the Priceless Child: The Changing Social Value of Children* (Princeton, 1994 [1985]), 209–11.

45. Margaret Sanger, *Woman and the New Race*, 52.

46. "Client" to ABCL, September 6, 1933, Planned Parenthood League of Massachusetts Papers, Sophia Smith Collection, Smith College, Box 19.

47. *BCR*, December 1924; MWDP, reel 18, 832; *BCR*, December 1922; MWDP, reel 18, 674; *BCR*, February 1925.

48. MWDP, reel 18, 761, 773; Client to Sanger, December 18, 1920. MSLOC, reel 26.

49. Margaret Sanger, *Woman and the New Race* (New York, 1920), 187; MWDP, reel 18, 669; Mary Ware Dennett, "Birth Control and the Law" Address at the Conference of the ABCL, November 19, 1929 (MSLOC, reel 9)

50. Upton Sinclair, *The Book of Life: Mind and Body* (Girard, Ks., 1922), 64; "Convictions in the Postal Law Cases" *Bulletin of Pharmacy* 27:2 (February 1913). Elliot described his case in a 1912 letter to the pre-Sanger birth control activist William Robinson. At the time he was two years into a ten-year sentence and had paid a fine of $10,000. "My conviction was secured upon that clause of the statute which refers to the giving of information ... The evidence consisted of two decoy letters written by an aide to the secret service department ... Owing to the tender pleadings of this woman's letter my

sympathies were aroused and I replied and gave said information gratis and as I believed consummated a most humanitarian act. After a Federal Grand Jury returned an indictment against me I sold my property, and the attorney's fees for my defense at the ensuing trial drained me of every dollar which I possessed" (William Robinson, *American Journal of Clinical Medicine* 18:6 (June, 1911). In 1915 Sanger reported that Elliott had been released after "some agitation" led to his pardon. (Sanger, "Birth Control in America," *Freedom: A Journal of Anarchist Communism*, 29:315 (July 1915). Though Sinclair received "hundreds of letters asking for information" after writing articles on birth control in various magazines in the 1910s, Elliot's imprisonment made him hesitate to reply for fear of entrapment by "Government spies" ("Progress or Comstock: Letters from our Readers," *The Masses*, April 1915).

51. MWDP, reel 18, 807, 661, 764. On the reasons few Americans feared the Comstock laws see Tone, *Devices and Desires*, 25–45.

52. "The Whys and Why-Nots of Birth Control," *Medical Times* 50:4 (April, 1922); Vreeland, "Process of Reform," 535. A doctor from Huntington, West Virginia, dismissing the relevance of contraceptive laws before a Congressional panel on birth control in 1934, noted that that seven of the town's nine drugstores sold contraceptives to "any man or woman, boy or girl," and that all seven had, "in the past year or so," displayed those supplies "in the window with advertising placards" (Testimony of Dr. James A. Klumpp before the U.S. House Committee on the Judiciary, Jan., 1934).

53. Margaret Sanger, *Woman and the New Race*, 204. On the theoretical role of clinics in eugenic reform see Hajo, *Birth Control*, 103–13.

54. ABCL circular letter, November 28, 1930, MSLOC, reel 9.

55. "Margaret Sanger and 'a Glorious Chain of Clinics,'" *Margaret Sanger Papers Project Newsletter* 9 (Winter 1994–1995); Hajo, *Birth Control*, 126; *BCR*, February 1919.

56. Hajo, *Birth Control*, 152; Kopp, *Birth Control in Practice*; Hajo, *Birth Control*, 125. Additional studies attesting to the popularity of these methods include Robert L. Dickinson and Lura Beam, *A Thousand Marriages: A Medical Study of Sex Adjustment* (Baltimore, 1931), 114; and (on England) Enid Charles, *The Practice of Birth Control: An Analysis of the Birth Control Experiences of Nine Hundred Women* (London, 1932), 50. Douching may have been more popular in the nineteenth century than in twentieth. See James Mahood and Kristine Wenburg, eds., *The Mosher Survey: Sexual Attitudes of 45 Victorian Women* (New York, 1980 [1892]).

57. Regine K. Stix and Frank W. Notestein, "Effectiveness of Birth Control: A Second Study of Contraceptive Practice in a Selected Group of New York Women," *Milbank Memorial Fund Quarterly* 13: 2 (April, 1935).

58. Hajo, *Birth Control*, 134, 152; Gilbert Wheeler Beebe, *Contraception and Fertility in the Southern Appalachians* (Baltimore, 1942), v.

59. MWDP, reel 18, 782; Client (Albany, GA) to Sanger, February 29, 1928, Sanger Papers, Collected Documents, reel 4.

60. On ergot, savin, and especially apiol, a once popular abortifacient, see Edward Shorter, *Women's Bodies: A Social History of Women's Encounter with Health, Ill-Health, and Medicine* (New York, 1992 [1982]), 208–24.

61. *BCR*, November 1925, October 1924.
62. *BCR*, April 1923. On class barriers and contraception see also Seccombe, "Starting to Stop," 166.
63. Hajo, *Birth Control*, 12; Sanger, *Woman and the New Race*, 203. Sanger's *Birth Control Review* occasionally carried more realistic estimates of the prevalence of adequate contraceptive knowledge among the poor. In 1922 a professor of public health at the Johns Hopkins University wrote in *BCR* that doctors considered birth control knowledge "widespread even among the poorest families," and that when such families were large it generally was due to a lack of "imagination" rather than technical knowledge (Reynold A. Spaeth, "Birth Control as a Public Health Measure," *BCR* August 1922).
64. Robinson, *Seventy Clinics*, 127, 119; Robinson to Sanger, January 19, 1929, MSLOC, reel 9; Raymond Pearl, "Statistical report on the first year's operations" in *First Report of the Bureau for Contraceptive Advice, Baltimore, Maryland* (1929), MSLOC, reel 4; Lena McQuade, "Troubling Reproduction: Sexuality, Race, and Colonialism in New Mexico, 1919–1945" (Ph.D. dissertation, Univ. of New Mexico, 2008), 114. Robinson gave $500 and pledged another $500 for a Philadelphia clinic but told Sanger "they are dreadfully discouraged right now because they have had no patients and really no prospects of any" (Robinson to Sanger, op. cit.). In the late 1920s, ABCL records indicated that all U.S. birth control clinics were treating "at most 5,000 patients per year" (Vreeland, "Process of Reform," 338).
65. At various times the ABCL also sent Sanger's *Family Limitation* pamphlet to inquirers who did not live near a clinic or sympathetic doctor. See McCann, *Birth Control Politics*, 76.
66. Engelman, *Birth Control*, 151, puts the number of doctors on the ABCL's "referral list" at over 28,000 in 1925, and Sanger later recalled the list containing "some twenty thousand" names in the mid-1920s (Sanger, *An Autobiography* (New York, 1938), 363). Francis Vreeland, as part of his doctoral fieldwork, counted 5,484 names in the League's "Doctors File" in 1927 (Vreeland, "Process of Reform," 280). Estimating the scope of the referral program requires informed guesswork. In 1924 the ABCL "read and answered" all of the 71,041 letters it received in the previous year. Not all correspondents needed a medical referral, nor did needy writers always receive one, and the ABCL did not sustain a 100 percent response rate. Letter volume also fell quickly: a 1931 ABCL memo logged 511 letters in the month of February, of which around 150 went unanswered ("Letters received during February 1931 and Answered," MSLOC, reel 22). However, if we assume a 80 percent response rate across the 1920s, and speculate that around half of writers ultimately received a referral, the program could have reached more than 100,000 people. Caroline Robinson's report suggests the broad plausibility of this figure. As of 1929, Robinson wrote, "the League was handling about twenty-five letters a day from appealing women, and to about one-fourth of these it was necessary to reply that there was no birth control clinic or listed physician within reach" (Robinson, *Seventy Clinics*, 50).
67. Sanger to Client (Selby, Iowa), October 12, 1928. Sanger papers, Collected Documents series, reel 4; Robinson, *Seventy Clinics*, 50. Another letter from

the same period asks for life enrollment as "evidence of your good faith" (Sanger to Client, October 15, 1928, Sanger Papers, Collected Documents series, reel 4, 796).

68. Robinson, *Seventy Clinics*, 223.

69. Sanger, *Woman and the New Race* (New York, 1920), 229. On Sanger's opportunistic courtship of eugenicists in the 1920s, see Chesler, *Woman of Valor*, 212–17. Less forgiving accounts of Sanger's tactics include Angela Franks, *Margaret Sanger's Eugenic Legacy: The Control of Fertility* (Jefferson, N.C., 2005) and Gordon, *Moral Property*, ch. 9. Sanger primarily supported policies designed to discourage reproduction among the poor and feeble-minded, as opposed to encouraging reproduction among the "fit." She largely abstained from the scientific racism sometimes associated with the eugenics movement. The *Review*'s early support for eugenics is evident in its third issue, which carried articles by the noted eugenicists Paul Popenoe and Roswell Johnson (*BCR*, April–May 1917). See also *The Pivot of Civilization* (1922), esp. ch. 8. Dennett was primarily interested in contraception as a means of liberating and demystifying sexuality. She endorsed eugenic goals without emphasizing their importance. On the appeal of eugenics among more conservative birth control advocates, see Carole Ruth McCann, *Birth Control Politics in the United States, 1916–1945* (Ithaca, N.Y., 1999), 99–134.

70. Josephine Hagen to Ben Lindsey, March 14, 1927. Benjamin Barr Lindsey Collection, Library of Congress, box 277.

71. *MIB*, 246, xii.

72. Mary Ware Dennett, "A Problem of Both," *BCR*, November 1918; Sanger, "Birth Control a Parents' Problem or Woman's?" *BCR*, November 1918; Sanger, *Woman and the New Race*, 98.

73. *BCR*, June 1921, November 1922, January 1926.

74. *MIB*, 183, 192, 283.

75. *MIB*, 239. The absence of hostile husbands may be partly due to self-selection, since women who were certain their husbands would refuse any contraceptive method might not have bothered to write. If this situation were widespread, however, we might expect writers to ask about methods that could be used without their husbands' knowledge. Only one such letter appears among the 556 sampled here, and no female writer appears to have been concerned that her husband might discover her correspondence with the ABCL.

76. *BCR*, February 1924, November 1925. Among immigrant populations in three U.S. industrial cities, "husbands had more influence in matters of birth control than in childbirth, using their own networks to provide information about birth control or to identify an abortionist." Susan Cotts Watkins and Angela D. Danzi, "Women's Gossip and Social Change: Childbirth and Fertility Control among Italian and Jewish Women in the United States, 1920–1940," *Gender and Society* 9: 4 (August, 1995), 480.

77. *BCR*, Sep. 1924, October 1925, November 1925.

78. *MWDP*, reel 18, 500. Eighty-two percent of writers to the Oslo Mothers' Clinic were female (Blom, "Master of Your Own Body," 60), as were about 80 percent of Marie Stopes' correspondents (Seccombe, "Starting to Stop,"

157), but just 43 percent of writers to Sweden's National Association for Sexuality Education (Kling, "Experiences of Childbearing," 181). Kling writes that despite the different interests and experiences of men and women within the reproductive couple, "contraception was usually a male responsibility," and that the letters lend "no support" to the idea that men left contraception to women as part of the female domestic sphere (p. 182n). Seccombe comes to similar conclusions with regard to the Stopes letters. A study of Stopes' Canadian writers, however, finds that these correspondents framed birth control "as very much a woman's responsibility" (Angus McLaren and Arlene Tigar McLaren, *The Bedroom and the State: The Changing Practices and Politics of Contraception and Abortion in Canada, 1880–1997* (Oxford, 1997), 27). Ethnographic studies of gendered reproductive agency in the late twentieth century have produced mixed results. For example, husbands' primary influence in fertility decisions is evident in Laurie F. DeRose, F. Nii-Amoo Dodoo, and Vrushali Patil, "Fertility Desires and Perceptions of Power in Reproductive Conflict in Ghana," *Gender and Society* 16:1 (February, 2002); and Laurie Derose and Alex Ezeh, "Men's Influence on the Onset and Progress of Fertility Decline in Ghana, 1988–98," *Population Studies* 59:2 (July 2005). Female subjects were more influential in Jessica Gipson and Michelle Hindin, "The Effect of Husbands' and Wives' Fertility Preferences on the Likelihood of a Subsequent Pregnancy, Bangladesh 1998–2003," *Population Studies* 63:2 (July 2009).

79. Katherine A. Lynch, "Theoretical and Analytical Approaches to Religious Beliefs, Values, and Identities during the Modern Fertility Transition" in Derosas and van Poppel, eds., *Religion and the Decline of Fertility*, 30. On spouses' differing interests and gendered expectations in Norway, and their frequent agreement on family limitation, see Sølvi Sogner, "Abortion, Birth Control, and Contraception: Fertility Decline in Norway," *Journal of Interdisciplinary History* 34:2 (Autumn, 2003), 230–34. On this dynamic in English women's letters to birth controllers, see Wally Seccombe, "Starting to Stop: Working-Class Fertility Decline in Britain," *Past & Present* 126 (February, 1990), esp. 173–78.

80. Margaret Sanger, *The Pivot of Civilization* (New York, 1922), 271; Dennett, *The Sex Side of Life* (New York, 1919), 4. David M. Kennedy, *Birth Control in America: The Career of Margaret Sanger* (New York, 1970), esp. 12–14, 62–71, focuses on Sanger's romantic view of sexuality as a central facet of her worldview. Ellen Chesler, *Woman of Valor: Margaret Sanger and the Birth Control Movement in America* (New York, 1992), 111–25, summarizes the influence of English sex reformer Havelock Ellis on Sanger.

81. Sanger, *Family Limitation* (New York, 1920 [1914]), 14; Dennett, *Sex Side of Life*, 4. On activists' rifts over sexual liberation see McCann, *Birth Control Politics*, 40; Gordon, *Moral Property*, ch. 4. On abstinence as a social ideal in nineteenth-century America and its effects on subjective well-being, see Gordon, *Moral Property*, 59–65, 117–18.

82. On companionate versus patriarchal marriages see Nancy Cott, *Public Vows: A History of Marriage and the Nation* (Cambridge, Mass.), ch. 7; Christina Simmons, *Making Marriage Modern: A History of Women's Sexuality*

(Oxford, 2009), ch. 3. Perceived connections between this marital ideal and low fertility go back at least to 1867, when a British chronicler of American manners reported that "in a hundred of the purest cities of America" good wives believed their "first thought should be for her husband, and for herself as his companion in the world." This "very strange and rather wide conspiracy," Dixon announced, had "no chiefs, no secretaries, no head-quarters," and if successful, would ensure that "there would be no more baby-shows in this country, since there would be no longer any Americans in America" (William Hepworth Dixon, *New America*, vol. 2 (London, 1867), 265–66).

83. BCR, November 1925; MWDP, reel 18, 863; BCR, July 1925, July 1923. On "antisexual feeling" among women fearful of pregnancy see Gordon, *Moral Property*, 62–65.

84. Angus McLaren finds evidence that "women were concerned with the 'romance' in their marriages" and "accepted the idea that the 'safeguarding of passion [was] of critical import for marital adjustment'" in a reading of some of the Sanger and Stopes letters (McLaren, *History of Contraception*, 221). In this chapter's letters, taken as a whole, such a reading would only be possible if one took an extremely broad view of marital romance and passion, where the desire not to worry about contraceptive failure was equivalent to a concern for romantic and sexual connection.

85. On delayed marriage and the "culture of abstinence" in early twentieth-century Britain (and before) see Szreter, *Fertility, Class and Gender*, 367–423; Seccombe, "Starting to Stop." Lee L. Bean, Geraldine P. Mineau, and Douglas L. Anderton, *Fertility Change on the American Frontier: Adaptation and Innovation* (Berkeley, Calif., 1990) present evidence for the prevalence of abstinence (as well as coitus interruptus and perhaps condoms) in the western United States during the nineteenth and early twentieth centuries. Explanations of fertility change in that region "need not stand or fall on the question of the availability of modern contraceptive technology" they observe (p. 32).

86. George Kneeland with Katherine Bement Davis, *Commercialized Prostitution in New York City* (New York, 1913), 100; Vice Commission of the City of Chicago, *The Social Evil in Chicago: A Study of Existing Conditions* (1911), 34. On prostitutes' birth control methods see Ruth Rosen, *The Lost Sisterhood: Prostitution in America, 1900–1918* (Baltimore, 1983), 99. The early birth control expert Dr. James F. Cooper reported that among 4,000 prostitutes in Detroit, "lathering the vagina with the fingers, and a swab, in the squatting position, has shown a high degree of safety" (James F. Cooper, *Technique of Contraception: The Principles and Practice of Anti-Conceptional Methods* (New York, 1928), 121).

87. Katherine Bement Davis, "A Study of Certain Auto-Erotic Practices," *Mental Hygiene* 8 (July 1924); Dickinson and Beam, *A Thousand Marriages*, 352; Francis Bliss to Ben Lindsey, March 12, 1927, Benjamin Barr Lindsey Collection, Library of Congress, box 155; Thomas W. Laqueur, *Solitary Sex: A Cultural History of Masturbation* (New York, 2004), 374.

88. Timothy Gilfoyle, *City of Eros: New York City, Prostitution, and the Commercialization of Sex* (New York, 1992), 176; Alfred Kinsey, *Sex Behavior in the Human Male* (Bloomington, Ind., 1998 [1948]), 367–70.

89. Dickinson and Beam, *A Thousand Marriages*, 81. On the ways early twentieth-century New Yorkers achieved sexual gratification while avoiding pregnancy, see Elizabeth Alice Clement, *Love for Sale: Courting, Treating, and Prostitution in New York City, 1900–1945* (Chapel Hill, NC, 2006), esp. 45–75. On sexual experimentation before marriage in the nineteenth century see Ellen K. Rothman, "Sex and Self-Control: Middle-Class Courtship in America, 1770–1870," *Journal of Social History* 15 (1982).

90. H.L. Mencken, *In Defense of Women* (New York, 1922), 182. On birth control, sex, and Americans' changing ideas about permissible public speech see Rochelle Gurstein, *The Repeal of Reticence: A History of America's Cultural and Legal Struggles Over Free Speech, Obscenity, Sexual Liberation, and Modern Art* (New York, 1996), 91–115. Gurstein sees Sanger as a leader of the intellectual movement to dethrone "the reticent sensibility," alongside figures such as Mencken and Theodore Dreiser. On Sanger's effect on the media see Chesler, *Woman of Valor*, 128–32, 192–99, 218–20.

91. On women's use of chastity or "passionlessness" as an ideological tool, as opposed to actual antieroticism, see Nancy F. Cott, "Passionlessness: An Interpretation of Victorian Sexual Ideology, 1790–1850," *Signs* 4:2 (1978).

92. On clinic patients' conservative sexual values see Hajo, *Birth Control*, 139.

5 MISSIONARY WORK: TOURING AMERICA FOR BIRTH CONTROL

1. Matthew Arnold, "In Harmony with Nature" in *Poetical Works of Matthew Arnold*, vol. 1 (London, 1905).

2. Warner Fite, "Birth Control and Biological Ethics," *International Journal of Ethics*, October 1916.

3. James Cooper to Anne Kennedy, February 24, 1925. American Birth Control League (ABCL) Records, Houghton Library, Harvard University. Kennedy was the ABCL's executive secretary at the time of Cooper's tours.

4. Cooper helped set up a contraceptive testing system at the ABCL's New York clinic, and checked in with other ABCL-affiliated clinics, but devoted most of his time to speaking.

5. Sanger to Leon Cole, July 17, 1925. Margaret Sanger Papers, Collected Documents Series, reel 3.

6. Ira S. Wile, "Introduction" in James F. Cooper, *An Outline of Contraceptive Methods* (New York, 1930). Cooper died of prostate cancer not long after the conclusion of his tours, in 1931.

7. Margaret Sanger, *An Autobiography* (New York, 1938), 362; Noah Slee to Anne Kennedy, June 16, 1926, ABCLR, Houghton Library, Harvard University [hereafter ABCLR]. On the ABCL's struggles in the 1920s, see Ellen Chesler, *Woman of Valor: Margaret Sanger and the Birth Control Movement in America* (New York, 1992), 224–26. The ABCL relied heavily on a few large donors, notably Slee, throughout its career. Among ABCL officers this was considered a grave weakness. It gave "the movement more of

the characteristics of a private philanthropy than a national social movement," observed Vreeland. However, Cooper's hiring, Vreeland thought, might prove a "new and effective method" of reaching physicians. He noted that between 1921 and 1924 the ABCL had placed envoys in front of eleven medical audiences, but in 1925–1926, as Cooper's tours began, they reached seventy-five such audiences. (Francis M. Vreeland, "The Process of Reform with Especial Reference to Reform Groups in the Field of Population," Ph.D. dissertation, University of Michigan (1929), 255, 265).

8. Cooper claimed to have addressed 172 county medical societies, but only reported on 151 medical meetings. He also spoke to 110 lay meetings and 12 mixed groups. Physicians' groups averaged 38 attendees; lay, 128. Sanger seems to have looked more favorably on Cooper's nonmedical work than Slee. Telegramming an associate in Denver, Sanger wrote "Cooper capable addressing medical social religious groups. Excellent speaker" (Sanger to Ruth Vincent, May 21, 1925 MSP, Collected Documents Series, reel 3).

9. Cooper reported on 253 audiences totaling 18,119 attendees. These figures exclude several hundred meetings with individuals or very small groups, plus 21 larger sessions for which Cooper did not report exact attendance. Of the 18,119 recorded attendees, 5,538 were physicians, 12,280 were laypeople, and 683 attended in mixed medical-lay groups.

10. Cooper's reports came at the insistence of Sanger and Slee, who were anxious to see immediate returns on Cooper's $10,000 salary and travel expenses.

11. Vreeland, "Process of Reform," 328.

12. Forty-six percent of doctors and 59 percent of laypeople lived in or near one of the country's hundred largest cities, which – with their suburbs, held about one-third of the U.S. population (core municipalities alone had 28 percent). The smallest of these 100 cities, South Bend, Indiana, had 70,983 inhabitants in 1920 (Campbell Gibson, "Population of the 100 Largest Cities and Other Urban Places in the United States: 1790 to 1990," Washington: U.S. Census Bureau, 1998). Socioeconomic status can be inferred from the types of groups Cooper addressed: doctors, nurses, clubmen and clubwomen, professors, postsecondary students, ministers, social workers, and parent-teacher associations, among others. Just three times did he address working-class audiences, all in New York City. Most of Cooper's medical audiences would have been entirely male; men made up approximately 95 percent of the medical profession throughout the 1920s. Most lay audiences included women; twelve were entirely female. Cooper addressed two African-American groups, one composed of doctors in New Jersey, the other of midwives in Mississippi. Twelve of Cooper's 274 reported meetings were with groups that possessed an identifiable reform agenda. Another seven were unofficial meetings convened by sympathetic members of groups that refused to hear Cooper as official bodies. Eight were addresses to social workers who may have been predisposed to favor social reforms like birth control. Five were "parlor meetings" arranged by sympathetic parties. Together these presumably sympathetic groups made up 13 percent of Cooper's meetings. When doctors agreed to join the ABCL's mailing list or doctors file, Cooper normally attached their business cards to his report. Because these cards are not

archived with the reports, the "cooperator" figure is based on thirty-two instances in which Cooper enumerated cooperators in the report itself. It is possible that his actual cooperation rate was less than one-quarter, since twenty-four of these thirty-two reports came from western states which Cooper found unusually friendly to his message.

13. "Notes," *Birth Control Review*, September 1925.

14. Cooper, Reports from Detroit, Mich., July 1925, November 1926, and December 1927. *All reports are in ABCLR, series 1, folders 143–50, 232–72, 368–80, and 455.*

15. Charles Knowlton, *A History of the Recent Excitement in Ashfield* (Ashfield, Mass., 1834), quoted in Janet Farrell Brodie, *Contraception and Abortion in Nineteenth Century America* (Ithaca, N.Y., 1994), 4. The manual was *Fruits of Philosophy*, first published (anonymously) in 1832.

16. Cooper, Reports from Dallas, Tex., October 1925, November 1925.

17. *Great Falls Tribune*, September 4, 1926. Kitty Marion, the *Birth Control Review* street vendor in New York City, also noticed changing public sentiment toward the cause in the mid-1920s. "We have torrents of abuse and insult and showers of compliments and encouragement," she wrote in 1925, reflecting on eight years on the job, "and as the former decreased the latter increased." Kitty Marion, "Address to International Malthusian Conference" (1925), ABCLR.

18. Cooper, Report from Detroit, Mich., December 1926; Beatrice Johnson to Cooper, April 9, 1926, Esther Katz, ed., Margaret Sanger Papers: Collected Documents Series (Sanger Papers); Cooper, Report from Lincoln, Neb.; Cooper to Anne Kennedy, September 26, 1926, ABCLR.

19. Cooper, Report from Wilmington, N.C. Cooper was explicitly denied meetings fifteen times. In seven of those cases he succeeded in setting up unofficial gatherings with sympathetic parties. Other times Cooper was unable to speak for ambiguous reasons. It is impossible to quantify this figure since Cooper did not always report the goals of his many private meetings with local leaders, many of which were aimed at laying the groundwork for future appearances.

20. Cooper, Report from Tacoma, Wash. Cooper reported opposition in twenty-six of his 253 meetings. No region of the United States was disproportionately represented in these incidents; nor were audiences inside or outside the country's largest 100 cities; nor were medical or lay audiences.

21. Cooper, Reports from Wyomissing, Penn., Greensboro, N.C., and Philadelphia, Penn. (February 1926); Cooper to Anne Cooper and Noah Slee, August 31, 1926, ABCLR.

22. Cooper, Report from Sioux Falls, S.D. Cooper's allusion to "wrong ideas" may be read as a reference to Americans' sometime failure to distinguish between "birth control" and abortion. This seems unlikely, however, since Cooper was not shy about mentioning this confusion in his reports and correspondence. Cooper's largest audience, in fact, consisted of 1,500 Brooklyn theater-goers who heard an "address given between 3rd and 4th acts of play entitled *Her Unborn Child*." "This play strongly infers that Birth Control and abortion are the same," Cooper reported. "Address of 20

minutes given to correct this erroneous impression ... Message well received by silent attention throughout with much appreciative applause at the conclusion."

23. Vreeland, "Process of Reform," 124; Sanger to Juliet Rublee, November 5, 1928. Margaret Sanger Papers, Collected Documents Series (College Park, Md., 1997), reel 4. Sanger reached a core of sympathetic women's clubs, reform groups, local birth control leagues, and college students (who welcomed her "because their ideas were not yet biased," recalled Sanger in her *Autobiography*, p. 364). For records of Sanger's speaking engagements see Sanger Papers, Collected Documents Series, reel 17. On her mixed effectiveness as a speaker see Engelman, *A History of the Birth Control Movement in America* (Santa Barbara, Cal., 2011), 64. On her difficulties securing support from politically moderate groups in the 1920s, see McCann, *Birth Control Politics*, 19, 212–215.

24. Elsie Sulzberger to P.B.P. Huse, December 17, 1928, MSLOC (italics original); Jean H. Baker, *Margaret Sanger: A Life of Passion* (New York, 2011), 250. On the consultancy's findings see Linda Gordon, *The Moral Property of Women: A History of Birth Control Politics in America* (Urbana, Ill., 2002), 222. On the efforts of Sanger-founded organizations to move away from Sanger's radical reputation and towards more technocratic approaches see Gordon, *Moral Property*, 242–54. Sanger's opposite number Anthony Comstock, for his part, also managed to alienate moderates. For the obituary in his hometown *New York Times* that noted the "ridicule" which followed him throughout his career see "Anthony Comstock Dies in His Crusade," *New York Times*, September 22, 1915.

25. On U.S. physicians' campaign against venereal disease and associated infecundity, see Allan M. Brandt, *No Magic Bullet: A Social History of Venereal Disease in the United States* (Oxford, 1987), ch. 1.

26. Vreeland, "Process of Reform," 283.

27. Noah Slee to Anne Kennedy, June 16, 1926, ABCLR.

28. Cooper to Anne Kennedy, August 31, 1926, ABCLR.

29. Cooper, Report from Walla Walla, Wash.

30. James F. Cooper, *Technique of Contraception: The Principles and Practice of Anti-Conceptional Methods* (New York, 1928).

31. James F. Cooper, "Some Reasons for the Popularity of the Birth Control Movement," New York: American Birth Control League [1925]. Birth control pamphlets collection, Widener Library, Harvard University. Cooper called this seven-page pamphlet the "condensed outline of the address I use a great deal in my public work" (Cooper to Beatrice Johnson, May 14, 1926, ABCLR). Newspaper accounts of Cooper's speaking engagements closely mirror its structure and talking points. During his tours Cooper repeatedly reprinted "Some Reasons" (sometimes at his own expense) as a means of distributing his views.

32. The use of science rhetoric has a long history in birth control. Robert Dale Owen probably chose the title *Moral Physiology* for his contraceptive tract because "physiology was a catchword ... with a poorly defined but scientific-sounding content in the public's mind" (Etienne van de Walle and Virginie De

Luca, "Birth Prevention in the American and French Fertility Transitions: Contrasts in Knowledge and Practice," *Population and Development Review* 32:3 (September 2006), 532. Philippe Ariès argued that "the interiorization of scientific determinism," above all, made mass contraception possible in the West. Ariès, "Two Successive Motivations for the Declining Birth Rate in the West," *Population and Development Review* 6:4 (December 1980).

33. Cooper, Reports from Haverford, Penn., Morehead, Ky. Cooper reported two boycotts (e.g. St. Albans, Vermont) and addressed at least four "unofficial" meetings (e.g. San Francisco). In Haverford, as in several other towns, Cooper reported addressing the "largest attendance in the history of the society." Medical audiences averaged thirty-eight attendees; lay audiences, 128.

34. "List of Medical Groups Inviting Dr. James F. Cooper," enclosed in Margaret Sanger to Leon Cole, July 17, 1925. Margaret Sanger Papers, Collected Documents Series, reel 3; Cooper, reports from, Wilmington, N.C., Muskogee, Ok., Aberdeen, S.D., Jonesboro, Ark. In the mid-1930s the Iowa Maternal Health League reported a "wall of indifference in our community" to League efforts at providing better contraception (IMHL to ABCL, no date, ABCLR, microfilm edition, series 1, folder 531).

35. Cooper, Reports from Fresno, Cal. and Williamstown, Mass.

36. Cooper, "Some Reasons." The ABCL initially distributed Cooper's contraceptive manual to doctors for free. Later they charged 50 cents for an abbreviated version. On physicians' self-perception as overseers of social as well as physical health see John S. and Robin M. Haller, *The Physician and Sexuality in Victorian America* (Urbana, Ill., 1974). On the growing "cultural authority" of scientific medicine in this period, see Paul Starr, *The Social Transformation of American Medicine: The Rise of a Sovereign Profession and the Making of a Vast Industry* (New York, 1982). Boston University School of Medicine was converting from homeopathic to "regular" medical standards at the time of Cooper's graduation in 1910. It is unclear how many of the doctors with whom Cooper spoke would have been aware of the school's homeopathic origins or seen this orientation as significant. On the status of homeopathic medical schools in the early twentieth century, and Boston University's conversation from homeopathy, see William G. Rothstein, *American Physicians in the Nineteenth Century: From Sects to Science* (Baltimore, 1972), 237–39, 296–97.

37. Margaret Sanger, *Autobiography*, 363. In 1926 the ABCL's executive secretary told Cooper of a letter from a doctor who had seen Cooper in upstate New York: "you made an excellent impression ... but it jarred the ethical sensibilities of certain physicians when you took a pessary out of your pocket and presented it." Sanger suggested he keep his pessaries under wraps until doctors asked to see them, "thus, it does not seem that you have an 'axe' to grind in the way of being an agent for pessaries" (Anne Kennedy to Cooper, April 1, 1926. Sanger Papers). See also Gordon, *Moral Property*, 182. Like other prominent doctors, Dickinson dismissed and sneered at "the radical wing of the birth control movement." See Robert L. Dickinson, "Foreword" in Caroline Hadley Robinson, *Seventy Birth Control Clinics: A Survey and*

Analysis Including the General Effects of Control on Size and Quality of Population (Baltimore, 1930). For more on Dickinson's role in the birth control movement, and as a liaison between the medical establishment and the ABCL, see McCann, *Birth Control Politics in the United States, 1916–1945* (Ithaca, 1999), 79–97; Reed, *Private Vice*, 143–93.

38. Raymond Pearl to Margaret Sanger, April 16, 1927, Margaret Sanger Papers, Collected Documents Series, reel 4

39. Cooper, Reports from Rutherfordton, N.C., and Walla Walla, Wash.

40. Cooper, Report from Anacortes, Wash. Bernice A. Pescosolido and Jack K. Martin, "Cultural Authority and the Sovereignty of American Medicine: The Role of Networks, Class, and Community," *Journal of Health Politics, Policy and Law* 29 (2004) argues for the importance of "social network ties among members of the middle classes" as a key factor in the consolidation of medical authority.

41. On the expansion of permissible public speech see Rochelle Gurstein, *The Repeal of Reticence: A History of America's Cultural and Legal Struggles Over Free Speech, Obscenity, Sexual Liberation, and Modern Art* (New York, 1996). On the declining association of sexual expression with illicit lust and prostitution, circa 1920, see Timothy Gilfoyle, *City of Eros: New York City, Prostitution, and the Commercialization of Sex* (New York, 1992), 311–14.

42. On sexual ideals and practices in the United States, see Karen Lystra, *Searching the Heart: Women, Men, and Romantic Love in Nineteenth-Century America* (Oxford, 1989), esp. ch. 3; Carl Degler, "What Ought to Be and What Was: Women's Sexuality in the Nineteenth Century," *American Historical Review* 79 (1974); Ronald G. Walters, *Primers for Prudery: Sexual Advice to Victorian America* (Baltimore, 2000 [1974]), 1–31.

43. Brodie, *Contraception and Abortion*, 181–82, 201; Martin Larmont, *Medical Adviser and Marriage Guide* (New York, 1861), 91; Delos F. Wilcox, *Ethical Marriage: A Discussion of the Relations of Sex from the Standpoint of Social Duty* (Ann Arbor, Mich., 1900), 5. Brodie notes that "although reproductive control publishing became a significant part of the publishing business in the decades between 1850 and 1875, it was neither openly accepted nor respectable" (p. 194). Writing in 1893, Dr. John S. Billings argued that a major cause of declining birthrates was "the diffusion of information with regard to the subject of generation by means of popular and school treatises on physiology and hygiene." He traced this diffusing trend to the 1850s and 1860s (John S. Billings, "The Diminishing Birth-Rate in the United States," *Forum* 15 (August 1893)). On sexual rhetoric and reality among nineteenth-century Americans see Lystra, *Searching the Heart* and Carl Degler, "What Ought to Be and What Was: Women's Sexuality in the Nineteenth Century," *American Historical Review* 79 (1974).

44. Robert and Helen Lynd, *Middletown: A Study in American Culture* (New York, 1929), 123

45. Walter Lippman, *A Preface to Morals* (New York, 1929), 284. On the sentencing of an ABCL operative in 1918, Sanger wrote: "Three judges, all married, one childless and two with but small families have sent Kitty Marion

to jail for thirty days for imparting information concerning contraceptives" (*Birth Control Review*, November 1918). On doctors' success in controlling their fertility see John E. Murray and Bradley A. Lagger, "Involuntary Childlessness and Voluntary Fertility Control during the Fertility Transition: Evidence from Men who Graduated from an American College," *Population Studies* 55:1 (2001).

46. Cooper to Anne Kennedy, July 22, 1926, ABCLR.
47. Cooper, Reports from Hamilton, Ont. and Toronto, Ont.
48. Cooper, Report from St. Louis (September 1925)
49. Cooper, "Some Reasons"; Transcription of Cooper's speech from *Los Angeles Educational Research Bulletin* 5:1 (September 1925).
50. Cooper to Anne Kennedy, July 22, 1926, ABCLR.
51. Cooper, "Some Reasons."
52. Frederick A. Erb to Cooper, September 1927, ABCLR.
53. Cooper, "Some Reasons." Cooper to Beatrice Johnson, May 1, 1926. Reports from Mansfield, Mo., and Grays Harbor, Wash. On eugenicists' support for birth control see, e.g., Simone Caron, *Who Chooses? American Reproductive History since 1830* (Gainesville, Fl., 2008), ch. 3; McCann, *Birth Control Politics*, ch. 4; Daniel Kevles, *In the Name of Eugenics: Genetics and the Uses of Human Heredity* (Berkeley, 1985), 88–92.
54. Cooper, Report from Utica, NY; Frank van de Bogert to Cooper, February 1926; *Los Angeles Times*, April 29, 1926.
55. Cooper, Reports from Summit, N.J., Syracuse, N.Y., Buffalo, N.Y., Rochester, N.Y., Batavia, N.Y., Niagara Falls, N.Y. Not all Cooper's opposition was Catholic, and his only generally hostile audience – the Brooklyn Heights Public Forum – was a non-denominational civic organization. Forum members did, however, "wander into religious vagaries."
56. Cooper, Reports from Tacoma, Wash., Sacramento, Cal.
57. Margaret Sanger, *An Autobiography* (New York, 1938), 200, 204.
58. Cooper, Reports from Middlebury, Vt., St. Albans, Vt., and Burlington, Vt.
59. Cooper, Reports from Reno, Nev., Everett, Wash., Birmingham, Ala., and Austin, Tex.
60. Cooper, Reports from Pawnee City, Neb., Devils Lake, N.D., and Geneva, Neb.

6 MARRIAGE AS IT IS

1. Ben Lindsey, "Address to National Motion Picture Conference," February 10, 1926. Benjamin Barr Lindsey Collection (BBLC), Library of Congress, Washington D.C., box 151.
2. Lindsey to Charles M. Richter, March 20, 1927. BBLC, box 155.
3. Lindsey, "Companionate Marriage (KOA)." Script of radio address read over KOA (Denver), March 13, 1927. BBLC, box 277. All capitalization original.
4. Ibid.
5. *American Magazine* poll cited in Rebecca L. Davis, "'Not Marriage at All, but Simple Harlotry': The Companionate Marriage Controversy," *Journal of American History* 94:4 (2008).

6. Lindsey's *The Revolt of Modern Youth* (1925) struck some conservatives and clergy as an apology for youth rebellion. But its relatively cautious claims failed to ignite the same controversy as companionate marriage.

7. Ida Stone to Ben Lindsey, March 12, 1927. BBLC; "A Few Rugged Individuals," *The New York Times*, September 19, 1930. Lindsey biographer Charles Larsen writes that this situation changed after the publication of the book version of *Companionate Marriage* later in 1927. "The largest number of letters the Judge received after publication ... fell into the 'Dear Abby' category. Thousands of ordinary people demonstrated the truth of Lindsey's assertion about the practical unavailability of reliable birth-control information when they wrote to ask his advice, particularly about 'the most effective method'" (Larsen, *Good Fight*, 178). I was unable to locate these letters. Lindsey's incoming correspondence regarding his articles in *Red Book* (later *Redbook*) was not dominated by requests for contraceptive advice.

8. Ben B. Lindsey and Wainwright Evans, *The Companionate Marriage* (Garden City, N.Y., 1929 [1927]), 173, 198; Lindsey, "Companionate Marriage (KOA)." Lindsey disparaged contraceptives "available ... via the drugstores, and without medical advice" as "usually crude and inadequate" but noted: "I don't say that such technique doesn't work. It does work in most cases when intelligently used" (Lindsey and Evans, *Companionate Marriage*, 137-38). Wainwright Evans, Lindsey's co-author, was a journalist who worked with Lindsey to structure the *Red Book* articles on which the book was based.

9. Lindsey also differed from other birth controllers in his attention to divorce. The judge's call to modernize divorce norms separated him not only from Sanger and colleagues but from the sympathy of some Americans who might otherwise have supported him. Divorce become procedurally and normatively easier in the early twentieth century, but only over strong objections from social conservatives. Criticism focused on two issues: divorces weakened homes as fundamental civic units and reflected individual failure to exercise personal and sexual self-restraint. Both these criticisms were also important arguments against birth control, but by the late 1920s, divorce may have carried a stronger stigma. In *Country Home*'s 1930 survey of 14,000 farm families, four-fifths of respondents were against making divorce easier, but two-thirds supported physician-prescribed birth control. Lindsey's marriage campaign focused more on birth control than divorce, however, and his respondents focused their comments on the ethics of separating sexuality from childbearing, not marital dissolution. The *Country Home* survey is summarized in "A Few Rugged Individuals," *The New York Times*, September 19, 1930. Later in the 1930s, George Gallup's cross-sectional polling on favorability to birth control returned similar figures (see Chapter 4). On divorce as a social issue in early twentieth-century America, see James P. Lichtenberger, *Divorce: A Study in Social Causation* (New York, 1909); Elaine Tyler May, *Great Expectations: Marriage and Divorce in Post-Victorian America* (Chicago, 1980).

10. Steven D. Anderson, "KOA" in Christopher H Sterling, ed., *Concise Encyclopedia of American Radio* (New York, 2010). Anderson notes that KOA focused its programming on issues of interest to farmers and ranchers.

In the late 1920s the northern Plains – the Dakotas, Montana, and Wyoming – had the country's highest proportion of ABCL members to native-born white population. The tabulator of that statistic, Francis Vreeland, attributed this to "certain magazines" but also to a recent political "ferment of ideas" in the northern plains, and to the people's relative isolation, youth, Protestantism, and economic precariousness (Francis M. Vreeland, "The Process of Reform with Especial Reference to Reform Groups in the Field of Population," Ph.D. dissertation, University of Michigan (1929), 166).

11. Robert S. Fortner, *Radio, Morality, and Culture: Britain, Canada, and the United States, 1919-1945* (Carbondale, Ill., 2005), 106; National Industrial Conference Board, *The Cost of Living in Twelve Industrial Cities* (New York, 1928), 21-26; United States Department of Agriculture, *The Agricultural Outlook for 1929* (Washington, 1929), 18-20.

12. *Knoxville Sentinel*, January 16, 1927.

13. Ben B. Lindsey, "The Moral Revolt" (part 5 of 7), *Red Book* (February 1927). *Red Book*'s circulation of around 790,000 made it one of the country's most popular magazines (*N.W. Ayer and Son's Newspaper Annual*, 1921). Like *Cosmopolitan*, it only became a women's magazine later in the century. Lindsey's *Red Book* editor apparently forbid the use of "birth control," but in the book version of the article Lindsey abandoned euphemism: "it would startle a good many smug persons if they knew how widespread among young people, in every class of society, is the knowledge and use of fairly effective contraceptive devices. They make use of them as a matter of course." (Lindsey and Evans, *Companionate Marriage*, 313).

14. Lindsey, "Moral Revolt" (*Red Book*).

15. The 123 articles came from thirty-three states. Seventy-one percent were editorials, columns, or articles written in the voice of the newspaper, while the remainder expressed the views of commentators outside the newspaper, including writers of letters to the editor.

16. Lindsey, "Companionate Marriage" (KOA).

17. *Council Bluffs Nonpareil*, January 17, 1927; *El Paso Herald*, January 14, 1927; "Would Companionate Marriage Remedy Modern Divorce Evil?" *San Francisco News*, January 20, 1927; *Rocky Mountain News*, January 18, 1927. Note that Lindsey's press clippings dealt with different issues, in different formats, than the newspapers surveyed in Chapters 2 and 3. In addition to major differences in content – particularly regarding divorce – Lindsey's clippings were mostly original editorials from newspapers in small cities, whereas this study's newspapers served relatively progressive audiences in large cities, and contained a mix of formats (editorials, letters to the editor, reporting) more narrowly focused on the issue of birth control and birthrates. The press materials from Chapters 1 and 2 are better compared to one than to other press.

18. Lindsey, "Companionate Marriage (KOA)"; Arthur N. Askire to KOA, March 14, 1927. The KOA announcer's disclaimer is recorded in Dr. E.D. Starbird to Lindsey, March 16, 1927, and "Milit." to KOA, March 14, 1927.

19. Mr. and Mrs. O.L. Alspach to KOA, March 14, 1927.

20. E.A. Williams to KOA, March 13, 1927, BLC, box 151; W.W. Whitmore to KOA, March 16, 1927.
21. J. Albert Smith to Lindsey, March 16, 1927; Frank Richard, Jr., to KOA, March 13, 1927; P.F.J. to KOA, March 20, 1927. The broadcast represented a risk for KOA. Because radio programming arrived "uninvited" and could be heard by entire families, early stations set themselves apart from other media and practiced tight self-censorship. Policies banning discussion of sexual topics lasted well into the 1930s at NBC, which acquired KOA in 1928. See Louise Benjamin, "Controversy for Controversy's Sake? Feminism and Early Radio Coverage of Birth Control in the U.S.," Paper presented at the annual meeting of the International Communication Association, Dresden, Germany, June 16, 2006. KOA emerged from the broadcast unscathed, but Lindsey – who lost his Denver judgeship in 1927 as a result of a preexisting legal fight with the Ku Klux Klan – may have been prevented from returning to the bench in Colorado by his marriage proposals. He eventually became a Superior Court judge in Los Angeles.
22. Lindsey, "Companionate Marriage (KOA)."
23. Mrs. L.E. Pettigrew to KOA, March 14, 1927; T.J. Morrow to KOA, March 13, 1927; Thomas Lipscomb to KOA, March 14, 1927; Anonymous (Leola, SD) to KOA, March 14, 1927.
24. A.W. Mershon to KOA, March 17, 1927; B.B. Pennington to KOA, March 22, 1927.
25. Walter A. Kreutzer to KOA, March 14, 1927; Mr. and Mrs. E.E. Burdick to KOA, March 1927. When reminded that God had commanded his people to "be fruitful and multiply," Margaret Sanger liked to drily note that at the time God issued his directive to Noah, the world's population was six.
26. Mrs. V.K. Benson to KOA, March 15, 1927; George Carter to KOA, March 14, 1927.
27. Walter A. Kreutzer to KOA, March 14, 1927.
28. L.R. Hill to KOA, March 17, 1927.
29. Ben Lindsey, "Address at the University of Colorado," February 6, 1927, Lindsey Papers, LOC, box 151; Lindsey, "Companionate Marriage (KOA)"; Lindsey, "The Moral Revolt" [italics original]. Lindsey was doubtless gratified when, three years after the companionate marriage controversy broke out, the Vatican indignantly denounced "'temporary,' 'experimental,' and 'companionate'" marriages, even if they were "suited . . . to the present temper of men and the times" (Pope Pius XI, "Casti Connubii," 1930).
30. J.A.V. to KOA, March 14, 1927; Anonymous (Cairo, Neb.) to KOA, March 21, 1927; P.H. Wright to KOA, March 15, 1927.
31. On the follow-up program, one week later, Lindsey answered questions and responded to letters. No transcript appears to have survived and the broadcast elicited few letters.
32. Lindsey, "Companionate Marriage (KOA)."
33. Ibid.
34. A.R. to KOA, March 14, 1927; A.T. Rogers to KOA, March 15, 1927.
35. Marie Levoy to KOA, March 15, 1927; Ralph Nichols to KOA, March 14, 1927.

36. D.S. Todd to KOA, March 13, 1927.
37. E.G. Lauckner to KOA, March 16, 1927.
38. Davis, "Companionate Marriage Controversy." See also Nancy Cott, *Public Vows: A History of Marriage and the Nation* (Cambridge, Mass.), ch. 7; Christina Simmons, *Making Marriage Modern: A History of Women's Sexuality* (Oxford, 2009), ch. 3.
39. Lindsey, "Companionate Marriage (KOA)"; Mrs. A.G. Symons to KOA, March 18, 1927.
40. P.F.J. to KOA, March 20, 1927.
41. G.A. Woodcock to KOA, March 24, 1927.
42. Göran Therborn, *Between Sex and Power: Family in the World 1900–2000* (London, 2004), 29–32; Frederick Jackson Turner, "The Significance of the Frontier in American History," *Annual Report of the American Historical Association* (1894). On Sanger's reception in the west, see her *Autobiography* (New York, 1938), 200–04.
43. Dean L. May, *Three Frontiers: Family, Land, and Society in the American West, 1850–1900* (Cambridge, Eng., 1994), 16.
44. John W. Bennett and Seena B. Kohl, *Settling the Canadian-American West, 1890–1915: Pioneer Adaptation and Community Building* (Lincoln, Neb., 1995), 116; Paula M. Nelson, *After the West Was Won: Homesteaders and Town-Builders in Western South Dakota, 1900–1917* (Iowa City, Ia., 1986), 62.
45. Richard White, *It's Your Misfortune and None of My Own: A New History of the American West* (Norman, Okla., 1991), 193; Bennett and Kohl, *Settling the Canadian-American West,* 111; David B. Danborn, *Sod Busting: How Families Made Farms on the Nineteenth-Century Plains* (Baltimore, 2014), 72; Herbert Klein, *A Population History of the United States* (Cambridge, Eng., 2004), 134.
46. Paul Mathews and Rebecca Sear, "Family and Fertility: Kin Influence on the Progression to a Second Birth in the British Household Panel Study," *Plos One* (March 2013).
47. Transcription of Lindsey-Shuler debate, Pomona, California, November 3, 1927. BBLC, box 277.
48. Ibid.
49. Lindsey, "Companionate Marriage" (KOA).

7 CONCLUSION AND EPILOGUE

1. Alexis de Tocqueville, *Democracy in America*, vol. 2, trans. Henry Reeve (New York, 1899 [1840]), 586.
2. Daniel Yankelovich, *The New Morality* (1974), quoted in James T. Patterson, *Grand Expectations: The United States, 1945–1974* (Oxford, 1996), 361.
3. I refer here to the most distilled version of the birth control narrative, which tends to privilege feminist actors over eugenicists and other social engineers.
4. For a sketch of a society in which both men and women work while substantially splitting childcare between themselves (and well-compensated

professional caregivers), see Janet Gornick and Marcia K. Meyers, "Introduction" in Gornick and Meyers, *Gender Equality: Transforming Family Divisions of Labor* (London, 2009).

5. Linda Gordon, "Citizenship and the Right to Birth Control," *Dissent* 4 (Fall 2012). Some critics have further argued that the definition of birth control as a women's issue allows men to pass responsibility for fertility control to women, and more broadly to naturalize connections between women and all things reproductive, including childrearing. See e.g. Lisa Campo-Engelstein, "Contraceptive Responsibility: Trust, Gender and Ideology," Ph.D. dissertation, Michigan State University, 2009. Over the long term, the assumption of female agency could become a liability for feminism in contexts of prolonged local below-replacement fertility. The demographers Kingsley Davis and Pietronella van den Oever, for example, write that "women in industrial societies today are not motivated to achieve replacement fertility but instead are rewarded for nonfamilial activities" and that "in the long run . . . such an arrangement is self-defeating." Norman Ryder, another demographer, argues that "perhaps the principal reason for the recent decline in fertility is the possibility now gradually opening for women to derive legitimate rewards in the pursuit of activities other than motherhood . . . our past success at population replacement, throughout all of human history, has been conditioned on the discriminatory treatment of women." Though such arguments may implicitly favor women's emancipation, they also imply that sustainable fertility is only attainable through social policies directed at women. Davis and van den Oever, "Demographic Foundations of New Sex Roles," *Population and Development Review* 8:3 (1982); Ryder, "The Future of American Fertility," *Social Problems* 26:3 (1979) quoted in John C. Caldwell and Thomas Schindlmayr, "Explanations of the Fertility Crisis in Modern Societies: A Search for Commonalities," *Population Studies* 57:3 (2003).

6. Ibid.

7. United Nations Population Division, *World Population Prospects* (2015).

8. Ibid. The United States has remained at or near replacement rate for most of this period, due in part to its unusual religious and migration dynamics. In Europe, France and Sweden have occasionally approached replacement rate, again due partly to relatively high fertility among first-generation immigrants. Note that China's relaxation of its one-child policy is unlikely to result in higher fertility, due to low desired fertility. See Stuart Basten and Quanbao Jiang, "Fertility in China: An Uncertain Future," *Population Studies* 69: s1 (2015).

9. By liberal or free societies, I mean democracies that seek to maximize individual freedom, equality, and opportunity; insure citizens' basic needs; guard against concentrations of power; and protect freedom of religion, expression and conscience. I do not claim that "free societies" confer perfect freedom, equality, and opportunity on all their citizens, only that they provide advantages relative to other countries, present and past. This use of "liberal" departs from narrower definitions such as those focused on free-market

economics, political rights, or – as in U.S. politics – progressive and socially activist government.

10. Benedict Anderson, *Imagined Communities: Reflections on the Origin and Spread of Nationalism* (New York, 2006 [1983]), 11–12. Anderson sees nations' transcendent importance rising, in particular, alongside secularization: "With the ebbing of religious belief the suffering which belief in part composed did not disappear. Disintegration of paradise: nothing makes fatality more arbitrary. Absurdity of salvation: nothing makes another style of continuity more necessary. What then was required was a secular transformation of fatality into continuity, contingency into meaning . . . Few things were (are) better suited to this end than an idea of nation." The demographer Geoffrey McNicoll underscores institutional continuity: "Almost by definition a society has a collective interest in preserving its image of itself over time. Tacit that interest may be, but if pressed on the matter the society's members, or most of them, would likely see themselves as stakeholders in an intertemporal entity, looking to a future that is culturally and institutionally a recognizable extension of the present. Part of their well-being is tied to the thought that they are participants in such an ongoing enterprise" (McNicoll, "Reflections on Post-Transition Demography," *Population and Development Review* 38:s1 (2013)). See also Andrew Delbanco, *The Real American Dream: A Meditation on Hope* (Cambridge, Mass., 1999), ch. 2.

11. "How Europe Is Slowly Dying Despite an Increasing World Population," *The Telegraph*, February 16, 2015; "Europe Needs Many More Babies to Avert a Population Disaster," *The Guardian*, August 22, 2015; "A Land Without Children," *Spiegel Online*, August 12, 2011; "Time Is Running out for Japan's Dwindling Population," *Yomiuri Shimbun*, March 14, 2011.

12. Singapore, for example, pays about a third of the cost of childrearing, but has a total fertility rate far below replacement. On policy measures to increase fertility see Peter McDonald, "Low Fertility and the State: The Efficacy of Policy," *Population and Development Review* 32:3 (September, 2006); Adriaan Kalwij, "The Impact of Family Policy Expenditure on Fertility in Western Europe," *Demography* 47:2 (May 2010); Anne H. Gauthier and Dimiter Philipov, "Can Policies Enhance Fertility in Europe?" *Vienna Yearbook of Population Research* (2008); Paul Demeny, "Population Policy and the Demographic Transition: Performance, Prospects, and Options," *Population and Development Review* 37:s1 (2011) State attempts to incentivize marriage and childbearing, especially with bachelor taxes, have a long history. For a remarkable catalog of these policies see "Wilhelm Roscher on Means of Promoting Population Increase," *Population and Development Review* 32:3 (2006). Plutarch records one such policy: "Lycurgus also put a kind of public stigma upon confirmed bachelors. They were excluded from the sight of the young men and maidens at their exercises, and in winter the magistrates ordered them to march round the market-place in their tunics only, and as they marched, they sang a certain song about themselves" (*Life of Lycurgus*, Book 15).

13. On migrants' assimilation of fertility norms see Emilio A. Parrado and S. Philip Morgan, "Intergenerational Fertility among Hispanic Women: New

Evidence of Immigrant Assimilation," *Demography* 45:3 (2008); Hill Kulu et al., "Fertility by Birth Order among the Descendants of Immigrants in Selected European Countries," *Population and Development Review* 43 (2017). For example, despite the perception across much of Europe that Muslim immigrants and their descendants have abnormally large families, the Muslim total fertility rate in Europe is 2.1, versus 1.6 for Christians and 1.4 for the religiously unaffiliated (Pew Research Center, *The Future of World Religions: Population Growth Projections, 2010–2050: Europe* (April, 2015)). On the strained relationship between legacy populations and new immigrants (especially Muslims) in Europe, see Pew Research Center, "In Europe, Sentiment against Immigrants, Minorities Runs High" (May 2014); Pew Global Attitudes Project, "Muslims in Europe: Economic Worries Top Concerns about Religious and Cultural Identity" (July 2006).

14. United Nations Population Division, *Replacement Migration: Is it a Solution to Declining and Aging Populations?* (New York, 2000); Jakub Bijak, Dorota Kupiszewska, and Marek Kupiszewski, "Replacement Migration Revisited: Simulations of the Effects of Selected Population and Labor Market Strategies for the Aging Europe, 2002–2052," *Population Research and Policy Review* 27:3 (2008). The UN report sparked considerable popular and scholarly interest; Bijek et al. contains an introduction to the debate surrounding the report's methods and implications.

15. On the Mexican strategy, Jay Winter and Michael Teitelbaum, *The Global Spread of Fertility Decline: Population, Fear, and Uncertainty* (New Haven, 2013), 209–11; on the Palestinian expression, Floya Anthias and Nira Yuval-Davis, "Contextualizing Feminism: Gender, Ethnic and Class Divisions" in Marco Martiniello and Jan Rath, eds., Selected Studies in International *Migration* and *Immigrant Incorporation* (Amsterdam, 2010), 482. See also Monica Duffy Toft, "Wombfare: The Religious and Political Dimensions of Fertility and Demographic Change" in Jack A. Goldstone, Eric P. Kaufmann, and Monica Duffy Toft, eds., *Political Demography: How Population Changes are Reshaping International Security and National Politics* (Boulder, Col., 2012).

16. Ron Lesthaeghe and Lisa Neidert, "The Second Demographic Transition in the United States: Exception or Textbook Example?" *Population and Development Review*, 32:4 (December 2006); Ron Lesthaeghe and Chris Wilson, "Modes of Production, Secularization, and the Pace of Fertility Decline in Western Europe, 1870–1930" in *The Decline of Fertility in Europe*, Ansley J. Coale and Susan Cotts Watkins, eds. (Princeton, 1986), 281; Michael Hout, Andrew Greeley, and Melissa J. Wilde, "The Demographic Imperative in Religious Change in the United States," *American Journal of Sociology* 107:2 (September 2001).

17. Phillip Longman, "The Return of Patriarchy," *Foreign Policy* 153 (2006). See also Longman's book-length development of this idea: Longman, *The Empty Cradle: How Falling Birthrates Threaten World Prosperity (And What to Do About It)* (New York, 2004); Russell Shorto, "No Babies?" *New York Times Magazine*, June 29, 2008. German center-left politician Thilo Sarrazin's *Deutschland schafft sich ab: Wie wir unser Land aufs Spiel setzen*

[*Germany Does Itself In*] (Munich, 2010) speculates that immigrants will assume control of Germany over the next few generations due to higher birthrates and refusal to assimilate. Michel Houellebecq fictionalizes a similar scenario in *Submission* (New York, 2015).

18. David Coleman, review of Jonathan V. Last, "What to Expect When No One's Expecting: America's Coming Demographic Disaster," *Population and Development Review* 39:4 (December 2013). Coleman spells out several reasons to question the disaster scenario in David Coleman and Stuart Basten, "The Death of the West: An Alternative View," *Population Studies* 69:S1 (2015). Apart from Last, the disaster demographers Coleman has in mind likely include Mark Steyn, Patrick J. Buchanan, Ben Wattenberg, and David P. Goldman. Coleman himself, however, has made dire predictions in more careful language. "A third demographic transition is underway in Europe and the United States," he writes: "With larger numbers, populations of foreign origin may feel less need to adapt to local norms . . . The population could become disconnected from the history of the territory in which they live, and from its values, shared identity, and legends. Distinct physical appearance would reinforce that discontinuity. As numerical balance changes, assimilation may become increasingly a two-way street, and old assumptions about majority values and shared identity may cease to be tenable. Literalist religion may thereby regain the salience that it has mostly lost in Western Europe." On this basis Coleman argues for "the rights of natives to conserve their own way of life," drawing an analogy between "the Yanomamö and Tapirapé of the Amazon forest" and "the inhabitants of Tower Hamlets or Toulouse" (David Coleman, "Immigration and Ethnic Change in Low-Fertility Countries: A Third Demographic Transition," *Population and Development Review* 32:3 (September 2006)).

19. Jennifer Glass, Vern L. Bengtson, and Charlotte Chorn Dunham, "Attitude Similarity in Three-Generation Families: Socialization, Status Inheritance, or Reciprocal Influence?" *American Sociological Review* 51:5 (October 1986); M. Kent Jennings, Laura Stoker, and Jake Bowers, "Politics across Generations: Family Transmission Reexamined," *The Journal of Politics* 71:3 (July 2009). For a challenge to this view see Christopher Ojeda and Peter K. Hatemi, "Accounting for the Child in the Transmission of Party Identification," *American Sociological Review* 80:6 (2015).

20. Viktor Gecas and Monica A. Seff, "Families and Adolescents: A Review of the 1980s," *Journal of Marriage and Family* 52:4 (November 1990); Jennings et al., "Politics across Generations." See also Vern L. Bengtson, *Families and Faith: How Religion is Passed Down across Generations* (Oxford, 2013).

21. Wolfgang Lutz, Vegard Skirbekk, and Maria Rita Testa, "The Low-Fertility Trap Hypothesis: Forces that May Lead to Further Postponement and Fewer Births in Europe," *Vienna Yearbook of Population Research* (2006). On the transmissibility of family size preferences see William G. Axinn, Marin E. Clarkberg, and Arland Thornton, "Family Influences on Family Size Preferences," *Demography* 31:1 (February 1994); Jennifer Barber, William Axinn, and Arland Thornton, "The Influence of Attitudes on Family Formation Processes," in Ron Lesthaeghe, ed., *Meaning and Choice: Value*

Orientations and Life Course Decisions (The Hague, 2002). On desired versus actual fertility, see Christine A. Bachrach and S. Philip Morgan, "A Cognitive–Social Model of Fertility Intentions," *Population and Development Review* 39:3 (September 2013).

22. Kevin Smith, John R. Alford, Peter K. Hatemi, Lindon J. Eaves, Carolyn Funk, and John R. Hibbing, "Biology, Ideology, and Epistemology: How Do We Know Political Attitudes Are Inherited and Why Should We Care?" *American Journal of Political Science* 56:1 (2011). A clearer picture of the relative importance of environmental and genetic factors in political behavior may emerge from new genome-wide analyses which began in 2013. Early research on the genomes of 13,000 people found several possible "genetic focal points" for "Conservative-Liberal orientations." This research provides "preliminary support to the hypothesis that whatever relationship exists between politics and genetics" may involve the "genetic loci that influence flexibility in information processing and cognition." Replication and refinement of these results would present compelling evidence for the so-called "partially genetic approach." To date "social, religious, and political attitudes have largely been ignored in the mainstream of modern genetic research," the authors write. Genetic science and its grantor agencies focus on medical issues, shying away from political research due to "concern about how to interpret the societal implications, if any, of a more complex model involving genetic as well as social factors" (Peter K. Hatemi et al., "A Genome-Wide Analysis of Liberal and Conservative Political Attitudes," *Journal of Politics* 73:1 (January 2011)).

23. Phyllis Moen, Mary Ann Erickson, and Donna Dempster-McClain, "Their Mother's Daughters? The Intergenerational Transmission of Gender Attitudes in a World of Changing Roles," *Journal of Marriage and the Family* 59 (1997). Among several hundred mother–daughter pairs in upstate New York, Moen et al. found that "mothers who held traditional (or egalitarian) gender role attitudes in the 1950s are likely to have adult daughters in the late 1980s with more traditional (or egalitarian) attitudes as well, even controlling for mothers' and daughters' experiences," but that sexual and gender norms nevertheless quickly and consistently liberalized in this time. Value transmission is also uneven because of variation in parents' tone and consistency. "Children may come to resemble their parents in one or another respect," M. Kent Jennings and colleagues write. "But only if parents hold consistent attitudes on topics spanning the political agenda will children reproduce their parents' political character to a much broader extent" (Jennings et al., "Politics Across Generations"). Frequent engagement with moral and political questions also aids transmission, though authoritarian parents may polarize their children, prompting some to reject their views entirely. See also Mick Cunningham, "The Influence of Parental Attitudes and Behaviors on Children's Attitudes toward Gender and Household Labor in Early Adulthood," *Journal of Marriage and Family* 63 (2001); Steven Hitlin and Jane Allyn Piliavin, "Values: Reviving a Dormant Concept," *Annual Review of Sociology* 30 (2004).

24. On the origins and consequences of "developmental idealism" see Arland Thornton, *Reading History Sideways: The Fallacy and Enduring Impact of the Developmental Paradigm on Family Life* (Chicago, 2005), esp. ch. 8.

25. "Pope Francis complains of 'haggard' Europe in Strasbourg," BBC News, November 25, 2014; "Falling birthrate is killing Europe," *The Guardian*, November 9, 2009. Though Islamic law tolerates contraception and other sexual arrangements forbidden by conservative Christians, political Islamism is rife with allusions to "Western" sexual sin and unnaturalness. On Qutb's early expressions of this sentiment in political Islam see John Calvert, *Sayyid Qutb and the Origins of Radical Islamism* (Oxford, 2013).

26. Tomáš Sobotka, "Does Persistent Low Fertility Threaten the Future of European Populations?" in Johan Surkyn, Patrick Deboosere, Jan Van Bavel, eds., *Demographic Challenges for the 21st Century: A State of the Art in Demography* (Brussels, 2008), 28; Stark and Kohler, *Popular Debate*, summarizing Stark and Kohler, "The Debate over Low Fertility in the Popular Press: A Cross-National Comparison, 1998–1999," *Population Research and Policy Review* 21:6 (2002).

27. Caldwell and Schindlmayer, "Explanations"; "Trump, in Poland, Asks if West Has the 'Will to Survive,'" *New York Times*, July 6, 2017; "Italy Is a 'Dying Country' Says Minister as Birth Rate Plummets," *The Guardian*, February 12, 2015; "In Rapidly Aging Japan, Adult Diaper Sales Are About to Surpass Baby Diapers," *The Atlantic*, July 11, 2013; Teitelbaum and Winter, *Fertility Decline*, 39, 25.

28. David Reher, "Economic and Social Implications of the Demographic Transition," *Population and Development Review* 37:s1 (2011); Lant Pritchett and Martina Viarengo, "Why Demographic Suicide? The Puzzles of European Fertility," *Population and Development Review* 38:s1 (2013); Caldwell and Schindlmayr, "Explanations."

29. Tooze, "Germany's Unsustainable Growth"; U.K. Office for National Statistics, "Statistical Bulletin: Births in England and Wales by Parents' Country of Birth, 2012" (2013); Paul Demeny, "Sub-Replacement Fertility in National Populations: Can it Be Raised?" *Population Studies* 69:s1 (2015); Walter Laqueur, *The Last Days of Europe: Epitaph for an Old Continent* (New York, 2007). On social strains and "competitive demography" caused by perceived low-fertility and a "general sense of worry about … population future," see Jennifer Aengst, "The Politics of Fertility: Population and Pronatalism in Ladakh," *Himalaya* 32:1.

30. On Hispanic and Asian integration see Pew Research, "Second-Generation Americans: A Portrait of the Adult Children of Immigrants" (February 2013). On generational differences in Europeans' tolerance for immigration see Pew Research, "A Global Generation Gap" (February 24, 2004). This long view of multiculturalism's career in America interprets Donald Trump's election (with a minority of the popular vote) as more anti-establishment than ethno-nationalist.

31. Edward J. Lincoln, "Japan's Long-Term Economic Challenges," *Comparative Economic Studies* 53:3 (2011); Landis MacKellar, Tatiana Ermolieva, David Horlacher, and Leslie Mayhew, *The Economic Impacts of*

Population Ageing in Japan (Northampton, Mass., 2004). See also David E. Bloom, David Canning, Günther Fink, and Jocelyn Finlay, "The Cost of Low Fertility in Europe," *European Journal of Population* 26:2 (2010); Adam Tooze, "Germany's Unsustainable Growth: Austerity Now, Stagnation Later," *Foreign Affairs* 91:5 (2012).

32. Geoffrey McNicoll, "Reflections"; Reiko Aoki, "A Demographic Perspective on Japan's 'Lost Decades,'" *Population and Development Review* 38:s1 (2013).

33. Elizabeth Krause, *A Crisis of Births: Population Politics and Family-Making in Italy* (Belmont, Cal., 2005), 179; *Suddeutsche Zeitung*, April 21, 2001, quoted in Laura Stark and Hans-Peter Kohler, "The Popular Debate about Low Fertility: An Analysis of the German Press, 1993–2001," *European Journal of Population* 20 (2004); Stark and Kohler, *Popular Debate*. See also C. Alison McIntosh, *Population Policy in Western Europe: Responses to Low Fertility in France, Sweden and West Germany* (New York, 1983).

34. Saeed Kamali Dehghan, "Iran Considers Ban on Vasectomies in Drive to Boost Birthrate," *The Guardian*, April 15, 2014; Winter and Teitelbaum, *Fertility Decline*, 52; Tomas Frejka and Sergei Zakharov, "The Apparent Failure of Russia's Pronatalist Family Policies," *Population and Development Review* 39:4 (2013). Russia's demographic trends have already inspired the term "depopulation bomb." See Nicholas Eberstadt, *Drunken Nation: Russia's Depopulation Bomb, World Affairs*, Spring 2009. On population control and its excesses see Matthew Connelly, *Fatal Misconception: The Struggle to Control World Population* (Cambridge, Mass., 2008). Iran's total fertility rate has been below replacement for decades, and one largely agrarian province, Gilan, has a fertility rate of 1.2, comparable to the world's lowest national fertility rates. Mohammad Jalal Abbasi-Shavazi, Peter McDonald, and Meimanat Hosseini-Chavoshi, *The Fertility Transition in Iran: Revolution and Reproduction* (Dordrecht, Neth., 2009), 180–82.

35. European Commission, *Europe's Demographic Future: Facts and Figures on Challenges and Opportunities*, pt. 3 (2007).

36. William P. Butz, "First, Do No Harm," *Vienna Yearbook of Population Research* (2008).

37. On gender equity and higher fertility see Peter McDonald, "Gender Equity in Theories of Fertility Transition," *Population and Development Review* 26:3 (2000); Massimo Livi Bacci, "Too Few Children and Too Much Family," *Daedalus* 130:3 (2001); Gøsta Esping-Andersen and Francesco Billari, "Re-Theorizing Family Demographics," *Population and Development Review* 41 (2015).

38. European Commission, "Europe's Demographic Future"; S. Philip Morgan and Kellie Hegewen, "Is Very Low Fertility Inevitable in America? Insights and Forecasts from an Integrative Model of Fertility" in Alan Booth and Ann C. Crouter, eds., *The New Population Problem: Why Families in Developed Countries are Shrinking and What it Means* (Mahwah, N.J., 2005), 23. Morgan and Hegewen consciously invert Judith Blake's 1974 call to dismantle "coercive" pronatal norms – though "coercion" is too strong a term in both cases. On disparities between actual and desired fertility see Gretchen

Livingston, "Birth Rates Lag in Europe and the U.S., but the Desire for Kids Does Not," available at www.pewresearch.org/fact-tank. On attempts to help citizens achieve desired fertility see Paul Demeny, "Population Policy Dilemmas in Europe at the Dawn of the Twenty-First Century," *Population and Development Review* 29 (2003).

39. Roderic Beaujot, Ching Jiangqin Du, and Zenaida Ravanera, "Family Policies in Quebec and the Rest of Canada: Implications for Fertility, Child-Care, Women's Paid Work, and Child Development Indicators," *Canadian Public Policy* 39:2 (2013); Roderic Beaujot and Juyan Wang, "Low Fertility in Canada: The Nordic Model in Quebec and the U.S. Model in Alberta," *Canadian Studies in Population* 37:3/4 (2010); Warren C. Sanderson and Sergei Scherbov, "A Near Electoral Majority of Pensioners: Prospects and Policies," *Population and Development Review* 33:3 (2007). One proposal for preventing an elderly electorate from awarding itself an ever-larger share of scarce resources is "Demeny voting," in which parents receive additional votes for any minor children. The proposal's namesake, demographer Paul Demeny, argues policies should seek to "reconnect the material status of elderly parents with the number and productivity of their children in the labor force." Paul Demeny, "Population Policy and the Demographic Transition: Performance, Prospects, and Options," *Population and Development Review* 37:s1 (2011). Nikolai Botev suggests that overtly pro-natalist policies may backfire by, first, creating expectations of extrinsic motivation for childbearing, and second, making childrearing appear to serve a controlling collective rather than an autonomous self. Botev, "Could Pronatalist Policies Discourage Childbearing?" *Population and Development Review* 41:2 (2015).

40. James Reed, *From Private Vice to Public Virtue: The Birth Control Movement and American Society since 1830* (New York, 1978), ix. Reed's assessment is based on his reading of anthropological field studies. On the prevalence within human societies of reproductive rules or preferences "which tend to preserve the structure of the groups concerned over time" see also Patrick Heady, "Fertility as a Process of Social Exchange," *Demographic Research* 17 (2007).

41. Arthur Schlesinger, Jr., *The Vital Center: The Politics of Freedom* (Boston, 1949), 245–48. Like Erich Fromm, Theodor Adorno, and other of his contemporaries, Schlesinger worried that democratic citizens might tire of "chamber-of-commerce banalities," turning instead to self-annihilating ecstasies of totalitarian political violence.

42. Robert N. Bellah, Richard Madsen, William M. Sullivan, Ann Swidler, and Steven M. Tipton, *Habits of the Heart: Individualism and Commitment in American Life* (New York, 1985), 140; Howard M. and Kathleen S. Bahr, "Families and Self-Sacrifice: Alternative Models and Meanings for Family Theory," *Social Forces* 79:4 (2001).

43. Peter M. Todd, Thomas T. Hills, Andrew T. Hendrickson, "Modeling Reproductive Decisions with Simple Heuristics," *Demographic Research* 29 (2013) speculate that heuristic intuition is *more* important than rational deliberation in fertility decisions. The importance of personal fulfillment is

heightened by the declining practical importance of local, informal communities in ensuring basic welfare.

44. David Bentley Hart, "Religion in America: Ancient and Modern," *New Criterion*, March, 2004; Eric P. Kaufmann, *Shall the Religious Inherit the Earth: Demography and Politics in the Twenty-First Century* (London, 2010), 269; Sarah R. Hayford and S. Philip Morgan, "Religiosity and Fertility in the United States: The Role of Fertility Intentions," *Social Forces* 86:3 (2008). Hart, a self-declared enemy of "the secular order," has suggested Christians adopt a "strategy … of militant fecundity: abundant, relentless, exuberant, and defiant childbearing" as the most effective possible means of "war" on modern godlessness (David Bentley Hart, "*Freedom and Decency*," *First Things*, June 2004). Pippa Norris and Ronald Inglehart outline two great cultural "survival strategies": "traditional" religiosity with high fertility, and "modern" secularism with subreplacement fertility. They note the higher living standards and subjective well-being in modern societies, but say "insofar as sheer numbers count, traditional societies are clearly winning" (Norris and Inglehart, *Sacred and Secular: Religion and Politics Worldwide* (Cambridge, Eng., 2004), 23). On the U.S. see Tomas Frejka and Charles F. Westoff, "Religion, Religiousness and Fertility in the U.S. and in Europe," *European Journal of Population* 24:1 (2008).

45. Pew Research Center, "2014 Religious Landscape Study," available at www .pewforum.org; Eric P. Kaufmann and Vegard Skirbekk, "'Go Forth and Multiply': The Politics of Religious Demography" in Goldstone et al., eds., *Political Demography*, 207. The Islamic State in Iraq and Syria, despite being theocratic, permits the use of modern hormonal contraception, and assumes that the world's Muslim population will be reduced to 5,000 before Jesus returns to Earth to lead Muslims to final victory over the West.

46. Tom Wolfe, "The 'Me' Decade and the Third Great Awakening," *New York*, August 23, 1976. Another communitarian social critic, Christopher Lasch, decried the "cultural devaluation of the past" as the ultimate loss in a "narcissistic" culture: "To live for the moment is the prevailing passion – to live for yourself, not for your predecessors or posterity. We are fast losing the sense of historical continuity, the sense of belonging to a succession of generations originating in the past and stretching into the future" (Lasch, *The Culture of Narcissism: American Life in an Age of Diminishing Expectations* (New York, 1979), xvii).

47. Gordon, *Moral Property*, 7.

48. Anti-abortion activists make frequent reference to nature as a prescriptive force, and paint their opponents as fundamentally opposed to "life." The sociologist Kristin Luker observes that understanding the abortion debate requires examination of "the meaning of life and death, the meaning of parenthood, the role of sexuality, what is 'natural' for men and women, and how morality is formed and experienced" (Luker, *Abortion and the Politics of Motherhood* (Berkeley, 1984), 8).

49. Oswald Spengler, *The Decline of the West*, vol. 1, trans. Charles Atkinson (1922), 104. Spengler's bestseller attributed "appalling depopulation" to the loss of a "peasant" sense of "enduring and inward union of eternal land and

eternal blood." Though Spengler dismissed Nazi anti-Semitism and anti-intellectualism and feuded with the Nazi race-theorist Alfred Rosenberg, his mystical vision inspired German organic nationalists including Adolf Hitler and Joseph Goebbels.

50. Nicholas W. Townshend, "Parenthood, Immortality, and the End of Childhood" in Graham Allan and Nathanael Thomas Lauster, eds., *The End of Children? Changing Trends in Childbearing and Childhood* (Vancouver, 2012), 102, 95. On the continued importance of naturist cosmology in reproductive behavior see Cynthia Woodsong, Michele Shedlin, and Helen Koo, "The 'Natural' Body, God and Contraceptive Use in the Southeastern United States," *Culture, Health & Sexuality* 6:1 (2004).

51. On pronatalism as coercion see Judith Blake, "Coercive Pronatalism and American Population Policy" in Ellen Peck and Judith Senderowitz, eds., *Pronatalism: The Myth of Mom and Apple Pie* (New York, 1974); Laura Lovett, *Conceiving the Future: Pronatalism, Reproduction and the Family in the United States, 1890–1930* (Chapel Hill, N.C., 2007).

52. On the increased chance of childbearing among Americans whose friends have recently had children, see Nicoletta Balbo and Nicola Barban, "Does Fertility Behavior Spread among Friends?" *American Sociological Review* 79:3 (2014).

53. Stable population may help create an environment more conducive to addressing other macro-level issues, such as climate change or inequality. "Over the long term, zero growth ... should be an attractive demographic objective: there is always a lot for any society to be worried about, but at least concerns about overall scale – too many people or too few – can then be set aside" (McNicoll, "Reflections on Post-Transition Demography").

54. Oswald Spengler, *The Decline of the West*, vol. 2, trans. Charles Francis Atkinson (London, 1928 [1922]), 103; Delos F. Wilcox, *Ethical Marriage* (Ann Arbor, Mich., 1900), 10, 20.

Bibliography

Abbasi-Shavazi, Mohammad Jalal, Peter McDonald, and Meimanat Hosseini-Chavoshi. *The Fertility Transition in Iran: Revolution and Reproduction* (Dordrecht, Neth., 2009)

Adams, Henry. *The Education of Henry Adams: An Autobiography* (Boston, 1918)

Ade, George. *Single Blessedness, and Other Observations* (New York, 1922)

Adsera, Alicia. "Religion and Changes in Family-Size Norms in Developed Countries," *Review of Religious Research* 47:3 (2006)

Aengst, Jennifer. "The Politics of Fertility: Population and Pronatalism in Ladakh," *Himalaya* 32:1

Allen, Grant. *Post-Prandial Philosophy* (London, 1894)

Allen, Nathan. "Changes in New England Population," *Popular Science* (August 1883)

Allen, Nathan. *Population – Its Law of Increase* (Lowell, Mass., 1870 [1868])

Anderson, Benedict. *Imagined Communities: Reflections on the Origin and Spread of Nationalism* (New York, 2006 [1983])

Anderson, Steven D. "KOA" in Christopher H Sterling, ed., *Concise Encyclopedia of American Radio* (New York, 2010)

Anthias, Floya and Nira Yuval-Davis. "Contextualizing Feminism: Gender, Ethnic and Class Divisions" in Marco Martiniello and Jan Rath, eds., *Selected Studies in International Migration and Immigrant Incorporation* (Amsterdam, 2010)

Aoki, Reiko. "A Demographic Perspective on Japan's 'Lost Decades,'" *Population and Development Review* 38:s1 (2013)

Ariès, Philippe. "Two Successive Motivations for the Declining Birth Rates in the West," *Population and Development Review* 6:4 (December 1980)

Armstrong, Elizabeth A. and Mary Bernstein. "Culture, Power, and Institutions: A Multi-Institutional Politics Approach to Social Movements," *Sociological Theory* 26:1 (2008)

Arnold, Matthew. "In Harmony with Nature" in *Poetical Works* (London, 1891).

Axinn, William G., Marin E. Clarkberg, and Arland Thornton. "Family Influences on Family Size Preferences," *Demography* 31:1 (February 1994)

Bachrach, Christine A. and S. Philip Morgan. "A Cognitive-Social Model of Fertility Intentions," *Population and Development Review* 39:3 (September 2013)

Bahr, Howard M. and Kathleen S. Bahr. "Families and Self-Sacrifice: Alternative Models and Meanings for Family Theory" *Social Forces* 79:4 (2001)

Bailey, Amy Kate. "How Personal Is the Political? Democratic Revolution and Fertility Decline," *Journal of Family History* 34:4 (October 2009)

Baker, Jean H. *Margaret Sanger: A Life of Passion* (New York, 2011)

Balbo, Nicoletta and Nicola Barban. "Does Fertility Behavior Spread among Friends?" *American Sociological Review* 79:3 (2014)

Banks, J.A. *Victorian Values: Secularism and the Size of Families* (London, 1981)

Banks, J.A. and Olive Banks. *Feminism and Family Planning* (London, 1964)

Barber, Jennifer, William Axinn, and Arland Thornton. "The Influence of Attitudes on Family Formation Processes" in Ron Lesthaeghe, ed., *Meaning and Choice: Value Orientations and Life Course Decisions* (The Hague, 2002)

Basten, Stuart and Quanbao Jiang. "Fertility in China: An Uncertain Future," *Population Studies* 69:S1 (2015)

Basu, Alaka Malwade and Sajeda Amin. "Conditioning Factors for Fertility Decline in Bengal: History, Language Identity, and Openness to Innovations," *Population and Development Review* 26:4 (December 2000)

Bauer, Martin W. "Classical Content Analysis: A Review" in Martin Bauer and George Gaskell, eds., *Qualitative Researching with Text, Image and Sound: A Practical Handbook* (Thousand Oaks, Cal., 2000)

Bean, Lee L., Geraldine P. Mineau, and Douglas L. Anderton. *Fertility Change on the American Frontier: Adaptation and Innovation* (Berkeley, 1990)

Beaujot, Roderic, Ching Jiangqin Du, and Zenaida Ravanera. "Family Policies in Quebec and the Rest of Canada: Implications for Fertility, Child-Care, Women's Paid Work, and Child Development Indicators," *Canadian Public Policy* 39:2 (2013)

Beaujot, Roderic and Juyan Wang. "Low Fertility in Canada: The Nordic Model in Quebec and the US Model in Alberta," *Canadian Studies in Population* 37:3/4 (2010)

Beck, Ulrich, Anthony Giddens, and Scott Lash. *Reflexive Modernization: Politics, Tradition and Aesthetics in the Modern Social Order* (Cambridge, Eng., 1994)

Beck, Ulrich, Wolfgang Bonss, and Christoph Lau. "The Theory of Reflexive Modernization: Problematic, Hypotheses and Research Programme," *Theory, Culture & Society* 20:2 (2003)

Becker, Gary S. "An Economic Analysis of Fertility" in Becker, ed., *Demographic and Economic Change in Developed Countries* (Princeton, 1960)

Becker, Gary S. and H.G. Lewis. "On the Interaction between the Quantity and Quality of Children," *Journal of Political Economy* 81:2 (1973)

Bederman, Gail. *Manliness and Civilization: A Cultural History of Gender and Race in the United States, 1880–1917* (Chicago, 1995)

Beebe, Gilbert Wheeler. *Contraception and Fertility in the Southern Appalachians* (Baltimore, 1942)

Bellah, Robert N., Richard Madsen, William M. Sullivan, Ann Swidler and Steven M. Tipton. *Habits of the Heart: Individualism and Commitment in American Life* (New York, 1985)

Beisel, Nicola. *Imperiled Innocents: Anthony Comstock and Family Reproduction in Victorian America* (Princeton, 1997)

Bendroth, Margaret Lamberts. *Growing Up Protestant: Parents, Children, and Mainline Churches* (New Brunswick, N.J., 2002)

Bengtson, Vern L. *Families and Faith: How Religion is Passed Down across Generations* (Oxford, 2013)

Benjamin, Daniel J., David Cesarini, Matthijs J. H. M. van der Loos, Christopher T. Dawes, Philipp D. Koellinger, Patrik K. E. Magnusson, Christopher F. Chabris, Dalton Conley, David Laibson, Magnus Johannesson, and Peter M. Visscher, "The Genetic Architecture of Economic and Political Preferences," *Proceedings of the National Academy of Sciences* 109:21 (2012)

Benjamin, Louise. "'Controversy for Controversy's Sake'? Feminism and Early Radio Coverage of Birth Control in the U.S." Paper presented at the annual meeting of the International Communication Association, Dresden, Germany, June 16, 2006

Bennett, John W. and Seena B. Kohl. *Settling the Canadian-American West, 1890–1915: Pioneer Adaptation and Community Building* (Lincoln, Neb., 1995)

Benz, Ernest. "Family Limitation among Political Catholics in Baden in 1869" in Renzo Derosas and Frans van Poppel, eds., *Religion and the Decline of Fertility in the Western World* (Dordrecht, 2006)

Berkman, Joyce. "The Fertility of Scholarship on the History of Reproductive Rights in the United States" *History Compass* 9:5 (2011)

Beveridge, Albert. *The Young Man and the World* (New York, 1905)

Bijak, Jakub, Dorota Kupiszewska, and Marek Kupiszewski. "Replacement Migration Revisited: Simulations of the Effects of Selected Population and Labor Market Strategies for the Aging Europe, 2002–2052," *Population Research and Policy Review* 27:3 (2008)

Billings, John S. "The Diminishing Birth-Rate in the United States," *Forum* 15 (August 1893)

Binion, Rudolph. "Marianne in the Home: Political Revolution and Fertility Transition in France and the United States," *Population: An English Selection* 13 (2001)

Blake, Judith. "Coercive Pronatalism and American Population Policy" in Ellen Peck and Judith Senderowitz, eds., *Pronatalism: The Myth of Mom and Apple Pie* (New York, 1974)

Bledsoe, Caroline. *Contingent Lives: Fertility, Time, and Aging in West Africa* (Chicago, 2002)

Blight, David W. "The Memory Boom: Why and Why Now?" in Pascal Boyer and James V. Wertsch, eds., *Memory in Mind and Culture* (Cambridge, Eng., 2009)

Blom, Ida. "'Master of Your Own Body and What Is in It' – Reducing Marital Fertility in Norway, 1890–1930" in Angelique Janssens, ed., *Gendering the Fertility Decline in the Western World* (Bern, 2007)

Bloom, David E., David Canning, Günther Fink, and Jocelyn Finlay. "The Cost of Low Fertility in Europe," *European Journal of Population* 26:2 (2010)

Bongaarts, John and Susan Cotts Watkins, "Social Interactions and Contemporary Fertility Transitions," *Population and Development Review* 22:4 (December 1996)

Botev, Nikolai. "Could Pronatalist Policies Discourage Childbearing?" *Population and Development Review* 41:2 (2015)

Boydston, Jeanne. "Gender as a Question of Historical Analysis," *Gender & History* 20:3 (2008)

Brandt, Allan M. *No Magic Bullet: A Social History of Venereal Disease in the United States* (Oxford, 1987)

Brodie, Janet Farrell. *Contraception and Abortion in Nineteenth Century America* (Ithaca, N.Y., 1994)

Bryant, John. "Theories of Fertility Decline and the Evidence from Development Indicators," *Population and Development Review* 33:1 (March 2007)

Bryce, James. *The American Commonwealth*, vol. 2 (London, 1888)

Bullough, Vern, ed., *Encyclopedia of Birth Control* (Santa Barbara, Cal., 2001)

Burch, Thomas K. "Demography in a New Key: A Theory of Population Theory" *Demographic Research* 9 (2003)

Burnham, John C. *Health Care in America: A History* (Baltimore, Md., 2015)

Butz, William P. "First, Do No Harm," *Vienna Yearbook of Population Research* (2008)

Byers, Edward. "Fertility Transition in an Early New England Commercial Center: Nantucket, Ma., 1680–1840," *Journal of Interdisciplinary History* 13 (1982)

Cain, Mead. "The Economic Activities of Children in a Village in Bangladesh," *Population and Development Review* 3:3, 1977

Caldwell, John C. "Demographic Theory: A Long View," *Population and Development Review* 30:2 (2004)

Caldwell, John C. "On Net Intergenerational Wealth Flows: An Update," *Population and Development Review* 31:4 (December 2005)

Caldwell, John C. "Three Fertility Compromises and Two Transitions," *Population Research and Policy Review* 27:4 (2008)

Caldwell, John C., Barkat-e-Khuda, Bruce Caldwell, Indrani Pieris and Pat Caldwell, "The Bangladesh Fertility Decline: An Interpretation," *Population and Development Review* 25:1 (March 1999)

Calhoun, Arthur. *A Social History of the American Family from Colonial Times to the Present*, vol. III (Cleveland, 1919)

Calvert, John. *Sayyid Qutb and the Origins of Radical Islamism* (Oxford, 2013)

Campo-Engelstein, Lisa. "Contraceptive Responsibility: Trust, Gender and Ideology," Ph.D. dissertation, Michigan State University (2009)

Carey, James. "A Cultural Approach to Communication" in Carey, ed., *Communication as Culture: Essays on Media and Society* (New York, 2009 [1975])

Caron, Simone. *Who Chooses? American Reproductive History since 1830* (Gainesville, Fl., 2008)

Carr-Saunders, A.M. *The Population Problem: A Study in Human Evolution* (Oxford, 1922)

Carter, Susan B., Roger L. Ransom, and Richard Sutch. "Family Matters: The Life-Cycle Transition and the Antebellum American Fertility Decline" in Timothy Guinnane, William Sundstrom and Warren Whatley, eds., *History Matters: Essays on Economic Growth, Technology, and Demographic Change* (Palo Alto, 2004)

Casterline, John B. "Introduction" in Casterline, ed., *Diffusion Processes and Fertility Transition: Selected Perspectives* (Washington, D.C., 2001)

Charles, Enid. *The Practice of Birth Control: An Analysis of the Birth Control Experiences of Nine Hundred Women* (London, 1932)

Charles, Enid. *The Twilight of Parenthood* (London, 1934)

Cherlin, Andrew. *Marriage, Divorce, Remarriage* (Cambridge, Mass., 1992 [1981])

Chesler, Ellen. *Woman of Valor: Margaret Sanger and the Birth Control Movement in America* (New York, 1992)

Chudacoff, Howard P. *The Age of the Bachelor: Creating an American Subculture* (Princeton, 1999)

Cleland, John and Christopher Wilson, "Demand Theories of the Fertility Transition: An Iconoclastic View," *Population Studies*, 41 (March 1987)

Clement, Elizabeth Alice. *Love for Sale: Courting, Treating, and Prostitution in New York City, 1900–1945* (Chapel Hill, N.C., 2006)

Coale, Ansley and Susan Cotts Watkins, eds., *The Decline of Fertility in Europe* (Princeton, 1986)

Coale, Ansley J. and Melvin Zelnik. *New Estimates of Fertility and Population in the United States* (Princeton, 1963)

Cohen, Lizabeth. *A Consumer's Republic: The Politics of Mass Consumption in Postwar America* (New York, 2003)

Coleman, David. "Why We Don't Have to Believe without Doubting in the 'Second Demographic Transition': Some Agnostic Comments," *Vienna Yearbook of Population Research* 2 (2004)

Coleman, David and Stuart Basten. "The Death of the West: An Alternative View," *Population Studies* 69:s1 (2015)

Coleman, David. Review of Jonathan V. Last, "What to Expect When No One's Expecting: America's Coming Demographic Disaster," *Population and Development Review* 39:4 (December 2013)

Coleman, David. "Immigration and Ethnic Change in Low-Fertility Countries: A Third Demographic Transition," *Population and Development Review* 32:3 (September 2006)

Commander, Lydia Kingsmill. *The American Idea: Does the National Tendency Toward a Small Family Point to Race Suicide or Race Development?* (New York, 1907)

Connelly, Matthew. *Fatal Misconception: The Struggle to Control World Population* (Cambridge, Mass., 2008)

Cooke, Kathy J. "The Limits of Heredity: Nature and Nurture in American Eugenics before 1915," *Journal of the History of Biology* 31:2 (1998)

Cooley, Charles Horton. *Human Nature and the Social Order* (New York, 1902).

Cooley, Charles Horton. *Social Organization: A Study of the Larger Mind* (New York, 1911)

Cooper, James F. *Technique of Contraception: The Principles and Practice of Anti-Conceptional Methods* (New York, 1928)

Cooper, James F. *An Outline of Contraceptive Methods* (New York, 1930)

Cooper, John M. *Birth Control* (Washington, D.C., 1923)

Cott, Nancy F. "Passionlessness: An Interpretation of Victorian Sexual Ideology, 1790–1850," *Signs* 4: 2 (Winter 1978)

Cott, Nancy. *Public Vows: A History of Marriage and the Nation* (Cambridge, Mass., 2000)

Craig, Lee A. *To Sow One Acre More: Childbearing and Farm Productivity in the Antebellum North* (Baltimore, 1993)

Cunningham, Mick. "The Influence of Parental Attitudes and Behaviors on Children's Attitudes toward Gender and Household Labor in Early Adulthood," *Journal of Marriage and Family* 63 (2001)

Danborn, David B. *Sod Busting: How Families Made Farms on the Nineteenth-Century Plains* (Baltimore, 2014)

Darnton, Robert. "The Library in the New Age," *New York Review of Books*, June 12, 2008

David, Paul A. and Warren C. Sanderson. "Rudimentary Contraceptive Methods and the American Transition to Marital Fertility Control, 1855–1915," in Stanley L. Engerman and Robert E. Gallman, eds., *Long-Term Factors in American Economic Growth* (Chicago, 1986)

David, Paul A. and Warren C. Sanderson. "The Emergence of a Two-Child Norm among American Birth-Controllers," *Population and Development Review* 13:1 (1987)

Davies, Margaret Llewelyn, ed. *Maternity: Letters from Working Women* (London, 1978 [1915])

Davis, David Brion. *The Problem of Slavery in the Age of Revolution, 1770–1823* (New York, 1999 [1975])

Davis, Katherine B. *Factors in the Sex Life of Twenty-Two Hundred Women* (New York, 1929)

Davis, Kingsley and Pietronella van den Oever. "Demographic Foundations of New Sex Roles," *Population and Development Review* 8:3 (1982)

Davis, Rebecca L. "'Not Marriage at All, but Simple Harlotry': The Companionate Marriage Controversy," *Journal of American History* 94:4 (2008).

DeFleur, Melvin L. and Sandra Ball-Rokeach. *Theories of Mass Communication* (New York, 1975)

Degler, Carl N. *At Odds: Women and the Family in America from the Revolution to the Present* (New York, 1980)

Degler, Carl N. "What Ought to Be and What Was: Women's Sexuality in the Nineteenth Century," *American Historical Review* 79 (1974)

Delbanco, Andrew. *The Real American Dream: A Meditation on Hope* (Cambridge, Mass., 1999)

Demeny, Paul. "Population Policy and the Demographic Transition: Performance, Prospects, and Options," *Population and Development Review* 37:s1 (2011)

Demeny, Paul. "Population Policy Dilemmas in Europe at the Dawn of the Twenty-First Century," *Population and Development Review* 29 (2003)

Demeny, Paul. "Sub-Replacement Fertility in National Populations: Can It Be Raised?" *Population Studies* 69:S1 (2015)

Demos, John. *Circles and Lines: The Shape of Life in Early America* (Cambridge, Mass., 2004)

Derose, Laurie F. and Alex Ezeh. "Men's Influence on the Onset and Progress of Fertility Decline in Ghana, 1988–98," *Population Studies* 59:2 (July 2005)

Derose, Laurie F., F. Nii-Amoo Dodoo, Vrushali Patil. "Fertility Desires and Perceptions of Power in Reproductive Conflict in Ghana," *Gender and Society* 16:1 (February 2002)

Dickinson, Robert L. and Lura Beam. *A Thousand Marriages: A Medical Study of Sex Adjustment* (Baltimore, 1931)

Du Bois, W.E.B. *The Negro Family* (Atlanta, 1908)

Dumont, Arsène. *Depopulation and Civilization: A Demographic Study* (1990 [1890])

Dyer, Thomas G. *Theodore Roosevelt and the Idea of Race* (Baton Rouge, La., 1980)

Easterlin, Richard, George Alter, and Gretchen Condran. "Farms and Farm Families in Old and New Areas: The Northern States in 1860" in Maris Vinovskis and Tamara Hervan, eds., *Family and Population in Nineteenth-Century America* (Princeton, 1978)

Easterlin, Richard. "The Economics and Sociology of Fertility: A Synthesis," in Charles Tilly, ed., *Historical Studies in Changing Fertility* (Princeton, 1978)

Eberstadt, Nicholas. "Drunken Nation: Russia's Depopulation Bomb," *World Affairs* (Spring 2009)

Edvinsson, Sören and Sofia Kling. "The Practice of Birth Control and Historical Fertility Change: Introduction," *The History of the Family* 15 (June 2010)

Elder, Glen, Jr. *Children of the Great Depression: Social Change in Life Experience* (Chicago, 1974)

Engelman, Peter. *A History of the Birth Control Movement in America* (Santa Barbara, Cal., 2011)

Esping-Andersen, Gøsta and Francesco Billari. "Re-theorizing Family Demographics," *Population and Development Review* 41 (2015)

European Commission, *Europe's Demographic Future: Facts and Figures on Challenges and Opportunities*, pt. 3 (2007)

Everaert, Huub. "Changes in Fertility and Mortality around the Abolition of Slavery in Suriname," *The History of the Family* 16:3 (August 2011)

Fass, Paula S. *The Damned and the Beautiful: American Youth in the 1920s* (Oxford, 1979)

Fass, Paula S. *The End of American Childhood: A History of Parenting from Life on the Frontier to the Managed Child* (Princeton, 2016)

Fellman, Anita Clair and Michael Fellman. *Making Sense of Self: Medical Advice Literature in Late Nineteenth Century America* (Philadelphia, 1981)

Finer, Lawrence B. and Mia R. Zolna. "Unintended Pregnancy in the United States: Incidence and Disparities, 2006," *Contraception* 84:5 (November 2011)

Fisher, Kate. *Birth Control, Sex, and Marriage in Britain, 1918–1960* (Oxford, 2006)

Fite, Warner. "Birth Control and Biological Ethics," *International Journal of Ethics* (October 1916)

Folbre, Nancy. *Greed, Lust and Gender: A History of Economic Ideas* (Oxford, 2010)

Fordham, Elias Pym. *Personal Narrative of Travels in Virginia, Maryland, Pennsylvania, Ohio, Indiana, Kentucky; and of a Residence in Illinois Territory: 1817–1818* [Frederic Austin Ogg, ed.] (Cleveland, 1906)

Forster, Colin and Graham Tucker. *Economic Opportunity and White American Fertility Ratios: 1800–1860* (New Haven, Ct., 1972)

Fortner, Robert S. *Radio, Morality, and Culture: Britain, Canada, and the United States, 1919–1945* (Carbondale, Ill., 2005)

Fowler, James H. and Christopher T. Dawes. "In Defense of Genopolitics," *American Political Science Review* 107:2 (May 2013).

Frank, Stephen M. *Life with Father: Parenthood and Masculinity in the Nineteenth Century American North* (Baltimore. 1998)

Franklin, Benjamin. "Observations Concerning the Increase of Mankind" (1751) in Alfred Henry Smith, ed., *Writings of Benjamin Franklin*, vol. III (New York, 1907)

Franks, Angela. *Margaret Sanger's Eugenic Legacy: The Control of Fertility* (Jefferson, N.C., 2005)

Freedman, Estelle B. "'Crimes which Startle and Horrify': Gender, Age, and the Racialization of Sexual Violence in White American Newspapers, 1870–1900," *Journal of the History of Sexuality* 20:3 (2011)

Freedman, Estelle B. and John D'Emilio. *Intimate Matters: A History of Sexuality in America* (New York, 1988)

Frejka, Tomas and Charles F. Westoff. "Religion, Religiousness and Fertility in the U.S. and in Europe," *European Journal of Population* 24:1 (2008)

Frejka, Tomas and Sergei Zakharov. "The Apparent Failure of Russia's Pronatalist Family Policies," *Population and Development Review* 39:4 (2013)

Friedlander, Dov, Barbara S. Okun, and Sharon Sega. "The Demographic Transition Then and Now: Processes, Perspectives, and Analyses," *Journal of Family History* 24:4 (1999)

Gauthier, Anne H. and Dimiter Philipov. "Can Policies Enhance Fertility in Europe?" *Vienna Yearbook of Population Research* (2008)

Gecas, Viktor and Monica A. Seff. "Families and Adolescents: A Review of the 1980s," *Journal of Marriage and Family* 52:4 (November 1990)

Gere, Anne Ruggles. *Intimate Practices: Literacy and Cultural Work in U.S. Women's Clubs, 1880–1920* (Urbana, Ill., 1997)

Gerstle, Gary. "Theodore Roosevelt and the Divided Character of American Nationalism," *Journal of American History* 86:3 (December 1999)

Gibson, Campbell. *"Population of the 100 Largest Cities and Other Urban Places in the United States: 1790 to 1990"* (Washington, 1998)

Giddens, Anthony. *Modernity and Self-Identity: Self and Society in the Late Modern Age* (Palo Alto, 1991)

Giddens, Anthony. *The Consequences of Modernity* (Palo Alto, 1990)

Gilfoyle, Timothy. *City of Eros: New York City, Prostitution, and the Commercialization of Sex* (New York, 1994)

Gipson, Jessica and Michelle Hindin. "The Effect of Husbands' and Wives' Fertility Preferences on the Likelihood of a Subsequent Pregnancy, Bangladesh 1998–2003," *Population Studies* 63:2 (July 2009)

Glass, Jennifer, Vern L. Bengtson and Charlotte Chorn Dunham. "Attitude Similarity in Three-Generation Families: Socialization, Status Inheritance, or Reciprocal Influence?" *American Sociological Review* 51:5 (October 1986)

Glynn, Carroll, Susan Herbst, Garrett O'Keefe, and Robert Y. Shapiro. *Public Opinion* (Boulder, Colo., 1999)

Golden, Janet. *A Social History of Wet Nursing in America: From Breast to Bottle* (Cambridge, Eng., 1996)

Goldscheider, Calvin and William D. Mosher. "Patterns of Contraceptive Use in the United States: The Importance of Religious Beliefs," *Studies in Family Planning* 22 (1991)

Goldstein, Cynthia. *The Press and the Beginning of the Birth Control Movement in the United States* (Ph.D. diss., Pennsylvania State University, 1985)

Goldstone, Jack A., Eric P. Kaufmann and Monica Duffy Toft, eds., *Political Demography: How Population Changes are Reshaping International Security and National Politics* (Boulder, Col., 2012)

Gordon, Linda. *The Moral Property of Women: A History of Birth Control Politics in America* (Urbana, Ill., 2002)

Gordon, Linda. *Woman's Body, Woman's Right: A Social History of Birth Control in America* (New York, 1976)

Gornick, Janet and Marcia K. Meyers, eds., *Gender Equality: Transforming Family Divisions of Labor* (London, 2009)

Greenhalgh, Susan. "Anthropology Theorizes Reproduction: Integrating Practice, Political Economic, and Feminist Perspectives" in Susan Greenhalgh, ed., *Situating Fertility: Anthropology and Demographic Inquiry* (Cambridge, Eng., 1995)

Gurstein, Rochelle. *The Repeal of Reticence: A History of America's Cultural and Legal Struggles Over Free Speech, Obscenity, Sexual Liberation, and Modern Art* (New York, 1996)

Hacker, J. David. "Child Naming, Religion, and the Decline of Marital Fertility in Nineteenth-Century America," *The History of the Family* 4:3 (1999)

Hacker, J. David. "Rethinking the 'Early' Decline of Marital Fertility in the United States," *Demography* 40 (2003)

Haines, Michael R. and Avery M. Guest. "Fertility in New York State in the Pre-Civil War Era," *Demography* 45 (2008)

Hajo, Cathy Moran. *Birth Control on Main Street: Organizing Clinics in the United States, 1916–1939* (Urbana, Ill., 2010)

Hall, Ruth, ed., *Dear Dr. Stopes: Sex in the 1920s* (London, 1978)

Haller, John S. and Robin M. Haller. *The Physician and Sexuality in Victorian America* (Urbana, Ill., 1974)

Hammel, E.A. "Theory of Culture for Demography," *Population and Development Review* 13:3 (1990)

Hansen, Randall and Desmond King. *Sterilized by the State: Eugenics, Race, and the Population Scare in Twentieth Century America* (Cambridge, Eng., 2013)

Harper, John Paull. *'Be fruitful and multiply': The reaction to family limitation in nineteenth-century America* (Ph.D. dissertation, Columbia University, 1975).

Hatemi, Peter K., Nathan A. Gillespie, Lindon J. Eaves, Brion S. Maher, Bradley T. Webb, Andrew C. Heath, Sarah E. Medland, David C. Smyth, Harry N. Beeby, Scott D. Gordon, Grant W. Montgomery, Ghu Zhu, Enda M. Byrne, and Nicholas G. Martin. "A Genome-Wide Analysis of Liberal and Conservative Political Attitudes," *Journal of Politics* 73:1 (January 2011)

Hayford, Sarah R. and S. Philip Morgan. "Religiosity and Fertility in the United States: The Role of Fertility Intentions," *Social Forces* 86:3 (2008)

Heady, Patrick. "Fertility as a Process of Social Exchange," *Demographic Research* 17 (2007)

Herman, Edward S. and Noam Chomsky. *Manufacturing Consent: The Political Economy of the Mass Media* (1988)

Himes, Norman E. *Medical History of Contraception* (New York, 1963 [1936])

Hirschman, Charles. "Why Fertility Changes," *Annual Review of Sociology* 20 (1994)

Hitlin, Steven and Jane Allyn Piliavin. "Values: Reviving a Dormant Concept," *Annual Review of Sociology* 30 (2004)

Hodgson, Dennis. "Demography as Social Science and Policy Science" *Population and Development Review* 9:1 (March 1983)

Hoffert, Sylvia D. *Private Matters: American Attitudes toward Childbearing and Infant Nurture in the Urban North, 1800–1860* (Urbana, Ill., 1989)

Holz, Rosemarie Petra. *The Birth Control Clinic in a Marketplace World* (Rochester, N.Y., 2012)

Houellebecq, Michel. *Submission* (New York, 2015)

Hout, Michael, Andrew Greeley, and Melissa J. Wilde. "The Demographic Imperative in Religious Change in the United States," *American Journal of Sociology* 107:2 (September 2001)

Hoyert, D.L. "Maternal Mortality and Related Concepts," *National Center for Health Statistics, Vital Health Stat* 3:33 (2007)

Hyatt, Harry Middleton. *Folk-Lore from Adams County Illinois* (New York: 1935)

Inglehart, Ronald and Wayne E. Baker. "Modernization, Cultural Change, and the Persistence of Traditional Values," *American Sociological Review* 65:1 (February 2000)

Inkeles, Alex and David H. Smith. *Becoming Modern: Individual Change in Six Developing Countries* (Cambridge, Mass., 1974)

Inkeles, Alex. *Exploring Individual Modernity* (New York, 2013 [1983])

Jameson, Elizabeth. *All that Glitters: Class, Conflict, and Community in Cripple Creek* (Urbana, Ill., 1998)

Janssens, Angélique, ed., *Gendering the Fertility Decline in the Western World* (Bern, 2007)

Jennings, M. Kent, Laura Stoker and Jake Bowers. "Politics across Generations: Family Transmission Reexamined," The Journal of Politics 71:3 (July 2009)

Johansen, Shawn. *Family Men: Middle-Class Fatherhood in Industrializing America* (Abingdon, Eng., 2015 [2001])

Johnson-Hanks, Jennifer A., Christine A. Bachrach, S. Philip Morgan, and Hans-Peter Kohler. *Understanding Family Change and Variation: Toward a Theory of Conjunctural Action* (Dordrecht, 2011)

Johnson-Hanks, Jennifer. "Demographic Transitions and Modernity," *Annual Review of Anthropology* 37 (October 2008)

Johnson-Hanks, Jennifer. "On the Modernity of Traditional Contraception: Time and the Social Context of Fertility," *Population and Development Review* 28:2 (2002)

Johnson-Hanks, Jennifer. *Uncertain Honor: Modern Motherhood in an African Crisis* (Chicago, 2006)

Juergensmeyer, Mark. *Global Rebellion: Religious Challenges to the Secular State* (Berkeley, 2008)

Kalwij, Adriaan. "The Impact of Family Policy Expenditure on Fertility in Western Europe," *Demography* 47:2 (May 2010)

Kanaanah, Rhoda Ann. *Birthing the Nation: Strategies of Palestinian Women in Israel* (Berkeley, 2002)

Kaufmann, Eric P. *Shall the Religious Inherit the Earth: Demography and Politics in the Twenty-First Century* (London, 2010)

Kennedy, David M. *Birth Control in America: The Career of Margaret Sanger* (New Haven, 1970)

Kertzer, David I. "Qualitative and Quantitative Approaches to Historical Demography," *Population and Development Review*, 23 (December, 1997)

Kertzer, David I. and Dennis P. Hogan, *Family, Political Economy, and Demographic Change: The Transformation of Life in Casalecchio, Italy, 1861–1921* (Madison, Wisc., 1989)

Kertzer, David I. and Tom Fricke, eds. *Anthropological Demography: Toward a New Synthesis* (Chicago, 1997)

Kevles, Daniel J. *In the Name of Eugenics: Genetics and the Uses of Human Heredity* (Berkeley, 1985)

Khawaja, Marwan. "The Recent Rise in Palestinian Fertility: Permanent or Transient?" *Population Studies* 54:3 (2000)

King, Rosalind Berkowitz. *Women's Fertility in Late Modernity* (Ph.D. dissertation, Univ. of Pennsylvania, 2000)

Kinsey, Alfred. *Sex Behavior in the Human Male* (Bloomington, Ind., 1998 [1948])

Kiser, Clyde. "The Indianapolis Fertility Study: An Example of Planned Observational Research," *The Public Opinion Quarterly* 17:4 (1953)

Klandermans, Bert and Conny Roggeband, eds. *Handbook of Social Movements across Disciplines* (New York, 2009)

Klein, Herbert. *A Population History of the United States* (Cambridge, Eng., 2004)

Klepp, Susan E. *Revolutionary Conceptions: Women, Fertility, and Family Limitation in America, 1760–1820* (Chapel Hill, 2009)

Kling, Sofia. "'I Think I'd Rather Die than Go through with a Pregnancy Again.' Experiences of Childbearing and Birth Control in Sweden in the 1930s" in Janssens, ed., *Gendering the Fertility Decline* (Bern, 2007)

Kneeland, George with Katherine Bement Davis. *Commercialized Prostitution in New York City* (New York, 1913)

Knowlton, Charles. *Fruits of Philosophy* (1832)

Kohler, Hans-Peter, Jere R. Behrman, and Susan C. Watkins. "The Density of Social Networks and Fertility Decisions: Evidence from South Nyanza District, Kenya," *Demography* 38:1 (2001)

Koonz, Claudia. *Mothers in the Fatherland: Women, the Family and Nazi Politics* (Abingdon. Eng., 1986)

Kopp, Marie E. *Birth Control in Practice: Analysis of Ten Thousand Case Histories of the Birth Control Clinical Research Bureau* (New York, 1930)

Kornhauser, Marjorie E. "Taxing Bachelors in America, 1895–1939" in John Tiley, ed., *Studies in the History of Tax Law*, vol. 6 (Cambridge, Eng., 2013)

Kramer, Karen. *Maya Children: Helpers at the Farm* (Cambridge, Mass., 2009)

Krause, Elizabeth. *A Crisis of Births: Population Politics and Family-making in Italy* (Belmont, Cal., 2005)

Kreager, Philip. "Aristotle and Open Population Thinking," *Population and Development Review* 34:4 (December 2008)

Kreager, Philip. "Demographic Regimes as Cultural Systems" in David Coleman, ed., *The State of Population Theory* (Oxford, 1986)

Krippendorff, Klaus. *Content Analysis: An Introduction to Its Methodology* (Thousand Oaks, Cal., 2013)

Kuczynski, R.R. "Fecundity of the Native and Foreign-Born Population in Massachusetts," *Quarterly Journal of Economics* 16 (1901)

Kulu, Hill et al. "Fertility by Birth Order among the Descendants of Immigrants in Selected European Countries," *Population and Development Review* 43 (2017)

Kyvig, David. *Repealing National Prohibition* (Chicago, 1979)

Ladd-Taylor, Molly, ed. *Raising a Baby the Government Way: Mothers' Letters to the Children's Bureau, 1915–1932* (New Brunswick, N.J., 1986)

Laqueur, Walter. *The Last Days of Europe: Epitaph for an Old Continent* (New York, 2007)

Laqueur, Thomas W. *Solitary Sex: A Cultural History of Masturbation* (New York, 2004)

Larsen, Charles. *The Good Fight: The Life and Times of Ben B. Lindsey* (Chicago, 1972)

Lasch, Christopher. *The Culture of Narcissism: American Life in an Age of Diminishing Expectations* (New York, 1979)

Lears, Jackson. *No Place of Grace: Antimodernism and the Transformation of American Culture, 1880–1920* (New York, 1981)

Leasure, J. William. "A Hypothesis about the Decline of Fertility: Evidence from the United States," *European Journal of Population* 5:1 (1989)

Leavitt, Judith Walzer. *Brought to Bed: Childbearing in America, 1750–1950* (Oxford, 1986)

Lee, Ronald. "Intergenerational Transfers, the Biological Life Cycle, and Human Society," *Population and Development Review* 38:s1 (February 2013)

Leet, Don R. "Population Pressure and Human Fertility Response: Ohio, 1810–1860," *The Journal of Economic History* 34:1 (March 1974)

Leete, Richard, ed., *Dynamics of Values in Fertility Change* (Oxford, 1999)

Lesthaeghe, Ron. "A Century of Demographic and Cultural Change in Western Europe: An Exploration of Underlying Dimensions," *Population and Development Review* 9:3 (1983)

Lesthaeghe, Ron. "The Second Demographic Transition in Western Countries: An Interpretation" in Karen Oppenheim Mason and An-Magritt Jensen, eds., *Gender and Family Change in Industrialized Countries* (Oxford, 2003 [1995]), 21

Lesthaeghe, Ron. "The Unfolding Story of the Second Demographic Transition," *Population and Development Review* 36:2 (2010)

Lesthaeghe, Ron and Lisa Neidert. "The Second Demographic Transition in the United States: Exception or Textbook Example?" *Population and Development Review*, 32:4 (2006)

Lesthaeghe, Ron and Johan Surkyn. "Cultural Dynamics and Economic Theories of Fertility Change," *Population and Development Review* 14:1 (Mar., 1988)

Lesthaeghe, Ron and Johan Surkyn. "Value Orientations and the Second Demographic Transition (SDT) in Northern, Western and Southern Europe: An Update," *Demographic Research* 3 (2004)

Lesthaeghe, Ron and Chris Wilson. "Modes of Production, Secularization, and the Pace of Fertility Decline in Western Europe, 1870–1930," in *The Decline of Fertility in Europe*, Ansley J. Coale and Susan Cotts Watkins, eds., (Princeton, 1986)

Lewis, Alfred Henry, ed. *Speeches and Messages of Theodore Roosevelt, 1901–1905* (Washington, D.C., 1906)

Lewis, Jan and Kenneth A. Lockridge. "'Sally Has Been Sick': Pregnancy and Family Limitation among Virginia Gentry Women, 1780–1830," *Journal of Social History* 22 (Autumn, 1988)

Lichtenberger, James P. *Divorce: A Study in Social Causation* (New York, 1909)

Lincoln, Abraham. "Second Annual Message to Congress," December 1, 1862

Lincoln, Edward J. "Japan's Long-Term Economic Challenges," *Comparative Economic Studies* 53:3 (2011)

Lindsey, Ben B. and Wainwright Evans. *The Companionate Marriage* (Garden City, N.Y., 1929 [1927])

Lippmann, Walter. *A Preface to Morals* (New York, 1929)

Lippmann, Walter. *Public Opinion* (New York, 1922)

Livi Bacci, Massimo. "Too Few Children and Too Much Family," *Daedalus* 130:3 (2001)

Longman, Phillip. "The Return of Patriarchy," *Foreign Policy* 153 (2006)

Longman, Phillip. *The Empty Cradle: How Falling Birthrates Threaten World Prosperity (And What to Do About It)* (New York, 2004)

Lovett, Laura. *Conceiving the Future: Pronatalism, Reproduction and the Family in the United States, 1890–1930* (Chapel Hill, N.C., 2007)

Luker, Kristin. *Abortion and the Politics of Motherhood* (Berkeley, 1984)

Lutz, Wolfgang, Vegard Skirbekk, and Maria Rita Testa. "The Low-Fertility Trap Hypothesis: Forces that May Lead to Further Postponement and Fewer Births in Europe," *Vienna Yearbook of Population Research* 4 (2006)

Lynch, Katherine A. "Theoretical and Analytical Approaches to Religious Beliefs, Values, and Identities during the Modern Fertility Transition" in Derosas and van Poppel, eds., *Religion and the Decline of Fertility*

Lynd, Robert S. and Helen Merrell Lynd. *Middletown: A Study in American Culture* (New York, 1929)

Lynd, Robert S. and Helen Merrell Lynd. *Middletown in Transition: A Study in Cultural Conflicts* (New York, 1937)

Lystra, Karen. *Searching the Heart: Women, Men, and Romantic Love in Nineteenth-Century America* (Oxford, 1987)

MacKellar, Landis, Tatiana Ermolieva, David Horlacher, and Leslie Mayhew. *The Economic Impacts of Population Ageing in Japan* (Northampton, Mass., 2004)

Mackinnon, Alison. "Were Women Present at the Demographic Transition? Questions from a Feminist Historian to Historical Demographers," *Gender & History* 7 (1995)

MacNamara, Trent. "Why 'Race Suicide'? Cultural Factors in U.S. Fertility Decline, 1903–1908," *Journal of Interdisciplinary History* 44:4 (2014)

Main, Gloria L. "Rocking the Cradle: Downsizing the New England Family," *Journal of Interdisciplinary History* 37:1 (2006)

Martinelli, Alberto. *Global Modernization: Rethinking the Project of Modernity* (Thousand Oaks, Cal., 2005)

Mason, Karen Oppenheim and Herbert L. Smith. "Husbands' versus Wives' Fertility Goals and Use of Contraception: The Influence of Gender Context in Five Asian Countries," *Demography* 37:3 (2000)

Mason, Karen Oppenheim. "Explaining Fertility Transitions," *Demography* 34:4 (November 1997)

May, Dean L. *Three Frontiers: Family, Land, and Society in the American West, 1850–1900* (Cambridge, Eng., 1994)

May, Elaine Tyler. *Great Expectations: Marriage and Divorce in Post-Victorian America* (Chicago, 1980)

May, Elaine Tyler. *Homeward Bound: American Families in the Cold War Era* (New York, 2008 [1988])

Macleod, David I. *The Age of the Child: Children in America, 1890–1920* (New York, 1998)

McCann, Carole Ruth. *Birth Control Politics in the United States, 1916–1945* (Ithaca, 1999)

McCurdy, John Gilbert. *Citizen Bachelors: Manhood and the Creation of the United States* (Ithaca, N.Y., 2009)

McDonald, Peter. "Gender Equity in Theories of Fertility Transition," *Population and Development Review* 26 (2000)

McDonald, Peter. "Low Fertility and the State: The Efficacy of Policy," *Population and Development Review* 32:3 (September 2006)

McLaren, Angus and Arlene Tigar McLaren. *The Bedroom and the State: The Changing Practices and Politics of Contraception and Abortion in Canada, 1880–1980* (Toronto, 1997)

McLaren, Angus. *A History of Contraception: From Antiquity to the Present Day* (Cambridge, Mass., 1990)

McLaren, Angus. *Sexuality and Social Order: The Debate over the Fertility of Women and Workers in France, 1770–1920* (New York, 1983)

McLaren, Angus. *Twentieth Century Sexuality: A History* (Oxford, 1999)

McNicoll, Geoffrey. "Legacy, Policy, and Circumstance in Fertility Transition," *Population and Development Review* 35:4 (December 2009)

McNicoll, Geoffrey. "Reflections on Post-Transition Demography," *Population and Development Review* 38:S1 (2013)

McNicoll, Geoffrey. "Taking Stock of Population Studies: A Review Essay," *Population and Development Review* 33:3 (2007)

McQuade, Lena. "Troubling Reproduction: Sexuality, Race, and Colonialism in New Mexico, 1919–1945," Ph.D. dissertation, University of New Mexico (2008)

McQuillan, Kevin. *Culture, Religion, and Demographic Behaviour: Catholics and Lutherans in Alsace, 1750–1870* (Montreal, 1999)

Mencken, H.L. *In Defense of Women* (New York, 1922)

Meyer, Wilkinson and Jimmy Elaine. *Any Friend of the Movement: Networking for Birth Control, 1920–1940* (Columbus, Oh., 2004)

Meyerowitz, Joanne. "Beyond the Feminine Mystique: A Reassessment of Postwar Mass Culture, 1946–1958," *Journal of American History* 79:4 (March 1993)

Mintz, Steven and Susan Kellogg. *Domestic Revolutions: A Social History of American Family Life* (New York, 1987)

Moen, Phyllis, Mary Ann Erickson and Donna Dempster-McClain. "Their Mother's Daughters? The Intergenerational Transmission of Gender Attitudes in a World of Changing Roles," *Journal of Marriage and the Family* 59 (1997)

Mohr, James. *Abortion in America: The Origins and Evolution of National Policy* (Oxford, 1979)

Molnos, Angela. *Attitudes towards Family Planning in East Africa* (Munich, 1968)

Montaigne, Michel. *Works*, ed., and trans. William Hazlitt (London, 1845)

Montgomery, Mark R. and Woojin Chung. "Social Networks and the Diffusion of Fertility Control in the Republic of Korea" in Richard Leete, ed., *Dynamics of Values in Fertility Change* (Oxford, 1999)

Montgomery, Mark R. and John B. Casterline. "Social Learning, Social Influence, and New Models of Fertility," *Population and Development Review* 22:S1 (1996)

More, Louise Bolard. *Wage-Earners' Budgets: A Study of Standards and Cost of Living in New York City* (New York, 1907)

Morgan, S. Philip and Kellie Hegewen. "Is Very Low Fertility Inevitable in America? Insights and Forecasts from an Integrative Model of Fertility" in Alan Booth and Ann C. Crouter, eds., *The New Population Problem: Why*

Families in Developed Countries are Shrinking and What it Means (Mahwah, N.J., 2005)

Morone, James A. *Hellfire Nation: The Politics of Sin in American History* (New Haven, 2003)

Mosher, Clelia Duel. *The Mosher Survey: Sexual Attitudes of 45 Victorian Women*, James Mahood and Kristine Wenburg, eds., (New York 1980)

Murray, John E. and Bradley A. Lagger, "Involuntary Childlessness and Voluntary Fertility Control during the Fertility Transition: Evidence from Men Who Graduated from an American College," *Population Studies* 55:1 (2001)

National Industrial Conference Board, *The Cost of Living in Twelve Industrial Cities* (New York, 1928)

Nelson, Paula M. *After the West Was Won: Homesteaders and Town-Builders in Western South Dakota, 1900–1917* (Iowa City, Ia., 1986)

Noonan, John T., Jr. "Demographic and Intellectual History," *Daedalus* (Spring 1968)

Noonan, John T., Jr., *Contraception: A History of its Treatment by the Catholic Theologians and Canonists* (Cambridge, Mass., 1965)

Norris, Pippa and Ronald Inglehart. *Sacred and Secular: Religion and Politics Worldwide* (Cambridge, Eng., 2004)

Notestein, Frank. "Population: The Long View" in Theodore W. Schultz, ed., *Food for the World* (Chicago, 1945)

Nugent, Jeffrey B. "The Old-Age Security Motive for Fertility," *Population and Development Review* 11:1 (March, 1985)

Ojeda, Christopher, and Peter K. Hatemi. "Accounting for the Child in the Transmission of Party Identification," *American Sociological Review* 80:6 (2015)

Parkerson, Donald H. and Jo Ann Parkerson. "'Fewer Children of Greater Spiritual Quality': Religion and the Decline of Fertility in Nineteenth-Century America," *Social Science History* 12:1 (1988)

Parrado, Emilio A. and S. Philip Morgan. "Intergenerational Fertility among Hispanic Women: New Evidence of Immigrant Assimilation," *Demography* 45:3 (2008)

Patterson, James T. *Grand Expectations: The United States, 1945–1974* (Oxford, 1996)

Pauly, John J. "Ritual Theory and the Media" in Robert S. Fortner, P. Mark Fackler, eds., *The Handbook of Media and Mass Communication Theory*, vol. 1 (Chichester, Eng., 2014)

Paxson, Heather. *Making Modern Mothers: Ethics and Family Planning in Urban Greece* (Berkeley, Cal., 2004)

Pernick, Martin. *The Black Stork: Eugenics and the Death of "Defective" Babies in American Medicine and Motion Pictures since 1915* (New York, 1996)

Pescosolido, Bernice A. and Jack K. Martin. "Cultural Authority and the Sovereignty of American Medicine: The Role of Networks, Class, and Community," *Journal of Health Politics, Policy and Law* 29 (2004)

Philipov, Dimiter, Zsolt Speder, and Francesco C. Billari. "Soon, Later, or Ever? The Impact of Anomie and Social Capital on Fertility Intentions in Bulgaria (2002) and Hungary (2001)," *Population Studies* 60:3 (2006)

Plant, Rebecca Jo. *Mom: The Transformation of Motherhood in Modern America* (Chicago, 2010)

Pollak, Robert A. and Susan C. Watkins. "Cultural and Economic Approaches to Fertility: Proper Marriage or Mesalliance?" *Population and Development Review* 19:3 (September 1993)

Polybius. *Histories*, vol. 2, trans. Evelyn Shuckburgh (London, 1889)

Pooley, Sian. "Parenthood, Child-Rearing and Fertility in England, 1850–1914," *The History of the Family* 18:1 (2013)

Popenoe, Paul and Roswell Johnson. *Applied Eugenics* (New York, 1918)

Preston, Samuel H. "Changing Values and Falling Birth Rates," *Population and Development Review* 12 (1986)

Pritchett, Lant and Martina Viarengo. "Why Demographic Suicide? The Puzzles of European Fertility," *Population and Development Review* 38:S1 (2013)

Rainwater, Lee. *And the Poor Get Children: Sex, Contraception and Family Planning in the Working Class* (Chicago, 1960)

Randolph, Vance. *Ozark Superstitions* (New York, 1947)

Ranum, Orest A., and Patricia Ranum, eds. *Popular Attitudes toward Birth Control in Pre-Industrial France and England* (New York, 1972)

Reagan, Leslie J. *When Abortion Was a Crime: Women, Medicine, and Law in the United States, 1867–1973* (Berkeley, 1997)

Reed, James. *From Private Vice to Public Virtue: The Birth Control Movement and American Society since 1830* (New York, 1978)

Reher, David. "Economic and Social Implications of the Demographic Transition," *Population and Development Review* 37:S1 (2011)

Riddle, John M. *Contraception and Abortion from the Ancient World to the Renaissance* (Cambridge, 1992)

Riddle, John M. *Eve's Herbs: A History of Contraception and Abortion in the West* (Cambridge, Eng., 1997)

Riley, John Winchell and Matilda White. "The Use of Various Methods of Contraception," *American Sociological Review* 5:6 (December 1940)

Riley, Nancy E. and James McCarthy. *Demography in the Age of the Postmodern* (Cambridge, Eng., 2003)

Robinson, Caroline Hadley. *Seventy Birth Control Clinics: A Survey and Analysis Including the General Effects of Control on Size and Quality of Population* (Baltimore, 1930)

Roosevelt, Theodore. "Biological Analogies in History," Romanes Lecture, Oxford, England, June 7, 1910 (New York, 1910)

Roosevelt, Theodore. *Presidential Addresses and State Papers* (New York, 1910)

Roosevelt, Theodore. *Realizable Ideals* (San Francisco, 1912)

Roscher, Wilhelm. "Wilhelm Roscher on Means of Promoting Population Increase," *Population and Development Review* 32:3 (2006)

Rosen, Christine. *Preaching Eugenics: Religious Leaders and the American Eugenics Movement* (New York, 2005)

Rosen, Ruth. *The Lost Sisterhood: Prostitution in America, 1900–1918* (Baltimore, 1983)

Ross, Edward A. "The Causes of Race Superiority," *Annals of the American Academy of Political and Social Science* 18 (July, 1901)

Ross, Edward A. *Seventy Years of It: An Autobiography* (New York, 1936)
Ross, Edward A. *Sin and Society, An Analysis of Latter-day Iniquity* (Boston, 1907)
Rothman, Ellen K. "Sex and Self-Control: Middle-Class Courtship in America, 1770–1870," *Journal of Social History* 15 (1982)
Rothman, Sheila M. *Women's Proper Place: A History of Changing Ideals and Practices, 1870 to the Present* (New York, 1978)
Rothstein, William G. *American Physicians in the Nineteenth Century: From Sects to Science* (Baltimore, 1972)
Rutenberg, Naomi and Susan Cotts Watkins. "The Buzz outside the Clinics: Conversations and Contraception in Nyanza Province, Kenya," *Studies in Family Planning* 28:4 (December 1997)
Ryan, Mary P. *Cradle of the Middle Class: The Family in Oneida County, New York, 1790–1865* (Cambridge, Eng., 1981)
Ryder, Norman. "The Future of American Fertility," *Social Problems* 26:3 (1979)
Sachsenmaier, Dominic, S.N. Eisenstadt, and Jens Riedel, eds. *Reflections on Multiple Modernities: European, Chinese and Other Interpretations* (Leiden, Neth., 2002)
Sanderson, Warren. "Below-Replacement Fertility in Nineteenth Century America," *Population and Development Review* 13:2 (June 1987)
Sanderson, Warren C., and Sergei Scherbov. "A Near Electoral Majority of Pensioners: Prospects and Policies," *Population and Development Review* 33:3 (2007)
Sanger, Margaret. *Autobiography* (New York, 1938)
Sanger, Margaret. *Motherhood in Bondage* (Columbus, Oh., 2000 [1928])
Sanger, Margaret. *The Pivot of Civilization* (New York, 1922)
Sanger, Margaret. *Woman and the New Race* (New York, 1920)
Sarrazin, Thilo. *Deutschland schafft sich ab: Wie wir unser Land aufs Spiel setzen [Germany Does Itself In]* (Munich, 2010)
Sauvy, Alfred. *Fertility and Survival: Population Problems from Malthus to Mao Tse-Tung* (New York, 1961)
Sauvy, Alfred. *General Theory of Population*, trans. Christophe Campos (London, 1969 [1966]), 388)
Schindlmayr, Thomas. "Explanations of the Fertility Crisis in Modern Societies: A Search for Commonalities," *Population Studies* 57:3 (2003)
Schoen, Johanna. *Choice and Coercion: Birth Control, Sterilization, and Abortion in Public Health and Welfare* (Chapel Hill, N.C., 2005)
Schneider, Jane C. and Peter T. Schneider. *Festival of the Poor: Fertility Decline and the Ideology of Class in Sicily, 1860–1980* (Tucson, Ariz., 1996)
Schlesinger, Arthur, Jr. *The Vital Center: The Politics of Freedom* (Boston, 1949)
Schwartz, Timothy T. *Fewer Men, More Babies: Sex, Family, and Fertility in Haiti* (Plymouth, Eng., 2009)
Seccombe, Wally. "Starting to Stop: Working-Class Fertility Decline in Britain," *Past & Present* 126 (February, 1990)
Shaw, George Bernard. *Getting Married* (New York, 1909)
Shorter, Edward. "Female Emancipation, Birth Control, and Fertility in European History," *American Historical Review* 78 (1973)

Shorter, Edward. *Women's Bodies: A Social History of Women's Encounter With Health, Ill-Health, and Medicine* (New York, 1992 [1982])

Simmons, Christina. *Making Marriage Modern: Women's Sexuality from the Progressive Era to World War II* (Oxford, 2009)

Sinclair, Upton. *The Book of Life: Mind and Body* (Girard, Ks., 1922)

Smith, Daniel Scott. "Family Limitation, Sexual Control, and Domestic Feminism in Victorian America," *Feminist Studies* 1:3, 1973

Smith, Kevin, John R. Alford, Peter K. Hatemi, Lindon J. Eaves, Carolyn Funk, and John R. Hibbing. "Biology, Ideology, and Epistemology: How Do We Know Political Attitudes Are Inherited and Why Should We Care?" *American Journal of Political Science* 56:1 (January 2012)

Sobotka, Tomáš. "Does Persistent Low Fertility Threaten the Future of European Populations?" in Johan Surkyn, Patrick Deboosere, Jan Van Bavel, eds., *Demographic Challenges for the 21st Century: A State of the Art in Demography* (Brussels, 2008)

Sogner, Sølvi. "Abortion, Birth Control, and Contraception: Fertility Decline in Norway," *Journal of Interdisciplinary History* 34:2 (Autumn 2003)

Solinger, Rickie. *Pregnancy and Power: A Short History of Reproductive Politics in America* (New York, 2005)

Solinger, Rickie. *Reproductive Politics: What Everyone Needs to Know* (Oxford, Eng., 2013)

Søland, Birgitte. *Becoming Modern: Young Women and the Reconstruction of Womanhood in the 1920s* (Princeton, 2000)

Spengler, Oswald. *The Decline of the West*, trans. Charles Francis Atkinson (London, 1928 [1922])

Stark, Laura and Hans-Peter Kohler. "The Debate over Low Fertility in the Popular Press: A Cross-National Comparison, 1998–1999," *Population Research and Policy Review* 21:6 (December 2002)

Stark, Laura and Hans-Peter Kohler. "The Popular Debate about Low Fertility: An Analysis of the German Press, 1993–2001," *European Journal of Population* 20:4 (December 2004)

Starr, Paul. *The Social Transformation of American Medicine: The Rise of a Sovereign Profession and the Making of a Vast Industry* (New York, 1982)

Stern, Alexandra. *Eugenic Nation: Faults and Frontiers of Better Breeding in Modern America* (Berkeley, 2005)

Stern, Paul C., Thomas Dietz, Troy Abel, Gregory A. Guagnano, and Linda Kalof. "A Value-Belief-Norm Theory of Support for Social Movements: The Case of Environmentalism," *Research in Human Ecology* 6:2 (1999)

Stix, Regine K. and Frank Notestein. "Effectiveness of Birth Control," *Milbank Memorial Fund Quarterly* 7:1 (January 1934)

Stix, Regine K. and Frank W. Notestein. "Effectiveness of Birth Control: A Second Study of Contraceptive Practice in a Selected Group of New York Women," *Milbank Memorial Fund Quarterly* 13:2 (1935)

Stone, Lawrence. *The Family, Sex, and Marriage in England, 1500–1800* (New York, 1977)

Stone, Lee Alexander. *Sex Searchlights and Sane Sex Ethics: An Anthology of Sexual Knowledge* (Chicago, 1922)

Stopes, Marie. *Mother England: A Contemporary History* (London, 1929)

Strangeland, Charles. *Pre-Malthusian Doctrines of Population: A Study in the History of Economic Theory* (New York, 1904)

Swidler, Ann. "Cultural Power and Social Movements" in Hank Johnston and Bert Klandermans, eds., *Social Movements and Culture* (Minneapolis, 2004 [1995])

Szoltysek, Mikolaj. "Science without Laws? Model Buliding, Micro Histories and the Fate of the Theory of Fertility Decline," *Historical Social Research* 32:2 (2007)

Szreter, Simon. *Fertility, Class and Gender in Britain, 1860–1940* (Cambridge, Eng., 1994)

Szreter, Simon, Robert A. Nye, and Frans van Poppel. "Fertility and Contraception during the Demographic Transition: Qualitative and Quantitative Approaches," *Journal of Interdisciplinary History* 34:2 (Autumn, 2003)

Teitelbaum, Michael. *The British Fertility Decline: Demographic Transition in the Crucible of the Industrial Revolution* (Princeton, 1984)

Temkin-Greener, Helena and Alan C. Swedlund. "Fertility Transition in the Connecticut Valley: 1740–1850," *Population Studies* 32:1 (1978)

Tentler, Leslie Woodcock. *Catholics and Contraception: An American History* (Ithaca, N.Y., 2004)

Tentler, Leslie Woodcock. "'The Abominable Crime of Onan': Catholic Pastoral Practice and Family Limitation in the United States, 1875–1919," *Church History* 71:2 (2002)

Therborn, Göran. *Between Sex and Power: Family in the World 1900–2000* (London, 2004)

Thompson, E.P. "The Moral Economy of the English Crowd in the Eighteenth Century," *Past & Present* 50:1 (1971)

Thomson, Elizabeth, Elaine McDonald, and Larry L. Bumpass. "Fertility Desires and Fertility: Hers, His, and Theirs," *Demography* 27:4 (November, 1990)

Thornton, Arland. "The Developmental Paradigm, Reading History Sideways, and Family Change," *Demography* 38:4 (2001)

Thornton, Arland. *Reading History Sideways: The Fallacy and Enduring Impact of the Developmental Paradigm on Family Life* (Chicago, 2005)

Tobin, Kathleen A. *The American Religious Debate over Birth Control, 1907–1937* (Jefferson, N.C., 2001)

de Tocqueville, Alexis. *Democracy in America*, trans. Arthur Goldhammer (New York, 2012 [1840])

Todd, Peter M., Thomas T. Hills, Andrew T. Hendrickson. "Modeling Reproductive Decisions with Simple Heuristics," *Demographic Research* 29 (2013)

Toft, Monica Duffy. "Wombfare: The Religious and Political Dimensions of Fertility and Demographic Change" in Jack A. Goldstone, Eric P. Kaufmann, and Monica Duffy Toft, eds., *Political Demography: How Population Changes are Reshaping International Security and National Politics* (Boulder, Col., 2012)

Tone, Andrea. *Devices and Desires: A History of Contraceptives in America* (New York, 2002)

Townshend, Nicholas W. "Parenthood, Immortality, and the End of Childhood" in Graham Allan and Nathanael Thomas Lauster, eds., *The End of Children?: Changing Trends in Childbearing and Childhood* (Vancouver, 2012)

Tooze, Adam. "Germany's Unsustainable Growth: Austerity Now, Stagnation Later," *Foreign Affairs* 91:5 (2012)

Tönnies, Ferdinand. *Critique of Public Opinion* (1922)

Tucker, George. *Progress of the United States in Population and Wealth in Fifty Years* (New York, 1843)

Turner, Frederick Jackson. "The Significance of the Frontier in American History" *Annual Report of the American Historical Association* (1894)

U.S. Centers for Disease Control. "Achievements in Public Health, 1900–1999: Healthier Mothers and Babies," *Morbidity and Mortality Weekly Report* 48:38 (October 1999)

United Nations Population Division. *Replacement Migration: Is it a Solution to Declining and Aging Populations?* (New York, 2000)

United Nations Population Division. *World Population Prospects* (New York, 2015)

United States Department of Agriculture. *The Agricultural Outlook for 1929* (Washington, 1929)

Van Bavel, January. "Subreplacement Fertility in the West Before the Baby Boom: Past and Current Perspectives," *Population Studies* 64 (March 2010)

Van Bavel, Jan and David Reher. "The Baby Boom and Its Causes: What We Know and What We Need to Know," *Population and Development Review* 39:2 (2013)

van de Kaa, Dirk. "Europe's Second Demographic Transition," *Population Bulletin* 42 (1987)

van de Kaa, Dirk. "The True Commonality: In Reflexive Modern Societies Fertility Is a Derivative," *Population Studies* 58:1 (2004)

van de Walle, Etienne. "Fertility Transition, Conscious Choice, and Numeracy," *Demography* 29:4 (1992)

van de Walle, Etienne. "Motivations and Technology in the Decline of French Fertility" in R. Wheaton and T. Hareven, eds., *Family and Sexuality in French History* (Philadelphia, 1980)

van de Walle, Etienne and Elisha P. Renne, eds. *Regulating Menstruation: Beliefs, Practices, Interpretations* (Chicago, 2001)

van de Walle, Etienne and Virginie De Luca. "Birth Prevention in the American and French Fertility Transitions: Contrasts in Knowledge and Practice," *Population And Development Review* 32:3 (September 2006)

van Poppel, Frans and Renzo De Rosas, eds. *Religion and the Decline of Fertility in Europe* (Dordrecht, 2007)

Van Vorst, Mrs. John [Bessie], and Marie Van Vorst. *The Woman Who Toils: Being the Experiences of Two Ladies as Factory Girls* (New York, 1903)

Vice Commission of the City of Chicago. *The Social Evil in Chicago: A Study of Existing Conditions* (1911)

Vinovskis, Maris A. "Socioeconomic Determinants of Interstate Fertility Differentials in the United States in 1850 and 1860," *The Journal of Interdisciplinary History* 6:3 (1976)

Vinovskis, Maris A. *Fertility in Massachusetts from the Revolution to the Civil War* (New York, 1981)

Vreeland, Francis M. "The Process of Reform with Especial Reference to Reform Groups in the Field of Population," Ph.D. dissertation, University of Michigan (1929)

Walker, Francis A. "Restriction of Immigration," *Atlantic Monthly* (June 1896)

Walters, Ronald G. *Primers for Prudery: Sexual Advice to Victorian America* (Baltimore, 2000 [1974])

Watkins, Susan Cotts and Angela D. Danzi. "Women's Gossip and Social Change: Childbirth and Fertility Control among Italian and Jewish Women in the United States, 1920–1940," *Gender and Society* 9:4 (August 1995)

Watkins, Susan Cotts. "Conclusions" in Watkins and Ansley Coale, eds., *The Decline of Fertility in Europe* (Princeton, 1986)

Watkins, Susan Cotts. "Fertility Determinants" in Edgar F. Borgatta and Rhonda J. V. Montgomery, eds., *Encyclopedia of Sociology*, 2nd edn., vol. 2 (New York, 2006)

Watkins, Susan Cotts. "If All We Knew about Women Was What We Read in 'Demography,' What Would We Know?" *Demography*, 30 (1993)

Watkins, Susan Cotts. "Local and Foreign Models of Reproduction in Nyanza Province, Kenya," *Population and Development Review* 26:4 (December 2000)

Weiss, Jessica. *To Have and to Hold: Marriage, the Baby Boom, and Social Change* (Chicago, 2000)

Welskopp, Thomas and Alan Lessoff. *Fractured Modernity: America Confronts Modern Times, 1890s to 1940s* (Munich, 2012)

Wells, Robert V. "Family History and Demographic Transition," *Journal of Social History* 9:1 (1975)

Wells, Robert V. "Family Size and Fertility Control in Eighteenth-Century America: A Study of Quaker Families," *Population Studies* 25:1 (1971)

Wertz, Richard W. and Dorothy C. Wertz. *Lying In: A History of Childbirth in America* (New Haven, 1989 [1977])

Westoff, Charles and Elise Jones. "The End of 'Catholic' Fertility," *Demography* 16:2 (1979)

White, Richard. *It's Your Misfortune and None of My Own: A New History of the American West* (Norman, Okla., 1991)

Wilcox, Delos F. *Ethical Marriage* (Ann Arbor, Mich., 1900)

Wilmoth, John R. and Patrick Ball. "The Population Debate in American Popular Magazines, 1946–90," *Population and Development Review* 18:4 (December 1992)

Winter, Jay and Michael Teitelbaum. *The Global Spread of Fertility Decline: Population, Fear, and Uncertainty* (New Haven, 2013)

Wolf, Jacqueline H. *Deliver Me from Pain: Anesthesia and Birth in America* (Baltimore, Md., 2009)

Woodsong, Cynthia, Michele Shedlin and Helen Koo. "The 'Natural' Body, God and Contraceptive Use in the Southeastern United States," *Culture, Health & Sexuality* 6:1 (2004)

Wrigley, E.A. "Fertility Strategy for the Individual and the Group" in
    Charles Tilly, ed., *Historical Studies of Changing Fertility* (Princeton, 1978)
Yang, C.K. *The Chinese Family in the Communist Revolution* (Cambridge, Mass.,
    1959)
Yasuba, Yasikichi. *Birthrates of the White Population of the United States,
    1800–1860: An Economic Study* (Baltimore, 1962)
Zelizer, Viviana A. *Pricing the Priceless Child: The Changing Social Value of
    Children* (Princeton, 1994 [1985])

PRESS SOURCES

Atlanta Constitution
Baltimore Sun
Birth Control Review
Boston Globe
Chicago Tribune
Council Bluffs Nonpareil
Denver Post
Der Spiegel
Dissent
Economist
El Paso Herald
Freedom
Great Falls Tribune
The Guardian
Hartford Courant
The Independent
Life
The Ladies' Home Journal
Los Angeles Times
Medical Age
New York Times
New York Tribune
Popular Science
Red Book
Rocky Mountain News
San Francisco News
The Telegraph
Trenton Evening Times
Washington Post

Index

CPSIA information can be obtained
at www.ICGtesting.com
Printed in the USA
LVHW092044090820
662761LV00001B/42